JONATHAN CAPE
PAPERBACK
JCP 23

THE WALL HAS TWO SIDES

FELIX GREENE

The Wall Has Two Sides

A Portrait of China Today

JONATHAN CAPE
THIRTY BEDFORD SQUARE LONDON

FIRST PUBLISHED 1962
THIS PAPERBACK EDITION FIRST PUBLISHED 1964
REPRINTED 1966
© 1961 BY FELIX GREENE

Printed in Great Britain by
Fletcher & Son Ltd, Norwich
and bound by
Richard Clay (The Chaucer Press) Ltd, Bungay, Suffolk

CONTENTS

5

CONTENTS

PREFACE TO THE ENGLISH EDITION

IN the past eleven years only nine Americans have set foot on the mainland of China with the approval of the United States Government.[1] It is, of course, well known in Britain that America doesn't approve of China, refuses to recognize her government and has for years successfully used her powerful influence to keep her out of the United Nations. But the full extent to which the United States has severed her relations is probably not generally realized. America was prepared to trade with the Soviet Union (and to allow her citizens to travel there) many years before she extended recognition, but with China she maintains a total trade embargo and a very strict control on travel. Some eminent American citizens who have wanted to go to China — including Members of Congress, a Justice of the Supreme Court and Mrs Eleanor Roosevelt — were forbidden by the State Department to do so. On occasions when American diplomats abroad might meet Chinese representatives they have been instructed neither to shake hands with them nor to speak to them except in formal conference, and on one occasion (so goes the story) were told that they must not even look at the Chinese!

Except in time of war it would be very difficult to find another example of a nation in the Western world that has so completely severed her communications with another people — yet in this case one is the most powerful industrial country in the world and the other comprises one quarter of the human race.

This book was commissioned by an American publisher and was originally written for American readers. Except for quite minor changes and the usual alterations in spelling and phraseology, the text is the same

---

[1] Six of the nine were relatives of United States prisoners and were permitted to visit China just for a few days; one was a lawyer who was allowed to go only after the courts had ordered the State Department to grant him a visa; two were correspondents. (A tenth United States citizen accompanied U.N. Secretary-General Hammarskjold on his visit to Peking but travelled with a U.N. passport and under U.N. jurisdiction.)

A few Americans have travelled to China without permission and have had their passports taken away on their return to America.

In December 1960 — shortly after my return from China — a new State Department regulation made it impossible for foreigners like myself resident in the United States to travel to China without forfeiting their privilege of re-entry to the United States.

as in the American edition. It is in itself an extraordinary fact that this book is the first general report about China written for American readers since the Communists took over in 1949.

As an Englishman resident in America I have been to China twice, travelling on a British passport. I went first in 1957, taking with me all the assumptions and apprehensions generally prevalent in the United States. I expected to find a country of vast impoverishment and dreadful squalor and disease. I prepared myself to see a people embittered by the rigid coercions of a police state. I expected to see fear as I had seen it in Russia in the early 'thirties and later in Germany and Italy. That was the China I expected but it was not the China that I found.

The discrepancy between what I had been led to expect and what I actually saw was at first bewildering and disturbing. No one can be in China for more than a few hours without sensing an almost tangible vitality and an enormous optimism. I saw in the people a buoyancy and confidence which was utterly unlike my expectations.

I had already travelled, either as a staff member of the B.B.C. or, later, on my own as a businessman and free-lance correspondent, to most of the countries of the world. I thought of myself as a hardened traveller. I was rather blasé. I did not think that seeing a new country could ever really stir or excite me again. But I was wrong. No experience in my life shook me so deeply as this first visit to China. I was not blind to the mistakes that were being made or the extent of the poverty that still existed. I knew something, too, of the suffering and bloodshed that had accompanied the birth of this new China. But all this took on a new meaning in the light of the accomplishments that I could see around me wherever I went. I came away certain that, whatever our view of it might be, what was taking place in China was one of the great historical events of our era.

But how was it possible that a journalist like myself, presumably well-informed on world events, could have gone to China so totally unprepared? The reason is simple. I had been living in the United States. Not only has America been cut off diplomatically from China but her people have been cut off also from any serious information about a country that is moving very quickly to the forefront of political and economic power. I am convinced that this ignorance is dangerous and detrimental to their interests.

PREFACE

In 1959 I went to Asia again — not to China, but to broadcast political commentaries from several of China's continental neighbours. I interviewed a number of Asian leaders. Among these were Mohammed Naim, Foreign Minister of Afghanistan; Prasad Koirala, Prime Minister of Nepal; the Dalai Lama; Dr Subandrio, Foreign Minister of Indonesia. I spent an evening of discussion with Mr Nehru. I also visited Burma, Thailand, Laos, Singapore and Japan. As a result of these talks, one thing became clear to me: that with a variety of hostile, friendly, or ambivalent feelings, Asian leaders are watching the transformation of China into a world power and are wondering when America will understand and come to terms with this reality.

*

Before we condemn America for an attitude towards China which might appear to us as being dangerously rigid and unrealistic we should remind ourselves of America's long and rather special relationship with China. For nearly a century Americans have looked on the Chinese almost as their protégés. Into China they poured help of all kinds — missions, schools, medical institutes, food, money. Hundreds of thousands of Americans were in one way or another involved with China. Of course commercial interests were bound up with all this, but it appeared to many Americans that it was their country's historic mission to help China out of her backwardness and to make her a modern nation — respectably capitalistic, democratic and — if possible — Christian. This sense of special obligation towards China engendered an unreal, a paternalistic, and often a sentimentalized, image of China in the minds of many Americans. They never allowed themselves to doubt China's admiration and gratitude towards her benefactor.

So when in 1949 America (in her terminology) 'lost' China to the Communists and relations were broken the initial response was one of shocked sadness — the end of an affectionate even though an unequal friendship. At this stage America (quite misjudging the nature of the Chinese revolution) believed that the Chinese would sooner or later overthrow their Communist masters and that the old American-Chinese relationship would somehow be restored. A year later, in Korea, China and America were engaged in a peculiarly horrible war.

9

The Chinese army (which under Chiang Kai-shek was viewed by the American military with derisive contempt) fought the Americans to a standstill and forced upon America an armistice she did not want. The mood of sadness changed to one of the most intense hostility and bitterness and it has remained so to this day.

It is still difficult for an American politician (or anyone else, for that matter) to say anything nice about China — much more difficult than to say something nice about Russia. Almost nothing can be said or written about China in the United States that isn't controversial — unless based on the assumption of her total malevolence. To question America's present attitudes and policy towards China, to analyse the structure of the Chinese Government, to try to learn what it is that is moving the Chinese people to such extraordinary efforts is, to many in America, positively subversive. The fact that this book does not attempt to engender hatred for the Chinese people, but to widen our understanding of what is going on in the country, will in itself be an offence in the eyes of many official propagandists.

The British, in the course of long experience, have learned that it is wise wherever possible to keep doors open rather than to slam them shut. They have learned that in the shifting tides of international relationships nothing remains the same for too long. The enemy of today may be the needed friend of tomorrow. The British decision to face realities and to recognize the Communist Government in 1950 — which after all represented a quarter of the world's population — was a wise one. It is rather fashionable in America to say that Britain's recognition has brought her no benefits and was a mistake. If it has been a somewhat restrained and unrewarding relationship is it not perhaps because it has never been full-hearted on Britain's side, and that whenever crucial decisions affecting China have had to be made — on trade, Formosa, Korea, representation in the U.N. — she has tended (for understandable reasons) to support Washington rather than to follow her own instincts?

Britain would have been a better friend to America — and would in no way have jeopardized her powerful bond with her — if she had more consistently followed her own highest interests and opened the channels of trade and communications with China more fully. Today America is at an impasse. Though some of her leaders have seen the necessity of improved relations with China they find themselves hampered by public sentiment which they themselves had previously encouraged. America in this dilemma needs a friend — not merely an ally who will acquiesce reluctantly in formal decisions. Nothing would more readily prepare the American public for the changes that are necessary than for Britain, on this issue of China, to speak her mind openly and act without equivocation.

*

In the summer of 1960 I went to China for the second time, under contract to write this book. And here I must make a personal explanation. I write as an Anglo-American. By this I mean that I am both, and could never again be exclusively one or the other. I have spent twenty-five years of my adult life in the United States, but I was born and educated in England. My legal residence is in America, but my mixed activities of correspondent and businessman bring me to England at least twice a year. Countless associations of business and friendship and family bind me to America, much of my work is there, my home is there, I married there, my child goes to school there: but technically, and, I think, in my outlook, I am British.

Only those who live in both Britain and America as I do can know how both countries can be *home*: how it is possible to feel loyalty to both with no essential conflict. I explain this to avoid what might otherwise seem confusing: for though I went to China on a British passport (and could not have gone on an American), and though this Preface to the English edition is written in England and in my role as an Englishman, the 'we' used in this book refers (by long habit of affectionate identification) to 'us' Americans.

*

A journey to Communist China, which so few Westerners have visited, immediately gives rise to a host of questions: Was I free to travel where I wished? Were places prettied up for my benefit? What restrictions were placed on my photography? Did I ever travel alone or was someone always accompanying me? Was I able to meet anybody opposed to the regime? And could they talk freely? Not all these questions can be answered with a simple yes or no, but I believe they are all in some way answered in the course of this book.

I have relied a great deal on my journal — the notes taken while I travelled; and I have also made use of letters which I sent from China to my wife Elena and others. My own fluctuating moods appear in these notes and letters, and that perhaps is as it should be. No one can travel in China without feeling enchanted, angry, overwhelmed, frustrated, touched, saddened, optimistic, puzzled — everything but bored. I do not think that anyone with a grain of human curiosity could feel bored in China today.

I have tried to cover some of the more important facets of Chinese life. There are serious and obvious gaps. Factual information is not easy to come by in China. There are no standard reference books such as one could expect to find in America or even in Russia. There are no resident correspondents who have lived in China for years and who could provide background material. The Western diplomatic corps, while friendly and helpful, are themselves able to see less of China than a travelling correspondent like myself. And, of course, with statistics you can never win. If you quote them, they will be 'unreliable'. If you do not, your report will not be 'factual' enough. I have included some essential data which I believe to be true and which British industrial experts, French economists and others have accepted as accurate.

What I have tried most of all to convey is the *feel* of China, what the people are like, how they live, what they think, how the country functions. There are many inconsistencies in my report, because China is a very inconsistent country. There's too much going on. The country is in full spate of experimentation. And it's changing all the time. No one reporter can do anything but touch the fringe of all this. China is in the middle of a gigantic social and industrial explosion, and explosions are not always ruled by consistency.

*

One important element in the whole China picture is her feelings about America. The intensity of her hostility colours her world perspective and profoundly influences her policies. It is altogether wrong to interpret this hostility (as some American writers do) as being deliberately engineered to maintain an otherwise uncertain unity at home. The causes have far deeper origins than that. Many Chinese (and especially those who have been educated in America) spelt out to me with considerable cogency and a wealth of documentation why they feel so bitterly towards the United States. I have assembled my notes of these talks and have compiled from them what I have called 'the Chinese case'. This may not make comfortable reading; but if we hope to understand China we had better know why she feels about America as she does.

*

When in 1960 I went back to China, I had many questions in mind. I had been impressed and surprised by much of what I saw in 1957, but what changes had taken place since then? Were the people still as solidly behind the government? Was their revolutionary enthusiasm beginning to flag? What new developments had taken place in education, in medicine? I wanted to know more about the basic structure of China's economy and more about law and how it was being applied. What about prisons? What about Sino-Russian relations? And above all there were the communes about which we had read such dire reports and which were not even heard of when I was there before.

To find answers to these and many other questions I spent nearly five months travelling over ten thousand miles. I talked with cabinet ministers and pedicab drivers, with heads of government departments and writers. I visited schools, factories, prisons, hospitals. I went to many communes, spent days with the peasants, and ate with them in their communal dining-halls. Before I left China I had a long talk with Premier Chou En-lai.

This book describes what I saw and what I learned.

ACKNOWLEDGMENT

IT would be impossible for me to list by name all those in Asia, England and America who have in one way or another contributed to this book, whether by assisting me in preparation of the manuscript, or by deepening my knowledge and understanding of events in China.

To all of them, I remain enormously indebted.

Especially, I would not wish this book to leave my hands without an expression of gratitude to the scores — the hundreds, actually — of individuals in China who extended to me hospitality, courtesy, and hours upon hours of time. These included peasants and scientists, labourers and engineers, bellboys and cabinet ministers. Among them were many in official positions, but by far the larger number were ordinary citizens.

They were as eager to tell me about their country as I was to learn. Otherwise, this book could not have been written.

I

Hong Kong

May 23rd

Mʏ last day in Hong Kong. The usual rush. All the things I had put off or forgotten, and a hundred others never before thought of. Fountain pen, extra notebook paper, colour filters, extra batteries for the new tape recorder. Every shop, of course, claiming the rock-bottom cut rates. I studied one of the new Bolex 16-mm. cameras, rapidly weakening. Would they ever permit taking movies of the communes? Probably not. But they might, they just might. I broke down: Bolex, zoom lens, all the gadgets, complete with the light-weight tripod which I think weighs half a ton. Sweating and en-cumbered, I dodged through the crowded streets of this summer city.

On my fourth trip to the China Travel Agency, bad news for the fourth time. Still no visa....

'It will be all right,' said the agent.

'But they definitely promised the confirmation from Canton.'

'It will be all right.'

I gave up. In any case the whole business was now out of my hands. And I wanted to look up Kwai-ling before I left.... Hailing a cab, I rode to the grocery where she worked ... where she *had* worked when I had last seen her the year before.

'Gone,' said the proprietor.

'Gone? Where?'

A shrug of the shoulders.

I went to the tenement she had lived in, across the bay in Kowloon. It was gone too. I mean the whole building was gone; they had pulled

15

it down. Nothing was there at all, no one to ask: a gaping hole in that ghastly row of structures. Disappointed, I found myself searching for her along the crowded street as if she might still be somewhere near. One face among three million; what a hope!

Late this afternoon I returned to my hotel. At the desk was a phone message, an invitation for cocktails at six, to one of the grand houses on the Peak. I got there by seven, and found a larger crowd than I had expected. I remembered a few faces from before ... some of the government people, several correspondents. Hong Kong is infested with correspondents. All hoping to get into China, all suspicious of those who do. But I am going in. I'm no longer part of this ... provided the visa comes through. I was too anxious, too excited, too close to China, to care very much what went on at a cocktail party.

Drink in hand, I stepped out on to the terrace.

Below, in its myriad winking lights, lay the city of Hong Kong and the harbour with its ships; and lights glimmering in the black water, and beyond the harbour the lights of Kowloon. Farther off, behind the dark hills, was China. I thought again of Kwai-ling, who had come from China, and wondered where she was now; and I thought for a moment of all the other Kwai-lings ... all these trim, twinkling, tragic, undaunted little Chinese girls of Hong Kong. How many thousands had traced out their lives through the darkness of those fantastic lights?

I had been introduced to Kwai-ling by mutual friends, distant relatives of hers, I believe, when I had been in Hong Kong on a reporting job the year before. She was a refugee ... nineteen, quick and slim, with a shy laugh. I took her out to dinner once or twice and she told me something about the living conditions of the refugees in Hong Kong. One day I went to the grocery where she worked.

'Kwai-ling,' I said, 'when you've finished work, let me see where you live.'

'Oh no, *no*!' she exclaimed. 'You wouldn't like it at all. It's a very bad home.'

'That's why I want to see it.'

She considered this for a moment. 'All right, you come. Then you must tell other people how girls in Hong Kong have to live.'

That afternoon, after work, we took the ferry across to Kowloon. Kwai-ling's home was in a seven-storey tenement off one of the main

16

streets. We climbed flights of creaking stairs, dark, stinking of urine. I remember that she took my hand to lead me down a black corridor. She knew the way as a blind person knows, with her feet. Opening a door, she switched on a light.

'This is where I live.'

The room was no larger than a closet.

The bed was a plank on brackets with mattress, and the room was exactly long enough for the bed and there was space beside to stand. That was all. No window. The only light came from the bare bulb in the ceiling.

'How long have you lived here?' I asked.

'Three years.'

Three walls were flimsy wallboard, one was made of cardboard. As we stood silent, I heard stirrings and movements around us, footsteps from the other side. The room, I remember, was meticulously clean, but everything, the air, the walls themselves, smelt of decay. One tiny cupboard held Kwai-ling's possessions. And there was a box too, the size of a shoe-box, upon which she had propped a photograph. It seemed inconceivable that this young girl, so precise and neat in her blue dress, could find only a hole like this to live in.

As there was no chair — there wasn't room for one — we sat on the bed.

She explained that this was a great improvement on the first place she had lived in because here at least she was alone.

I picked up the photograph. It showed a large family group in a garden, posed rather formally.

'That's my father and that's my mother,' Kwai-ling told me. 'And that little girl is me.' She pointed out her sisters, her aunts and uncles. 'The picture was taken in Canton before the trouble began. My father is dead now and my mother is back in Canton, though.I don't know where. I have a brother in Taiwan, a sister in America.... '

A very usual Chinese story....

She took the photograph from me, held it in both her hands and looked at it as if she hoped that by gazing at it long enough she could will herself back into that garden.

'Would you like to go back?' I asked.

She said nothing for quite a long time. 'I think we all want to go back. It's our country. More and more of us are going back. But I'm frightened. What would it be like? What would they do to me? And if I couldn't stand it ... could I get out again? There are still some who get out and come here to Hong Kong ... and they tell us such different stories ... and why doesn't my mother write? I don't know. I can't stay here, but I don't know where to go. The American quota is closed, or I might be able to join my sister there. I just don't know. And now that you've seen where I live, you'd better leave.'

'Come along. Let's go and find somewhere to eat.'

But she was still looking at the photograph and shook her head.

I said goodbye, and found my own way down the dark staircase.

That was a year ago.

And where was she? Back in China? Or still fleeing it, still somewhere in the city below?

I heard a burst of music from inside as someone fiddled with the record player. A man I didn't know, an American, joined me on the terrace with a glass in his hand.

We stood looking over the harbour of Hong Kong and the lights of Kowloon, at the distant hills.

'I hear you're off to the promised land.'

'Yes. Tomorrow.'

'How in hell did you manage a visa? Special pull?'

'No. I've been waiting a long time. Of course,' I added, 'it helps to have chosen a British father.'

He fingered his glass. 'Never mind,' he said. 'Hong Kong has its compensations ... no slogans, no communes, no production statistics ... and the girls! I bet you'll be mighty happy to see Hong Kong again when you're through getting led around those communes. And just bear this in mind. You're jail meat if you so much as wink at a girl. China? Boy — you can have it!'

II

Going In

May 24th

FAR too early, I arrived at Kowloon station.

The confirmation had not yet come. 'But it will be all right,' the travel representative once more assured me. 'It will be at the border.' But will it? Who can tell? I already imagined the border official, polite, smiling: 'So sorry, Mr Greene, it will not, after all, be quite convenient for you to enter China just now.... ' It had happened to others — the last-minute change of mind in Peking. But at least I was not afraid today, as I had been three years before. I was actually half hoping, then, that I *would* be turned back at the border. There had been so many warnings from Hong Kong friends. 'You're a damn fool to be going in,' they had told me. 'They know you live in America. They'll trump up some spy charge against you. Then you've had it.' Another had said, 'Everybody is followed continuously, of course, and your letters will be opened and phone calls tapped. Watch your step, man!' Most disturbing of all was the dapper little Chinese who had approached me in the hotel entrance the night before I left. (Who *was* he, anyway?) Slipping an innocuous picture postcard into my hand, he had said in perfect English, 'If you get into trouble, Mr Greene, or if you think they are about to arrest you, post this and we will see what we can do.' He had disappeared before I could even say 'Hey, wait a minute!' I tore the postcard up.

Despite the frightful warnings, I had gone into China, spent four or five weeks, and lived to see Hong Kong again. So I knew better this time. My only real anxiety now was that delayed confirmation from Canton.

At 10.20, on schedule, the train pulled out of Kowloon and headed for the border. We meandered past vegetable plots and rice paddies, among the low hills, the lakes and inlets of the New Territories. At each stop a few more passengers left our first-class coach. None got on. At last there were only three of us left. Nothing could have conveyed to me more eloquently how cut off China is from the Western world. There are two ways by which Westerners can enter China: from Russia (there's a jet plane service twice a week from Moscow to Peking), and this daily 10.20 train out of Hong Kong. Into Britain more than four thousand travellers come every day. New York alone receives at least a thousand daily by ship and by air. Here, going into China (which has almost three times the population of the United States and Britain combined), just three of us.

My two fellow-travellers, I learned, were Australians on their way to Peking to sell wool. Friends, but representing different companies. One was tall, distinguished, of English background; he fitted my mental image of a director of the Bank of England. The other was short and tough, humorous in an American style (and originally was American). He introduced himself as Hank. The 'director' had never been to China before and didn't want to go. He seemed as nervous as I had been three years earlier. He believed, I think, that his chances of ever coming out hung by the slenderest of threads. Hank, who had been on regular circuit to Peking for the last five years, kept up a running patter which did nothing to cheer his friend.

Fifty minutes after leaving Kowloon the train clanked to a halt. We were at the border.

Instantly, from other carriages, hundreds of Chinese swarmed down and scurried off towards the insignificant iron bridge that links China with British territory. They were families returning from visits to friends and relatives in Hong Kong, or people from Hong Kong going on visits to China; or students home for the holidays; or small business-men, merchants, pedlars — all struggling with bundles and baskets, nets of fruit, chickens, boxes, suitcases, great bundles of bedding; and everyone laughing and chattering as if it were a great spree. They all seemed to know where to go. The three of us did not. We stood, self-conscious and uncertain, till we were ushered to a small waiting-room by a Travel Service man.

'We have sent your passports across,' he told us. 'When your visas are stamped, they will send them back and you can go.'

We waited twenty, thirty minutes. Some hitch, I thought. The 'director' closed his eyes, pressing his finger-tips to his forehead. Hank was telling me about a deal he had made last week in Cairo — but I wasn't listening. There's been a hitch, I told myself. There's been some hitch.

Our turn came at last. A Chinese official in spotless white jacket came to us and said, 'I have your visas — will you please come?'

As we trudged across the bridge towards Shumchun, the railway station on the Chinese side, I recalled my 1957 trek and made some mental comparisons. There were still guard towers on each side, but this time I caught no glint of bayonets. I saw no machine-guns, no barbed wire, no officers peering through field-glasses. On the Chinese side only one somewhat bored khaki-clad soldier leaned on his rifle.

Most of our bags had already been carried across the bridge by porters — the last time, I had had to carry them myself. And there was solid wood planking to walk on rather than tiptoeing on the sleepers. Precisely at the centre of this undramatic iron bridge the three of us walked into China. I glanced at my companions. The 'director', tall, erect and pale, advanced to his doom. Hank, irrepressible, was trying his handful of Chinese words on the official beside him. All I could think was, My God, I'm really in!

*

All borders are a separation. And this trivial, almost unguarded bridge much more than most. To some this bridge has represented hope, to some disenchantment and despair. To all of us it has become a wall of ignorance and fear. But walls have two sides, and I have breached it, and now my work is ahead of me, difficult and defined: to see and report as fairly as I can what it looks like here on the other side.

III

Peking Express

SLUNG with Bolex, exposure meters, gadget bags, my Zeiss cameras, and that 'light-weight' half-ton tripod, I staggered after the others. Health certificates first. In another waiting-room, another long form to fill in — border stations are the same all over the world. Camera numbers? Quantity of unexposed film? The usual questions.

Next, to the examination of baggage.

My miniature tape recorder intrigued the examiner.

'It's very small,' he said.

I nodded. He was, I think, an electronics engineer at heart. He fingered the recorder affectionately. 'Nickel cadmium batteries?'

'Yes.'

'Does it have a wide frequency range?'

'No, but good enough for speech.' I knew what he wanted and waited for him to ask.

'May I switch it on?' He was like a small boy.

'Of course.'

The night before, in my hotel room, to test the thing, I had picked up an old copy of an American magazine, I have forgotten which, and read from the first page that fell open. What was it I had read? Panic as it came to me — too late. From the tiny machine, my own voice spoke, clear, distinct: 'With the use of modern infra-red film and stereo lenses wide areas of territory can today be photographed from high altitudes.... '

Why had I chosen *that*, of all pieces to read? Why not a symphony review or a marriage announcement? Why in the name of heaven had I not washed the thing off? The customs man, expressionless, was listening intently. I saw my China trip ending here ... held for investigation

... tape sent to Peking for analysis ... an international incident ... British spy ... American saboteur ... *idiot!*

The voice finally petered out.

The customs inspector switched the machine off and gently closed the lid. 'Thank you,' he said, 'thank you very much. Very interesting. Very good voice reproduction.' He held out his hand. 'We hope you have a pleasant stay in China, Mr Greene. The train to Canton will leave in an hour. There is a restaurant upstairs.'

'Goodbye,' I said. 'And thank *you* very much.'

Upstairs, I found my two Australians studying the luncheon menu. The restaurant looked clean and bright with white tablecloths and flowers. The 'director' was a man reprieved but not yet altogether out of the shadows. No firing squad, just life imprisonment. 'I must admit,' he said, with admirable Anglo-Saxon sportsmanship, 'that these officials couldn't have treated us with greater courtesy.' But he added, 'We have to realize, of course, it's all part of the plan to create a good first impression.'

The Canton train was in by the time we finished lunch. Passengers again with bundles, chickens, babies, boxes, children, stood waiting to board. Soldiers were in the line too — there was no priority. And no one shoving or pushing, but everyone talking at a great rate. We were led to an observation car at the end of the train — our bags were already aboard. Soon after, to a great blast of music from loudspeakers on the lamp poles, and another loud blast (with a different tune) from speakers on the train, the train rolled out of the station.

*

This was a fancy coach, better than anything I had seen three years before. Leather chairs faced each other, set far enough apart for plenty of leg-room. At the rear was a potted tree, and several smaller shrubs, like a conservatory; and there were flowers and ferns on the tables between the chairs. Two rosy-cheeked, pigtailed girls, looking astonishingly young, in grey-blue skirts and white blouses, kept dusting and cleaning, and fetched us tea at frequent intervals. The coach was not full. There were perhaps ten others, apart from the Australians and myself. All were young men in T-shirts. When I opened my Bolex

23

and threaded a reel of film, they gathered round to watch. Everything was very informal. Catch a Chinese eye and it invariably responds with a smile.

The view from the train windows was like a scene from a Sung painting, even more Chinese than I had remembered. Old clustered villages with their curved roofs among the terraced rice fields. Tiny silver waterfalls sparkled from terrace to terrace, an irrigation system two thousand years old and still working. Peasants in the fields in their wide cone hats, at work, or walking languidly with rake or hoe over their shoulders. And water buffalo. And brakes of bamboo and banana trees; everything green and lush.

There were young trees everywhere, I noted, especially along the sides of the railway track, five, eight, ten rows deep. Acacia, pine, eucalyptus. Trees — miles and miles of them. I remembered them as not much more than twigs three years ago. Now they are eight and ten feet tall. There are almost no large trees visible. China must have been a treeless land. Now, looking back from the observation car, the track runs endlessly between groves of young trees, their branches wildly waving with the rush of wind from the train.

*

We rolled into Canton late in the afternoon; there would be a two-hour wait for the train to Peking. I had asked at the border for an interpreter to meet me in Canton, and the Travel Agency had wired ahead. Mr Chin was waiting on the platform. He was friendly, eager to help. He slung some of my cameras over his shoulders and arranged for a porter to carry the other luggage. We went to a large waiting-room, cool, with white slip-covers on the furniture and a large fan spinning silently overhead. A young woman in plaits and trousers brought us tea.

Mr Chin said, 'How long did you work with the B.B.C., Mr Greene?'
I glanced up, surprised.
'Oh, I remember you well from your last visit,' he told me.
We talked then about some of the other foreigners he had helped on their way through Canton. His comments were witty and perceptive.

I asked what had become of my Australian companions, and learned that arrangements had been made for them to go on to Peking by air.

It was very hot. Obviously Mr Chin was sleepy, and I was too, but I wanted to see something of the town. I suggested that he should stay while I went out for a stroll. At this he looked dubious. 'You might get lost,' he warned. But the thought of a short nap in the cool waiting-room must have appealed to him. 'Be sure to come back in plenty of time,' he called, and settled himself into one of the armchairs.

Historically, Canton has long been a city of insurrection — it was here the Opium War started, and the Sun Yat-sen revolution; this is where the Communist movement in the 'twenties reached its greatest ferment and where it was ruthlessly crushed by Chiang Kai-shek. It was a city of secret societies and dark assassinations. It was from here that the Chinese travelled to make new homes in South-east Asia, in Hawaii, in America. Today the largest industrial city of south China, it seems the least touched by the great clean-up, the least refurbished, of any Chinese city. Grey and sprawling, crowded and dirty, Canton spans the Pearl River. On the river the tugs hoot and push their way among the thousands of sampans and junks with patched and tattered sails, on which Chinese still are born and live and die.

In the streets, I walked into the throbbing life of a Chinese city. The poverty hit me almost like a physical blow! I had forgotten how poor the Chinese are. But it's not a sullen or apathetic poverty; not like India — not a sitting-around-waiting-for-something-to-happen kind of poverty. Here, in spite of squalid surroundings, a general atmosphere of vitality. Children playing lustily everywhere — some followed me, giggling.

At a lumber yard, tiny, slight men, stripped to the waist, backs glistening with sweat, were carrying waterlogged tree trunks from a river — each one fifteen feet long and at least six inches or more thick, a load for four or six men at home. Staggering, they carried these immense weights up a slope, then across a busy street to the sawmills. Unbelievable that these thin bodies could bear so heavy a load. I also stopped to watch some small-scale iron-casting — men hauling tremendous buckets of molten iron drawn from a kiln and pouring it into sand moulds. Four men to a load. Rough ground. A single stumble and the bucket would have spilled, with dreadful consequences.

Vitality and poverty. Children and laughter. Shrill music from loudspeakers. Women sitting on doorsteps chattering, men calling to each other across the street. The noise, the children, the squalor, the buoyancy — I knew I was really back in China.

On the Train to Peking

I said goodbye to Mr Chin at Canton. I'm on my own and have just finished a splendid dinner — pressed duck, fish fried in batter with sweet-sour sauce, shredded onions, small peas, and rice, topped off with a huge bowl of soup. Soup ends the meal in China. All this with beer cost 8s. 6d. (The official rate of exchange is 6·859 yuan to £1. For simplicity I have translated yuan values throughout at the rate of 1 yuan = 3s.)

The dining-car is clean and continually swept and dusted. I watched them dusting even around picture frames and over the mouldings. The tables have white cloths and covers of transparent plastic, easy to wipe down. General atmosphere informal and relaxed. I realize again that China is a workers' country. The ordinary people have taken over. It's their show. The men wear T-shirts. Easy-going, a good deal of joking. No one pays much attention to me — except the children, of course, who always think foreigners are funny. There is no menu. The waiter tells people what's available and they order by word of mouth. Service is quick. Among the diners I could spot, here and there, serious young men in glasses, obviously intellectuals. Schoolteachers perhaps, or scientists. They wear the same clothes, but seem a little quieter than the others, though they join easily enough in the general talk.

I think I am the only foreigner on this twelve-coach train. The train is not at all crowded. I have the compartment to myself, so far. My books, cameras, typewriter are scattered on the other beds. Nearly every hour the girl knocks and fills my tea mug from a huge can of steaming water. We try and talk together. Pointing, she tells me the Chinese for 'tea', for 'mug', for 'bed', for 'book' (*cha, bei, chuang, shu*). Then she points to her hot-water can to indicate that she must be off on her rounds.

I get down at most station stops, partly for exercise, partly to sniff the atmosphere. As in America, an attendant stands at the coach entrance wiping the handles. The railway staff has a passion for cleanliness. At several of the longer stops girls with long-handled brooms and buckets of water wash down the outside of the coaches.

The coach I am travelling in was made in China in 1957. It isn't sleek. No air-conditioning, no vista-dome, no chairs that tilt back at the touch of a button. Simple, utilitarian. There are two classes. I'm travelling first class, which means a compartment with four berths, each berth with sheets, a blanket, and one not very soft pillow. There are double windows — the lower half of the outside pane is a fine screen, which dims the view and holds back the larger lumps of soot (all trains are coal burners) but allows the fine dust to get in. The Chinese have built several diesel-electric locomotives but they are not yet on regular runs.

Above the window is a loudspeaker; a strident woman's voice and the piercing wail of Chinese music, with now and again a more melodic tune that reminds me of a Scots lament. The perpetual music and running commentary was driving me mad till I discovered a control knob under the table, by which the volume could be lowered or the loudspeaker turned off altogether.

Cost of Travel: Canton–Peking, forty hours, more than a thousand miles, with sleeper for two nights: 117 yuan, or £17 11s. Air fare: 159 yuan, or £23 17s.

Meals: Western breakfast of three fried eggs with ham, tea, toast, butter, and jam, usually around 3s. 6d.; Chinese dinner and lunch (quite lavish, with beer or wine) around 8s. 6d.

Hints to Travellers: Take your interpreter to the dining-car before the train starts and you are left to your own devices. Through him let the chef know you like Chinese food and leave the choice to him. Ask when they would like you to come for meals. He will then do his best — some of the tastiest meals I have had in China were on the railways. There's no tipping in China, *anywhere*. Don't even *try* to tip, it will be as embarrassing as if you tried to tip an airline hostess. Receipts are given for everything, even the twopence you pay for the packets of tea and hot water, which are brought continuously to your compartment.

Before you go to China, try and learn a *few* Chinese characters and words. It pays off in the appreciation that is apparent everywhere. A little book put out by the Foreign Language Press in Peking, *English-Chinese Conversation*, is quite helpful. Having learnt a few words I was able to say to the waiter in the dining-car, '*Fan hen hao chih!*' (the food is excellent). I was not quite certain he understood, but a few moments later the chef popped his head round from the kitchen and gave me a wave — my message had reached its destination.

Leave everything in your compartment. Nothing is stolen. Beer is all in *large* bottles and very good. Today, I tried some red wine, which is good too, though rather sweet. Take your own towels. They *do* provide toilet paper, but it's like sandpaper. Toilets on the trains are not clean by American standards, but I have seen worse in Britain and France.

Just accept the fact that on a long journey you will get black. Don't wear white clothing. There's a choice — open your window and let the fine dust through the screening and *breathe*, or close the window, keep clean, and *suffocate*. I chose the dirt and air.

*

At one station during a ten-minute stop a crowd of interested young men gathered round me as I was making a recording of some station sounds. A policeman shooed them away — thought they were worrying me, and I couldn't get him to understand that I didn't mind. They moved off sullenly. When the policeman had gone I waved them back and they came grinning.

We are moving north across the Yangtze Valley and soon will be crossing the Yangtze River over the famous new bridge. From the train window, mile upon mile of rice terraces, in all shades of green, many with water standing on them. These terraced fields are so old, conform so gently to the contour of the land, that they seem to have become part of the natural landscape. Rice apparently has no season. I saw some being planted — girls with rolled-up trousers calf-deep in water, bending, with swift, deft movements planting the green tufts. Elsewhere peasants were harvesting. In some villages I saw them tossing the rice into the air, letting the wind do the winnowing, in the ancient way.

Almost all of this main line is now double-tracked. The new track, especially, appears well ditched and ballasted. Kilometres, in quarters, marked off along the track. I watched the locomotive being oiled last night under floodlights. A swarm of oilers were at work while the engine driver stood with list in hand and checked off the bearings as the oilers reported to him. Only when the list was fully checked did he signal that the locomotive was ready to go.

At all stops of ten minutes or longer, wheel tappers go down both sides of the train inspecting the wheels, lifting journal-box covers, feeling for the heat of the bearings. I watched a maintenance man check the adjoining track, both for level and for gauge. He could read on a rotating dial the amount of any deviation. I walked with him for a few moments and watched him closely as he moved down the line. The tolerance permitted seemed a narrow one. Each deviation beyond this tolerance he carefully recorded in a book. Trains in China ride astonishingly smoothly, even at high speeds.

At Canton I had walked up to the locomotive before we started. In the cab was a round-faced girl engine driver. She wore a peaked cap stuck jauntily on the back of her head. By her confident looks and gestures one felt how proud she was at having stepped into this man's world. There was an engineer, a man, with her. Both wore white cotton gloves.

Last night, at one of the stops, there was a gaily-covered booth with curved roof selling toilet articles. I bought a plastic soap box and a face-cloth. Lots of business. I lined up with the rest waiting my turn. When the girl looked up and saw I was a foreigner, she broke into a delighted grin.

A security policeman travels with the train. He seems to be always putting on his jacket, which is never properly buttoned up. I prefer this to the over-correct. Before we come into a station he hastily buttons up and puts on a belt. I often see him in the dining-car chatting with the train crew over a cigarette. Old-timers in China later told me that security police who travelled with the trains in Chiang Kai-shek's time were pretty tough.

May 26th

As we approached Peking, the excitement grew. I was summoned to lunch very early and I understood why later, when I saw the tables in the dining-car being scrubbed, chairs piled high, soy-sauce bottles emptied and washed. In the sleeping-car, carpets were lifted and the floors mopped down. During the forty-hour journey from Canton I estimated that the outsides of the coaches must have been washed down at least ten times. The train arrived as bright and shiny as when it left Canton.

I went into the kitchen after my last meal to shake hands with the four cooks and thank them. '*Shieh-shieh ni.*' They were delighted. '*Hen hao, hen hao,*' they said: very good, very good. When I got back to my compartment, the train was slowing down; we passed the city wall and slid slowly into a brand-new station. Potted plants stood in rows along the platform; and from the inevitable loudspeakers came the blare of a Sousa-type march, 'Socialism Is Good'.

We arrived two minutes ahead of schedule.

IV

A Banquet

THE Intourist representative was waiting for me at the station. An intense young man, apparently just on the boil under the surface, with unexpressed feelings and wordless passions. He was somewhat brusque. He conveyed that I was not to expect any little insincere speech of welcome from him, and I liked him for it. Whisking me through the ticket barrier, he said, 'This is our new station, you can see it all later'; and with that, we were into a taxi and off through the wide and tree-lined streets of Peking to the Hsin Chiao Hotel.

The Hsin Chiao, a large grey structure built in 1954 for returning Overseas Chinese, is now one of the main centres for foreign visitors. The much grander Peking Hotel is known as 'The Mausoleum', and I was glad not to be there. Accommodation at the Hsin Chiao is unpretentious but adequate. Each room has a private bath, telephone, desk, and two easy chairs, but, curiously, no chest of drawers. A message awaiting me at the desk requested me to call at the Information Office of the Ministry of Foreign Affairs at my earliest convenience.

I unpacked, sent my 'good' suit to be pressed, and set off by taxi for the Ministry. I should, I supposed, very shortly learn something of what was in store for me. Would the government be helpful? Would they be suspicious or friendly? What facilities would be given me to photograph? To travel? To interview those I wanted to see? There was also the question of extending my visa, which had been issued for only a month. I should need much longer than that to gather material for my book. I felt I should soon know the answer to these questions. But in China such matters are not decided so quickly.

I learned that I was at liberty to photograph whatever I wished excepting military installations. As to motion pictures, that was a different story. I could put my request in writing. Extension of the visa? Maybe so, maybe not; perhaps best to leave that till a little later on, Mr Greene. Meanwhile, would I submit a list of things I wished to see while in Peking? I agreed that I would; and as I took my departure, I was presented with an invitation to a banquet being given by Premier Chou En-lai that evening for the visiting guest-of-state, Field-Marshal Montgomery.

It was after six-thirty when I got back to my hotel. The banquet was to start within forty-five minutes. No suit! 'Sorry,' said the floor boy. 'Pressing department is close. Suit ready tomorrow morning.'

'But I'm invited to a banquet with Mr Chou En-lai!'

'Excuse — we shall see.' He took off down the corridor at a run. Fifteen, twenty minutes went by; time to leave. I hurried downstairs, found no one who spoke English. I tried the telephone. 'Sorry,' said the phone girl. 'Laundry and pressing room are close.'

Where's that floor boy? Had he gone home? I waited, and there at last he was, like a relay runner, the suit on its hanger extended at arm's length. And beautifully pressed!

Cars were drawing up when I arrived at the great curved ramp at the northern entrance to the Great Hall of the People. Police, in white jackets, were directing the flow of traffic. There was no confusion. An immaculately uniformed soldier stood motionless on each side of the wide doors. No one asked to see my invitation or checked my credentials. Under the crystal chandeliers the new arrivals were moving slowly up a lane of heavy carpet laid across a vast foyer towards a magnificent flight of stairs. I glanced around at my fellow-guests. Many looked like senior government officials; there were military officers, some young men in workers' uniform, girls — some in skirts, others in trousers. Here and there were members of China's many minorities in vivid national costumes.

I knew no one.

At the head of the stairs we were directed to a reception room where the official whom I had met earlier at the Ministry of Foreign Affairs at once came forward to greet me and to introduce me to others. Here I met Ron Farquhar, of Reuters. Only two Western news agencies have permanent representatives in China — Reuters and Agence France Presse. I talked to some officials from the British Embassy. Strictly speaking, there is no British Embassy in Peking (as there is no Chinese

Embassy in London), for the two countries have not yet exchanged ambassadors. It is officially 'The Office of the British Chargé d'Affaires'. Britain is represented there by a Minister. I was also introduced to Madame Kung Peng, Director of the Information Department at the Foreign Ministry. I was immensely glad to meet her. Madame Kung has become something of a legend among foreign writers who have visited China. I first heard of her from James Cameron of the *News Chronicle*. Sooner or later her name crops up in any conversation among journalists dealing with China news.

Madame Kung was dressed in black. Her manner was quiet. She spoke in a low voice, pausing for a moment's reflection before answering my questions. I had been warned that she was somewhat 'formidable'. Certainly she appeared composed and self-possessed, and I judged that not much would escape that level, kindly, and slightly ironic gaze. She was a person, I felt sure, not much interested in the minor social flatteries, but once her interest was engaged on a serious level the sense of formality vanished. I found her not at all formidable.

Madame Kung Peng pointed out several of the guests who were seated in a central group of chairs. There was Henry Pu-yi, last of the Chinese Emperors, who had been released from confinement only eight months ago. Henry Pu-yi had 'ruled' China from the age of two until he was six. The Japanese brought him back in 1932 as Emperor of their puppet state of Manchukuo. He was then called K'ang Te. Not far from the former Emperor sat Marshal Chen Yi, now Foreign Minister, the Communist general whose forces captured Shanghai in 1949. Beyond Chen Yi were several other generals who had fought under Chiang Kai-shek against the Communists. One of these, Tu Yu-ming, had at one time been Chiang's commander-in-chief in Manchuria. He had led the Kuomintang forces in one of the last decisive battles of the civil war, in which he had been routed by the Communist armies under General Chen Yi. Later Tu had been condemned as a war criminal, and, like the one-time Emperor, had only recently emerged from prison. Here they all were, ex-prisoners and high officials, chatting pleasantly together at an official banquet!

The Prime Minister, Chou En-lai himself, now came in with the guest of honour, Field-Marshal Montgomery. Monty looked trim and alert, though rather older than I had expected. Chou En-lai, apparently ageless (he is now in his early sixties) appeared dapper, suave, thoroughly at ease in a simple grey Chinese jacket and trousers. I watched this man, fascinated by his gestures and by the rapid alternation of his expressions. An extraordinarily mobile face — now ironical, now jesting, now, at some comment from Montgomery, instantly alert and attentive.

Here, without doubt, was one of the most outstanding figures of modern history. He had been in the thick of it from the very start; a founder of the Chinese Communist Party in 1921, a soldier on the Long March, a leader throughout more than twenty years of civil war and a decade of war against the Japanese. He had led a life of miraculous escapes. Captured and imprisoned by Chiang's forces, he had more than once slipped through their fingers. A quarter of a million dollars on his head, he had walked unguarded among the peasants. Several times he had survived what for most human beings must have been total and annihilating defeat — and now he was Prime Minister, chief executive officer of the People's Republic of China. Hero to millions, devil to millions of others. What was one to read in such a face? Tenacity, a lively humour, the keenest intelligence, certainly; a man fully committed, without divisions within himself; yet also, perhaps, able to stand outside, watching, cool, detached, thoughtful....

I was quite close as Chou introduced Monty to Henry Pu-yi. Monty asked if he was happy. The last of the Manchu Emperors replied:

'I am a gardener now and I have never been happier in my life. It is much better to be a gardener than to sit on the throne of the Imperial Palace doing just what you're told to do.'

Chou laughed. Monty looked bewildered. I wondered if he knew who Pu-yi was. The Prime Minister now turned to the generals who had risen from their chairs and were waiting to be introduced. Pointing to Tu Yu-ming and Chen Yi, the Prime Minister said, 'These two fought each other. This one lost.'

'How many men did you have?' Montgomery asked Tu.

'A million.'

'Why did you lose if you had a million men?'

'They all ran over to his side,' said Tu, nodding towards Chen Yi. Chou En-lai threw back his head and laughed.

*

A BANQUET

We moved on to the banquet hall for dinner. This chamber, I was told, can seat five thousand guests at five hundred round tables. To-night there were only a hundred or a hundred and fifty people, but the room had been skilfully reduced in size by screens of potted plants. At one end was a stage hung with curtains of heavy gold brocade. Between courses, the curtains were drawn back and a programme of Chinese singing and dancing was presented, both classical and modern, ending with a professional performance of Western classics by the Central Philharmonic Symphony Orchestra. The entire programme was magnificent. And the food! Well, these were some of the items (among a good many others) on the menu:

> Jasmine chicken soup
> Three-coloured sharks' fins
> Green peas in chicken oil
> Steamed shad
> Roast-pork slices
> Duck with tea flavour
> Strawberries with cream

There were also red and white wines, Chinese brandy, and *mao tai*, a distilled liquor rather like a fierce vodka. We were served by young women who moved about with so little fuss and clatter that you scarcely noticed the constant reappearance of steaming platters in front of you.

Chou En-lai made a short speech of welcome to the visiting field-marshal. He offered a toast to the British people. We all stood while the band played 'God Save the Queen'. Then Chou walked from table to table — he came to ours and I tipped glasses with him. Monty, glass in hand, then made his reply:

'I should like very much to extend to Prime Minister Chou En-lai a very warm invitation to visit me personally as my private guest at my home in England so that I can show him my country and I hope very much that he will come.'

This was translated and brought a burst of applause from the guests.

Monty continued: 'Old China suffered many years of external aggression in which perhaps we British were not completely blameless, and suffered internal oppression of a feudal nature. You have swept away

35

emperors, war lords, absentee landlords, and foreign devils. All have gone.

'There is a new China under a new leadership which is determined to be master in its land and to plan its own destiny in its own way without any outside interference. From what I have seen, I like the new China better than the old.

'Now there are great misconceptions in the Western world about the new China. I find the Chinese people to be happy and cheerful, whereas in the Western world it is considered that the Chinese people are very depressed and unhappy.... '

When General A. C. Wedemeyer, U.S. Army, retired, read this speech, he challenged the British field-marshal in a letter to the Washington *Star*. (See Kaleidoscope 2.)

*

I walk home alone.

The night is warm. Everywhere about me I see the changes that have taken place since my previous visit. Tien An Men Square has been enormously enlarged. Old buildings are gone, walls gone, tram-lines gone. There are new buildings, new trees. Tien An Men itself, the main gate to what once were the Imperial Palaces, softly lighted, its roofs curved like a tent, still broods majestically over the capital of China.

Shi Chang An Chieh, the main boulevard which crosses the city from east to west, is ablaze with lights. But there are not many people out at this late hour. A few young men, nearly all in white open-necked shirts, and women in trousers and coloured blouses, stroll homeward along the pavements. The last cars from the banquet hall go speeding by; and a late pedicab trundles down the wide avenue carrying a prodigious load of furniture. I walk past Peking Hotel, then along Tai Chi Chang to what I still can only think of as 'Legation Street'. The Hsin Chiao is only a few blocks beyond.

I am tired; but the long suspense is over. I am *here*. Back in Peking. I feel again the enchantment, the strange and subtle spell that this extraordinary city casts on all who come here. I sniff the night air and am deeply content. I feel confident that all will go well with my undertakings....

PART TWO

V

Peking, the Old and the New

IN 1949 when the Communists marched into Peking, the city, with a population of not much more than a million and a half, was almost wholly enclosed within its walls. As in the days of the Emperors the gates of the city were shut at night. Immediately beyond the walls were the rice fields and vegetable gardens. Today, eleven years later, with a population that has soared to four million (seven and a half million if the whole municipal area is included), Peking has burst through its walled enclosure and has burgeoned outwards in every direction. The forty-foot-thick walls have been pierced to allow new boulevards to radiate from the city, and the walls are now not much more than picturesque reminders of a legendary past.

Peking continues to be the heart, the mind, the controlling centre, of China.

It is a very ancient city; its origins are buried in the far past. Records show that over four thousand years ago there was already a settlement at the spot where the present city stands. By the twelfth century the city, known then as Chungtu, was playing an important role as a commercial centre and as headquarters for the forces protecting the country from the encroachments of nomadic tribes from the north. When Genghis Khan swooped down from beyond the northern deserts he captured Chungtu. A hundred years later his grandson Kublai Khan, having conquered the whole of China, rebuilt the city and renamed it Tatu — the Great Capital. Called Peiping (Northern Peace) in the Ming dynasty, its name was changed in 1420 to Peking (Northern Capital), which it retained until 1928 when Chiang Kai-shek moved his capital south to Nanking and it was known again as Peiping.

Laid out when London was still a village, Peking has been burned, rebuilt, sacked, demolished by earthquakes, and rebuilt again; for six centuries it has been the city in which China's learning and wealth, culture and politics, found their national focus.

In October 1949, when the Chinese People's Republic was established, its position as the national capital and its name were restored, and it is today known as Peking throughout the world — except in the United States, in deference to the myth that Chiang Kai-shek is still the ruler of China. (To call it Peking would imply that the capital of China is there and not in Taipei, on the island of Taiwan.)

Peking is a city built on an ancient Chinese pattern, a series of rect-angles enclosed by walls. Its primary purpose was to enshrine the Imperial Palace. Peking, though its avenues are wide and straight, is a city of walls, of walls within walls. There is the wall of the Chinese City and the wall of the Tartar City; within the walls of the Tartar City are the walls of the Imperial City; and finally, within these are the rust-red walls of the Imperial Palace, the Forbidden City itself. In this inmost sanctuary are the golden-roofed palaces, the courtyards and the gardens from which successive Emperors held sway over the vast expanses of China — *Chung Kuo*, the Middle Kingdom. The architecture is mas-sive but of flawless proportion. One feels that these buildings, like China herself, will be here for ever. Never before, not even in Greece and Rome, have I felt so powerful a sense of the continuity of human history as I have in these palaces of Peking. Walking through the courtyards, it is not difficult to imagine their past glory and their almost total isolation from the teeming, hungry life of the ordinary mortals who lived beyond the walls.

The Forbidden City is no longer forbidden. It is open — free to children, and to anyone else who can raise the equivalent of twopence for admission. The halls, the temples, the living-quarters of the Emperors, most painstakingly and beautifully restored, are now national museums. Days can be spent here strolling through palaces with absurd and poetic names — the Hall of Supreme Harmony, the Palace of Heavenly Peace, the Hall of Mental Cultivation, the Palace of Earthly Tranquillity. Crossing the Golden Water on bridges of white marble you mingle with the crowds of visitors — soldiers walking hand in hand, Tibetans in hats, Africans slung with cameras, schoolchildren with bright-red scarves, babies carried piggy-back by brothers and sisters scarcely older than themselves. Pools reflect the drooping willow trees, butterflies hover over silent lotus ponds; and on a stool, watched by wide-eyed children sucking frozen sugar-water sticks, a man sits carving the sayings of Confucius on a single grain of rice.

Today, the city in no sense seems enclosed, but rather of limitless physical expansion. To this capital come visitors from almost every country on the globe. To millions of Asians, Latin Americans, and Africans, Peking has become the new Mecca.

Walking through the city one is given a strong impression of living in two eras. Peking is a big, clean, well-functioning modern city; it is also — one is reminded of this everywhere — a city that has just stepped out of the Middle Ages. From my hotel window I can see the Great Hall of the People, completed in 1958, and almost in the same glance my eye catches one of Peking's ancient gates — the Chien Men. Everywhere the old, the new. In the street below me a caravan of pedicab drivers will, on their makeshift and dilapidated tricycles, be transporting the latest delicate apparatus from an electronics plant.

There are more theatres in Peking today than in New York. Most of the fifty-five cinemas — some have wide-screen projectors — were built in the last ten years. There are sixteen main hotels, nearly all have gone up since 1950; they are up-to-date, with private bathrooms and telephones in every room. Unlike Moscow, everything — plumbing, hot water, room service — really *works*.

The postal service with 350 post offices in the city and suburbs is efficient and deliveries are rapid. China is a member of the International Postal Union and letters can be sent from here to anywhere in the world, including the United States. For reasons unknown I discovered that mail to America arrived much sooner if Hong Kong could be avoided. This could be done by writing 'via Moscow' on the envelope.

Officially there is no censorship of mail in China and I have no reason to suspect that any of my letters were read, but other Westerners, permanently resident in Peking, feel certain that some of their letters are opened. But *where* they are opened (in China or somewhere else along the route) is anybody's guess. When I questioned the head of the incoming foreign-mail department at the Peking central post office, he swore that mail was never tampered with in China.

You can cable from Peking to any country in the world. I received many cables from the United States and sent many, and they all went through without a hitch. One cable sent from California reached me in Peking in two hours. The domestic telegraph service is cheap and fast — there is a flat rate, regardless of distance, of the equivalent of one shilling for ten words, with an additional $1\frac{1}{4}d$. for each additional word. Documents or other written material can be sent by facsimile to most of the main cities of China for five shillings a sheet.

You can telephone from Peking to almost every country in the world *except* the United States. Telephone communication with Canada is possible, and I tried once to telephone to my wife in California *through* Canada. The Chinese accepted my call and said they would do their best to put it through, but rang back later and told me that the United States would not accept this arrangement. Long-distance calls to cities within China are subject to delays, and often the circuits are poor. In Peking itself there is a dial system a great deal more efficient than the London service, which, I admit, is not saying much. Again unlike Moscow, there are plenty of telephone directories, though unless you are an advanced scholar in Chinese, to find a number is a hopeless proposition. Local calls cost the equivalent of $1\frac{1}{2}d$. from a booth, but hotels make no charge for calls. If you dial 07 you will be given the time; if you dial 05 you can ask for a weather report, learn what's on at the theatres, or subscribe to a newspaper or magazine.

Other developments that have brought Peking into the twentieth century are the hospitals — at least thirty large new ones have been built, and some of these are as up-to-date as any in the West; more about these later; a modern sewage system, and water which is safe to drink. The Chinese have become very 'public-hygiene conscious'; people with colds are expected to wear surgical masks — this is a common sight. The streets — even the small lanes which are still of tamped earth — are swept and sprinkled down every day. Big water trucks are constantly washing down the wider streets. Peking is as clean or cleaner than many of the cities of England or America. No piles of garbage, no refuse, no smells, no cigarette stubs — and (it's true) almost no flies. China is now so clean that I broke what is otherwise one of my iron rules of travelling

— namely, never to eat uncooked vegetables or salads. In China I did both for nearly five months, including meals on the train, and suffered neither anxiety nor ill effects. I know of no other country in Asia where this is even thinkable.

The sheer volume of building construction going on in China — and I found this to be true in all the cities I visited — is overwhelming. New offices, hotels, museums, schools, blocks of flats, colleges, technical institutes, stadiums, gymnasiums, swimming pools, are going up in such numbers and at such a speed that it has to be seen to be believed. The construction — I have had some experience in the building line — is without question superior in technical quality to the buildings I watched being erected in the Soviet Union, where the engineering is sometimes inferior.

In speed of construction the Chinese have far out-Americanized America. By 1954 they had mastered the problems of smooth organization, a steady supply of materials to the building sites, and round-the-clock continuous operation. James Cameron of the *News Chronicle*, who was in China that year, reported in his book, *Mandarin Red*, how even then the pace of building was, unless you watched it yourself, unbelievable; how four new hospitals, six factories, and eleven full-scale Ministerial blocks, had been laid out, started, completed, and inhabited, in a matter of weeks. The hotel I stayed in in Nanking in 1957 — a four-hundred-room hotel with tiled bathroom to every room, telephones, lifts, all equipment — was (I was assured by a British resident who had watched it) completed in seventeen weeks, including the landscaping with almost full-grown trees brought in. James Cameron saw the Chinese genius for rapid construction in 1954; I saw it first in 1957; and now in 1960 they were outdoing even these earlier efforts.

To celebrate the *tenth* anniversary of the regime (1959), the government determined in 1958 that Peking would undertake *ten* major building projects and complete them in *ten* months. (The Chinese are fond of this kind of play with numbers. The revolution led by Sun Yat-sen was celebrated as Double Ten (October 10) and still is on Taiwan.) Two of these projects were the construction of the Museum of Chinese History and the Great Hall of the People. These vast buildings stand each side of Tien An Men Square. The square itself was enlarged from twenty-seven to nearly one hundred acres in extent, five times the size of St Peter's in Rome, and it is now the largest, and I think perhaps one of the most pleasing, squares in the world.

On the east of the square is the new Museum of Chinese History. Here you can trace the history of China through its art from its earliest beginnings to the modern era. This is now the repository of China's finest artistic treasures. Air-conditioned, beautifully lighted, and with its displays presented with the taste one would expect from these artistic people, this will one day be known as one of the great museums of the world.

Facing it across the square — the square is five hundred yards wide — stands another new building, the one that takes pride of place in the hearts of all Peking — the Great Hall of the People. Size and taste don't often go together. Here they do. The size of this building is staggering, its proportions and simplicity are noble. Eleven hundred feet long, fronted by ten columns, this building contains within it not only the five-thousand-seat banqueting hall where the dinner to Montgomery was held, and twenty-odd reception rooms each as big as a normal ballroom, but the Great Hall itself. With two sweeping, unsupported balconies, this auditorium holds ten thousand people, and it is here that the National People's Congress meets, and all the other great political meetings and rallies, as well as the large concerts, are held.

There are several novel features about this hall. Its design breaks every known rule of acoustics, but you can, in spite of its size, hear distinctly in every part of it. Unknown to you, the sound from the stage is reaching you from ten thousand small loudspeakers — one is installed at the back of every chair. All seats on the ground floor are equipped with ear-phones through which you can hear a simultaneous translation of a speech in any one of twelve different dialects or languages. Russian and English are invariably among these. Another interesting fact about this hall is that while fourteen thousand workers were employed in its construction, citizens of Peking could give whatever volunteer help they wanted, and many thousands did so at week-ends, in the evenings, or during their holidays. One of my interpreters, a girl, once pointed to the building as we passed it in a car and said, 'I helped to build that hall!'

If this hall (even with the help of volunteers) had been built in ten years, it would still have been an architectural triumph. Designed, built, equipped, landscaped and fully completed in ten months, it is a miracle.

The ugly grey Hsin Chiao Hotel, ten minutes' walk from Tien An Men Square at the end of Sungcheng Street, is my home base. It is from here that I set out every morning for the day's activities. Soon after my arrival in Peking I was asked by the Information Department at the Ministry of Foreign Affairs for my list of what I wanted to do in Peking and the people I wanted to see. I spent my first week-end preparing my list, which filled fifteen typewritten sheets. (As I handed this formidable document to an official, he blanched, and for a moment I felt he was about to lose his composure. 'It is a very long list ... we cannot promise ... we will do our best.... ') And now, working heroically through this list, Mr Shen Shou-yuan is on the phone every morning at eight o'clock to check with me the arrangements for the day.

It is from the Hsin Chiao that I step out strong, fresh, rested, eager for whatever the day may bring; new films in my cameras, lenses cleaned, and a semi-Western breakfast under my belt. And it is back to the Hsin Chiao that I limp in the evening, dirty, sweaty, tired, my eyes red with coal dust from a visit to a factory, or boots muddy from a five-mile trudge across the fields of a commune. Or I may come back clean, but with my head spinning with facts and figures and analyses presented at some long briefing at a government department — and knowing that it will take six more hours of work to make sense of all this information and record it in my journal before I am deluged with yet more material the next day. I have worked on other reporting jobs under much more trying conditions; I have never worked harder than in those first few weeks in Peking; and I've never enjoyed a job more.

From time to time, when the pressure was too great, I would phone Mr Shen and, after the necessary courteous formalities of inquiring after each other's health, tell him that this day I wanted to look round on my own.

It was on these 'off' days when, in the soft Peking light, I strolled alone through the streets that I came gradually to terms with this amazing city. I began to learn what trolley buses would take me where. I was (at times) even understood when I ventured to ask my way. Peking still held me in a magic spell (and I think it always will), but I began to wake up in the mornings without a sense of stupefaction just at the thought of being there. I learned my way around the labyrinth of little lanes, the *hutungs*; how to reach the Street of Beautiful Objects to browse among antiques, or the Street of Silks, where I fingered the rich fabrics which I could admire but could not buy, since nothing made in China can be imported into the United States. I would idle for an hour watching the children play among themselves; I stood to listen to the traffic policeman calling to pedestrians through his megaphone, telling them they must hurry please across the road before the light changed, or shouting at the boy on a bicycle that he would most certainly meet his death if he didn't stop wobbling all over the street. On these days I would stroll to the parks, join the easygoing holiday-makers on the pleasure boats, and watch the children career down slides or, like children everywhere, play with endless fascination in the sand. I explored the restaurants. I began to know where to go for Peking Duck; where to find 'Instant Boiled Mutton' Mongolian style, or the hot spicy food of Szechwan province. And when thirsty I would sit on the pavement with a row of others, sipping pale tea which I had bought from a vendor for just one fen. Always something new. One day it's the tinker who comes by, tools balanced on his head, beating a little wooden drum; or boys carrying slogans which I cannot read; or a women's militia brigade trying to look earnest and efficient but not quite managing to keep in step.

And the tree-planting. Trees everywhere. Nine million trees (they tell me) have been planted in Peking alone, and I believe it. Trees line every street — and not just a sober row or two along each avenue, but eight rows or ten or twelve. Down one new avenue beyond the walls I counted trees *twenty* rows deep on either side. Around Tien An Men they have not planted small trees and waited for them to grow but brought in grown ones, pines and evergreens, roots carefully boxed. Not just a few but hundreds. One day I watched several more coming in on a lorry and a giant crane lifting them each in turn, and lowering them gently, almost lovingly, into the waiting cavity below. Peking that was once treeless is now a city of trees.

*

Up before five today and off for a walk. The hotel was quiet, everyone asleep except the man at the desk. He appeared undismayed at seeing a guest out so early and paid no attention to me as I went by.

PEKING, THE OLD AND THE NEW

I walked in the cool daybreak past Chungwenmen (which old China hands used to call Hatamen). The first sun was just touching the top of this great gate and thousands of swallows swooped in the pale sky. The streets were almost deserted. I passed a few old men walking in great dignity with hands tucked in their sleeves. After strolling along Chungwenmen Tachieh, I turned off into the maze of little grey alleys — the *hutungs*.

Here and there a rooster crowed; smoke curled up from breakfast fires. Householders sprinkled down the dust in front of their doorways. At one corner a group had collected around a vendor of brown, fried bean curd; a father was feeding his little son. Little by little the pavements became crowded. I heard the motors start up in a small machine shop, the rasp and pull of a handsaw from a cabinet maker's.

Men and women, buttoning their jackets, hurried along to the bus stops. No one appeared to notice me as a foreigner, no one bothered to look my way — a big difference from three years ago. It was a good walk. It reminded me that the great Tien An Men Square and the Imperial Palaces and the Hall of the People, where I had been a guest at the banquet for Monty, are staging — they provide the necessary heroic form to these stirring times. But the people of Peking were going about their daily, commonplace routines, as were the people of all other great cities of the globe this morning.

Back at the hotel for breakfast I share a table with a young Dutchman. We have met several times already. He is a businessman, here to sign a big contract. He is alert, sharp, likeable, and impatient. When fully three or four minutes have passed since he sat down and no waitress has taken his order, he snaps his fingers. The waitresses look across but don't hurry. 'They're impossible,' he said. He has been here six weeks dickering over the contract, always on the verge of agreement; I think it will be another six weeks before he's finished. Snapping one's fingers is not the way to produce results in China today.

Mr Shen was on the phone at eight o'clock. What shall it be today? A children's hospital? a commune? a museum? an interview with a cabinet minister? Today it's steel. 'May I photograph?' 'Of course.'

Yen Chao-hua, my interpreter, was waiting for me in the hall. Tall, loose-limbed, casual, Yen reminds me of an American college boy. His blue jacket is usually unbuttoned. He is always pleasantly at ease. He talks to a steelworker or a pedicab driver in exactly the same tone as he does to a cabinet minister — he's invariably polite, never servile, never ruffled. And he enjoys his work. And because he enjoys it he is a rattling good interpreter. If he knows I am to visit a lawyer, he will study legal terms; or before a visit to a hospital he will have spent the night before with a medical dictionary. A bad interpreter can ruin an interview; a good one can almost make one forget that the conversation is being interpreted at all. Yen is one of the best. He tells me nothing about his own life — the Chinese feel more than we do that that is their own affair — but in the course of time I learn that he is twenty-six years old and is married, and that's about all I ever learned about him.

*

China is a country of infinite and bewildering variety; but these official visits — whether it is to a government department, a commune, a school, or a prison — seem to follow a standardized procedure. So on this day I knew ahead of time that the director of the steel mill would be waiting to greet me as I stepped out of the car. How long, I have sometimes wondered, have I kept these busy people waiting? Friends of mine who have visited Mao Tse-tung were astonished to find him standing waiting to greet them as they alighted from their car. Great stress is placed on this act of courtesy; which, of course, makes punctuality enormously important. Our first stop will not be the blast furnaces or rolling mills, but a quiet reception room where, over tea and cigarettes, I shall be given a detailed briefing and have a chance to ask my questions.

The director of a large steel plant must obviously be a very busy man. Yet however much work he has piled on his desk, however many urgent telephone calls his secretaries may be receiving for him, he will not by the least gesture show impatience. If an interview is once granted, no time limit is imposed on it. It was not unusual for my talks to last four hours; I caught nobody surreptitiously looking at a watch. No secretary ever breaks in. Tea is poured, cigarettes are passed, and the talk continues. Almost always there will be one or two others in the room who take no part in the conversation. I am never introduced to them. They take notes assiduously. I am never told who they are. Probably members of the Party, which keeps an eye on everything that goes on, anywhere, everywhere, in China. I learned from visitors who were not journalists that no one took notes of their discussions. This procedure may be followed only when there might be need to check the accuracy of a published report.

*

'This factory,' the director was saying, 'was started in 1918 by the war lord Tuan Chi-jui. Those were times of great strife, and during the next three years only 36,000 tons of pig iron were produced....

'During 1959 the plant turned out 740,000 tons of iron and 170,000 tons of steel. We have just opened a new blast furnace with an annual capacity of 500,000 tons.... '

This, too, is the pattern of all such discussions: *growth* — over the cups of tea the facts and figures of a fantastic expansion. And whether or not one cared to question the figures, the *fact*, in broad outline, was indisputable. I needed only to glance out of the window to see it: the chimneys, the columns of yellow smoke slanting across the blue sky.

'We employ fifty-one thousand workers today! Two years ago it was only twelve thousand! We are leaping forward year by year and the lives of the workers are improving every day!' Everything was exclamatory. The director rocked forward on the edge of his chair, cigarette in hand, ejecting puffs of smoke like a forced draught engine. I never found out whether he was married or got along well with children, or what sort of problems he was having with his mother-in-law. But this man was enjoying life. He was tough and hard and vital, like a successful Texas oil-man. He was, one felt, an individual functioning to capacity. His work was his life.

'To what,' I asked, 'do you attribute your advances?'

I was bowling him a slow ball. And back it came, as I expected, without a second's hesitation. 'The reasons? First: the correct leadership of the Party and Chairman Mao. Second: the unselfish assistance of our brother countries, especially the Soviet Union. Third: the growing political awareness of the workers.... '

After two hours of background briefing and questions we went on a tour of the plant. I have been through steel plants in Pittsburgh and Sheffield, and this one looked exactly the same — the same roar of

47

machinery, the screech of switch engines from the shunting yard, the hiss of steam; the same huge cranes moving through the same kind of fiery glare, and the same perpetual rain of fine soot.

The new welded steel tube plant was half a mile away. It was almost completely automated. In an enormous, cheerfully lighted building, a handful of workers, several of them women, were minding sets of electric relay switches. Rolls of steel plate, fed in at one end, emerged at the other as completed tubes, cut to length, counted, bundled, and tied and were whisked away to be loaded on to railway flatcars. This monster was of Russian construction, but I saw only one Russian keeping a rather casual eye on the operations.

While we watched, one of the relays went out of kilter and the whole show came to a halt. A girl on the control platform, with a smear of oil across her cheek and her cap on the back of her head, flicked open one of the switch panels, but obviously didn't know what to do next. The Russian, though he was standing near by, made no effort to intervene. The girl called to another man (Chinese), who strolled over (there was, in all this, no sense of pressure, although the entire assembly line was now waiting), produced a screwdriver from a pocket of his overalls, fiddled with something inside, and closed the cover. The girl then pressed the warning signal and the line began to move again. But she had forgotten to switch on the high-voltage welder. There was a good deal of kidding, which I took to be the equivalent of, 'Hey there, wake up! Why don't you do your sleeping at night?'

She seemed not in the least abashed — she flicked the switch and shouted some answer which set all the others laughing.

VI

'We Clap Our Hands, We Are So Happy'

I RECEIVED an invitation yesterday to a children's party. June 1st in China is 'Children's Day'. So I set out that evening for Chungshan Park, and at the gate met a Frenchman who seemed rather an unlikely candidate for a children's party. I think he considered Peking rather dusty, the Chinese tiresome, the regime appalling.

The park was like a fairyland. Thousands of tiny coloured lights had been strung between the trees, and beneath them some fifteen to twenty thousand children were playing, dancing, laughing. Troupes of jugglers, clowns, actors, acrobats, performed to audiences that shrieked and applauded with delight. It was an amazing spectacle.

'It is all so *organized*,' said the Frenchman. *'C'est si enrégimenté.'*

Enrégimenté or not, I thought, if London could put on a carnival like this in Hyde Park, or Paris in the Bois de Boulogne, we would have reason to be pleased with ourselves. These kids were having the time of their lives.

Yet they never forgot to be polite. We couldn't stop at any show without a dozen little boys and girls leaping up to offer us their seats. In a way this was all part of the fun. Wherever we went, the children clapped us (as foreign friends, I think, not foreign devils). And then we had to clap back — that is the custom here; and the kids would clap in rhythm simply exploding with merriment, sometimes bringing the shows to a halt. Then the performers clapped too, everybody clapped, till we waved and moved along.

I noticed the Frenchman fingering the palms of his hands as if they were getting rather tender, and he raised his eyebrows, shook his head. This was, after all, a sufficiently tedious affair....

*

49

I went out the other day to visit a kindergarten near Peihai Park. There was, of course, the usual briefing on general background, over cups of tea; the same emphasis on growth ('We started our kindergarten in 1949 with thirty children; today we have four hundred.') And here too, 1958, the 'Year of the Great Leap Forward', had been decisive, because that was the year in which perhaps tens of thousands of mothers went out to work for the first time in industry. There was also the same sense of boundless optimism, the same conviction that human happiness would be achieved through solution of immediate tasks. It would have been senseless, here, to have raised a question as to the *purpose* of education. The purpose was to produce citizens each of whom would carry his fair share of the burden of socialist society — just as the purpose of the steel mill was to produce those structural members which would support the roofs and bridges of socialism.

My hostess, Miss Chiang, was the teacher in charge. She sat very trim and neat in a blue skirt and rose-coloured blouse. Rather 'correct' — like schoolteachers all over the world. Her voice was gentle, but I suspected this concealed a very determined and efficient nature. The room we sat in was full of sunlight and we could hear the children at play outside. 'Our children,' Miss Chiang said, 'when they grow up, will take their place in the country's work — they will be children trained in communist ideals. They will love labour. They will respect people.'

'How can you teach them proletarian politics at four?' I inquired.

'The principles of the education of children,' said Miss Chiang, 'are expressed in the *Five Loves*: 1. Love of Motherland, 2. Love for People, 3. Love of Work, 4. Love for Knowledge, 5. Respect for Public Property.'

'How ... ' I began.

'These principles,' Miss Chiang continued, 'are taught according to age levels, in conversation, songs, nursery rhymes, art and games.'

I went with her into several of the classrooms. In some the children ran up to me, catching me by the hands and tugging me this way and that to see the things in their room. (How much of all this, I wondered, was really spontaneous?) They seemed not at all disturbed by the arrival of a stranger, and a foreigner at that. In one room I found the class gathered in a circle around the teacher, all singing together while the children took turns at acting the parts of the song. They performed their parts with much gusto. One little boy, when his turn came, leaped to his feet and shouted his lines at the top of his lungs. I asked what the song was, and learned it was about the pig-breeding campaign on the farms and a man who raised a pig that weighed half a ton.

Here are the words of other songs they were singing, as they were translated to me word for word:

> I have a good mother,
> She works in the fields;
> She works so hard that the commune
> Has presented her with a red flower.
> Our mothers are all good.
> All are working
> For the benefit of our new country.
>
> ———
>
> We clap our hands, we are so happy!
> The communes are so powerful!
> My father works in a factory!
> Our country is led by the Communist Party!
> My brother drives the tractor,
> My sister works the loom,
> The electric light lights every household.

As I walked back to the reception room with Miss Chiang, I learned more about the kindergarten.

Many of the children go home every evening, some stay from Monday to Saturday. The school keeps in close touch with parents, and parents may visit whenever they wish. Some children, having lived happy-go-lucky lives at home, find it difficult to adjust themselves, at first, to the ordered routine, and particularly in the all-week group, children get homesick when they first arrive. For this, there is a period of 'full-time looking after' — which means that a single nurse or one of the younger teachers is in constant contact with the child, and becomes (though this was not the term Miss Chiang used) a mother-substitute. The child looks to this person for comfort and help, and the teacher or nurse, by watching the child closely, learns what his problems are: eating and sleeping habits, likes and dislikes. In this way the child learns quite quickly to adjust itself to the community life of the school.

Personal possessions are not allowed. Everything is *ours*, nothing is *mine*. Toys brought by the children are put into the common pool.

I asked about the signs one looks for in emotionally disturbed children. About bed-wetting. Very infrequent. Nurses on duty at night know the ones who need to be wakened during the night. Thumb-sucking? Only a few suck their thumbs when they first come — but it doesn't last long. Night terrors? Never!

'None of the teachers is permitted to tell gruesome or frightening stories,' Miss Chiang told me quite severely. 'If you walk around the bedrooms at night, you might hear children laughing in their sleep. Fears are very rare.'

'Temper tantrums?' I had to describe the symptoms.

'No, we never see children in that condition,' Miss Chiang said. 'We have naughty children, of course. But we always believe that these naughty children are the clever, specially-gifted ones — we just have to direct their energies. So we let a naughty child be captain of a ship, or locomotive driver. We let him use his talents and he ceases to be the naughty one.'

'Do you teach them,' I asked, 'about American imperialism?'

'Yes, we do, as far as they can understand it. We tell them that American imperialism is the greatest enemy of the world. But the ordinary people of the world, even the ordinary workers and farmers of America, are their friends. The teachers here, for example, took part in the great anti-American rally a few weeks ago and they told the children about it.'

Miss Chiang filled the teacups. We were now back in the reception room bright with chintz slip-covers and sunlight. There was a fragrance of incense in the room, and from outside, the sound of the children calling to each other on the playground. Flowering quince brushed the open window and beyond I could see the shadow of a willow tree against a wall. A Chinese miniature.

'Do you not think,' I asked Miss Chiang, 'that these international enmities will have been resolved by the time these little children grow up? And what can children of four or five understand about these affairs so far removed from their young lives? What can they possibly *mean* to them?'

Miss Chiang replied, 'We are socialists and proletarians. Imperialism exists. It is a fact. And we believe it to be the greatest single danger to our world. Even children must know these realities. We tell them about China's past, too. These children were born after liberation, but they must know something of conditions before that. They ask, "Did you have kindergartens then?" No, we were so poor we could hardly keep ourselves alive, we tell them; and many of us died of hunger. You from the West can have no conception of our poverty and hopelessness in those days. But our children must understand this. They must know of our past, our present, and our future — and the dangers that lie ahead from imperialism.

'We have a Chinese proverb: "When you drink water think of its source." We want our children to think of the source of their improved lives when they enjoy playing and eating and singing at a nursery school like this. The source is the socialist state which we are building.... '

And with steady hand Miss Chiang refilled our cups.

Letter to a Friend, a child
psychologist in California. June 18th

Dear Isabel,

Hardly a day goes by without my wishing you were here so we could talk. There's so much going on — this country is in full creative ferment, but much of it remains a puzzle to me. The *outside* stuff is reasonably easy to follow — the material progress since I was here before: the schools, the new hospitals (hundreds of them), factories, kindergartens. Vitality and confidence in the future are apparent everywhere — you should just see the young gals stepping down the street with pigtails swinging, as if the wide world belonged to them. And the kindness they show to each other and to strangers! That's fine; one can make some sense of all this. But what goes on *inside* — especially what goes on inside children? It's just here I am most baffled....

I have spent a lot of time watching children playing in the streets — little tots all on their own. They are endlessly inventive in their games — a piece of wood or a bit of string will keep them happy for hours. They never fight! *Why* don't they? They never snatch — never 'that's *mine*!' They seem to have almost no *personal* achievement motive, no combativeness; another child coming along will immediately be included in the group (no exclusive 'gang' feeling); and no apparent anxiety about absence of adults. They not only never fight but they *never cry*. The only child I have heard crying was one who was physically hurt. *What's* going on?

Some of this can be explained by the almost total permissiveness in the handling of children. I saw a small boy piddle in the middle of a big shop. *He* didn't mind, his *mother* didn't mind, other people didn't mind; the shop attendant who came to mop up smiled as if it were his special pleasure to mop up little boys' messes. I have seen a child squat outside a shop front, and the shopkeeper came out with brush and pan and stood courteously waiting till the boy had finished. A small child can do no wrong, and is surrounded by people who look after him. If he is travelling alone in a bus, an adult gives him a seat. To him *all* adults are 'uncles' and 'aunts' and so the need for the presence of his *own* parents seems less important. His assurance comes from the adult world in general, not his own parents in particular. All this must have a very profound effect on a child and his feelings about himself.

But that's too simple and too pat. Because from the point of view of Western psychiatry these Chinese children are *too good*. It seems as if total permissiveness leads to total docility — and a docility that continues into adulthood. I have never known a people who all think so much alike — and they *really* do, it isn't put on for reasons of political security. I am quite convinced that if there was an absolutely free vote in this country, an overwhelming majority — way up in the 90 per cent bracket — would vote the same way. It is a monolithic structure, *not* based on external coercions but on what is much more powerful — a psychological unity. This in the end may have its profound weaknesses, too.

I have tried to make some cross-checks about children in the kindergartens and hospitals — places where young children would be away from home. Bed-wetting? Very rare. Only in three- and four-year-olds. At the big nursery I visited today, the teacher could recall only one instance of persistent bed-wetting at the six-year level — and this turned out to be a girl with a physical bladder ailment. Homesickness? A little at first. Easily handled Crying at night? No known cases. Temper tantrums? Lying on the back, kicking the heels, screaming? They look at one another in amazement. No they have not had any problems like *that*! Fights? Very rare. Their idea of genuinely *naughty* behaviour seemed to be for one child to push another. At the kindergarten I visited, and in several nursery schools, I have asked, 'Do they own anything of their *own*? A doll? A toy?' And the answer is *no*. If the child brings something from home, it is put in with all the other toys.

Here they have a great many toys that belong to all of them, was what the teacher at the kindergarten told me. They don't want anything of their own.

But *don't* they? If they do, and are angry about having to give up their own particular toy, where does the anger go? Where is the aggression going? What's happening to the normal childhood hatreds? I haven't the faintest idea, and I can find no clue. The collective, *national* aggression finds outlet through hatred of an externalized enemy, *America*; but this cannot be an adequate channel for individual frustration among the young.

Here are some other facts to throw into the melting pot: young children take on responsibility very early. You see a child of four caring for a baby of one — feeding it, playing with it, keeping it warm, carrying the baby for blocks, staggering under the weight. Also helping with family chores, cutting up vegetables — really tiny children.

Adult docility. I went to Peking's only prison a few days ago, having been interested in penal reform in England, and here I found the Chinese doing what we had been trying to get the English authorities to do for years without success. Mainly, of course, to get the stigma, the moral stigma, out of imprisonment. The 'security' is minimal. There is one guard at the gate with a rifle (the gates are open) and there is one guard in a tower. No one else is armed. The walls are low. No locks anywhere. The window bars have been replaced by large casement windows. In one workshop of about fifty prisoners I asked where the guard was and was introduced to a smiling youngster in a T-shirt who was showing a prisoner how to fix a machine — he was the only warder in this room. If these were American prisoners they would all be out of that place inside three minutes. Why don't they escape? Here is docility taken to an extreme. They have great re-education sessions — 'reform through education' is the slogan.

Now to my point ... Can it be that the Chinese child, having had a total sense of *belonging* when young, has a permanent, built-in dread of being 'outside', of *not* belonging? A Chinese child, unlike ours, has never had to learn to be on his own, resisting opinion around him, has never learned to stand on his own rock. So that the worst possible psychological pain to a Chinese adult might be to be socially outcast. Is this at the back of their 're-education' process? Is it the permissiveness, the total security for the Chinese child, that makes possible the mono-lithic quality of their social structure? In other words, that dissent be-comes almost a psychological impossibility?

Or is the structure of the unconscious itself different? After all, the Chinese developed their society for four thousand years uninfluenced by Western concepts and behaviour patterns. Is it possible that the highly separate, individuated consciousness which some of our psycho-logical historians believe developed in Western man only at the time of the Renaissance, has never had to evolve here? In other words, that the consciousness of *I* being separate from *you* is not so sharp here as it is with us? *Me* and *not-me* tend to merge in the collective *we*?

If we are to understand the Chinese we simply cannot go on taking for granted some of our own psychological assumptions. I stand here baffled at behaviour which seems to turn some of our neat conclusions upside down — behaviour which cannot adequately be explained by any of our accepted theories....

VII

Peking Incidents

'WHAT do you take me for — an *imbecile*? Do you think I've flown six thousand kilometres from Paris in the utmost discomfort to see an old railway station?' Her voice was shrill and contemptuous; she was a free-lance journalist on an assignment from a French left-wing magazine.

'It isn't an old station' (it was Hsu doing his best), 'it's really quite new.' She didn't want to hear.

'I come to China to see communism, I come to see Mao Tse-tung, I come to see the rebirth of a great and glorious people — and you say go to a railway station!' and out of Mr Hsu's little office she flounced.

'What's all this about, Hsu?'

Hsu, my original Intourist greeter to Peking, had become something of a friend. We shared a mutual dislike for Peking opera and a mutual attachment to ballet and some of the new dance-dramas that are being developed in China today. He seemed to have a miraculous ability to get seats at the last minute for most of the shows I wanted to see — on one occasion (I only learned this afterwards) giving up his own long-awaited chance to see a particular play so that I could go. I liked him enormously, especially his capacity for anger.

One day in his office in the Hsin Chiao I sat, fascinated, listening to him conduct a fifteen-minute uninterrupted high-speed high-temper tirade on the telephone which even with my ignorance of the Chinese language I knew was making the wires sizzle, and then at the end, having slammed the receiver down, he turned to me without a second's pause, flourishing a ticket in the air. 'Mr Greene, I have a seat for you for *Swan Lake* tonight!'

'What's all this about, Hsu?'

57

'It's our new station — she didn't want to see it.'

'Is it worth seeing? What's special about it?'

'Go to it — you'll see.'

And Hsu being Hsu, I went.

Someone had phoned ahead, so Mr Wang, the deputy station-master, was waiting to greet me. He took me across the huge central concourse (the ceiling is 120 feet high!) to one of the six V.I.P. waiting-rooms — this was as large as a ballroom — for the tea and briefing, and then for a tour.

This station is impressive. There are four main escalators (made in Shanghai) to take passengers to an upper floor where there are seventeen waiting-rooms, seating in all 17,000 people. There are several interesting features. Platform entrances and exits are arranged so that incoming passengers and outgoing never intermingle though using the same platform; each long-distance train has its own waiting-room, so that when the train is ready, all (except mothers and children, who go ahead of the others) can board at the same time. It was fascinating to see the gay national costumes of the people waiting to board the train, which follows the old silk route to Urumchi in Sinkiang; and in another waiting-room those, again many in national costume, about to start on their long journey to Munankwan on the Vietnam border in the south. The restaurant (open day and night) seats seven hundred people at a time — a bright clean place with a fountain bubbling at one end. There are four rooms reserved for children, and two nurseries for infants, where mothers can leave their children under the care of young trained nurses. In one of the nurseries I saw rows of little tots fast asleep in their cots.

Tickets can be ordered by telephone from anywhere in the Peking area and will be delivered by messenger promptly. Eighty-five per cent of all long-distance tickets are sold before the date of departure and no more tickets are sold than the number of seats in the train. For incoming passengers there are service bureaux for those who haven't made hotel reservations, need to find their relatives, or arrive without money; interpreters in all dialects and for Russian and English are available. There are reading-rooms and TV rooms for those who have a long wait between trains. Everything is spotlessly clean. I watched the sweepers with mops six feet wide on rollers mop down the immense areas of terrazzo and marble flooring.

Every waiting-room has telephones connected with a central inquiry booth, and — this was the feature that most intrigued me — dotted here and there were closed-circuit TV inquiry stations. Standing in front of one of these gadgets the inquirer is immediately seen by the young ladies in the central inquiry bureau. While in this bureau I watched a child, not more than ten years old, come on to one of the screens to inquire anxiously about her train. She was afraid she had missed it. As it turned out she still had another half-hour to wait. She was asked whether she was travelling alone, and when she said yes, one of the other clerks picked up a phone and spoke to an attendant in the waiting-room where the child was, suggesting that she should be given special attention. With this explained, the little girl's face gradually changed from anxiety to a broad grin. 'Have a happy journey,' the clerk said through the TV circuit.

There's probably not another station like this in China; nor, perhaps, anywhere else. Mr Hsu was right, the French journalist should have gone.

Letter to Elena. *June 21st*

Almost a month here already ... the days go fluttering by like leaves in the wind. I try to wring the fullest meaning out of every moment but am horribly conscious of how much I'm misreading, how much I'm not even *seeing*....

Last night, partly impelled by loneliness, partly because I have so far refused every other invitation from the Embassy, I went for a while to the 'club' (at the British Embassy) for a dance they hold there every few weeks for the Western community. Germans, Swedes, Finns, Indians, Dutch — they were all there, but it was unmistakably a *British* party. The tasteless music blaring too loudly from a loudspeaker, the 'bar' around which most of the men clustered, leaving the women stranded like islands in a receding sea; nothing — not a flower, not an ornament — to give the rather drab room a little gaiety or beauty. It could have been a Saturday-night dance at a second-class commercial hotel in Bristol. In America they do these things better, always with greater taste and flair.

I shouldn't have gone. It's the problem of the exiled foreigners. I have seen this all over the world. But the 'enclave' mentality is always most acute in the countries 'behind the curtain'. The small group of Westerners huddle together, not because they specially like each other, but because there are so few, and it's difficult to make adequate social contacts with those among whom they live. It's difficult enough to become friends with Russians in Moscow; I think it is even more difficult for the Westerners here ever to strike up friendships with the Chinese. But because one can explain it, it doesn't make the consequences any more happy. Unavoidably, it seems, this isolation leads to an 'us' and 'they' attitude, and 'they' are always 'quite impossible!'

But what I, as a visitor, find especially trying is the tacit assumption among my compatriots that I also think in terms of 'us' and 'they' — in fact, that if I don't it's disloyal, that in some obscure way I'm letting the side down; and that, of course, I also feel that 'they' are really 'quite impossible'. But I reject this assumption, and I don't feel 'they' (in this case the Chinese) are any more 'impossible' than we are. If I remain silent, their assumption is strengthened; if I say what I think, there is an argument and nothing is gained either.

That's why I shouldn't have gone.

Then the giant judgments based on the tiniest personal grievances! I had a fine example of this at the dance last night. I was dancing with a Swiss woman — she's been here three years. 'Have you *ever*, in all your life, seen such *lazy* people!' (Of course she was referring to 'them'.) I stopped dead in my tracks. I thought I had heard the Chinese people called everything under the sun — but never *lazy*!

'Yes, downright lazy,' she went on. 'This morning I went up to a rickshaw driver [that's what she called him — there haven't been any rickshaws in Peking for years] and told him to take me home — and they know perfectly well we Europeans always have to pay them more than the Chinese do [she's wrong]. And do you know what the man said? He said, "I can't because I'm just going to have my lunch." See what I mean? Lazy!'

I looked at her. She was youngish and rather pretty. We were still standing at one side of the dance floor. I said, 'I think you have missed the meaning of this small event. The pedicab man wasn't lazy. But this is the first time a pedicab driver can say "no" to a foreigner, and it's the first time for 2,000 years that he can say "no" because he has a lunch to go to.' She looked at me strangely and walked away. I wasn't living up to the rules.

The evening ended with my being asked to convey a drunken business-man back to the Hsin Chiao. He's here to sell steel. We were driven back in a bouncy embassy jeep. The businessman was telling me how he had been shown the Great Hall of the People that day. 'And do you know what I did there?' he asked, and he heaved with laughter at the memory. 'Told my beads, that's what I did! Didn't let on of course— hah, hah — had my rosary in my jacket pocket — told my beads all the time they were talking ... and [very confidentially] I think that was *historical* ... yes, really historical ... because I bet you ten pounds that no one ever has told beads in that hall before.'

He was very drunk. At the hotel I propped him up on my shoulder and we wove our way to his bedroom. He clung to me. ' ... C'mon in ... just one last little one ... ' I pushed him on to his bed and went along to my room.

```
**********************************
*                                *
*          PART THREE            *
*                                *
**********************************
```

VIII

Assembly Lines

THE North-east (formerly known as Manchuria) is historically the oldest industrialized area of China, and contains enormous deposits of coal and iron ore. Foundries and steel mills were established in Mukden and Anshan by the Japanese early in this century.

Until 1880 entry into the land of the Manchus was forbidden by decree of the Emperors. By 1900, however, land-hungry peasants from North China — Shantung province in particular — were encouraged to immigrate. This sprawling area of some half a million square miles then had a population density of only seventy persons per square mile compared with more than five hundred in some areas of China proper.

The North-east, despite its severe winters, has rich farmlands as well as great mineral wealth. Principal crops are kaoliang, soybeans, wheat, millet, flax, beet, rice, and in the hot summers cotton can be grown.

The Russians had for many years claimed a vague suzerainty over large areas of Manchuria; and after the completion of the Trans-Siberian railway and the suppression of the Boxer Rebellion in 1901 they pushed southwards to the warm-water ports of Port Arthur and Dairen. But after Russia's defeat by the Japanese in 1905, Japan took possession of the richer part of Manchuria, the south; the Russians continued to occupy the northern half until the Russian Revolution, when they formally withdrew. In 1931 the Japanese drove the Chinese out of Mukden and took over all Manchuria.

The Japanese exploited the area's rich resources. They built roads, railways and factories, and set up a typically colonial regime which shipped raw materials and semi-finished products to Japan. In 1932 the puppet state of Manchukuo was established and the North-east's resources and manpower were utilized as cogs in the machinery of Japan's growing industrial and military empire.

After Japan's defeat in 1945 there followed a period of almost indescribable chaos and destruction; the Russian army moved in and stripped many plants that fell under their control, as did Chiang Kai-shek's officials. The Chinese today refuse to acknowledge any Russian looting, but the removal of great quantities of machinery from the factories in the North-east and its shipment to Russia is well documented. Most of the larger cities were taken over by Kuomintang troops, while Mao Tse-tung's army controlled almost all of the countryside.

It is interesting to recall that at this time the Russians were still helping Chiang. While the Communists were taking over the countryside, the Russian army, which had smashed the crack Japanese Kwantung Army in August 1945, was helping to install Kuomintang officials in the cities. The Russians were even asked to remain longer than originally requested in order to give Chiang more time for the Americans to transport his troops from south China.

Nearly 200,000 Kuomintang troops were rushed to the North-east by American naval vessels and planes immediately following VJ Day. After the Russians evacuated Harbin and other cities in the north, Chiang, with five American-equipped armies, began a drive from the south against the Communist forces.

The Kuomintang, however, military and civil administration alike, was already far advanced into that state of decay which was to ensure its defeat. Officials were, for the most part, more interested in looting industrial properties and selling on the black market than they were in getting factories and mines into operation. The great open-cast coal mines of Fushun, for example, which under the Japanese had been turning out 25,000 tons a day, was reduced to 2,000 tons a day. The Anshan steel mills, which produced 840,000 tons for the Japanese in 1943, yielded less than 9,000 tons in twenty-two months of Kuomintang control. At one time this steel centre had 100,000 workers in its mills. In 1948 there were less than 10,000.

With the renewal of open civil war in 1947 Chiang was soon thrown back on to the defensive in the North-east. The Communists controlled most of the region, two-thirds of the railways, and the majority of the food-producing land. The Kuomintang controlled the big cities and industry. By the end of the year, a good part of seven Kuomintang armies, trained and equipped by Americans, had been shattered by the Communist General Lin Piao. Moreover, as in the case of the Formosans, the good will of the people had been lost; however, instead of revolting as the Formosans did in 1947, the people of the North-east went over to the Communists. (See Part Six for an account of the Formosan revolt.)

In the early autumn of 1948 the Communist armies, for the first time, launched an offensive aimed at taking major cities. The fall of Changchun and Mukden in October signalled the complete collapse of the Kuomintang in the North-east, and heralded the final victory of the revolution in all of China. Within fifteen months Chiang Kai-shek had fled to Taiwan.

Thus it was not until 1949 that a stable Chinese government controlled the North-east. Slowly the new regime set about picking up the pieces and straightening out the frightful shambles which was all that remained of this once important industrial centre.

After more than a month in and around Peking I set out on a tour through this industrial North-east.

From My Journal. July 1st — Harbin

Up at four, and boarded the airline bus at the terminal near the Peking Hotel. The driver couldn't get it to start. Some of us jumped out and tried pushing. No use, something was really jammed. Another bus towed us — a huge racket and the wheels locked when the bus was put into gear. It sounded as though every gear would be stripped. This went on for a couple of miles, when suddenly our engine turned over and we proceeded to the airport without further mishap.

The new Peking airport seems spacious enough for present needs. Quiet (almost hushed), very orderly, and with a good restaurant. Visitors who arrive here by jet from Russia invariably contrast it with the noise and unutterable confusion of the Moscow airport.

Only fifteen kilos (thirty-three pounds) are allowed for personal baggage. Flight designation is not by flight number but by plane number, which is stamped on your ticket when you buy it. Each plane has a number, written large, on its sides. Thus, if several planes are lined up, the passenger knows which one to board. There is no checking at the gate, but loudspeaker announcements are made every few minutes. As I couldn't understand these I just wandered out when the time was near and boarded the plane with the right number.

The plane was a Russian version of a DC-3 — twin engines and unpressurized. Pilots and crew were Chinese. As in Russia, there were no seat belts. The stewardess, minus insignia, dressed in white blouse and blue skirt, brought us tea in glasses, and sweets. A large clock in front with two dials, one indicating air speed, the other altitude. The girl noticed that my chair would not tip back because of the tightly-wedged mail-bags in the seat behind. She had these rearranged without my mentioning it.

At the second stop I wandered into the airport building. I didn't realize it was Harbin and the end of my journey until the stewardess appeared carrying my bags, books, typewriter and cameras, which I had left on the plane. There was no one to meet me. No one spoke English. Long conversations on the phone. An Intourist man finally got on the phone and told me he'd be right over. The reason he wasn't there? The plane had arrived an hour ahead of schedule.

Letter to Elena. July 2nd

... I flew up here from Peking yesterday. I was pleasantly surprised at this city. I expected a vast, dreary, smoke-laden industrial town like Pittsburgh or Manchester; but instead I find it a city of trees and green lawns and girls in bright skirts. There are lots of parks. There's an absolutely delightful one running for two miles or more along the edge of the river. Here couples were sitting under trees, little boys with nets were trying to catch fish, a man with a concertina was entrancing a dozen eager-eyed children. Hundreds of people were strolling at leisure eating ice-cream; and a group of Buddhist monks — shaved heads and all — strolled by. At one end of the park there is a restaurant (at one time a Japanese officers' club which now belongs to the Railway

Union). It's open to the public every night for dancing. Along the river, boats are for hire and there they bob up and down in the waves with laughing youngsters getting their oars all mixed up. This city seems so relaxed after Peking. No one walks fast, just strolls along as if they have all the time in the world, often arm-in-arm....

And under this almost casual swagger a tremendous sense of pride at accomplishments. I stopped to talk to this group or that — each person bursting to tell me what he's doing.

But it is an industrial city for all that. I have spent today, this morning, going through a city commune — a huge one. 162,000 people, eighteen large factories, dozens of small neighbourhood workshops, 356 public dining-rooms, 433 nurseries for children, 184 kindergartens — the figures make one's head reel. The size, the scope, the liveliness, the sheer volume of production, the new blocks of flats, the range and variety of experimentation — who will believe me when I get home? Everyone doing something, no one idle, all find a place in this vast resurgence. In Peking I studied the theory and the figures — now I am seeing it function in reality. The impact is overwhelming....

Small workshops and factories are scattered everywhere. You pass what looks like an old cowshed built of mud bricks — roof patched, one wall propped up, plaster peeling — and you look inside to find 150 young women in overalls tending precision lathes turning out some part for a larger factory, or making electric motors or radio sets or what have you. Most of these girls were illiterate three years ago; now they go to schools and technical colleges; they have language courses, drama groups, music lessons. A whole country in creative ferment — it has to be seen to be even faintly believed ... and the production potentials that have been revealed!

*

They took me off to lunch, the director of a commune at Harbin and some of his officials. All young. The director, about thirty, the others younger. I asked about the industrial production in this commune. More figures. In 1958 (the year the commune started) industrial production 10 million yuan (about £1½ million); last year this had jumped to 22 million yuan; and in the first five months of this year, 30 million. The commune now owns one hundred small factories.

'The large state-owned factories in our area form the core of our industrial work,' the director said; and he described how all the commune factories and workshops were integrated with these larger manufacturing plants. Until recently these large plants would get their parts made all over China; now the idea is to get everything they need locally made, with a tremendous saving in transportation costs. What is more, these parent plants can supervise production, train the workers, and adjust supply quickly to production changes.

After lunch I went round to some of these small commune factories. One — now an electrical instrument factory — was started a year and a half ago by three men (two watch-repairers and a seal engraver) who had the idea of making things out of scrap and left-overs too small to be of use elsewhere. In a lean-to shed they began making miniature apparatus out of brass filings, end-runs of plastic tape, steel shavings from lathes. Like so many of these commune factories this one mushroomed — it now employs 512 people, and otherwise unusable scrap is brought to their newly built plant from all over Harbin.

Again, there was a small plant in this neighbourhood which was employing thirty-five women — all unskilled peasants — to make rope from twisted straw. A near-by state-owned fork-lift-hoist factory was looking for a local source for its ball bearings. They moved into the straw-rope plant, set up the necessary equipment, trained the women, and began to turn out ball bearings. The factory, greatly enlarged of course, now employs 678 people, and supplies ball bearings to many other local factories. I found one of the original straw-rope makers — she was in the quality-control department checking ball bearings on a precision machine. Other plants that I went to that had been established since 1958 were turning out saws, heavy-duty electric motors, soft-drink bottles and furniture.

'Where do people get their hair cut?' I asked.

'Come along and see ... ' and they took me to the barber's shop serving a new housing estate. It was in a wooden hut, neat as a pin. About eighteen girls in spotless white coats. Clippers, combs, and towels sterilized in a home-made steam contraption. Special sterilization for Mohammedans, who mustn't use the instruments and towels used by non-Mohammedans!

'May I have a shave?' (I hadn't shaved that morning.) They grinned, terribly pleased. I waited until a chair was free, and a girl who looked about sixteen (but was really twenty-four), with two white ribbons set jauntily on each side of her head, set to work. I got a 'Chinese shave', not only my whiskers, but everywhere — over my forehead, over my nose, round the back of my neck, every inch which wasn't actually my hair. Lots of hot towels. They wouldn't let me pay — normal cost is a shilling for haircut, shampoo and shave. The barber's shop runs on a no-profit, no-loss basis.

One more surprise. As I was leaving, my eye caught sight of a wooden box from which protruded a mass of wires. 'What's *that*?' I asked. 'That's a portable, home-made permanent waver. It's portable because some of the women can't get here and we go and do their hair in their homes. And look — in the box is a small radio, so that while the women are having their hair done they can listen to music!'

Then across a football (soccer) field to a huge new housing estate. The exterior was depressing. No trees, no grass — just these giant structures. I knocked at one or two doors and was answered with an immediate smile and a 'please come in'. Neat and clean, all of them, but really terribly poor. Usually two huge beds in one room, on which the whole family sleep. In one a crib suspended over the bed for the small baby. The pattern in each was about the same — each flat has two rooms, a small kitchen and sink, and a private toilet. No bath-room — there are communal bath-houses quite near. In nearly all of them there was a radio, Thermos flask, sheets and blankets piled neatly on the bed; most of them had rather garish pictures on the wall. Some had vivid imitation flowers on the table. I took photographs and they didn't seem to mind. These people's welcome was so spontaneous that had I not chosen these flats at random myself, I would have felt sure that these families had been specially told to be ready to meet a foreign guest.

The rent? Some three yuan, others four yuan a month (nine shillings and twelve shillings), *including light and water*!

Who is given these flats? The street committee decides who needs the housing most urgently — usually those with children are given first choice. There's still a terrible housing shortage.

The hotel here reminds me of Russian hotels — a huge room, old-fashioned and Edwardian; plush furniture, easy chairs covered with white slip-covers. A Thermos on the table. The bed is hard but good, covered with an enormous eiderdown as in Switzerland. Either roast or freeze here. Nothing working too well in the bathroom — again like Moscow.

Rates are cheaper than in Peking, eight yuan a day. Food is cheaper, too. I had an excellent dinner last night: black caviare, a locally made vodka, a meat dish, soup, and sour milk all for 1·60 yuan (4s. 9½d.) — the caviare accounted for half of this.

Signs of Harbin's former large Russian colony are everywhere (there once were almost 50,000 White Russian refugees here) — the wide streets, shops, buildings, and even in some of the dress. My hunch is there are still more than three or four thousand, the figure given me by my guide. He said most Russians went back to the Soviet Union after this area was 'liberated' by the Soviet armies in 1945. Those still here are referred to as Soviet overseas citizens. Quite a few have become Chinese citizens.

Notices, menus, signs in Chinese and Russian. I seem to be a rarity here, for few English-speaking visitors turn up. There should be more, since it is an impressive city.

On the Train

We are leaving behind a great city, chimneys pouring smoke, dark, rain-swept buildings, power pylons, coal heaps, more and more smoke-stacks; the jagged angles of factories. Then newer and pleasanter-looking houses, not yet smoke-grimed, with red roofs and young fruit trees and patches of garden like English allotments.

A young man with a red armband interrupts my typing. He sits down and we have a long, uncomprehending conversation. I think he's asking me what time I want to eat lunch. But he may be the security guard, or just someone who wants to try his easily exhaustible English vocabulary on me.

'*Yi dien tzoong*' (one o'clock), I say. He seems to understand. I try some more: '*Pi jiou*' (beer), and he nods. He must be from the dining-car. So I rattle off, '*Tzoong gwo tsai — tzu row, bai tsai*' (Chinese food — pork, cabbage). I revert to English: 'Stewed fruit.' He shakes his head. Rice (my mind gropes), bread and butter — hell, I don't really want that. We sit silently for a few moments, he gazing at my portable typewriter. A few minutes later he gets up, smiles, says 'Please', and vanishes down the gangway.

I never did find out who he was; but at one o'clock I went into the dining-car and the food, as usual on Chinese trains, was delicious.

Changchun: Facts, Figures, and Slogans

I suppose the Changchun lorry factory visit was jinxed from the start. That incredible man who turned up as my interpreter! I should have taken that as an omen. I am as irritable as most people, and this fellow annoyed me from the moment he met me at the station. 'You have arrived late, and you shouldn't have come on a Sunday morning — everything is closed.' These were his first words. Dressed in white shirt and white trousers, he made me feel under-dressed in my blue polo shirt and baggy flannels. He ordered a porter to take my heavy bag, but didn't offer to help with the two I was carrying. 'Unreconstructed Shanghai type,' I thought. He told me his name was — well, it *sounded* like *Nng*, and that was the nearest I ever got to it. Definitely, we didn't get off to a good start!

The next morning began badly, too. I was about to take a photograph of the largest, shiniest car made in China today — the Red Flag (like a slightly enlarged Cadillac) — which was standing outside the hotel. 'You must get permission to photograph that car' — it was Mr Nng at my side — 'it is a private car and we should get the permission of the owner.' I didn't even trouble to reply.

Arriving at the lorry factory, because time was so limited I suggested to the officials who met us that we leave the 'background' briefing until afterwards and get straight on to my questions. I hoped to eliminate the political stuff and get some facts if I could. This insistence on reversing usual procedure may well have touched off the difficulties.

Our conversation, according to my notes, went as follows:

Q. What are the principal products of this factory?
A. Heavy-duty lorries, the new Red Flag saloon, some variations on the basic design for lorries for special use, engines for combine harvesters, motors for pumping, for irrigation.

Q. How many units in each category did you make during the last three years?

A. The factory was designed to make 30,000 lorries a year.

Q. Have you achieved that?

A. Due to leadership of the Party, Mao Tse-tung ... etc., workers showing tremendous enthusiasm for increasing production, technical innovations, the Great Leap Forward, etc., etc., etc....

Q. (breaking in) How many lorries did you make in 1959?

A. There was a slight shortage of material last year so we just about filled the capacity of the plant.

Q. You mean you produced 30,000 lorries in 1959?

A. I do not know the exact figure....

Q. What about 1958 ... was it in the neighbourhood of 30,000?

A. But the figures are issued by another department, I really couldn't be certain.

Q. (trying another tack) How many people do you employ here?

A. I'm not sure, I haven't got the figures. I think the number of women is increasing. The Soviet Government gave us all-round and unstinted help in setting up this factory — a large number of our technicians, as well as the administrative staff, went to the U.S.S.R. to study their methods; a great many Russians came here.

Q. How can I get the figures of production and of personnel?

A. A great many of the technical innovations were initiated by the workers, especially since 1958 when the general line was laid down and the Communist Party of this district ...

Q. Who can give me the figures? May I see the Managing Director — could he give me them?

A. We didn't know when you came which figures you would want, so we were not able to gather the right facts together.

Q. Look! I have been to a number of factories since coming to China — they have always known exactly what their production figures were. As for not knowing what questions would be asked, it's surely obvious when one goes to *any* factory, it doesn't matter *what* it is — shoes or toothbrushes — one of the *first* questions is 'How many of these things do you make?' I am here to write a book about China. I want to write a fair and honest book. How can I if I can't get any facts? You say you haven't got figures about the number of lorries you make or people you employ. Let's be frank. Every factory knows how many people it employs — at least approximately — and how many units it manufactures....

A. But this factory is so much larger than others — it's difficult to assemble the facts ... if we had known this was the sort of information you required ...

Q. (I just had to!) I have been round car factories twenty times the size of this one and they know how many people they employ.

At this a huddled, whispered conversation between the chief and one of the 'silent men' (Party members?) who always sit in. The chief then says that the production figures will be difficult to get unless the chief of the planning department is available. However, the number of employees is available and his colleague will go to phone the personnel department.

While waiting I tell them that I understand that *every* country has certain figures which it doesn't make public for security and other reasons. If their production figures are not revealed for such reasons I should understand and respect that. But I think we ought to be frank and say so.

That's about as far as the conversation went. We were not too friendly, though on the surface things were all right. I didn't like being told untruths and they didn't like my pressing them and making them admit it.

Eventually the man came back and said that as far as he could determine the round figure of employees was about 23,000.

As time was growing short, I broke off the questioning and asked to see the plant itself. We walked quickly through nearly all the main construction departments, hurrying, not because they set the pace but because of the enormous size of the factory.

Designed and equipped by the Russians, the plant began operations in August 1956. It is self-contained; it has its own foundry, forging plant, motor-tools and assembly unit, body works, and main assembly lines.

Because this was the first factory in China to turn out motor vehicles, the Chinese are immensely proud of it. To them it represents a step into the age of mass production. Perhaps it may seem impressive by Russian standards; by American standards it has a long way to go.

I listed in my notes nine weak points in this factory: 1. An array of parts lying about between the buildings, many of them rusting. 2. Too many people not doing anything, a general lack of drive and precision. 3. Too much being carried by hand; a single part would be tugged along by a couple of men while other parts are moved on electric carts. All of this through a good deal of disordered rubbish. 4. Where there is good equipment it isn't being properly used. For example, main body frames are pressed out on a 3,500-ton press. The press itself is fine; but a lot of time has to be spent prying the part loose from the press, by hand, with levers. The pressing takes five seconds, while removing the part takes half a minute. A few well-placed automatic punches from inside could eject each part instantaneously. 5. Too much disorganized work: a man fixes one part with a welder and turns to do something else. 6. Poor lighting — even though it *was* a rainy day. 7. Assembly line moved so slowly it was difficult to see if it was moving at all. I timed it: a foot every twenty seconds. Lorries were spaced twenty-five feet apart, so this means that maximum output would be only 115 per sixteen-hour shift, or 34,500 per three-hundred-day year. Even this is more than estimated. 8. Sloppy assembly-line techniques include passing tools from one side to another — not enough tools — and lack of testing, no checking anywhere. Lights were not adjusted for alignment, brakes not tested, and it took a long time to work petrol into carburettor; I saw water leaking from a hose-pipe insecurely fastened. 9. Lack of minimum safety precautions, e.g., there was no fire extinguisher visible near the petrol supply.

I stood for ten minutes watching lorries being driven off. If general carelessness was the case at this final stage, it can be assumed that a lack of precision is true all along. The appearance of the factory supports this.

In general I would say from what I saw that the equipment in the factory is at least fair, if not good, but is not being used to best advantage. Given some technical planning advice and know-how by a crew from Detroit or France, a general cleaning-up of the factory, and a rearrangement of feed-ins, etc., my layman's guess is that with existing equipment plus some minor auxiliary stuff which could be made in China, and given an adequate and continuous supply of raw materials, this factory could turn out several times its present production, which is probably only one-third of the total capacity.

*

The trip to the Changchun lorry factory was a useful reminder. The industries in the communes, the developments in heavy and light industry, the colossal human effort going into production all over China, still do not add up to a thoroughly industrialized nation.

If the Chinese believe this plant shows that they are ready to turn out all the lorries needed, they are simply deceiving themselves. With tremendous muddle and waste they are producing in a year what Detroit could run off in a single day without turning a hair.

As to the product itself, by examining the lorry, bouncing on it, listening to the engine, seeing it in operation under all kinds of loads, I would say it is a sturdy, no-nonsense vehicle without frills to go wrong; rather rough in the engine. I imagine it could stand a great deal of abuse and poor driving, bad petrol and overloading. Exactly what is most suited to China's present needs.

About a month after I was there, in August, another correspondent visited the factory. He told me afterwards that it was operating much more efficiently than when I had seen it. He said they were expanding production and now expected to turn out 70,000 lorries a year. I think our diverging experiences proved to some extent the variability and inconsistency of so much of Chinese industry at this stage of development. Considering the lack of technological experience the Chinese had ten years ago, progress has been very considerable.

IX

Shenyang: Pittsburgh of China

THE final stage of the train journey to Shenyang — once known as Mukden — the largest city in the North-east. Population nearly three million. As the train nears the city new factories, new blast furnaces, poke up through the rice paddies and kaoliang fields; then the scene becomes a jumble of industrial plants, smoking chimneys, and endless grey streets.

Shenyang is the main rail centre for the southern part of the industrial North-east, and is the focus of nearly a dozen major cities. In 1952, on the eve of the First Five-Year Plan, more than 50 per cent of China's industrial production came out of the North-east. In terms of sheer industry, Shenyang makes Harbin and Changchun seem small-scale. There is simply no comparison. One could spend weeks here going through factories. I went through many — some as muddled as the Changchun lorry factory; some in a curious state of transition, factories in which age-old hand methods were combined with modern stream-lined techniques ('walking on two legs' the Chinese call this); and some that I think could, as smooth-running operations, compare with any in the Western world.

The Shenyang Number 1 Machine Tool Factory presents a sharp contrast to the lorry factory I saw a few days ago. It took a bit of doing to discover the number of lathes being manufactured. I had hardly sat down when Mr Nieh Tseng-kuo, deputy-director of the factory, con-fronted me with a base of 100 for 1956 and then proceeded to rattle off yearly increases of 180 per cent, 280, 350, etc. I shook my head, and asked him for something more concrete. After all, percentages based on a hypothetical 100 base are quite meaningless. I came right to the point and asked Mr Nieh how many lathes were being turned out.

The first response to this was, 'Our objective this year will be over-fulfilled,' and so forth.

'You must understand my difficulty,' I broke in. 'You give me a base of 100 for 1956 and then tell me that production has increased and you expect to overfulfil your target. Really, that means very little. Supposing your production one year was five lathes, and the next year you made ten. Production would have gone up 100 per cent. It might sound good, but you still would only have produced ten lathes!'

We were sitting (a refreshing change) in his office, not in the usual reception room. A secretary sat at another desk and occasionally answered a phone call, but was otherwise busily engaged, and paid no attention to what went on. No one else here this time taking notes. In a bowl on the table before us two goldfish were swimming inexhaustibly round a submerged Temple of Heaven.

Mr Nieh was looking at me steadily.

'You are right. We are not revealing our annual figures, but I can tell you this. Our factory at present is turning out more than a thousand lathes of all sizes in our standard patterns each month,' and he here listed the dimensions and capacities; the smallest of the standard lathes was five tons in weight. 'We hope to continue to increase this number during the rest of the year, provided supplies of raw materials continue to be made available. I can also tell you that a thousand lathes a month is 50 per cent more than our average production in 1959.'

I felt like a winner of an international chess match who gains an unexpected victory. I had been given an actual figure — and I believed it to be a true one. This man was an engineer, not a propagandist.

'Is this the largest factory of its kind in China?' I asked.

'No, no. There are many far larger. This is not a large factory. It is listed as a medium-sized factory. I have seen many much larger than this.'

I liked Mr Nieh. He was direct. He hardly mentioned 'the correct line' or the 'inspiring leadership of the Communist Party'. He answered my questions promptly and always to the point. Here are some of the facts I was given as I jotted them down in my notebook:

Twelve per cent of the six thousand workers are women, and they get the same pay as men. There is no piecework at all in this factory. The wage scale is comparable to other factories — the average wage for the entire factory is 70 yuan (£10. 10s.) a month, the lowest wage for un-skilled beginners who are being trained is a little over 30 yuan (£4. 10s.), and the highest-paid technicians get something over 100 yuan (£15). The director gets less than his chief engineer, the highest-paid individual in the plant, who gets 200 yuan (£30). There are the usual welfare schemes — free medical aid, eight weeks' maternity leave on full pay, etc., as in other factories.

The educational facilities provided by the factory are extensive — there are spare-time schools for adults who missed schooling, from primary level right through to college, and technically more advanced courses for those who want to go further. Writers from the Shenyang Writers' Union hold classes for creative writing; there is an amateur drama group, a sports and recreation club, and a documentary-film unit for those interested in making films. Ninety-five per cent of the workers make use of the educational facilities. There are the usual nurseries and kindergartens.

'Percentage of illiterates?' I asked.

Mr Nieh (with a grin): 'In this factory now — none. The last group passed their literacy test two or three weeks ago. We have very few old people and the young are very eager. Of course "literacy" is a vague term. Our standard here is not especially high — I believe we have set it at fifteen hundred characters.'

The factory itself is almost fully self-contained. Some smaller components and some electric motors are made by the commune workshops in the neighbourhood, supervised by the factory technicians, who set rigid quality standards. Rejects from the commune workshops were high at first. 'After all,' Mr Nieh said, 'the workers were almost all women who had never handled a machine before, but now rejects are comparatively rare.'

Before starting our tour of the factory I asked whether I could take photographs. 'Take whatever you like,' Mr Nieh answered.

I expected that the quality of directness and competence that Mr Nieh showed would be reflected in the factory itself, and I was not dis-appointed. If nothing else, my journey to this factory has revived my belief that the Chinese are capable of efficient large-scale organization. Watching the lathes roll off the line, the special train backed into a siding for easy handling, and the general efficiency here, I feel that this factory really is producing lathes in considerable numbers. My guess is that the plant is working at 80 to 85 per cent of capacity. There were very few machines idle, and an absolute minimum of people just standing about.

The Chinese are not just talking when they talk about workers' innovations. Many were pointed out to me. There were automatic grinders which can now be attended to by one man instead of four, a bit clamp which can be tightened by one twist instead of being locked by tightening three clamps. A huge multiple plane was shown me as being a 'technical innovation'. I didn't understand this, as it was of Russian manufacture. The answer was that the design was based on suggestions made by Chinese workers.

Quality and finish seemed excellent. The assembly line moved smoothly, seemingly without much pressure on those working on the line. Every part is individually checked before assembly, checked after attachment to the main frame, and the completed machine is tested in a special room after coming off the assembly line. After this it is painted, greased, wrapped, and crated for shipment. Some of the lathes being crated were going to India.

There was a noticeable air of intense concentration on the faces of many of the workers. Each one seemed to pay close attention to the job at hand, with an eager look almost like students who have just mastered some new skill. I watched many at close range. They handled their tools well, seemed to know what they were doing — always with this eager quality. Perhaps this is just Chinese!

Letter to Elena. *July 5th*

I've just had dinner and feel comfortable and expansive, having had some excellent caviare and half a bottle of Shenyang wine. It's hot — 95 degrees. I am sitting by the open window and from the street comes the sound of children at play. Far too sticky for them to go to bed yet and so there they are down there in the dark, inventive as always, playing their wonderful games, shouting and laughing.

Yesterday the lorry works at Changchun — very evasive about figures, and in a way I don't blame them, for the figures would have revealed too much what a mixed-up place it was. Ford à la Russia in Chinese style ...

Here I have a room in a hotel built by the Japanese, although German-designed. Huge, ornate, but with remarkably pleasant rooms. This could be a rather good New York hotel. From the entrance hall is the door to a tiled bathroom, also American in style. There's a lace curtain between the entrance hall and the bedroom (they *had* to bring the lace in somewhere), which isn't Western, but otherwise this bedroom could be anywhere. The bed beautifully comfortable.

I have four nights in this capitalistic and unregenerate hotel. It's not too wildly unregenerate, of course. There's a bar, which never opens, and a billiard room which closes at nine. Earlier this evening I walked around the city to learn what was going on — I had a choice of a circus, cinema, Peking opera, and the hotel billiard room. I decided to have a good dinner and write up my notes — which I better get to right now....

*

En route to Anshan, which is about seventy-five miles south of Shenyang, accompanied by Chang Yung-tse, one of the very nicest and most intelligent of interpreters. I've seen so many factories in the past week or so that I'm beginning to feel like Chaplin in *Modern Times*. Anshan is the last stop on this North-east tour.

Over the train loudspeakers the strains of the current hit, 'Socialism Is Good', as we pull out of Shenyang station. Then the girl's voice (she really throws herself into it): 'Now with the start of the train our life of travel begins.... We are moving across the face of our beloved mother-land.... We all have different destinations but we all have one aim, to reconstruct our country quickly.... ' More music.

After a while I dropped into the broadcasting booth in the middle of the train — the girl looked about fifteen. She told me she hadn't been doing this for very long. She apologized because the gramophone was an old one and had to be wound by hand, and sometimes when the train joggled it would send the needle off the groove. As an old radio hand I complimented her on the way she faded the music and brought her voice in over it. 'I think it's fun,' she said. 'Excuse me a moment,' and while fading the music with one hand she announced through the microphone, 'We shall be arriving at ... [the train seemed to stop at every town between Shenyang and Anshan] in two minutes. If this is your stop, please get ready and get off quickly since we are staying there only briefly. Do not rush or you may have an accident. Be sure you take all your things and help anyone who needs help.'

Later, when I was back in my seat, I heard her make the following announcement: 'On behalf of the railway administration and the train crew we wish to apologize for the fact that the train is very crowded today and some passengers are standing. Many soldiers have had to travel with us unexpectedly and we were unable to add more coaches at short notice. Will the younger people please give their seats to the older ones, and everyone please see that no woman with a child has to stand. When unexpected difficulties such as these occur we must all help each other as much as we can. We promise you that all of us who serve on this train will have a serious discussion when this trip is over to see how we can avoid the mistake of not having enough seats in the future.'

There is a real network of railway tracks in this part of the country. From my window, at times, I can count as many as seven tracks, with many branch lines going off on both sides. We pass long freight trains carrying coal. There is also a network of power lines. And as always, new factories everywhere rising out of the fields.

At one stop, looking out on a grey and drizzly landscape of tracks and coal trucks, I thought how tediously like all other shunting yards these in China were. This could be Chicago, London... Just then a locomotive puffed by, and riding on its boiler was a magnificently fierce, brightly painted dragon!

After one stop about a dozen soldiers came and sat down in the empty seats directly across the gangway from myself and Chang. They were travelling 'soft' — coaches in China have two classes, 'soft seats', first class, and 'hard seats', second class.

Their loose-fitting khaki trousers and jackets were unpressed, and all but one wore the usual gym shoes. These men were officers, but except for the collar tabs which denote rank, they wear the same clothes as a private. Each wore a wrist watch and had a fountain-pen clipped to the upper pocket of his jacket.

After a bit of eavesdropping I leaned across the gangway trying to strike up a conversation. They took me at first, I think, for a Russian. When one of them asked what country I was from, I replied quickly before Chang could answer, '*Wo shih Meigworen*' (I'm an American), to see what the response would be.

There was no particular show of interest. 'Are you travelling alone?' And then we went on to other things. This is an example of the astonishing lack of curiosity about the United States which I have noticed everywhere. What a contrast to Russia! Or even China three years ago. Here was a lively bunch of officers and not a question about the country they are always so vehemently denouncing.

I learned that the soldiers were an army basket-ball team on the way to a game in Anshan. I also discovered that there is no compulsory military service in China because the number who want to join is far more than the army can absorb. Any able-bodied man can apply, but only a certain number are selected after physical and mental examinations. Length of service is three years.

But at this point, to exhortations from our girl in the radio booth to be careful and to help each other, we arrived at Anshan station.

X

Anshan: Steel City

A MR LIU TIEN-YI, an official of the steel company, met us at the station. 'Let's have lunch,' he said. I thought this an admirable beginning to a trip round a steelworks.

Liu was affable. Driving to one of the company's dining-rooms he said, 'I'll tell you the background, then you ask me questions.' Swaying along through streets crowded with workers, bicycles, donkey carts, lorries, I jotted down some reminders.

'All this,' Liu said with a grand sweep of his arm, 'is part of the Anshan Iron and Steel Company. We have forty mines, mills, and fabricating plants — all under the same management — and we employ 170,000 people. The highest production before liberation was in 1943 — 840,000 tons — then it dropped almost to nothing. But by 1949 Russian technical experts were helping us to rebuild. It was a fearful mess. We didn't finish reconstruction of these plants until 1953. We've opened up some new open-hearth furnaces, several rolling mills, an automated seamless-steel-tube factory. By the end of 1957 we were turning out nearly three million tons and this year we will be topping six million — almost one-third of the national total.'

We swung off the street to the company's head office. Lunch had already been ordered. We sat in our shirt-sleeves in a room to ourselves. Good food, good beer. Chang, Liu, and I forgot about steel for a while. These young men were clearly of university graduate level. They had never met before. I asked them about themselves.

Chang Yung-tse's family came to Shenyang from Shantung province. He had been a studious boy, and his family, who owned a hardware shop, were able to send him to college.

In the early summer of 1948 Chang was one of a group of students

83

from the North-east who made their way down to Peking to petition the Kuomintang authorities for promised school funds. This was at a time when Peking's students were protesting against arbitrary arrests in the schools. One night — Chang's group was camped in an old Buddhist temple — the secret police rounded them up and took them all off to jail.

'How'd you get out?' I asked.

'My father got word of what had happened, and after a few months enough money was raised in Peking to buy me out of jail.'

Chang remained in Peking — some of his friends crossed the lines into Communist territory — and after liberation he entered the Foreign Language Institute in Peking.

All this was said rather hesitatingly and seriously.

Liu Tien-yi was a blunter type. His family had been connected with the steel companies in this area. The father worked here under the Japanese, for a pittance.

'Sometimes my father brought back so little at the end of a week's work that we had no food. I mean my mother and the children had none. Mother made my father eat, because if he lost his health and lost his job we should all have starved.'

After the Japanese were defeated the works were taken over by the Kuomintang and things got worse. Many of the mills closed. There was no work. 'My father was ingenious and became a street hawker selling small necessities which he often made himself out of metal scrap that he would go out and steal — things like small pots and frying pans.

'After liberation, of course, things picked up. As many as possible were put to work clearing the rubble and cleaning up the destroyed factories. At first for little wages, but just to be doing something again was a help. When the Metallurgical Institute was opened here, I applied, passed the examinations, and got a four-year training course — then was taken on almost automatically by the steel company. My father is still working here — he's too old to be in the furnace plants, he works in the tube mill.'

We had more beer. The room was full of smoke, and the relating of these stories (so unusual for Chinese to be so outspoken about themselves) had brought a certain atmosphere of intimacy between us.

We were silent for a few moments. Why wouldn't young men like this be behind the regime, I thought. But such musings could wait. I wanted to make the most of the present atmosphere to ask questions that had always somehow been evaded.

'If a boy sees a girl that he takes a fancy to, how does he get to know her?'

They both smile at this sudden switch in conversation. Apparently he does what young men all over the world do — he might wait for her outside the factory gate, make some excuse for talking to her, ask her out to a cinema.

'And if he wants to marry her?'

'I don't think he would ask her himself,' Liu said. 'A few might, but not most. Not right out like that. He would first get a friend to ask her if it would be all right for him to ask her to marry him ... and in that way he wouldn't make it embarrassing for her to say "no" if she didn't want to, or embarrassing to himself to be rejected. Then, of course, there might be a good deal of discussion between the two families — but the decision is entirely up to the couple. If everything is all right, then they must both get a health certificate. Then they can get married.'

'What ceremony is performed?'

'Usually none at all, except, of course, the families will come together to celebrate with a small dinner. Then the couple are given a three-day holiday with pay by way of a honeymoon.'

'Of course,' added the serious Chang, 'the boy and girl would ask each other about their political views in order to be sure to marry someone who is politically mature.'

And now an even more delicate question.

'What about boys and girls sleeping together before they are married? Does it happen often?'

'Oh yes, of course it does happen,' Chang said. 'But it's against the law.'

'No, no,' said Liu, 'it's not against the law, but it's frowned on. Not that we mind about people sleeping together from any old-fashioned moralistic ideas or religious notions — nothing of that kind; but if they sleep together they might have children, and anyway, isn't it better to get married?'

Mr Liu, looking at his watch: 'We'd better get going if we are to see the steel mills.'

*

For the rest of the afternoon I went round the steel plant. It seemed in full production. There were no idle men, nothing that gave any sense of inefficiency or lack of direction. A constant pouring of metals, men sweating, steam, coal dust — a nightmare vision of what hell must be like.

The rolling mills seemed to be working full speed. Tremendous chunks of bright-red steel were being pushed around, flattened, squeezed through giant rollers till they went leaping, one hundred and fifty feet long, back and forth between the rollers like red serpents.

High above was the control room. The driving mechanisms below were operated by three men seated at the electric switches. Even here the heat was overwhelming, and the nineteen-year-old at the centre controls was unable to prevent sweat running down his face. Over his head was a large mirror in which he could watch the incandescent snakes as they lashed out beneath him.

Below, the circular saws with a screech and a shower of sparks parted the snake into five rails. Forty-four miles a day, enough for twenty-two miles of track. I timed the cutting and worked out the equation. It came to almost what Mr Liu had claimed. If one were to discount half that amount for replacement use, the availability of even eleven miles of new track per day from this plant seems quite good.

At this point Liu said he wanted to run me out to one of the smaller steel plants which the mother-company operates on the outskirts of Anshan. I said fine, anything to get away from the dust, the glare, the crash of cranes....

We drove thirty miles. On the way I asked Liu to tell me what had happened to the small back-yard furnaces I had heard so much about. He said that in the summer of 1958 there were hundreds of thousands of these small furnaces all over China. 'Everyone was making steel in home-made furnaces, some of them just a cubic metre or a metre-and-a-half capacity. Foreigners laughed at us about these furnaces, and of course they were very inefficient. But they missed the point. The iron

86

and steel that these furnaces turned out were never included in the national production figures, the iron wasn't good enough for industrial use.'

In a thirty-five-page report, the United States Department of the Interior, referring to the period of back-yard furnaces, stated:

As many as sixty million people were taken off the farms to look for minerals, work in coal mines and smelt iron. Although this programme dislocated the country's economy as a whole ... it served a useful purpose to the mineral industry with regard to the accumulation of information on resources and training a large number of persons in the fundamentals of mineral extraction. The by-product of this programme was another great increase in mineral production, coal and steel output being respectively more than 100 per cent and 50 per cent greater in 1958 than in 1957. The back-yard programme has since been junked, but it set the stage for many small and medium semi-modern industries.

This revealing report, which makes some of my conclusions about China's industry seem almost conservative, appears in Special Supplement No. 59, March 1960, *Mineral Trade Notes of the Bureau of Mines*, United States Department of the Interior.

'It wasn't production that these furnaces accomplished,' Liu went on, 'it was education. Our people, especially our peasants, have never been around machines as your people have been. They were completely un-mechanically minded. Many of them were in awe of technological processes. But now they were encouraged to make their own simple tools — wheelbarrow wheels, gate hinges, even their own ball bearings in a pestle and mortar — and out of iron they themselves had smelted! In one summer's hectic activity, our peasants learned not to be afraid of "technique". It lost its mystery. People who have actually poured their own steel and made things with it feel they can do anything. I don't know if that was really the reason why these furnaces were started — but the effect has been just what I said. In six months it was all over.

'There were other side benefits. The peasants discovered many unsuspected sources of ore and coal, which we can now exploit. Now integrated plants — medium-sized furnaces — have taken the place of the back-yard furnaces, and these are now dotted all over China. The steel they produce is as good as anything we turn out at Anshan. What we are going to see is one of the integrated plants which developed out of the little furnaces.'

This enterprise (rising out of the rice fields) consisted of fourteen furnaces, each with a capacity of fifty-five cubic metres.

The entire plant was set up in three months. Of the sixteen hundred workers — four hundred are women — almost all were peasants a few years ago, only eight men have any advanced technical skill. To construct these furnaces and produce steel with such an unskilled work force, my guides told me, would have been impossible except for the experiment with the back-yard furnaces. These provided a cram-course in applied metallurgy. Millions of peasants who had never conceived of making steel learned enough of the rudimentary principles to be able to come into a medium-sized operation like this integrated plant almost without technical direction from above.

In the Train Going Back to Shenyang

Exhausted, Chang and I arrived at the railway station on time, with Liu to see us off. Late evening and a slow trip back to Shenyang. A tremendous crowd on the station — a new one is being built and this temporary one has no cover. The train is late and in the darkening light a fine drizzle begins. Men turn up their collars, women pull scarves over their heads.

A message comes down to us: Would the foreigner not prefer to go to the station office to keep dry? I say, no thanks: but Liu and Chang say, of course. The station office is a tiny room, full of banners and paintings by workers. Innumerable telephones keep ringing and no one answers. One wall is covered with pieces of coloured paper with black Chinese characters on them. I asked what they were — I should have known. 'They are suggestions from the railway workers as to how we can do our work better.'

The train finally steams in. It is dark now, and we have difficulty in finding the 'soft seat' compartment, and when we do discover it, it is an old coach, musty, with an unused, shabby look.

As the train pulls out, a delegation of three wait on us — two pretty girls and the head of the train crew. They stand looking very serious.

Very formally the head man begins. 'We have come,' he says, 'on behalf of the railway administration, to offer our apologies for the state of the coach in which you will have to sit on your journey. Our own coach unexpectedly had to go in for repairs this morning and we borrowed this old one from the Dairen headquarters.' A deep breath. He is steeling himself to tell the worst. 'We have no way of making you tea. We ask you to forgive us.'

There they stand, the three of them, in such charming and obvious distress, that I laugh and readily forgive them, and they go off in better spirits, but still, I am sure, feeling that in some terrible way they have brought disgrace to the People's Republic.

Within a few minutes, Chang on one seat, I on the other, we are fast asleep.

I woke at one stop and peered out through the rain. My window by chance was opposite a signal and switch-control tower. It was well lighted and I watched, fascinated. It was a fully automatic control system; on a panel rows of illuminated push buttons; above the operator's head was a complete visual layout of his section of the track and the station yards showing, by indicator lights, the location of each train, and each switch and signal light. I have never seen anything more up-to-date. It was worthy of the New York Central.

The train moved on and I settled down again to sleep.

XI

China an Industrial Power

CHINESE technical and industrial advances, hitherto (in the words of the *New York Times*) 'only a rumble as far as most Americans are concerned', are now coming through 'with thundering reality'. This is no place to make a detailed and definitive assessment of China's industrial and commercial potential, and any such attempt would be rich in error. The technological revolution in China is too vast, is changing too rapidly, is too new for a single reporter to cover. It would require an army of experts, production managers, statisticians, economists, geologists, and agronomists to visit China and interpret their findings for us; but by the time their reports were written their information would be out of date.

There are, nevertheless, some broad questions which can be asked and answered: How much credence can be given to Chinese statistics? Has China adequate mineral resources to enable her to become a first-class industrial power? Has she the technical know-how? We acknowledge that China is advancing industrially, but what is the pace of this advance? To what extent has she developed her international commerce? What particular technological problems does China face in the future?

Chinese figures — can we believe them?

A number of distinguished economists and industrialists from European and Asian countries have in the past few years visited China, and I am impressed with the fact that they make much use of Chinese figures in their reports. These men would quickly detect any sustained and deliberate attempts to mislead. No centrally planned economy can function without reasonably accurate statistics, and a nation consistently cooking its accounts would soon land itself into the most appalling troubles. Nor could it do so for long without its published figures revealing obvious contradictions. This does not mean that all Chinese statistics are accurate — they clearly are not; nor that we have anything like full information — for there is much that is still hidden. In some cases (notably the 1958 agricultural returns) the original figures were grossly inflated. Statistical skills grow with experience. Great mistakes have been made; but the Chinese authorities appear to be following the practice of publicly correcting figures which are found to have been inaccurate.

There are innumerable government agencies and academic institutions in the United States which scrutinize, sift, and analyse every available Chinese document. In England there are commercial and industrial research organizations which do the same; and in their case, findings can often be verified by personal visits to China. All these reports provide a useful, interlocking cross-check of Chinese statistical data. After studying them one is impressed with the general unanimity of their conclusions.

In December 1960 the American Association for the Advancement of Science held a two-day symposium in New York designed to assess China's progress in science and technology — we shall be referring to this meeting several times. The *Christian Science Monitor* for December 29th wrote of the reports given at this symposium: 'They were based mainly on published Chinese Communist literature. But in the few cases where experts had also first-hand experience, conclusions based on the literature jibed reasonably well with what they had seen.'

We have learned no longer to scoff at Russian statistical claims — they have too often been found to be of very sobering accuracy. I think that we will learn that this is true of China also.

Has China adequate natural resources?

The chief resources needed for large-scale industrialization are iron, coal, and petroleum. For many years, largely because no one had looked for them, it was assumed that China lacked adequate reserves of these minerals. That assumption must now be corrected.

The *New York Times* of December 27th, 1960, reported:

Intensive geological prospecting on the Chinese mainland in the last decade has disclosed mineral resources so extensive that they appear to make China one of the world's chief reservoirs of raw material.... Discoveries of raw material were described by Edward C. T. Chao of the United States Geological Survey. After World War II he said there were fewer than 200 active geologists in China.... Now there are 21,000 'geological workers'.... Also 400 foreign geologists have been brought in, mostly from the Soviet Union and Eastern Europe. Discovered in the exploration of the hinterlands, was an unsuspected reservoir of 7,000,000,000 tons of iron ore in the Shansi area of Central China. Another deposit estimated at 3,000,000,000 tons has been found in Honan Province. It assays at more than 50% iron oxide.

As a measure of comparison and to appreciate the magnitude of these figures the *New York Times* in this report said: 'One pillar of industrial growth in the United States has been the Mesabi range in Minnesota. From 1892 to 1950 some 1,500,000,000 tons of ore were removed from it.'

As for coal, all reports indicate that China has very large reserves. In its report the U.S. Bureau of Mines lists China's supply of both coal and coking coal as being in the 'first rank'. A British book (*The Economic Development of Communist China, 1949–1958* by T. J. Hughes and D. E. T. Luard) states: 'China has much greater coal resources than any other country in Asia. They are probably inferior only to those of the Soviet Union and the United States.' Another British report (*Chinese Trade and Economic News Letter*, London, June 1958) said that China's known coal reserves are adequate for centuries and are well-distributed over the country.

China's chief weakness appeared, until recently, to be in petroleum. The fields in operation in Kansu, Sinkiang, Szechwan, and elsewhere were not able to keep up with China's growing demands and much oil has had to be imported from the Soviet Union.

However, the picture has altered radically. Very intensive surveys have apparently met with success. I met an East-European in China, an oil expert, who was convinced that recent new discoveries will in time make China 'one of the great oil-producing countries of the world'. It will take some years to bring these new fields into production. The U.S. Bureau of Mines report (already referred to) appears to confirm this: 'Petroleum is inadequate but extensive exploration in recent years shows that the country will be prominent in this field five to ten years from now.... The country should no longer be considered poor in oil.'

As to other minerals, China's position is exceptionally strong in tin, tungsten, molybdenum, and mercury (in all of which she has the largest reserves in the world); and in chromium, nickel, asbestos, and diamonds.

To sum up: There appears no doubt whatever that China, in the words of the U.S. report, 'has a sufficiently diversified mineral base to become a first rank industrial power'.

Is China developing the technical knowledge
and skill to develop these resources?

'The Communist regime fully realizes', says the same report, 'that the key to China's industrial progress lies in the uncovering and efficient utilization of its mineral wealth.... Geological, mining, and metallurgical techniques are constantly being improved. It is a fallacy to assume that the Chinese Communists are not cost-conscious and do not believe in efficient practices. Great strides have also been made in training technicians and industrial workers to supply the manpower needed in mineral development.... If energy can be considered a good gauge of gross national product for a country, it is pertinent to mention that the 1959 output of coal, which is the main source of energy in mainland China, was about five times that of the pre-1949 peak year.... Many other minerals industries are undergoing rapid expansion.... The so-called modern operations which produce most of the mineral products in the country, are fairly up-to-date from the engineering point of view, but, while comparing favourably with European and Japanese practices, are much lower in productivity than U.S. operations. The reason again is that in any Asiatic country "poor man's engineering" must be applied which is good in quality but not in productivity. Generally speaking, the over-all level of mineral technology in Communist China has advanced rapidly in the past decade; the technological gap between the Orient and the West is narrowing. In fact some practices in Communist

China compare with the best in the world.... The fact that Communist China will soon have approximately a 100,000,000-ton-per-annum capacity in coal-cleaning facilities ... speaks well for technological process in controlling coal quality. Developments in mine construction and coal extraction are equally impressive; productivity is approaching European standards and advanced techniques like cutter-loader and underground hydraulic operations are employed at all large mines.'

It would be a mistake to think that the technological advances in China have been limited to the development of mineral resources, or that scientific training has in any way been neglected. The advance has been a *general* one.

Dr J. Tuzo Wilson, an eminent Canadian scientist from the University of Toronto, travelled to China in 1958 as President of the International Union of Geodesy and Geophysics. He has described what is going on in China as a scientific 'renaissance'. 'The government clearly believes in, and supports, education and science,' he told the Council of Scientific Societies of the Dallas–Fort Worth area on December 1st, 1960. 'Many scientists from the old regime, old universities and old institutes, are flourishing. They have never had so much support before.... I was impressed by the many new buildings and universities. The equipment was simple but far better and more abundant than I would have expected.... Some people have expressed a fear that scientific training in communist countries will produce nations of evil robots. I think this is balderdash. I saw no evidence of it.'

Dr Wilson, in the same lecture, mentioned conditions in the universities in Taiwan: 'One thing which I found particularly sad on Taiwan was that although Taiwan is often called "free" China, the universities there have had less support and fewer new buildings in recent years than those on the mainland; the libraries were poorer and the scientific equipment was less good than that which I had seen during the previous month in Peking, Sian, Lanchow, and Canton.'

Sir Cyril Hinshelwood, who as President of the Royal Society visited China in 1959, reported on the Chinese scientific effort in *The New Scientist*:

My Western prejudices against highly centralized organizations were very much mitigated by the open-minded and experimental view which I found prevalent.... I received the general impression of something rather more flexible than I had normally read of and would judge that even here the experimental method is rather widely understood and appreciated....

Laboratories and equipment are good ... the vast and well-equipped workshops I found a revelation. Library facilities, both in books and journals, are admirable. I have seldom, if ever, seen such extensive collections of scientific journals in all languages as I saw in several universities and Academic Institutes.... Students now learn both Russian and English, and many seemed to be making practical use of their knowledge in the libraries.... Although there is no question whatever of neglecting the basic sciences, there is much more conscious effort to mix fundamentals with practical applications at an early stage.... Among the students and the young research workers in the Institutes there seemed to be an atmosphere of enthusiasm....

... In some places, especially in Shanghai, there are well-established research schools of very high quality. The topics of investigation and the methods of approach do not differ much from those met with in Western laboratories....

I would not say that any of the research is influenced by ideology....

Further evidence that Chinese technological skills were advancing rapidly was given in the New York symposium already referred to (*New York Times*, December 27th, 28th, 1960, and San Francisco *Chronicle*, December 27th, 1960). T. C. Tsao of Columbia University reported that China had installed four nuclear reactors, and said that in view of China's rapid technological advances it would not be surprising if that country produced a nuclear explosion 'in the near future'. The per capita consumption of electric power, he said, has increased by 800 per cent since 1952.

In regard to technical literature available in China, Dr John M. H. Lindbeck of Harvard reported that between 1956 and 1957 the Chinese spent nearly £3¼ million to purchase scientific literature from non-communist countries. Dr Robert T. Beyer, a Brown University physicist, pointed out that 'about one-third of the scientific papers originating at the nuclear research centre at Dubna, near Moscow, have Chinese names attached to them.'

The rapidity of developments in the last decade was attributed, according to the *New York Times* reports, to such factors as: 'the existence for the first time in many decades of a strong central government; the allocation by that government of extensive funds for science; and a sudden release of enthusiasm and interest in a scientifically-minded population'.

I think enough has been said to indicate that there is no reason to doubt that the Chinese possess the scientific genius and talent to meet the technological demands of a modern industrialized state.

How fast is China's industry advancing?

To evaluate China's industrial progress a differentiation must be made between the absolute quantitative production, which reflects the nation's over-all strength, and the per capita production that reflects living standards. It is, I think, an accurate generalization to say that while China as a nation is rapidly approaching world-power status, the living standard of her people will remain relatively low for a long time.

China in 1949, even by Indian standards, was industrially an extremely backward country. So another warning must be given. Percentage increases may seem phenomenal because China started with so little. A workshop that formerly made ten bicycles in a given time and now makes a hundred has increased its production by 900 per cent, but it may have little significance in absolute terms.

Nevertheless, bearing these factors in mind, the *pace* of China's industrial development until 1960 outstripped all anticipations and was unprecedented in history. Dr Charles Bettelheim of the Sorbonne, who was one of a group of French economists who visited China in 1958, reported (in *The Economic Weekly*, Bombay, November 22nd, 1958): 'But above all, the feeling prevailing with my economist colleagues and myself is that of finding ourselves in a country that goes ahead at an unbelievable speed and which, in this respect, outdoes all the performances that could have been achieved elsewhere.'

Dr Bettelheim compares China's progress with the progress made by the U.S.S.R. at equivalent stages of her industrial expansion. During

China's First Five-Year Plan (1953–7) her expansion was approximately at the same rate as Russia's during its First Five-Year Plan (1927–8 to 1932). Both expanded at about 19·2 per cent annually. The new factor in China was the enormous acceleration of China's industrial growth that began in 1958. Within one year, Dr Bettelheim says, Chinese production was raised from a lower level than that of the U.S.S.R. in 1932 to a level not reached by the Soviet Union until after the Second World War, thirteen or fourteen years later. (China, of course, had the benefits of aid from an already established communist state which the Soviet Union did not have.)

The rapidity of expansion reported by Dr Bettelheim in 1958 did not appreciably decline until 1961. For example, steel production for 1960 reached a total of 18,450,000 tons. This is a net increase of more than five million tons over 1959 and over 50 per cent more than the production originally set as the target for 1962, the end of the Second Five-Year Plan. In other words, steel production increased by nearly 350 per cent in three years, i.e. from 5,350,000 tons in 1957 to 18,450,000 in 1960, an average increase of 4,300,000 tons. (The average annual increase in the First Five-Year Plan was only 800,000 tons.)

In almost all sections of industrial production, increases of an unprecedented character were reported. In February 1961 the *China Trade and Economic News Letter* stated: 'It may be conservatively estimated that gross industrial output rose by not less than one-fifth, and perhaps as much as one-quarter in 1960 [over 1959].' And this same report states that the increase in steel itself will almost *equal the total 1957 output*.

China's industrial advance was severely affected by the agricultural setback that began in the latter part of 1960. (See appendix: A Postscript on China's Economic Problems 1960–62.) Production in the heavy industries was drastically curtailed as the major emphasis was placed on those branches of manufacture that would most directly improve agricultural output. The production of tractors, harrows, sowing machines, reapers, water pumps, as well as fertilizers and insecticides, was rapidly expanded. Though overall industrial production was considerably cut back, China's production *potential* is indicated by the fact that in coal production she had become the third largest producer in the world; in machine tools she had surpassed Britain and West

Germany; in cotton production she had during one year surpassed the United States; and in textiles the city of Shanghai alone was for a period out-producing Britain. It is too soon to determine when China will have overcome her agricultural difficulties, but some Westerners who have been to China recently have reported that within a few years China is likely to resume rapid industrial expansion.

However severe the industrial retrenchment has been, general technological advance is reflected throughout Chinese life today.

Though still far from being able to manufacture in sufficient volume to meet her own needs, there is almost nothing that China requires that she is not making herself, whether it is diesel-electric locomotives for her railways, jet fighters for her air force, heavy tanks for her army, ships of 16,000-tons displacement, or advanced electronic computers.

Having seen China three years earlier, I can attest to the marked increase in the range and variety of products that were being offered for sale in the shops of the larger cities in 1960; and China's mastery of technological skills is even more dramatically shown in the permanent exhibitions (such as the Industrial Exhibition at Shanghai) which are primarily intended for overseas buyers. Here is a list, jotted down at random:

Stainless-steel blades for steam turbines, TV cameras and transmitting apparatus, TV sets, a forty-five-ton press for the making of tissue-paper, a machine for making 100,000 medicinal tablets per hour, automatic double-end grinding wheels, valve-testers, automatic chemical analysis machines, record-players, watches, clocks, cameras, grand pianos, motor-cycles (and racing motor-cycles, too), precision balances accurate to 0·0001 mg., and bathroom fixtures in three different sizes and five different shades!

As far as consumer goods are concerned, though it will be a long time before the average Chinese will even remotely approach the living standards of Europe, the knowledge of manufacture is there, the skills are being learned. Already, it would be difficult to find in a Sears Roebuck catalogue anything that China is not now making.

Industry Is People

Sustaining all these gigantic endeavours are the minds, the muscles, and the sinews of the largest population on earth. It is on the long-term readiness of the people of China to support these great plans that the country's success or failure will depend.

There is a prevailing opinion in America that the Chinese are being threatened, brainwashed, or bludgeoned into this work of national industrialization; that a small group of power-hungry Communist leaders have fastened themselves on to an unwilling and resentful population and are driving them fiercely forward against their will. Indeed, for nearly a decade America's national policy was based on the openly expressed hope that sooner or later the people of China would rise against their 'oppressors'.

I believe this picture is the very opposite of the truth.

And so do others who have seen the country for themselves. On his return from China in 1958 Mr James Muir, President of the Royal Bank of Canada, reported to his shareholders (in the *Royal Bank Magazine*, October 1958) as follows:

> The growth in industry, the change in living standards, the modernization of everything and anything, the feats of human effort and colossal impact of human labour are not within our power to describe and still give a worthwhile picture of the scene. All I can say is that it must be seen to be believed. It is truly stupendous.... We think the vast majority of the people of China have a government they want, a government which is improving their lot, a government in which they have confidence, a government which stands no chance of being supplanted.

Mr Muir, in a letter to me, expressed his view that America's policy towards China was 'one of the greatest diplomatic tragedies of the century'.

Another more recent visitor to China was Mr Kurt Mendelssohn of Oxford University. An author of several books on physics, Mr Mendelssohn was on his return invited by the B.B.C. to discuss the impact of technology on the Chinese people, and his words were published in *The Listener*, February 9th, 1961:

> Technology is not only based on machines but also on people: people with emotions, people who can be hostile to a programme, or indifferent, or enthusiastic.... For the worker in the West ...

99

industrialization always savours of enslavement and exploitation. The industrial revolution has left a bitter taste. Things are different for the Chinese. There, the Communists are not, as with us, a force which tries to destroy a well-established pattern of society. On the contrary, they have brought order and peace to a country which was torn by civil war. When the Chinese speak of liberation, they mean it; liberation from a nightmare which lasted half a century.... Technology is a great and joyful experience, an adventure into which they have thrown themselves with enormous enthusiasm. Anyone watching them at work will be struck by this enthusiasm which, to me at least, appears the most significant feature of their technological advance....

... It [is] said that being told constantly what to do is the price which the Chinese have to pay for development. We might consider being ordered about as tiresome, but I am fairly certain that the average Chinese does not feel like that at all. There is this exciting development going on in which they are all interested, and they expect — and enjoy — being given a lead and advice and hearing all about it. Contrary to the old days of Mandarin rule, the government now addresses the common people directly and they feel that they are being taken into their ruler's confidence.... What may appear as boring indoctrination to us is likely to be of absorbing interest for them....

In Moscow my colleagues told me that the Chinese students coming to work in the Soviet Union are gifted and incredibly hard-working, and that they are often at the top of their classes ... when they enter the field of industrial competition in earnest, they are likely to do so in their own right and not merely as imitators of Western methods. Discussing scientific or technological problems with the Chinese, one becomes acutely aware of many centuries of mental schooling. Their arguments are clever, shrewd, and to the point, and one feels that the minds which for more than a thousand years have been sharpened by classical training find little difficulty in making the change to science ...

One of the many slogans which has caught on particularly well is 'Learn while you work'.... I was told that at the building of the great Yangtze Bridge they started with a fairly small number of skilled crews. The others watched. Soon many more could do the skilled work, and so it went on in a chain reaction of learning.... The workers of China have this immense desire to learn because they enjoy it and not just because they want better jobs. In terms of industrial production this means that the Chinese scientists and engineers will be backed by a good supply of eager and enthusiastic technicians, a grade in which our own industry is lamentably short.

It is a sad reflection that the East should have succeeded where we seem to have failed.... The great advances which we have achieved in man's domination of the forces of nature ... have been met in the West with nothing better than apathy or even revulsion. The Chinese ... take these same things as exciting new developments, destined to enrich the life of human society....

However modern the political and economic views of one's Chinese friends may be, subconsciously they are backed by the past greatness of China. When the mind of China now turns to technology, it does so with the moral strength of historical success.... Wherever one goes and whoever one may talk to in the new China, these 2,000 years of unbroken civilization are in evidence. The buildings and monuments of the old China are receiving the same love and care as the new machines. One is made to feel that, to the Chinese, technology is not an aim in itself or a copy from the West, but simply another chapter in their long and glorious history: if you like, a new mandate of heaven.

China Kaleidoscope 1

NOTES FROM MY JOURNAL AND LETTERS

Are things specially arranged for foreigners?

Yes and no. *No* in any significant sense, such as changing things to impress a visitor. Often the foreigner is alone, as I am. Are they going to disrupt a factory employing 25,000 just so that one person will be pleasantly surprised by what he sees? I have often at the last minute changed my plans and decided to see *this* instead of *that*. Are they going to go to much trouble for a plan that might be changed by a visitor's whim?

Secondly: they simply don't care! They are not very concerned with what we think. They are enormously busy — as a nation at war is busy. We don't care in the middle of a war whether some foreign journalist gets the 'right' impression or not. It is part of our self-importance to think that our opinion matters so much to them.

But *yes* in a different sense. Preparations are made; a hotel room is booked; certain plans are arranged for, the picnic lunch is packed. The most 'casual' day, you can see afterwards, was most carefully thought out — mostly for your own comfort. The Chinese have a rare sensitivity about a traveller's needs. They seem to know exactly when he's had enough, when he wants to be alone, when he needs a nap, when he needs a beer. Chinese are among the best hosts in the world, and the least formal. You can have a good time and laugh with them. Or be silent with them. Silences are not uncomfortable socially as they are with us.

At Anshan, after a beer or two with Mr Liu, who had been showing us round, we became rather cheerfully friendly, and he told me some of the difficulties from their side. 'You know,' he said, 'we Chinese like to be hospitable, but we often don't know how to be. We haven't travelled, we don't know your customs and we often haven't the faintest idea of what you really want to do. We try our best but we are never quite sure, especially as you come from so many different countries, all with different customs. We never feel certain as to whether we are doing the right things for our guests.'

Sense of Equality

This is an important aspect of Chinese life. I remember my surprise, when I first came to America from England, on seeing a senior surgeon in a hospital lining up at the cafeteria with nurses and orderlies — this simply couldn't have happened in pre-war England — and, on another occasion, seeing the head of a company having to wait for a lift because the office boy got there first. China is like this, but more so.

It runs through their entire life. Yen, my current interpreter, feels perfectly at ease with cabinet ministers when I go for interviews. He shows respect, of course, but speaks as an equal. I have been told by one of the diplomatic people here that when Mao visits a farm or a factory, people are eager to talk to him, and do so without becoming fluttery and nervous. The judge at the court, the guard on a train, the head of a factory, the senior engineer on a hydro-electric dam project, all of them, I have noticed, walk about among the workers but never as 'bosses'. No one is obsequious. No one makes way specially for them — they aren't even noticed very much. They are another kind of worker doing their job.

Letter to Elena. June 15th

... This afternoon I saw the floor boys in a huddle in the private dining-room opposite the lift. The double doors were open and I stood and watched six or seven of them around a table, talking. Later I asked one of them if it had been their regular political meeting. He said, no, it was a meeting to discuss how they could become better floor boys, manage things better, be of better service to the guests.

Everywhere this passion for improvement! I believe that hotel boys in England or America would not meet like this; or if they did they would be talking about how to get more money, or how to wangle a better job.

But perhaps in the West it's not so much the desire for money that drives us, as much as the need to feel important. We all have need to *be* somebody. The personal-importance motive doesn't seem to operate here in the same way, or possibly it's submerged in a collective drive for mass advance. American corporations often secure the allegiance of an employee, not by more money, but by giving him more importance — a new title, a carpet, his name on the door, etc. I don't believe that would work here.

I have come to believe that the Chinese derive their deepest emotional satisfactions not from a sense of personal importance, but from sharing in activities which have aims beyond the individual. The government here has been extremely skilful in giving nearly everyone a sense that his work fits in somewhere. A floor boy in this hotel feels that he is participating in the rebirth of China every bit as much as a big shot in the government. All of them, down to those who do the most menial jobs — pedicab drivers, say — are made to feel they are an essential part of the whole show.

Item for Stamp Collectors

A recent stamp issue included paintings of about a dozen different varieties of goldfish. Others are of animals and birds, some are of children running and skipping. During the 'grow more pigs' drive a series came out with pictures of fat porkers. Domestic postage rates are four yen, less than a penny in our money.

One of China's less sticky problems comes up almost daily. They have no adhesive on their stamps. Post-offices provide small paste pots, and you do your best with both stamps and envelopes. It is quite a tedious and messy business, and if one has a pile of letters not only does it take some time, but the letters tend to stick together because the paste always oozes on to the back of the envelope. The reason given for continuing this absurdity (it started long before 1949) is that licking stamps is 'unhygienic'.

Here at the hotel post-office a damp hand-cloth is supplied to wipe the paste off one's hands.

Letter to Elena. June 24th

... Another appallingly frustrating day. I phoned the Ministry again today, but couldn't get anywhere; no answer, not even 'no'. The Chinese have a highly developed sense of *timing*. They will wait until *they* think it is time to act. And then, if need be, they can act quickly. But they *won't* be *pushed*!

I have never in my entire life come up against this in quite the form it takes here. It is like being pitted against a solid wall of rock. There is no way to climb it or push it, or to get round the ends. It is just there: a colossal disregard for anything but that which they consider important. There is tremendous strength in this, and it creates havoc with anyone who cannot bend a bit.

This is what the early Europeans found when dealing with the Emperors. This is what the Americans found when negotiating with the Chinese in Korea. This is what has been going on for more than five years of ambassadorial meetings in Warsaw. The Chinese are ready to meet, ready to talk, but not ready to compromise on a single basic principle.

It has been a difficult lesson for me. I'm usually impatient, as you know, to get things *done*. But the Chinese refuse to be hurried or made to do something in a way that is not right to *them*. One sees it, too, in the ordinary people everywhere. They are never rushed, never petulant, never impatient; they go their own way and at their own speed.

Sex and Rumours of Sex

China is going through a period of intense sexual morality. The authorities are determined not to allow foreigners to make sexual liaisons with Chinese girls. This is less likely to happen with Russian and East European technicians who come for a year or more with their wives and families. The problem is with foreign students. There's a rumour (I distrust rumours) that seven or eight foreign students are now in jail in Peking awaiting transportation back to their own countries because of illicit sexual relations with local girls.

A Hungarian technician (this is another story that's going the rounds) who was here fell in love with a Chinese girl and wanted to sleep with her. She said she had to get permission from her organization first. The next thing the man knew was that his visa had been cancelled, and he's now on his way to Budapest.

An African student (this, I believe, is a true story) who travelled to college every day on the bus was attracted by a girl conductor. He made sure he caught the same bus every day. An after-work meeting was arranged and he invited the girl to his hotel room.

The girl arrived accompanied by a friend, whom she hoped to leave downstairs. However, the hotel management wouldn't allow a single woman in a foreigner's room, so both went up. They all had a pleasant time — but perhaps not the kind the man had hoped for.

The incident got back to the girl's superiors and she was reprimanded. She didn't lose her job, but was transferred to another route. The student soon discovered that his studies were being rather mysteriously curtailed, and his visa was not extended. He sent the girl a letter and a small gift, offering his apologies. The gift was returned and the letter remained unanswered.

Burial Mounds

From the windows of trains I frequently see burial mounds scattered over fields; they take up valuable space and make mechanical cultivation difficult. The government rule apparently is strictly adhered to — no removal of graves without permission of the families. The government knows its people too well to interfere in a matter which touches them so deeply. And it is only a matter of time, they think, before the younger, less superstitious generation will give the necessary permission. All grave removals are done with the family present and at government expense. Ancestral remains are removed with appropriate ceremony to new cemeteries.

Sunday Church

Up early and caught the Number 10 trolley bus to the Catholic church near the East Wall. I wanted to find out about the attendance and see what sort of people they were. Was astonished to find this large church more than half filled. More women than men. Children everywhere, allowed to laugh and run about. Two confessional boxes in operation.

My guess was that half the congregation was under forty; about 20 per cent of *these* were in their teens or early twenties. The priest was young, assisted by a man in his working clothes — the priest in a robe of the most lovely apple green. The singing was fervent — chanting rather than singing. This church is *alive*. There was no national flag here as I had seen at the Protestant church last week. Dodged out early to count the people coming out — 540. Outside the church people stood around chatting — gave me the 'after-church' feeling as in England.

Chinese Puzzle

When I first went to Russia in 1931, the government was using the churches in Moscow for anti-God museums, for birth-control clinics, and even for stables. But here things are done more deftly. A few days ago I learned from the Reverend Chao Fu-san (he's a Protestant pastor and a teacher at the Peking Theological Seminary) that while the government gives the Christian organizations no moral support at all, it does give them some material help. He said that all church property is tax-exempt and that repairs are paid for by the government. Also, when the various religions hold their national conventions the government gives delegates free rail transport and helps them to get hotel accommodation. (I learned from a priest today that this is true for Catholic churches too.) When I asked the Reverend Chao 'Why?'— he said (this country is really full of paradoxes!), 'Oh, because they have to — the constitution guarantees freedom of religion!'

Conflict

When China's proverbial courtesy to strangers and official political antagonism meet — what happens? Which wins? I found myself one afternoon in a large and violent 'anti-American rally'. Around me were thousands shouting slogans and brandishing clenched fists. 'America get out of Taiwan! America get out of South Korea! Down with American imperialism!' Someone asked me where I was from. 'America,' I said. Immediately friendly grins and handshakes and applause from those standing near 'for our foreign friend'.

Shuo Fu

Today, near the covered market on Wang Fu Ching, a pedicab, loaded with bolts of cotton from a textile factory, went across a red light. These Peking pedicab drivers are cheeky to the traffic police — like the cockneys in London. The police carry small megaphones and yell through them, but pedicab drivers seem to make a point of never paying the slightest attention, and usually get away with it. However, today the policeman ran after the driver and made him pull over and stop. We were standing near by, so I waited to see what would happen. The policeman talked and talked while the pedicab driver, an old hand at this, said nothing but kept mopping his sweaty face. I asked my guide what the policeman was saying. Apparently he was delivering the man a lecture on what socialism means, the responsibility all have for the safety of everyone, and what would happen if everyone disobeyed the lights, and pointing out that if China was to become great, her people must be socially conscious. It went on and on — a long lecture, nothing more. No summons. This is an example of what the Chinese call 'shuo fu' (to convince by talk). The idea that explanation, talk, discussion, will eventually convince, runs through Chinese society today.

The incident today reminded me of another example of *shuo fu* when I was in China three years ago. October 1st was the day of the big national parade in Peking and the people got up early to get good positions along the route. I got up early, too, to see how they handled the crowds. By eight o'clock, two hours before starting time, I was standing under the trees not far from Tien An Men. Thousands of people were already lining the wide street. But apparently a mistake had been made; the section where I was standing was supposed to have been kept clear. An officer with a megaphone was shouting at the crowd, insisting that they move along — the space was reserved for the army.

But the people had already been there for several hours and they were damned if they were going to move. The officer shouted and gesticulated, but there was no response whatever. Presently several lorry-loads of white-jacketed police arrived. They linked hands and began to push. The crowd wasn't having any of this and stood its ground. More police arrived. They began to push those already pushing, and the pressure on the crowd was now quite tremendous. Yet it was all surprisingly good-humoured, with lots of kidding between the police and the people. It reminded me of bobbies and a London crowd.

The crowd was now losing ground and was just about to be pushed into the street, when — the idea must have occurred to them all simultaneously — they all sat down! That did it. The police were left with nothing to push. Kids, running in and out under the linked arms of the police, made it all appear quite ridiculous. I was watching the officer. He gave some new orders; the police piled into their lorries and off they went. The officer too. Good for the crowd, I thought. They've won.

But I had forgotten *shuo fu*, the appeal to reason. In about fifteen minutes, a small platform lorry arrived and parked in front of the crowd. Out of the cab jumped a young man who hung up a couple of loudspeakers, climbed on the lorry, and began talking. He didn't yell, he just talked. And he talked and talked. No one seemed to be listening. They sat there on the ground, looking anywhere but at the speaker This went on for more than thirty minutes. Then all at once the crowd got up, laughing and clapping, and he laughed and clapped at them; and they streamed away down the street. Yelling hadn't done it; pushing hadn't done it; but *shuo fu* did the trick.

```
*********************************
*                               *
*          PART FOUR            *
*                               *
*********************************
```

XII

How the Communes Started

IT was in the autumn of 1958 that the word *commune* first began to appear in the American press. There were rumours of something big developing in China — some new, ominous upheaval. Details were lacking at first, but the word itself held sinister connotations: and in any case, nothing good could be happening in mainland China. If it weren't good, clearly it was the duty of honest statesmen — not to mention news analysts — to say so.

They did. On November 14th, the Secretary of State, Mr Dulles, informed representatives of the Colombo Plan nations assembled in Seattle that the Chinese were 'imposing mass slavery on 650 million people'. They had 'degraded the dignity of the human individual'. They had created 'a vast slave state'.

Scripps-Howard newspapers featured a series of articles entitled 'Chain Gang Empire'. I recall that one of the cartoons illustrating this series offered a row of skulls above a blood-spattered wall, upon which was written (in words of blood): 'Family destruction', 'bestiality', 'slave labour'. And *Life* magazine presented pictures (artists' drawings, that is) of burning villages and weeping women.

I was in America when the commune movement began. I felt I knew enough about the Chinese people (and by this time enough about how the press was treating news from China) to discount most of the stories about 'breaking up the families' and about men and women being segregated and herded into barracks. What is more, some European reports were presenting a rather different version of events in China. But the horrible accounts of the communes must, I felt, be based on something. So I was looking forward with the keenest curiosity, and also a little apprehension, to learning for myself what the communes really were. I give here what I was able to learn pretty much as it came to me in discussions with European agrarian specialists, through talks with staff members of the Peking Agricultural College and, later, through a careful personal study of about fifteen different communes.

How It Began

Only one-ninth of China's land area has, until recently, been arable. But 80 per cent of the Chinese people are peasants — at present more than 550 million of them.

Professor Keith M. Buchanan, of the University of Wellington in New Zealand, who was making a study of agriculture in the Chinese countryside in October 1958, once said: 'We must keep in our minds a picture of old China — not the China of exquisite jade carvings and golden-roofed pagodas and elegant scholarship, but a country of poverty and exploitation. A country where children with swollen bellies died by the wayside and peasants ate roots and grass.'

For the past three thousand years the chronic semi-starvation of this vast mass of human beings has broken the 'exquisite' surface of Chinese history like a great barrier reef.

A feudal system of land tenure, a pyramided landlord-serf relationship, had been fastened upon the peasantry at least ten centuries before the beginnings of feudalism in Europe. Buttressed by beliefs and superstitions which demanded unconditional respect for tradition; patriarchal, isolated, each village hardly in touch with the next, the system maintained itself with amazing durability into the fourth decade of the present century.

Nine hundred years ago a Sung dynasty writer, Su Shiun, said:

The soil has ceased to belong to those who till it, and they who have the owning thereof toil not in the fields. Of their yield the landlord takes one-half; for every ten farmers there numbers but one proprietor and thus it is that, daily laying his share aside, he fattens in prosperity, whilst the others, exhausting theirs in order to keep every day alive, sink into poverty and hunger. And there is naught they can do.

And as recently as 1946, only three years before Chiang Kai-shek was driven from the mainland to Taiwan, Theodore H. White wrote in *Thunder out of China*:

> The ancient trinity of landlord, loanshark and merchant is a symbol hated throughout Chinese history. It represents a system that has shackled China's development for five centuries. During the last century, however, the system has tightened about the Chinese peasant as never before because of the impact of the West, by commerce and violence, on its time-worn apparatus....

The plight of the Chinese peasantry has been documented in countless studies by Western writers and scholars. The need for reform was recognized, theoretically at least, by the Chiang Kai-shek government. In fact, a land-reform programme was projected in 1948, by Americans working with the Kuomintang, which included a five-year plan for transforming all tenants into independent proprietors.

Like most other reforms under the Chiang regime, this land programme came too late (only when his position had become desperate) and was never implemented.

It was, fundamentally, the revolt of the peasantry which destroyed the Kuomintang on mainland China. The Communists gave leadership to the long-overdue agrarian revolution. This was their 'secret weapon', against which Chiang, with all his American equipment, remained powerless. In every district where the Communists came to power, there followed a confiscation of all landlords' land (above a certain minimum, which the landlord could stay and work for himself if he cared to), and division of the land among the landless peasants. After the Communists took over the national government in 1949, a redistribution (or 'land reform' as it was called) spread rapidly, and by 1952 had been carried through over the entire country, with the exception of certain remote areas.

The leaders of the new government, however, did not regard this as a final solution. As early as 1943 Mao Tse-tung had stated that: 'the one way in which the peasants can overthrow their poverty is progressively collectivizing; and according to Lenin, the one way to collectivization is via co-operatives'. Article 34 of China's provisional constitution, the Common Programme, in force from 1949 to 1954, admonished the government to ' ... gradually lead the peasants into organizing various forms of mutual aid in work and of co-operation in production'.

Distribution of land, the wiping out of feudal landlordism, was a first step, but small-scale farming by individual owners could not meet the need for basic modernization and mechanization of agriculture. Without this, China's chronic food shortage must continue. The peasants had become proprietors. They were free of the enormous burden of rent and debt, but this didn't help them much. The plots were too small; most peasants had no tools; land improvement, the making of ditches and repairing of dykes, had to be done together. The farmers were persuaded, and in some cases bullied, into forming mutual-aid teams, pooling resources to work together, and learning how to co-operate. The pressures on them were great, but they didn't have to join these mutual-aid teams, and some didn't. And when mutual aid later developed into co-operatives, some rugged individualists stayed out of those too — I met a few of them in 1957. But as the years passed and the advantages of co-operative farming became more evident in terms of equipment and per capita production as compared with private farming, most farmers joined them.

Thus, the mutual-aid team was the first step towards collectivization. By 1955 many of these small mutual-aid groups had joined together in voluntary co-operatives. At this stage the co-operatives were of a simple kind; land was still owned individually but worked collectively as one big farm; then from this there developed the 'advanced' type of co-operative, in which land and farm-implements were held in common, and at harvest-time profits were divided among the families in proportion to the days of labour each family had contributed. By the end of 1957, 97 per cent of China's peasants were in advanced co-operatives.

However, even these co-operatives, averaging less than two hundred families, were still too small. No real modernization plans could be based on these small units. And what is more, they were incapable of solving the chronic under-employment of the Chinese peasantry. No under-developed country that was hoping, as China was, to move quickly into the modern world could afford to have four-fifths of her people working less than half-time. The situation was ripe for the next stage.

During the winter of 1957–8 the government initiated a nation-wide water-conservation and irrigation programme. Considerable attention had already been given to irrigation as a means of raising the country's food production, some four and a half million acres having been brought under irrigation since 1950. The winter projects, however, dwarfed everything that had gone before. Tens of millions of peasants, together with volunteers from the cities, turned out to build dams, dredge canals and ditches, dig water storage ponds, and drill wells. During these months of massive effort nearly fourteen million additional acres were brought under irrigation, which made possible the large agricultural yields of the following summer.

But the irrigation drive had outstripped the capabilities of the co-ops. They were too small. For the large dams and canals necessary for effective irrigation, many co-operatives, often the people of an entire county, had to pool their labour, machinery, and materials. The same was true of tree-planting. One village had plenty of barren land in need of afforestation, but no extra labour force. Another might have the man-power but no land. The same for mining. Also, at this time the government was pushing mechanization of agriculture, but farm machinery was too expensive for many individual co-ops to finance on their own.

For these compelling reasons, informal mergers of co-ops began taking place in various parts of the country. Such mergers were called *ta shê*, 'co-op federations' or 'enlarged co-operatives'. They were an indication that the co-operatives were no longer able to meet the demands being made upon them.

Apparently the commune movement as such really got under way first in Honan Province. In Sueiping County in that province, twenty-seven co-ops merged in April 1958 — a combination of 9,300 families (more than 40,000 persons). Following the usual procedures, leaders were elected and the peasants divided themselves into work-groups. With a larger pool of man-power to draw from, nurseries were set up for mothers working in the fields. Some of the women banded together to start a kitchen to bring food out to the field gangs during the spring harvest. After a period of trial and error, and the usual group discussions, the merger of these twenty-seven co-ops was formalized and a set of by-laws adopted. They called themselves the *Weihsing* (Sputnik) Enlarged Co-operative. There was nothing very unusual about all this.

These peasants in Honan were concerned only with their own affairs and probably had no idea that they were initiating a movement which was soon to sweep the entire country.

One can assume from a reading of his earlier works that Mao Tse-tung had for some time had some such system as the communes in mind. That he was not expecting such a movement to start at the time it did is indicated by an article in the official English-language weekly, *Peking Review*, on June 10th, 1958. Mao, while commending a co-operative that had done particularly well, makes no mention of any imminent new developments. In *Socialist Upsurge in China's Country-side*, published in 1957, he said:

> Most of our present semi-socialist co-ops have only twenty or thirty families in them, because co-operatives of that size are easy to run and they give the administrative staff and the members an opportunity to gain experience quickly. They cannot operate on a large scale or use machinery. The development of their forces of production is still hampered. They should not stay in this position too long, but should go on to combine with other co-operatives.

Mao apparently concluded from these first mergers that the time was ready; and gave them the official support which got the movement off to a flying start. The Chinese attribute the use of the word 'commune' for the enlarged co-ops to Mao himself.

From that moment on, the Chinese press was filled with reports of co-operatives throughout China merging with their neighbours. Details of the Sputnik were publicized, and it is said that 85,000 people visited it to see how it worked. Within a few months the movement had swept through the country. By the end of the year almost every farm family in China was in a people's commune.

Chinese rural life had been reorganized three times within a decade — land reform, the co-operatives, and now the communes. This three-stage development, the Chinese believe, has taken the earth's most atomized and least-productive farm systems to the threshold of becoming one of the most consolidated and potentially most productive systems in the world.

XIII

Basic Structure and Finances

RETURNING to China in 1960, I brought with me a host of preconceived ideas — as well as apprehensions — about the communes. Many of these were centred on the accusations of forcible break-up of families, which I will touch on later. As for the communes themselves, I imagined some sort of physical structure into which one could walk and say, 'Now I am in a commune.' The fact is that wherever you are in the countryside in China today, you are 'in a commune'— just as in America or England, you are always in some particular county. At first you might have walked through hundreds of villages without noticing anything new, because the change is primarily administrative and social. Today, however, you would see changes in the form of new buildings: commune schools, canteens, kindergartens, factories, and workshops.

In extent, the commune equals roughly the basic political division of the Chinese countryside — the *hsiang*, equivalent to an American township. Ordinarily a *hsiang* comprises several villages with a total of from five to ten thousand families, although they can be considerably larger. And some of the really large communes cover several *hsiangs*.

The commune took over responsibility not only for agricultural work in its area but for all those functions usually assigned to local government. Primary and secondary schools, nurseries, kindergartens, 'spare-time' (adult-education) schools, canteens, industries, clinics and hospitals, banking, housing, barbers' shops, repairs, markets, libraries, theatres, sports, vital statistics, the care of those 'senior citizens' who had no families — all these, and many others, are today administered by the communes.

Communes are self-financing. Their products, over and above what is consumed by the commune members, are sold either through government purchasing agencies, or directly, to national or provincial factories. Prices are fixed by the government on the basis of a national average of production costs. They seem to have remained stable. Comparing present prices for staples such as wheat and rice, in town and country, with those obtaining during my past visit, I noted they had not varied.

Commune expenditures fall into the following main categories: production costs, depreciation of public property, state taxes, free food distribution, basic wages and bonus awards, public welfare funds, and an accumulation fund for capital investment. In 1960 communes were taxed 6 per cent of their total production value. This, nationally, amounted to 4,100 million yuan and represented only 5·9 per cent of the total national budget revenue.

The bonus payments (if a profit remains after other expenses have been met) are awarded, after public discussion, to the work-brigades that have done especially well. Sometimes these bonus payments take the form of small presents — notebooks, the works of Mao Tse-tung, ball-point pens, or a citation to be hung on a wall. The accumulation fund provides the financial resources for school and hospital buildings, tractors and machinery for the workshops, capital improvement of the land by dams, electric pumps, irrigation projects, etc. Tractors and industrial machinery can be bought from the factories on an instalment plan without interest charges. It is not lack of money, but the shortage of industrial output that prevents the communes from mechanizing as fast as they would wish. The welfare fund provides the cost of free education, medical care, maternity benefits, entertainment, burial allowance, pensions, and a home for old people who have no family, as well as a reserve fund to help any family through an emergency.

The method of determining money wages varies from commune to commune and comparisons are difficult. Broadly speaking, however, one can say that a worker in a commune will earn 7 to 12 yuan a month as a basic wage (21s. to 36s.). This is, of course, in addition to the free food. Wages are paid monthly and are not (as formerly) paid only to the husband, but to the individuals — including wives or children — who have actually earned it. Most families have several wage-earning members.

To the Western observer, these payments appear pitifully low, as indeed they are. But it must be remembered that cash wages form only a part of the commune member's real income. One of the first demands in nearly all communes was for a comprehensive system of social security, and the greatest security for the Chinese peasant is food. To him, money — for the first time the peasant is receiving a wage — is less important than the assurance of food. Thus, from the very beginning, communes have undertaken to provide 'free' food to all (some give only grain, some furnish all foods). In addition, there is housing, education, medical care, and all the rest. Wages may be low, food at times scarce, and the work extremely hard. But to the Chinese peasant, life in the commune represents a real improvement over the conditions of the yet-very-recent past.

Visible signs of the upswing of living standards (with the exception of food, which was in short supply in 1960 because of recent poor harvests) struck me forcibly after an absence of three years. Many peasants now were blossoming out in 'Sunday clothes'. There were more bicycles. Inside the cottages I sometimes noticed radios and clocks. I frequently saw piles of new blankets.

One would not have imagined that wages of less than 36s. a month would leave much to spare for savings. But the fact is that in all the communes I visited, an appreciable number of peasants had opened savings accounts on which they were earning from 3 to 8 per cent interest. Many savings were on a modest scale. In a commune I visited in Honan Province — a poor area — total personal savings averaged only 6 yuan (18s.). In the 'Green for Four Seasons' commune in Hopei Province, on the other hand, 57 per cent of all families held savings accounts with an average value of 97 yuan (£14. 11s.) per family. A decade ago bank savings of any kind were unheard-of among the peasants. (A friend of mine who lived in China for many years exclaimed, upon reading the above paragraph: 'Impossible! I know a great many things have changed, but I simply can't believe that peasants have bank accounts, let alone radios and clocks!')

A major objective of the commune movement, along with increasing national agricultural production, was to develop the industrial potential of the countryside and to use much more fully the huge under-employed resources of man-power. To do this, tens of thousands — perhaps even hundreds of thousands — of small factories or workshops were built in villages and towns throughout China. I will later describe several of the workshops which I visited.

Here let me point out that beyond these aims having to do with production, appear others of a less tangible nature. There is, for example, the growing wish in China to lessen the gap between city and country life — to give country people the cultural opportunities and the technical conveniences enjoyed by those living in cities; and, closely linked to this, the hope that gradually the differences between workers and intellectuals can be reduced. Behind this is a concept that workers should also be thinkers, and that intellectuals should also be able to work — that is, that the range of man's experience in life can be widened, once these arbitrary classifications are removed.

'We want to release the buried talents in ourselves and others' is a phrase I heard in various forms from many people active in the commune movement. In more strictly Chinese Marxist terms, the objective of the communes is to move the country forward to the time when full communism can be established — that is, a classless society governed by the principle 'From everyone according to his ability, to everyone according to his needs'.

During the first hectic months these long-range objectives had to take a second place. Organizing elections, working out details of management, new construction, the building of clinics and hospitals, the starting of schools, the establishing of communal kitchens, the equipping of workshops, the setting up of kindergartens and nurseries, and the training of young people to look after the children — these and a thousand other activities kept everyone at full stretch; and all this at a time when the work in the fields and the normal routines of harvesting, ploughing, and sowing had to be sustained! Exhausting as those months must have been, I found that many of the people I talked to looked back on 1958 as a high point in their lives — a 'great time to have lived' — very much as the British still look back on the blitz, or the French on their resistance.

XIV

The National Picture

THE reasons why the national government determined to press forward with the commune movement become obvious when one moves from an examination of the individual commune to an assessment of the effects on the nation as a whole.

In any under-developed economy one of the chronic problems is agrarian under-employment. At peak times, as during harvesting, there may be work for all, but mostly there is a severe shortage of work. This has been a centuries-old riddle for China, as it still is in more than half the world. The peasants of China represented a huge surplus labour force. A pre-war survey by Professor J. R. Buck, covering seventeen provinces, showed that the average days (or day equivalents) worked per year by men was 133. Thus for almost two-thirds of his life the average peasant was without employment and without earnings. The above appeared in an article by Shigeru Ishikawa of the Institute of Economic Research, Hitotsubashi University, Japan, in the *Far Eastern Economic Review*, September 29th, 1960. I am much indebted to Professor Ishikawa for his lucid discussion of this aspect of the communes.

Even by the mid-'fifties this condition had not fundamentally changed. A survey undertaken in 1955 estimated the working year for men and women in a 'lower co-operative' as totalling only 130 days (the figure would have been higher for men alone). Although the survey related to a single province, Anwhei, the editor of the report notes it as reflecting a general situation. By 1957 (the last year before the communes) men working in 'higher co-operatives' were still only working the equivalent of 161 days a year.

Governments of most countries in the world, confronted by the under-employment of their rural population, have looked for a solution to the expansion of urban industry and the gradual movement of surplus rural population into the cities. This pattern has been seen in the U.S.S.R., Japan, and many other countries. The process has been at best a slow and costly one, and offers a somewhat questionable 'solution', since the mushrooming of industrial cities (as many nations have learned to their cost) tends to create as many new problems as it solves old ones. In Soviet Russia the rural population began to decrease from the 'thirties onwards and it was expected that a similar trend, sooner or later, must appear in China. China's difficulties were aggravated by unemployment already existing in her cities — the whole problem being further intensified by the rate of population increase. Any real solution to rural unemployment in China, therefore, was remote.

The commune movement appears to have tackled this problem directly. Surplus labour in the country has found employment without migration to the cities. A survey taken in China in 1959, the first year after the communes, indicated that peasant working days had risen to 300 per year. This tremendous increase from the figure of 161 days only two years earlier reflects the results of establishing small rural industrial plants in the communes and of the use of labour surplus for agricultural capital construction (soil conservation, afforestation, dams, irrigation). China thus appears to be approaching what no other under-developed country has yet achieved — a solution to the riddle of rural under-employment. I was informed, and I believe correctly, that today in a number of areas there is actually a labour shortage — astonishing as this may seem for a country of such enormous population.

I met, while in Peking, an Indian active in trade-union work. He told me that of all that he had seen in China, the absence of unemployment was, in his view, the single most impressive achievement. I experienced in a small personal way what this means. I carried with me in China a good deal of photographic equipment — movie camera, tripod, still cameras, etc. I asked everywhere if I could hire a man to help to carry this stuff. Invariably the reply came back, 'We are very sorry, it would mean taking someone off his regular work.' Anyone who has been to India, of course, knows that if you so much as whisper the fact that you might need a carrier, several dozen applicants would be waiting on your doorstep within minutes.

One of the most significant features, economically, of the commune system is that it enables the country to finance agricultural improvements and to establish rural industries with almost no help from central funds. Large sums are being ploughed back into capital investment rather than being used to increase the standard of living. The productivity of the Chinese peasant today is rising far more steeply than is the increase of his individual purchasing power, the difference representing commune investment in capital equipment and capital improvement of the land.

This idea of holding down the rate of increase of wages is explicitly spelled out, and in discussions with the peasants I found they were well aware of its significance. The pitifully low wages referred to in the previous chapter are, in part at least, voluntary. In the constitution of the Sputnik Commune, Article 22 declares:

> When the average wages (including grain supply) of members of the commune rise to a level that guarantees a living standard equivalent to that of the well-to-do middle peasant, the rate of increase in wages should be reduced to ensure the rapid growth of industry, the mechanization of farming, and the electrification of rural areas in the shortest possible time.

Wages, of course, *are* increasing, but not as fast as productivity.

Still other benefits, nationally, are accruing from the commune movement. Larger units of cultivation make possible more advanced technique. (How rapidly, one wonders, could American agriculture have advanced had it been limited to the old-fashioned units of single-family-size farms?) Mechanization, spread of scientific information, proper use of fertilizer, pest control, experiments in hybridization of seed corn — all become vastly easier.

Meanwhile the workshops in the communes not only are adding to national output, but are converting a peasantry innocent of any previous contact with machines into a labour force with considerable mechanical know-how. Millions of men and women, who until a few years ago were unable to read or write, are now interpreting blue-prints, operating precision lathes, turning out work to decimal-point tolerance. This is not likely to be a disadvantage for a nation driving, as China is, towards industrialization.

One further national asset growing out of the communes should be mentioned, and that is strategic invulnerability. Decentralization of governmental functions and administrative apparatus and the scattering of industry provide a security not enjoyed by other industrial nations. Add to this the plans for regional self-sufficiency, the growing capability of local industry to meet local needs, and it becomes conceivable that a third or a half of China might be destroyed or overrun without too severe a dislocation in the remainder. The survival capacity of such a nation is enormous.

Clearly Chinese agriculture still has a long way to go, as the inadequate harvests of 1959–60 indicate. The Chinese themselves are more than ready to admit that by comparison with advanced Western countries, their methods remain extraordinarily primitive. They point out, however, that their very successes are responsible for many of the strains on their resources.

For example, a study completed in the autumn of 1960 demonstrated that the change from partial employment to full employment involved a greater consumption of food. Women who yesterday were pottering around their small houses, today are out in the fields and the workshops. They eat more. The government estimates that with the establishment of community dining-rooms in the communes, grain consumption by former poor peasants and lower-middle peasants has risen to the level of middle peasants.[1]

The great improvement in clothing everywhere (one of the first things I noticed on my return in 1960) keeps cotton in short supply, despite the fact that cotton production is reported to have more than quadrupled in the past ten years. By mid-1960 the Minister of Agriculture, Liao Lu-yen, summed up the situation as follows:

> With the development of industry ... the amount of grain to be supplied to the cities has increased.... The amount of grain to be

[1] During land reform the Communists divided the peasantry into rough categories. 'Poor peasants' were peasants who had no land and worked entirely for others; 'lower-middle peasants' owned some land but not enough to support themselves and so worked part-time as hired hands; 'middle peasants' owned enough land and could support themselves without employing others 'rich peasants' not only owned land and worked on it themselves but could employ other peasants to help them; and 'landlords' referred to those who owned land and were rich enough to enjoy its benefits without working themselves, could lease land to others.

supplied to the cities in 1960 is estimated to be nearly twice as much as in 1953, the first year of the Five-Year Plan.... Ours is a country where industry is not well developed.... It needs to import a certain amount of machinery and equipment which it cannot produce as yet or of which its output still fails to meet the demand. In order to import we have to export. In 1959 China's total exports nearly quadrupled compared with 1950. Of the exports more than 70 per cent were farm produce or processed farm produce....

The average annual rate of increase in China's grain output for the last ten years has reached 9·6 per cent ... but its per capita grain output is still comparatively low....

It is not difficult to solve the question of providing the productive equipment for the development of light industry; the question is where to get the necessary raw materials, especially the supply of farm products which are the main raw materials for light industry. For instance ... there is no difficulty in building in a year ten or even more textile mills, each with 100,000 spindles. But to provide the raw materials needed by ten mills in a year ... we shall probably have to build up cotton-production bases with an area of several million or even up to ten million mu....

Agricultural production in our country is still done almost entirely by manual labour. Most of the semi-mechanized farm-implements are also operated by animal traction and man-power.... The present task is to equip the people's communes with modern farm-machines so as to carry through the mechanization and modernization of our agriculture....

The switch-over to the people's communes and the level already attained in industrialization have prepared the necessary conditions for the mechanization of agriculture.... The areas cultivated by farm-machinery in 1959 constituted only about 5 per cent of the country's cultivated land.

This statement by the Minister of Agriculture indicates that the leaders are under no illusions about the backward state of Chinese agriculture.

If their agriculture is backward, the Chinese still believe that the communes give the best prospect for advance. Progressively greater national resources will be deflected to help them. Steel allocation for agricultural mechanization in 1960 was double the allocation for 1959, and in 1961 may well be doubled again. Confidence in the system itself remains unshaken; the communes will continue to be the basic unit of Chinese rural life. And it must be admitted that the results have been impressive. The 'disasters' prophesied by Western writers in the early days simply haven't happened. Even the reasoned doubts expressed by some responsible economists and agronomists have not been fulfilled. Professor Shigeru Ishikawa, whom I have quoted before, frankly admits this. 'About two years ago, when Agricultural Producers' Co-operatives were abruptly being reorganized into Rural Communes, I entertained a doubt about the stability of the new organization and its contemplated effect on production.... However, my fears have not materialized.... On the contrary, the organization of Rural Communes has persisted and played a crucial role in promoting changes in the economic structure of Mainland China which may have far-reaching implications in the future.... '

XV

Some Key Questions Answered

SINCE returning to the United States I have lectured extensively on my experiences in China. There are certain questions about the communes which I am asked by almost every audience: Wasn't it a system ruthlessly imposed by the government? Were there not terrible blunders committed by the Communists? Hasn't the family system been destroyed? These are key questions; and unless we understand the answers we can make no meaningful appraisal of the communes. These questions, I believe, have been inadequately dealt with in the press, and I am therefore attempting in this chapter to give what *seem to me the answers*.

1. *Were the communes imposed ruthlessly from above?*

I believe the answer is no.

No comment, prediction, or exhortation by Chinese officialdom before the summer of 1958 gives so much as a hint that something new was imminent. Yet it would be completely out of character for the leadership to have embarked on such a programme (had they known they were going to do so) without a long, careful 'discussion and education' period beforehand.

Nothing important happens in China without the direction of the Communist Party, and it is a party that keeps its ear very close to the ground. But after talking to many Westerners who watched this sudden, rural eruption in 1958, I have come to believe that the government was taken by surprise, if not by the movement itself, by the extent to which the peasants seized the initiative. A re-reading of the Chinese press of that time confirms the reports that local initiative was consistently outrunning government expectations, and that one of the government's primary concerns was how to control popular enthusiasm without diminishing the energies that had been released.

The first public comment by the Communist Party was not made till the end of August 1958, after a number of communes had already been established. The Communist Party Resolution of August 29th urged the peasants not to carry out mergers too hurriedly, to be sure 'to adapt their plans to local conditions', and to take steps 'only after full discussion'. Decisions about private plots of land need not be dealt with hurriedly; 'clear-cut decisions' could be postponed. It further urged that no change of ownership be made 'beyond the desires of the owner'.

On September 1st an editorial in *Hongqi* (*Red Flag*), the fortnightly publication of the Central Committee, followed this up:

> Only through a full airing of views and debates, only when the people in a locality are willing to go in for it entirely of their own accord, should the agricultural producers' co-operatives be transformed into people's communes.

On September 3rd, the Peking *Renmin Ribao* (*People's Daily*) said:

> People's communes must be set up on the basis of full discussion by the people concerned and it must be a matter of the people's own choice. No rash, impetuous, or domineering attitude should be taken, especially on the question concerning change in the ownership of the means of production.

All this has the sound of brakes being applied.

But once mass support for the communes had become evident, government and Party both gave full support.

2. *Have there not been disastrous psychological and economic blunders in the commune movement?*

From all I could learn there were at first plenty of mistakes.

The gravest apparently arose from over-enthusiasm. The promised day had arrived: the Kitchen God was smiling; free food — who had ever heard of free food in China before? So why not free clothes, free shoes, free everything? Even some Party cadres were, it seems, caught up in the general fiesta and began to force the pace too hard. It must have been a rousing sight to see the new production brigades on their way to work with their flags and drums (how the Chinese love a good show!), and difficult to keep a cool head amid such general excitement. Everything seemed to be going right. Even the harvest was a bumper one — the largest in China's history. In many areas there was talk (not officially encouraged) of how communism was 'just around the corner, if only we could work a little harder yet'.

The initial mistakes, the bungling, the overwork, are admitted today, but in the light of the total advances are accepted as inevitable, rather than serious.

'Research' became a magic word. As communes pooled their resources, they found they had extra funds and with these began to build 'experimental' and 'research' centres long before they had adequate technical knowledge. In some communes the excitement and novelty of starting industrial workshops (this was the first time many young peasants had ever been near machines) led to neglect of the farm work. In others, a drive to pile up record grain production meant that not enough attention was given to pig-breeding or poultry-raising. When the communal dining-halls were established, women, in their relief at not having to cook any more, turned in their pots and pans for the 'steel drive', and later, when they wanted to do some cooking at home, found they had nothing to cook in.

In nothing did the Western press so widely miss the mark as in its attacks on the communal dining-halls. Although I heard scattered complaints about the cooking, I found no women who looked at the dining-halls as anything but a blessed innovation. The virtues of Chinese food are well appreciated by Westerners, but anyone who has seen women bent over the crude charcoal or wood stoves in the country cottages, fanning the flames, or thought of the time and effort that go into cutting vegetables for a single dish, will appreciate the collective sigh of feminine relief that must have gone up when the communal dining-rooms were started. While I was in China I visited the elderly mother of a Chinese friend, a professor in an American university, and

E

asked her what special message she would like me to take back to her son. Her first words were, 'Since the beginning of the communal dining-rooms my life has become much happier....' She went on to describe how, being elderly, if she found it difficult to walk to the cafeteria, especially in rainy weather, some young person would bring the food to her at home. 'Of course,' she added, 'we cook at home when we have friends in or at festival times.'

There were more serious breakdowns. The rise of the communes coincided with a sudden astonishing increase in industrial production. This combined to create an enormous strain on an inadequate transportation system. Food grown in one area could not be moved to another because the railways were clogged with freight trains handling industrial shipments. On-the-spot shortages were common. Deliveries, even those for export, were delayed for weeks at a time. Statistical surveys broke down. No uniform system of estimating, or even of measuring, grain yields had yet been established. Storage capacity was inadequate for the unprecedented harvest. Even when grain was properly measured, some of it was lost by rotting before it could be used.

The government failed to realize the extent to which the agricultural figures pouring in from the countryside were wildly optimistic. All China, during this hectic summer and autumn, was in a state, it seems, of national euphoria. Before long, however, the practical quality of the Chinese people reasserted itself, and they began, with cooler heads, to tackle stubborn agricultural problems which do not easily yield to sudden onslaughts.

Mistakes were remedied. Hours of work were normalized. Collectivized vegetable plots, pigs, chickens, fruit-trees were returned to their original owners. Bicycles were 'decommunized'. Undoubtedly new problems will arise and adjustments will continue to be made.

That the communes had over-extended themselves is now generally conceded. As a result, some of the authority taken on by some commune organizations was whittled down and handed over to the smaller units: the production brigade (about two hundred households), which usually takes in the whole village, and the production team (the work unit). While I was still in China the orders were sent out that temporary helpers and government cadres from the cities were here to help the teams and brigades, rather than to order and direct policy.

The commune will retain its over-all administrative responsibility and will supervise the industrial workshops and the varied aspects of the people's welfare; but the individual peasant will once more feel himself working as part of a smaller group — his neighbours and friends — rather than the more impersonal commune with its tens of thousands. Rather larger opportunities are now being given the individual household to earn a little money on the side, and (this was true even while I was there) peasants are being encouraged once more to develop small private plots of ground for their own family use.

Some interpreters of China in the West have seen these moves as a retreat and a turning-away from the original aim of the communes. Less restrained quarters have even proclaimed that the communes have been 'abolished'. The Chinese take a different view, claiming that it is an attempt to give the peasant more of a say in how things shall be run.

In my judgment these adjustments, in relation to the whole, are relatively small. They indicate, of course, that mistakes were made, but when one considers the magnitude of the changes that took place — that the whole management of local government, agriculture, welfare, education, and industry was being taken over by half a billion peasants most of whom could not read a few years ago — one remains astonished, not that mistakes were made, but that the movement did not collapse in colossal confusion.

The first effervescent phase of the commune movement is now over. The next, I suspect, will be a period of consolidation. Looking back over this first period the Chinese would say that the mistakes and muddles arose from 'positive' causes, that in great measure they came from unexpectedly high production, from enthusiasm, in short from success, rather than from conflict or failure. They were growing pains. The Chinese, who are fond of catchy phrases, talk about this period as a period of 'dynamic unbalance'. 'When things are static,' an economist said to me, 'they are dead. We would rather have things unbalanced but moving forward, than have things balanced and nothing much happening. Mistakes we can always rectify.' And he finished with a phrase which I had heard before: 'Yo kwun nan, yo ban fa' — where there are difficulties there is a way.

By the beginning of 1961, a few months after I returned from China, new ways of meeting difficulties were being found. Changes in the administration of the communes were announced, continuations of adjustments which were getting under way before I left China.

Emphasis was placed on the recognition that in farming the long experience of the peasants themselves is often more valuable than theory, so the major change was a yet greater measure of freedom for the small production brigade to decide on the nature of the crops to be raised, and the time and manner of cultivation. Encouragement was also given to spare-time cultivation of private plots, and in addition, brigade members, actively engaged in food-growing, are no longer to be at the beck and call of the commune for other temporary tasks.

According to the Chinese press the small production brigade is to have 'the right of reforming cultivation methods' as well as deciding 'the number of the labour force, and the right of managing animals and implements.... Members' activity in raising livestock and the carrying on of domestic industries and tilling their own land should be encouraged. The state still allows the existence of village markets.'

Once again the Chinese government has shown extraordinary flexibility when confronted with problems or actual mistakes, and responsiveness to the actual needs of the farmers themselves. There is, apparently, to be less administrative control of the communes by the party cadres, for — in the words of the government — the 'masses must be daringly trusted'.

3. *Have the communes destroyed family life?*

It is my opinion that they have not and that they were not intended to.

I have, I suppose, discussed developments in China with at least fifty trained observers — Canadians, British, New Zealanders, Australians, French, Indians, and others. Some of these have known China for years and speak Chinese fluently; all have travelled extensively and visited many communes. I have yet to meet one who has seen any evidence of the forcible separation of husbands and wives; or of children being taken from mothers.

The only 'barracks' that I (or any of the others I spoke to) have seen, are temporary structures at some large construction projects far from any city. Since women as well as men work on these projects, there are of necessity separate barracks. All the new housing I saw in the communes had obviously been planned for families.

This does not mean that family life in China has not undergone some profound changes. The old, enclosed, 'feudal' family system has all but vanished. Men can no longer treat their wives as property. Today women have equal rights before the law; they receive equal pay for equal work and their wages are paid directly to them. Women have equal rights concerning marriage and divorce. (See the Chinese Marriage Law, in the Appendix.) The sociological and psychological changes that this has involved have been considerable. Professor Chao Kuo-chun, visiting professor at the Indian School of International Studies, in New Delhi, who was in China in 1960, describes the impact of the communes as follows (*Far Eastern Economic Review*, Hong Kong, September 29th, 1960):

The people's communes are affecting not only many social institutions (such as the ways of family life) but also values and even personal relationships. It is true from what I observed during my visit to more than a dozen cities in China; I found no evidence that the nucleus family was being broken up by the commune movement or any wholesale transfer of residents from one place to another occurring. However, the husband-wife relationship or the status of the housewife in a joint family could never be the same once she joins work at the commune. Not only her independent source of income but also her new, broader social contacts enable her to foster a new sense of self-confidence and personal dignity. Many city women, now relieved of the bulk of household chores, develop a higher spirit and are readier to enjoy recreational and cultural activities ... many ceased to be idle gossipers or quarrelsome over trivial matters. Their husbands are the first to benefit from such changes.

Before leaving this question it might be well to see what the Communist Party itself has to say on the matter. I quote from the official text of the 'Party Resolution on Questions concerning People's Communes', dated December 10th, 1958 (the italics are mine):

Nurseries and kindergartens should be run well, so that every child can live better and receive a better education there than at home, and so that the children are willing to stay there and the parents are willing to put them there. *The parents may decide whether their children need to board there, and may take them back at any time they wish.* The old existing houses must be reconstructed step by step; new, picturesque townships and village settlements must be built by stages and in groups; these will include residential quarters, community dining-rooms, nurseries, kindergartens, the Homes to Honour the Aged ... schools, hospitals, clubs, cinemas, sports grounds, baths, and latrines. The construction plans of townships and village settlements should be thoroughly discussed by the masses. We stand for the abolition of the irrational, patriarchal system inherited from the past and for the development of family life in which there is democracy and unity.... Therefore in building residential quarters, attention must be paid to making the houses suited to the *living together* of men and women, the aged and young of each family.

It is true that the Chinese people have broken the feudal patriarchal [family] system. It must be known that this patriarchal system has long since ceased to exist in capitalist society and this is a matter of capitalist progress.

It would be unwise of us, I think, to dismiss this merely as Communist propaganda. It is an official pronouncement on family life in the communes which has been nationally publicized, read and re-read by the people whom it concerns, all 550 million of them. It forms the official policy instructions to be followed by all members of the Communist Party.

I certainly am not in a position to say that these instructions have in every case been carried out; but from everything I saw and learned while in China, the pronouncement by the government does reflect the general sentiment of the Chinese who live in the communes; the new home construction that I saw was invariably designed for families living together (and in China 'families' always means three generations). Any Chinese government that tried to 'break up the family' would, I think, meet insurmountable popular opposition.

XVI

Coverage by the American Press

DEVELOPMENTS in China since the revolution have been most inadequately reported by the American press, and much of what was written has been tendentious. It is through newspaper stories and news-agency reports on radio and TV that the American public forms its opinions. Whether or not the American people are correctly informed may have a considerable bearing upon the survival of Western democracy, and perhaps upon the survival of mankind itself. I am not one who believes that any vigorous people need be shielded from the facts.

Unable to send its own reporters to China, the American press seems to have abandoned all attempts at any serious analysis of what is actually happening there. China's economic achievements have now (belatedly) been conceded, though sometimes sceptically. Reports trickling in from British and Canadian travellers, the accounts given by responsible international scientists of the tremendous advances made in Chinese science, and some blunt warnings from British and other industrialists that China may be the third largest industrial power within a decade, have made it impossible to conceal that some very rapid and striking advances have indeed taken place there. These advances have been explained in the American press by what one might call the 'slave-labour' theory. According to this, the Chinese government has dragooned their population. By driving the 500 million Chinese peasants into communes, by uprooting traditional family patterns and working the entire population fantastically long hours, enormous resources of man-power have been made available for agriculture and industry. In other words, material gains have been achieved by what Joseph C. Harsch in the *Christian Science Monitor* (December 24th,

1958) described as 'the greatest mass sacrifice of human heritage, human comfort and human effort in all time'.

Here are some examples of how the American press in general dealt with the communes.

Herald Tribune (New York, November 25th, 1958)

REDS' REGIMENTATION IN CHINA TOPS RUSSIA. PEASANTS LIKE AN ARMY MARCH FROM BARRACKS TO THE FIELDS

... Regimentation ... finds women 'liberated' from their homes and placed in barracks separated from their husbands and everyone from teen-age youth to oldster trained to put gun worship over ancestor worship — and commune life also requires them to march off to assigned tasks in preassembled squads; to eat, sleep, according to plan worked out by somebody else.

The peasants were severed from the small amount of acreage they had.... Their homes were either torn down or made into supply depots and they and their families were placed in barracks....

Christian Science Monitor (December 17th, 1958 headline)

RED CHINA PACKS PEASANTS INTO COMMUNES

[A news story two days later, by staff writer Takashi Oka, begins:] Now that almost all of mainland China's 500 million peasants have been herded into 'people's communes' ...

United Press International

[A story date-lined Tokyo appeared on December 18th, 1959, reporting that in the communes:] ... normal family life is wiped out by this latest Chinese Communist instrument.

... Some quarters on the outside are speculating that the love-every-two-weeks policy established within the communes actually may be a birth-control technique conceived by Peiping to halt population growth.

To control and push their millions of commune workers, the Communists are reported to be sending more and more arms to distant areas. As more and more arms are sent out to control the restless masses, the greater become the chances of these arms falling into the hands of revolutionaries. Western intelligence sources have reported there is reason to believe the people within Communist China would give considerable support to a Nationalist China landing force, if they thought it had a fair chance of success.

Scripps-Howard

[A series of four articles entitled 'Chain Gang Empire' by staff writer R. H. Shackford is introduced on December 17th, 1958, with the following editorial note:] *The Chinese have always been devoted to their family life. What is happening in Red China today as the regime tries to weld its teeming millions into a faceless mass existing only for service to the state? The following article tells the grim story.*

[Mr Shackford himself begins in the following words:]

Abolition of the family is an avowed, primary sociological objective of Red China's new commune system — the first serious effort in history to put a whole nation on what amounts to a prison chain gang. [And later:] The regime does not hide its determination to abolish the family. In fact, it callously boasts of it. Segregated barracks for men and women are replacing cottages.

Life (January 5th, 1959)

MISERY, OPPRESSION, FEAR INSIDE CHINA'S COMMUNES...

Two Chinese who escaped tell of Reds' harsh regimentation which tears families apart, puts children in barracks, even regulates sex — by James Bell.

All over China the family-centred, individualistic Chinese are being reduced to 653 million indistinguishable and interchangeable parts in a vast, inhuman machine. This machine is the commune, the most frightful form of regimentation in history.

The newspapers and periodicals cited above represent some of the more distinguished organs of American journalism. Their coverage represents a fair sample of how the rise and the development of a highly significant aspect of Chinese life was purveyed to the American public. One need only look through back files to discover a high degree of uniformity in all the newspapers. There were variations, of course, but the central theme was the same — the Chinese people were the helpless slaves in the grip of a ruthless and malevolent leadership.

My two trips to China have given rise to the serious belief that much of this information has been woefully inaccurate and that many of the conclusions Americans have drawn are erroneous. Civil wars are always among the most cruel of human conflicts. No one can claim that either side in China did not inflict the most enormous suffering on the other. None of the great historic revolts of a people against unendurable suffering and injustice has ever been a picnic and the contemporary world always recoils aghast at the violence that accompanies them. This was true of the French and American revolutions; it was equally true of the Chinese revolution.

While in Peking I talked with the ambassadors and staffs of most of the Western and neutral embassies. I also had discussions with many well-informed Europeans who have lived in China for many years. Their reports on the present leadership in China were impressively similar in substance. China is not being led by a group of men hungry for personal power who have fastened themselves on a resentful population. It is, rather, a leadership that has shown itself genuinely concerned with the welfare of the people. Though changes in the leadership take place from time to time, there is no evidence of that jockeying for power or of the personal rivalry that we have so often seen in the Kremlin.

I have come to believe that Mao Tse-tung is not surrounded by yes-men fearful of arousing his displeasure. We are not dealing with a Hitler or Mussolini, or a latter-day Stalin whose moral judgments were poisoned by a paranoiac mistrust of those around him. China is being led by historically conscious, strong, and enormously competent men who as far back as the 1920s identified themselves with the people and knew their needs. They won their revolution because they carried out the demands of a people driven to extremities of suffering, and who were determined to end the disease, hunger, and corruption which had held them in subjugation for centuries. If ever in history there was a people's revolution, this was it.

Clearly the original ban by the State Department on trips by American journalists, and now the reluctance of the Chinese government to come to an understanding on this matter, has posed a serious handicap for the American press, and I, for one, hope sincerely that a free flow of information in both directions will soon become possible.

But this is only half the problem.

As matters now stand I doubt that allowing American newspapers to send correspondents to China will by itself ensure an accurate picture of events. The disturbing element is that before and during the same period when the news stories quoted above were being published in the United States, a growing body of factual material — the first-hand observations of many reporters and reputable Western scientists — was available to people in Western Europe, in Canada, in India, in Australia, but was hardly ever mentioned by the American press.

I have already referred to some of this material in earlier chapters. Let me offer some further samples, the italics being mine:

Le Monde (Paris, October 12th, 1958)

René Dumont, Professor of Comparative Agriculture at the Agronomic Institute, Paris, in an article entitled 'Chinese Agriculture':

> Without the *active and voluntary participation of the majority*, the mountains would not have been terraced nor would the terraces have been held in place by gravel, nor would the gravel have been humped, basket by basket, from the river beds. It is my impression that the Chinese Party has succeeded, after due deliberation, in marrying its authority to the peasant's consent, a consent obtained by protracted explanations.

Maclean's Magazine (Canada, November 22nd, 1958)

Edward B. Joliffe, lawyer, leader of the Co-operative Commonwealth Federation of Ontario:

> Having visited such communities this year — and having entered many a peasant home forty years ago — I am amused by the story, zealously spread by certain writers from their posts in Hong Kong and Formosa, that the peasants (five hundred million of them) are kept in the co-ops by coercion and terror.

Economic Weekly (Bombay, November 22nd, 1958)

An article by Professor Charles Bettelheim of the Sorbonne, entitled 'China's Economic Growth', states:

> I think that one must first of all recognize that the manner in which Chinese economy and society are developing presupposes an essentially energetic direction which can be neither of a bureaucratic nor of an administrative nature, nor, still less, come in the

shape of pressure from the police (as some people imagine). Such growth implies great clearness of thought, a lucid vision of all the possibilities of development, of the manner in which these possibilities are interconnected, of the effort which each and every one is prepared to make in order to transform these possibilities into reality. This development also implies that this lucid vision does not remain the privilege of some people who keep aloof from the masses, but on the contrary, is shared by the masses.... Once the masses understand that technique has nothing mysterious about it, one witnesses the extraordinary development of enterprises run by local authorities and co-operatives, one witnesses a real technical revolution coming from the masses themselves.

New Statesman (London, December 20th, 1958)

Dr Joseph Needham of Cambridge University, eminent historian of Chinese science and Sinologist, who served during World War II as scientific attaché to the British embassy in Chungking, writing of a trip made to China in 1958:

I travelled some 12,000 miles within the country ... meeting hundreds not only of scientists and scholars but all sorts and conditions of men. My most outstanding impression of China this year was of the unreality of ideas so cherished in the West that the population is dragooned to perform its tasks. On the contrary, everywhere one sees spontaneity (sometimes overrunning government planning), enthusiasm for increasing production and modernization, pride in an ancient culture equipping itself to take its rightful place in the modern world. What has been done in public health, social services, industrial development, and advancing amenities of all kinds and what one sees going on under one's own eyes would be absolutely impossible without the *willing and convinced co-operation* of all types of workers, manual and intellectual.

New Statesman (January 10th, 1959)

R. H. S. Crossman, M.P., generally a sharp critic of developments in China, writes of a visit to several communes:

On each visit I was able to select a village for inspection.... Every village I visited was equipped with a crèche, a kindergarten, a primary school and canteens — with the result that women were out at work and the labour force had been doubled. Of course, a foreigner who knows no Chinese must be wary on this subject, but I saw no signs that family life was being destroyed. Families were sleeping, as usual, in one bed; and I do not believe that communal feeding will destroy a relation with children as tenacious and affectionate as any I have seen....

I am inclined to conclude ... that the movement for the People's Communes did indeed come not from a remote official stratosphere but from that hard puritan elite of Peasant Communists.... If I am right, this episode confirms that Chinese Communism still remains a dynamic mass movement and that its leaders still respond to pressures from below.

Sunday Times (London, June 19th, 1960)

An article by Field-Marshal Viscount Montgomery:

For China today the commune system seems to be necessary; indeed it is essential if the problems of a poor and backward nation are to be solved.... One hears it said that children in the communes are removed from their parents. I investigated this and found it to be totally untrue.

There are great misconceptions in the Western world about this new China, particularly in the United States ... and that cannot be stated too clearly.

The Oxford Magazine (Oxford, November 5th, 1960)

'A Visit to China' by Sir Cyril Hinshelwood, President of the Royal Society:

There is much that is tremendously impressive and admirable in the New China: there is, of course, no doubt that an upheaval of a far-reaching kind has taken place: there are some aspects of the socialist state which are uncongenial to a Westerner: but most of the things for which, at a distance, I had admired and loved the Old China, seemed to me to be intact, and some indeed appeared to be fostered more sedulously than ever. China possesses, of course, a communist organization with what most of us here regard as the inevitable restrictions associated with it. But the Chinese people never had much personal liberty and it is quite likely that many of them are now freer in some ways than they have ever been. And certainly the constructive achievements are very impressive indeed....

The total picture was warmer and more human than I had been led to expect....

The [commune] I visited, I must confess, did not seem an unhappy sort of place.

The sources from which I have drawn the foregoing extracts contain a wealth of reliable information on what is actually happening in China. There are other reports too — medical reports from British doctors, articles by British industrialists and scientists, technical papers by French, British, and Canadian economists, reports by Indians on advances made in Chinese village life; all this has been available to any newspaper.

In all fairness it should be noted that there have been times when unbiased reports have appeared in the American press, originating from inside China. The British news agency Reuters has been operating in China for several years. On occasion some of the larger American papers, the *New York Times*, the *Christian Science Monitor*, and a few others, have used its reports. Nevertheless, the over-all image of China in the public mind in the U.S.A. has been similar to that conveyed by the press coverage of the communes.

The present phase of American reporting about China is strongly reminiscent of what happened after the Russian Revolution in 1917. For the first four years there were no competent American correspondents in Moscow or anywhere else in the U.S.S.R. Nearly all Russian news came from violently anti-Russian sources at Riga (then not under Russian control). The result was a mass of material very similar to what Americans are getting today about China, mostly from Hong Kong. Families in Russia also were reported as being deliberately 'broken up'; Lenin and Trotsky had quarrelled; Lenin had had Trotsky shot; Trotsky had shot Lenin; both had killed themselves in a suicide pact; women had been nationalized (which meant that all women were public prostitutes operating without fees), etc., etc. The public believed these stories because they had nothing else to go on.

THE WALL HAS TWO SIDES

On August 4th, 1920, Charles Merz, who was later to become an editor of the *New York Times*, and Walter Lippmann wrote a famous supplement to *The New Republic*, 'A Test of the News', analysing press coverage of the early years of the then new Russian government.

In this famous article, Lippmann and Merz wrote:

> From the point of view of professional journalism the reporting of the Russian Revolution is nothing short of disaster.
> ... On the essential questions the net effect was almost always misleading, and misleading news is worse than none at all.

And that, I believe, is true of American reporting on China today.

XVII

Visit to a Rural Commune

Chengchow, Honan Province

Today I went to a rural commune near this city, which lies in the Yellow River valley.

Honan Province has always been one of the poorest areas of China. Last night, when they asked me what kind of commune I wanted to see, I said, 'Your worst.' They didn't seem to resent this. The commune I saw today was, they said, the poorest within driving distance, and after seeing it I can believe it. So much for the story that visitors see only the show places.

We left at eight. They had a Russian car for me today, small but brand-new, and we drove out of Chengchow over a reasonably good dirt road. (They drive with more zip here and without that maddening habit of rushing ahead and then coasting, which the Peking drivers are convinced saves petrol.) After half an hour we branched off and for another thirty minutes we bounced along a cart track. It was already hot. The sky was pale blue; there were no clouds.

Groups of peasants in wide straw hats were in the fields at work with hoes and rakes. Some were resting. The land here reminds me of parts of northern Spain, arid and barren, and the crops of wheat and millet looked sparse. The whole area has been badly hit by drought.

My interpreter told me this was the first time he had been in this part of China. It seems that there was no Intourist interpreter in Chengchow and he had been sent from Wuhan to meet me. A foot infection held me up in Peking, and he'd been hanging around for ten days waiting for me. He told me all this while we were lurching and bumping over the cart track, I wildly clutching my precious Zeiss cameras and praying for the Bolex in the boot.

Behind us we left a cloud of dust.

We came finally to a small village, with a faded banner strung across the street, and the car turned into a courtyard enclosed by low white-washed buildings. More flags and pictures and slogans painted across the walls. Mr Chiao, the director of the commune, was waiting to greet us, and he invited us in for the usual preliminary talk over a cup of tea. The room he took us into was long and narrow, with a table and benches running the full length. This was the meeting-room of the commune management committee. From the wall at one end Mao Tse-tung smiled benignly down at us; at the other were portraits of Liu Shao-chi, Chou En-lai, Chu Teh — the four heroes of the revolution. With Mr Chiao were two others who accompanied us all day, but they left the talking to Mr Chiao. Occasionally one or the other would bring out a notebook and record some question and answer. I never did learn quite what their function was; but I have become accustomed by now to these silent observers at my interviews.

As we sipped our tea Mr Chiao gave me the background picture. The basic problems of this commune were poor land and difficult climate. There was constant alternation between flood and drought. Five rivers, all flowing finally into the Yellow River, cross the commune land. Before liberation no one bothered to tend the dikes or clean out the canals, which were constantly silting up. Only a small rise brought the rivers to flood stage. Eight inches of rainfall in a season meant certain inundation.

Crop yields had almost always been poor. A high grain harvest for the region would be 60 catties per mu, or mou. (Approximately 6·9 bushels per acre. More prosperous communes I visited were harvesting as much as 1,000 catties per mu — 114·6 bushels per acre. By way of comparison, according to the *Statistical Abstract of the United States, 1960*, American output in 1959 was 21·3 bushels of wheat per acre.) Some years there had been no crop at all. In 1942, for instance — a year which the peasants still look back on with horror — during an autumn, winter, summer, and succeeding autumn no grain grew. More than two thousand families left the area to go and beg. Three hundred and twenty-seven people died of starvation in this immediate vicinity. Two hundred children were sold by families unable to feed them. People were eating the dry roots of grass and the bark of trees.

Most of the land was tenant-farmed. The Communists arrived in October 1948, and plans for land reform were started almost immediately. This area went through the same general stages as most other sections of China — mutual-aid teams, early co-operative period, advanced co-operatives, and now, the people's commune. Even the advanced co-ops, Mr Chiao felt, had been incapable of meeting basic agricultural needs. In the matter of water conservation, for example, those higher up the river might take too much, leaving those farther down with not enough. Or in flood-time some ill-considered action upstream could increase the flood level lower down. Also, the co-ops were too small to mechanize effectively. Tractors were scarce, and as they were under the control of central tractor stations, the co-ops had to apply in advance for them. In rush seasons tractors would arrive too early or too late.

When news of the Sputnik Commune spread across the country, peasants here at once began debating whether to form one of 'these new communes'. Everyone seemed in favour, representatives were sent to the county government to apply. The county approved and the commune was formally organized on August 17th, 1958.

The first thing they did was to tackle water conservation. Armed with picks and shovels, and carrying baskets, thousands of men and women, working after the autumn harvest and before spring sowing, had constructed five new reservoirs with storage capacity for 506 million gallons, as well as a network of drainage and irrigation canals. As much as twelve inches of rainfall now would not cause flooding, Mr Chiao thought; and despite the serious drought conditions for the past two years, some crops have been saved.

'What is your current crop yield?' I asked.

'Poor. The drought now is just as bad as 1942. The last two hundred days of last year there was no real rain at all, just a few sprinkles, and this year [1960] not a single drop. The water level is really low. The irrigation ditches helped our crop last autumn, but this year we have had to replant some of our fields four times and each planting has dried up. We are carrying water by hand and we have laid temporary piping. The crop will be far below normal, much less than we had hoped for. But we shall have something. No one will starve. There will be no 1942.'

I watched Mr Chiao as he recited these facts. He was, I judged, about thirty-five. He had muscular arms and calloused hands. In shirt-sleeves, elbows on the table, he looked straight across at me out of a tanned, weather-beaten face. Here was no city commissar. This man was from the land and part of the land. I could well understand why he had been elected to direct the commune.

'Come,' he said. 'I'd like to show you what we're doing.'

We stepped out, shielding our eyes, into the blaze of mid-morning sunlight. Our driver had pulled the car into the shade of a near-by tree and was fast asleep. We woke him, piled in, and headed for the tractor station. Tractors, clearly, were one of Mr Chiao's favourite topics. He told me the commune now owned thirty-five, in addition to four com-bine harvesters and fifty-one power machines, including some large pumps. At the tractor station we saw a repair shop equipped with several lathes, and mechanics at work on some dismantled machines. The tractors were lined up outside. I counted thirty-eight, plus five combines. Mr Chiao apologized. He said he had given me last year's figures; recently they had bought three more tractors and another combine.

One of the tractors here was of Chinese manufacture, from the near-by works at Loyang. The rest were Czech or Bulgarian. When I asked about performance, Mr Chiao said the Loyang and Czech were the best. The Chinese tractors have most power and can draw two combines, while the others draw one.

Into the car again, and as we drove Mr Chiao continued to bombard me with information about the many activities of his commune. They manufacture paper and chemical fertilizer; bottle wine and vinegar; raise fish which they sell to near-by markets; they have several assembly shops associated with large state factories. They also have a brickworks and are under contract to supply two million bricks this year to the city of Chengchow. The commune owns 6,000 pigs. (There is a national 'pig drive' this year, I learned, aimed at doubling China's pig popula-tion.) As to livestock, Mr Chiao told me, the commune has 160 horses, 4,000 chickens, and 1,500 ducks. When I said this seemed a surprisingly low figure (one chicken to every ten people) the director explained that *privately*-owned animals and poultry were not included in the figures he had given.

I asked if the members were allowed to keep their own chickens and ducks and to cultivate vegetable patches.

'They are not only allowed,' he replied, 'but encouraged. We have another drive on right now. [I had lost count of the drives.] We call it the *"Use-the-ten-edges campaign"*. Use every little strip of land around you. The edge of the road, the edge of the river, the edge of the orchard....'

At this point the car came to a halt in front of a new brick building — the ball-bearing plant — and we climbed out. Actually this was an assembly shop rather than a factory, the parts themselves being sent out from Chengchow. We saw some two hundred girls in blue overalls, seated at benches, and assembling various types of bearings to the accompaniment of music from a loudspeaker. I stopped by one bench where a girl — the prettiest of the lot — was bending over her work. She was so absorbed that she did not notice me till she heard the click of the camera. Then she looked up and broke into a delightful half-shy grin.

I asked her name.

'Shu Shao-yen,' she said. (Shao-yen, the interpreter told me, means 'swallow'.)

'How old are you, Shu Shao-yen?'

'Eighteen.'

'Can you read and write?'

'Yes — but I am still going to spare-time school to learn more characters.'

'Do you like your work?'

'I like it. And that we can help, too.'

'Help? How do you mean?'

'It helps our country,' she said, 'to build socialism.'

The ball-bearing shop seemed quite up-to-date and efficient, which was not the case with the other industries we visited that day. Nevertheless, the one that fascinated me most was not the ball-bearing plant but a paper mill, because of its Robinson-Crusoe, do-it-yourself quality. Here was a series of home-made wooden machines booming and thumping away like the big wheel and little wheel in the spiritual, which ran by faith and the grace of God. But they *were* running, and while straw and leaves were pushed into a primitive pulping machine (powered by a donkey) at one end of the shed, out from the other end between two rollers made of logs jerked a ribbon of wet paper, the coarsest I had ever laid eyes on. However, intended for packaging, it was quite adequate.

No problem of modern mechanics, I thought, would long resist the ingenuity that turned this collection of barrel-staves and tree-trunks into a paper mill.

On the way back to commune headquarters I asked Mr Chiao how much members were earning. He gave the figures for the commune's single complete year, 1959. The average cash wage was 6·80 yuan a month. Food, education, medical care, housing are free. The food distribution he estimated as 53 per cent of the total payment.

'Are you building new housing?' I asked.

Mr Chiao said they were, but not very fast. During 1959 they had added eight hundred new rooms, a total of 140,000 square feet. (This would represent approximately 120 two-bedroom-size American housing estate homes, and there are 8,000 families in the commune, most of them still living in small huts and cottages.)

'There are so many things that have to come first,' Mr Chiao said.

*

It was good to pause for a while in the committee room, good to get out of the glare. We were parched, dehydrated, and soaked with sweat. As we sat down again at the long table a girl brought in tea, and cold wet towels with which we mopped our faces. For a few minutes we silently sipped our tea. I dusted the camera lenses and put another hundred feet of film into the Bolex. Then, back to work.

'Tell me about education,' I said.

'To start with the little ones,' Mr Chiao replied, 'we run 120 nurseries and 89 kindergartens.' I interrupted to ask if all small children went to these. 'Oh no,' he said, 'we couldn't take care of them if they did. Only about 40 per cent of the children go — the rest stay at home with the grandparents. Then, in this commune we have 44 primary schools, 16 of which are run by the state.'

'Why doesn't the state run them all?' I asked. 'Isn't it the national policy to give primary schooling to every child?'

'Yes, but it would be impossible at this stage for the central government to set up schools in all our scattered villages. Besides, we like to run our own affairs. It makes good sense, too. We have the houses and we now have young people with enough training to be teachers, or we can get them from the colleges in the city.

'We provide spare-time education for adults too. Not only for the illiterate but for anyone who feels he hasn't had enough schooling. The majority of our members had no education at all when they were children. Now they can get it later in life. It doesn't matter what age they are, they can start as low as the first form if they want to and go through the schooling that they missed.'

'How many are still illiterate? And what is your definition of "literacy"?'

'There are a good many people who are just too old to learn to read and write. We don't press them. Spare-time education is only useful for those who really want it — and we have thousands of our adults enrolled in classes. But about 20 per cent will never become literate. By literate we mean knowing how to read and write about twelve hundred characters — that's enough to be able to read a newspaper. In cities the test is usually higher — two thousand characters or more. But here in the country ... ' He wiped his face again on the towel. 'In the country we have to take things as they are. And it's quite an event when one of our people passes the literacy test. We have a little celebration for them. Do you know what they nearly all want to do first? Write to Chairman Mao to tell him they have learned to write! He must get thousands of letters like that every day.

'You must understand, the communes have three purposes. They are to develop agriculture, to build local industry, and to advance education and culture. We want eventually to give people in the country the same opportunities as city people. One day the communes will have colleges and technical schools, their own theatres and schools of music, drama schools....' His voice trailed off and he leaned back, looking through half-closed eyes at the ceiling.

This seemed like a good time to ask a question, one I asked in every commune I visited. 'Have you ever,' I asked Mr Chiao, 'found it

151

necessary, perhaps for a short period, to house husbands and wives in separate buildings?' Mr Chiao asked the interpreter to repeat the question and the interpreter turned back to me. I repeated it.

The interpreter began to laugh and the director and the other members joined in. Mr Chiao, still laughing, said something and the interpreter said, 'Mr Chiao wants to know if that's what they do in England.' The widely publicized Party Resolution of December 1958 had ridiculed Mr Dulles's speech in Seattle in which he had informed the world that Chinese families were being broken up. Cartoons of Dulles and Eisenhower were often painted on commune and factory wall-boards. In all communes my question about family separation provoked mirth, except in one where the director said with a certain contempt, 'You have been reading Mr Dulles!'

'What do you do,' I asked, 'about a boy and girl who fall in love and have a child before they are married? Or before legal marriage age?'

The interpreter's translation of this question was followed by a rather lengthy silence. It was obviously an unusual question. The others at the table became very busy readjusting their notebooks and examining the points of their ball-point pens. The girl who was picking up the wet towels paused to listen.

'There is no problem now about marriage,' said Mr Chiao. 'Formerly, many could not afford to marry. But that is no hindrance now. Formerly also, the low level of education made some fall into wrong habits. That does not happen any more.'

'But human nature is human nature,' I insisted. 'You just can't expect me to believe that babies are never born to unwed parents.'

Mr Chiao shook his head.

I pressed the point as far as I felt I could go. It would hardly do to dispute the director's accuracy; I could not go out, after all, and count the babies as I had counted the tractors in the tractor yard. And who knows? — he may have been right. I told him that officials in Peking and elsewhere, people at the university and in the health office, discussed these problems as a matter of reality....

Mr Chiao, however, stood his ground. 'You may not believe me,' he said, 'but we really have none of these problems now.'

I nodded and changed the subject.

China is today an intensely, almost compulsively 'moral' society. Of the many communes I visited, all except one denied any knowledge of any children born out of wedlock. In the one exception, two cases were cited, both involving parents who were under the legal marriage age (twenty for boys and eighteen for girls). Both cases were resolved in the same way: by court orders permitting early marriage, 'in the interest of the child'.

I had by this time formed a high opinion of Mr Chiao. Despite his official position, he was neither servile nor overbearing in his manner. I noted that he spoke to those who were 'under' him in the same tone that he used to me, or to my interpreter. Besides that, I liked him for his obvious enjoyment of his job. He must be working like mad most of the time to keep up with this three-ring circus, and loving every moment of it.

I asked him to tell me about himself.

He shrugged the question aside, but as I persisted, he finally told me he had been born in a near-by village, not in what was now this commune, but in a neighbouring county. His father was a lower-middle peasant. The family owned a plot of land, too small to live off, and worked for a landlord and rented an extra field from him too. They never got out of debt. After liberation the family received eight mu of land, still inadequate for a living; but with mutual aid they began for the first time to move ahead.

'When did you learn to read and write?' I asked.

'At the spare-time school, six years ago.'

In these few and rather unwillingly spoken words, it seemed to me, lay a large part of the secret of the Chinese Revolution: the release of buried creative potential.

Ten years earlier Mr Chiao was grubbing out his life on half an acre. Today he is dreaming of power stations, technical colleges, schools of music. And not only Mr Chiao, but the girls in the ball-bearing factory, the youngsters who had dreamed up the fantastic 'paper mill', the nurses in the kindergarten, the men installing a new (commune-made) electric irrigation pump. Just in this one morning's visit I had seen hundreds who were using talents that would previously have remained immobilized. I remembered a slogan I had seen some days before painted in bold, red characters across a commune building: *Don't be frightened of the experts — compete with them!* They appear to be learning that technique has nothing mysterious about it; they are not waiting for the state to tell them how....

Mr Chiao brought me back. 'There's time to show you the hospital before lunch,' he said. 'I'd like you to see the hospital.'

Three Buns for Lunch

I was glad the hospital was only a short walk from headquarters. It was a simple structure of white-washed brick, less than a year old, with clean earth floors and a little tiling. On each side of a central corridor were small single rooms — thirty in all — with a nurse's office at the middle. There were ten patients at the time, and two neatly-dressed nurses were on duty.

A doctor arrived while I was there and I had a brief talk with him. He told me there were twelve doctors attached to this commune, and they spend most of their time on rounds in the villages. Six doctors are trained in Western, and six in traditional Chinese medicine. Only two of the Western doctors are fully qualified.

In addition to this small hospital, which he regarded as inadequate, they have set up sixteen 'hygiene stations' serving groups of villages (there are ninety villages altogether). These are clinics which can handle simple first-aid and immunization. They try to see that every infant gets B.C.G. at ten days and is later vaccinated against smallpox, diphtheria, and epidemic encephalitis (Japanese B).

The commune medical staff is still too small, 120 in all, including doctors, nurses, and technicians. They conduct continual educational programmes on health matters among the peasants by means of posters, films, and lectures. This, and the immunization programme, are paying dividends. There have been no cases of smallpox since the commune started, no cholera, no venereal disease, which used to be one of the worst problems here. They have been burning off the banks of the rivers and have virtually eliminated schistosomiasis, a disease caused by the ova of a blood-fluke to which a small water-snail plays host. The ova develop into minute, free-swimming cercariae which can penetrate the skin of a human being who wades in the water or even wets his hand while filling a pail. Elimination of the snail is the most direct way to break the cycle. Symptoms of the disease are severe, and include enormous extension of the spleen and progressive enfeeblement of the victim. This remains one of the most serious medical problems of China. There are still an estimated ten million cases.

In this commune bacillary dysentery is the most stubborn problem. Midwives are now trained, and the days when umbilical cords were cut with unsterilized scissors and bleeding stopped by dirt are past. Infant mortality has dropped, though the hospital was unable to give me the figures as the records were kept in the hygiene stations.

I asked whether the hospital was sufficiently equipped to perform an appendectomy. One of the doctors said they are treating most cases of appendicitis by traditional methods, not by surgery. (They told me the same story in Peking, and claimed a number of cures. See the chapter on medicine for a further discussion of this question.) But on being pressed the doctor admitted that all advanced cases were operated on. Most surgical cases from this commune would be taken to one of the modern, fully equipped hospitals I had seen in Chengchow.

After the hospital Mr Chiao, on behalf of the commune, extended to me an invitation to lunch.

I would stay, I said, provided I could eat in one of the canteens exactly as the commune members were eating. They agreed to this. But on our return to headquarters the meal was already spread out on the table in the meeting-chamber. I argued and begged. So did Mr Chiao. This would be so much more convenient, we could talk more easily, and particularly now the table was set....

But I insisted.

The canteen, one of 119 in the commune, was a pleasant, airy room, fifty or sixty feet long. Straw matting hung under the slope of the tile roof and at one end there was a portrait of Mao.

By this time it was well past two o'clock and most of the members had already eaten. But a few were still drifting in from the fields. The only table at which there were chopsticks was obviously ours: the five of us and the driver of the car sat down. Three or four dishes of vegetables and a platter piled high with steamed dough buns were brought in. There were no bowls or plates; nothing to drink; we pitched in out of the common platters. When I looked to see what was being served at the other tables, I understood their reluctance to bring me to the canteen. The workers were eating nothing but the dough buns (*man tow*). I tried one. These buns were about the size of a woman's fist, of dark wheat flour. Inside were about two teaspoonsful of chopped cabbage. This was the entire meal. Each worker had three; the children one.

I have seen poverty in many countries — in Mexico, in South America, in India — and I have always found it difficult to understand how a human body could go on day after day with so little nourishment. Here, then, was the bare truth. The people of this commune were desperately poor. I could hardly bear to watch these men coming in tired after working in the fields since daybreak; stopping at the kitchen to pick up their three buns; sitting down quietly to eat them. And the children, munching without a word!

Chalked on a blackboard I noted what looked like a menu for the week. I asked for a translation. Tonight, noodles. Anything else? No, just noodles. Tomorrow for breakfast, these same *man tow* but without the vegetable filling. Lunch, the same, but with something else inside. Tomorrow night, soup; and so it went on.

'How often do you eat meat?' I asked.

Chiao hedged. 'Not very often.'

'How often?'

'On festival days we have meat, and sometimes fish. On three festival days we eat meat, and on three days fish. But this will improve as time goes on.... '

'You mean three days in the whole year?'

'Yes, in the year.'

'And that's all the meat or fish you eat?'

'For the present, yes.'

What of those six thousand pigs I had heard about, I wondered. Or the fish-breeding pools from which they sent fish to the Chengchow market. There was a contradiction here I could not understand.

'May I see your fish-breeding ponds?' I asked.

And into the car we piled again to go bouncing over some very rough roads for twenty minutes or half an hour. The fish project, Mr Chiao explained, was the second task to which the new commune had turned its energies after water-conservation problems had been taken care of. Fish-breeding, it seemed, was completely new in this area. They had reclaimed some otherwise useless swamp-land, and in the first complete year of operation (1959) bred 29 million fish, of which they sold 313,000 pounds on the Chengchow market.

I was impressed by the figures.

I was even more impressed by the fisheries themselves. These were, I think, one of the most remarkable features of the entire commune. Over many acres of low-lying ground between two rivers, shallow ponds had been made with well-banked divisions. Each division had its own generation of fish. Each was neatly labelled as to date and type. Mostly silver carp. Young men, wading thigh-deep in the ponds, swung their nets over their heads, letting them balloon out in a wide circle before falling into the water. A universal method this, always fascinating to watch. Slowly the nets would be gathered in and every throw would collect thirty or forty slithering, fighting silver fish, all of uniform size, probably four or five pounds each.

After I had photographed these young fish-catchers, some of them walked back with me to the car. The sun was horribly hot. I suggested we sit for a while under a tree. One of the young men went off and brought back an armful of small melons — I don't know what kind they were, but they were juicy and ripe and we sat under the tree eating them, spitting out the seeds.

Then I raised the question which had been troubling me.

'You eat fish in your communal dining-rooms only three times a year. To judge by your menu you are not eating very well. You are not getting enough protein. Sooner or later your health will suffer. Why don't you eat the fish you raise in your own commune?'

There was a general outburst of talk, everyone saying something at once. Finally I sorted out what they were trying to tell me. This question of eating the fish from their own fisheries had been a matter of considerable controversy in the commune. They had had several meetings, mass discussions, special sessions of the management committee.

'But what are the objections?' I asked. 'Why *not* eat the fish?'

'Money,' they said. 'We need to earn more money.'

'Money for what?'

'Listen,' one young man told me, 'we only have one rather poor hospital. We should have a properly equipped one — and the instruments and the buildings and the X-ray equipment and all that costs money. Point one. Point two: look at some of our primary schools —

housed in old sheds. A disgrace. Point three: we need libraries. We've seen them in other communes. We haven't got any. Oh yes, we have so-called reading-rooms, but they are mostly for kids. We need a place where we can stock books and read, and have rooms in the different villages and the books can go from one village to another. Point four: we want some decent film equipment. You should see the old projector we have — well, we have two, but only one works. It goes the rounds of the villages, but that means we only see a show once every week or so. We need at least ten good projectors. All this costs money. Point five: the old people's homes. Go and see them. We have two that are all right — the others, well, they are nothing to be proud of.'

The young fellow paused long enough to spit out some seeds, and continued, 'What we have to understand is that we are a very poor commune. Other communes can do all these things because their land and conditions are better. So some of us think, "let's put off eating more fish until we get ahead and have done these things which need doing". Of course, others think that food is more important. But they don't understand that we are building a socialist country [he spoke scornfully], they are not politically aware and mature.'

'But what about health — isn't that important, too?'

'Look at us,' they said, laughing, 'do we look weak?' and they flexed their arms and showed their muscles. 'And the women and children who need more food get it.'

Perhaps here, sitting under the tree with these young men, I had hit on one element that, above all else, was enabling China to move forward so rapidly — the sense of self-restraint, the awareness that sacrifices now were necessary to lay the foundation of future prosperity. The almost unbelievable fact is that they are doing it, and to a great extent, voluntarily. Of course, the peasant cadres, the dedicated, professional, hard core of Communist youth, are giving the lead. I'm sure they do a lot of the talking at these public meetings and discussion circles and their powers of persuasion are great. But the people are let in — they can say what they feel, just as these young men under the tree were saying what they felt. The fish are sold to the city, but not 'by decree', which would leave a sullen and resentful peasantry who would do their best to sabotage the plan as soon as the leaders' backs were turned. The sacrifices, the self-restraint are not being imposed by young men with machine-guns, but by young men who talk — and there's a world of difference.

All this went through my mind as we drove back to the central village. But *had* there been an improvement? I wondered. How far were they 'shooting a line' about the bad old days? How much worse than this could it really have been? I made the suggestion that I would be interested in talking to some of the commune members in their own homes. Mr Chiao agreed; and even offered no objection to my seeing them on my own — on my own, that is, with the interpreter. As we climbed out of the car in front of headquarters, he waved us down the street and called, 'See who you can find at home,' and disappeared inside.

Personal Histories

Half a block farther along I pointed to a door at random, in a row of newish houses. The interpreter knocked and the door was opened by a woman with two children at her side who at once asked us in. Her name was Mrs Chang. The house consisted of two rooms and a small kitchen. Along one side of the living-room was a wide brick ledge (*kang*) upon which the entire family would sleep at night.

The room was not much larger, I think, than ten feet by twelve. The floor was tamped earth. There were four children in all, the two who had come to the door and a four-month-old baby in the lap of a five-year-old who was squatting on the floor. The baby had a dark area on its head, like a burn or some fungus. Mrs Chang was pert and eager. She wore a blue shirt-blouse with bright-green plastic buttons, and the usual work-trousers. I asked her later how old she was and she said thirty-two, but she looked older than that. She was self-possessed, not at all put out by having two strangers burst in on her, and one a foreigner. Her face was serious, but pleasantly so, and she showed occasional flashes of humour. Her hands were delicate and clean. (I have often noticed how well the Chinese, even the very poorest, keep their hands.)

As we talked her story came out little by little, hesitatingly at first, then more readily; and sometimes, as memories stirred her feelings, the story came with great fluency. I took it down precisely as she gave it to me:

'I was born in this very village. My father was already fairly old when

I was born, and my mother was blind, from an illness that she had had some years earlier. I was the eldest child of three — a brother and a sister. We had no land and my father worked for a landowner. The hut we lived in was very tumbledown, grass on the roof and so on. As my mother was blind, we depended entirely on my father's work, but as he was already fairly old, however hard he worked he could never get enough to support my mother and three children.

'I was the biggest, so when I was eight my mother and I would go out regularly every day to beg. I was still fairly small when we began this, so we were limited — we could just go about five li a day. Nineteen forty-two was especially bad for us. It was a drought year, my father was ill. We had nothing we could sell and couldn't send my father to be cared for. He was very thin from lack of food and his illness, but he kept on trying to go out. On the second of July in that year he went out, but he fell in the street and died there — it was really half due to his illness and half due to not having eaten anything for so long.

'His death was a disaster for us. My mother couldn't work, I was thirteen, my brother was eleven and my little sister was five. It was really a bad year. Later it rained a great deal and one day there was a tremendous storm — it was still summer-time, I remember — and the roof of our house fell in. We got out our bedding and took it to the temple. That winter, too, was cold. My mother and I would go out begging every day and sometimes our young brother would come too. One day, I remember, he fell into a deep hole full of snow. It was cold and we didn't have any clothes for that kind of weather. Nothing happened to my brother, we fished him out.

'The next really bad year was 1944 — another snowstorm. My sister was very ill and we had just nothing at all to feed her on. By this time we had moved from the temple to a kind of shack where we lived. It was just when my sister was so ill that the big snowstorm began — it lasted for three days and my mother and I couldn't get out at all. Only seven, sister was terribly ill and terribly undernourished. She died, during those three days of storm.

'After the death of my sister there were only three of us left to feed, which made it a little easier, but even so we never seemed to have enough. My brother and I used to go to the fields and pick up grains of rice or wheat which had dropped after harvesting, grain by grain. We would sometimes go to the market and pick up the little bits that were dropped on the ground. This sounds as if we were in an extra bad position, but we were not. This was the normal way of living for many people around us those years. There were some actually much worse off than we were.

'This area was liberated in 1948. The Japanese never actually occupied this area — they were north of the Yellow River — and the fighting between the Kuomintang and the P.L.A. [People's Liberation Army] took place about twelve miles from here, so we didn't see any actual fighting. The first time I saw the P.L.A. men come here I was very frightened. The P.L.A. sent some officials to us to explain things and tell us not to be frightened, but most of us were; we didn't believe them. They tried to organize us into an agricultural district and asked our family to join, but we were not sure what they were really after and we didn't join. We were only convinced when we were actually given some land under the land reform and when we really got rid of the landlords. That convinced us.

'At land-reform time my brother and I were old enough to till the land. The family got nine mu of land. The landlord pretended to be willing to distribute his land but in his heart he wasn't satisfied. So we held big speaking-bitterness meetings to tell the landlord what we thought of him and to calculate how much he had exploited the peasants on his land. We held several meetings to speak our bitterness to him. Sometimes at the big meetings there was only one landlord, sometimes several. We finally convinced this landlord that he had done terrible things to the peasants and he was ready to hand over his land. He was given his share of land — he is now somewhere in this commune but not in this section of it.

'I never went to school as a child, but in 1950 I went to a spare-time school and now I know enough characters to write letters and to read the newspaper. I'm working in the fields most of the time now, but also do work with pregnant women, especially to see when they should stop working. I got married in 1949 and have four children — these two go to kindergarten, the girl of two goes to nursery, and this baby as well, when I am busy and can't look after him.'

*

161

From Mrs Chang's we crossed the street to another house which turned out to belong to a cheerful-looking chap with bad teeth by the name of Yang Chin-li. His hair was cut very short and there were many crinkles around his eyes as if he laughed a great deal. His ears were slightly pointed and the skin drawn up, which gave him a bit of a puckish look. During our conversation he seemed to be always on the verge of bursting out laughing, as if all this business of recounting events out of the past was a great joke, another example of how odd foreigners could be.

Here is Mr Yang's story as he told it:

'My father was a poor peasant and worked for a landlord. I went to school when I was seven, but only stayed one year as my parents hadn't enough money to pay for me. There were six of us — my parents and four children. I have one sister older than I am and the rest are younger. My father rented eight mu of land — but rented land is always the worst, for the landlord kept the best land for himself, and usually for about eight months of the year we never had enough to live on. We kept on trying different crops and filled every corner, but we never made enough to pay the landlord and our debts to him kept growing. We did have a donkey and during the idle season when we didn't need him we rented him out to others and made a little that way.

'Our debt to the landlord was not money — it was in crops. The actual rent was paid for in wheat and sorghum. But that wasn't all. Before harvest time when we had no food my father would borrow from the landlord — but for every bushel of grain we borrowed we would have to pay back double after the harvest. We sometimes could pay off a little of the debt by working — one day's work was the equivalent of a quarter of a bushel of grain. We never got out of debt.

'We were always in trouble until I was sixteen years old. At that time we planted nearly thirty mu of land — the landlord lent us the additional land. But this land was paid for by an arrangement whereby we gave 80 per cent of the crop to the landlord and kept 20 per cent ourselves. We had to work very hard. Our living — our food — was better at this time but our debts never got smaller. We never did get out of this trouble until liberation, when under the land reform we got eighteen mu of land. It was fairly good land, too, and we could get a living off it, but we had some economic difficulties too, due to the climate — some harvests were good, others were bad. The government subsidized us when we had serious difficulties.

'At the bitterness meetings we all calculated how much the land-owners had exploited us, charging us too much rent and too much interest, and we showed how the landlord owed *us* debts rather than that we owed *him* debts. He had complete control over my family for years. The landlord ran away after one of these big meetings, but I believe he came back later.

'I can read and write now. I started in the spare-time school in 1953, and by 1956 had learned to read. It was difficult, but I always wanted to finish school and this was too good a chance to miss.

'When land reform changed to mutual aid and then to the co-op period, it meant that we had to give up this land that had been given us. It was difficult for many peasants to see the advantages of this and some wouldn't. I could already see that we would never really get ahead just working our own land, so I was ready to join the co-op, but a lot of the others weren't. What we did then was to give them time. The co-ops were voluntary, so those of us who wanted to joined up, those who didn't stayed out. But little by little they saw that we were doing better than they were and most of them joined up when they saw it worked.

'I think all the changes have worked out pretty well. This commune idea is working. It's ten thousand times better now than when I was a child! Look, I have five children — a girl in secondary school, a boy and a girl in primary school, a girl in kindergarten, and another girl in the nursery — *and with no money worry!* My mother is living with us — she's very old — but she's taken care of, too. Five children being taken care of — and my parents couldn't keep just one child at school!'

*

Out once more into the heat. The sun was lower now and its sting had gone, but the grey earth had absorbed the heat all day and was now reflecting it like a furnace. A few peasants were beginning to straggle back from the fields in twos and threes, men and women, and the dust whirled up in little puffs from under their feet. They looked tired and walked tired, saying very little. A few dropped into the general store to make some purchases. One man was walking alone and I greeted him as he went by. He stopped immediately, and with a show of courtesy took off his wide straw hat. His face was withered and his clothes were patched, and he, like the child I had seen earlier, had a blue mottled stain over one side of his face. I asked him his name and what work he had been doing. 'Hoeing,' he said. (He told me his name but I made no record of it.)

'What were you doing before liberation?' I asked him. He glanced at me with a wry grin: 'Me? Oh, I was a landlord.' 'How much land did you own?' Waving his hat vaguely around, he said, 'All this....' I asked him to tell me about it, and he did, but before he began we walked across to the shady side of the street and sat, leaning our backs against the mud walls of a house. He didn't speak as fluently as the others I had questioned. Perhaps there were too many painful memories involved. Perhaps the presence of my interpreter restrained him. But this is the story as it came out little by little:

When the Communist army came through in 1948 he tried to escape, but the village was surrounded and there was no way out. His land was not immediately confiscated, though he realized that there was no chance of his keeping it if the Communists won the civil war. There was no formal trial, but the villagers organized 'speaking-bitterness' meetings in which he was put on a platform and all those who had rented land from him could come and speak their mind.

'These meetings,' he said, 'were very difficult. Sometimes I was alone and the people would be shouting at me all the things they thought I had done wrong; sometimes they would have several of us at these meetings and the crowd would then be larger. Anyone who had any grievance against us could come to these meetings and speak their mind. The people were sometimes very angry. I didn't understand any of it at first; I didn't know they had any special grievance against me. They then added up all the money they thought I owed them, so they said that the land I owned was really theirs now, for they had worked it for years for too little. I was, they said, a rich landlord, because I didn't have to do work myself; but I don't think I was nearly as rich as they thought I was and I had plenty of economic troubles too.

'When the village committee was established to settle how my land was to be divided up, there was some argument among the peasants themselves, but they got it settled. All my land was taken from me.'

'All?' I asked.

'All except a small piece which they said was my share. It was very poor land, the poorest, but I was allowed to build a small house on it and that is where I and my family lived. The first few years were very hard. No one would speak to us and we could hardly earn enough from the land to keep going. When mutual aid came in they did help me a little, but never as comrades; we were always shunned. I had to attend political-instruction meetings twice a week.

'When the co-ops came I thought I'd better join in and I asked that my piece of land should be included. They did this, and it helped me; but we were not real members of the co-op. We couldn't go to the public meetings, we couldn't vote, but they began to talk to us more freely in the fields.'

'Are you now a member of the commune?'

'Yes. When the commune came in they had some meetings to decide which of the former landlords should be allowed in. As I had co-operated in the fields and because they felt I was beginning to understand what they were trying to do, they allowed me to join. Some of the others are not yet full members, they cannot vote or go to meetings. But I am a full member.'

'They speak to you now?'

'Oh, yes. They accept me. I do my share of work.'

'Looking back on all this,' I asked, 'do you think things were handled well or badly?'

'I was very bitter at first, because I couldn't understand what I had done wrong. But I think I understand it now. Yes, I suppose it was a necessary thing. Some of us have suffered, but things before were very bad for most people. There are some things to be grateful for. My grandchildren go to school. They learn to read and write. I was a landlord but I never learned how to read and write.'

'Were any landlords in this area killed by the people, or by the courts?'

'Not here. Some ran away and disappeared and we don't know where they are. None of us who stayed were killed. There are many former landlords in the commune. Yes,' he said, looking at my interpreter, 'socialism is a fine thing.'

And with that he cleared his throat and let loose a wad of spit.

Peasant Poets

As we turned back towards the main commune building to say good-bye to Mr Chiao and the others, we passed the main shop; there was also a barber's shop, a small radio station, a post-office, and a repair shop for clocks and radios. But what particularly interested me was the village notice-board.

Notice-boards play an altogether unique part in Chinese life today. I have never seen any to compare with them. Every factory, institution, school, or college has its notice-board — sometimes a whole series of them. Their Chinese name describes them well — *ta tzebao* (big character news). Opinions, information, complaints, suggestions, are all publicized in this way. Every factory has a special *ta tzebao* for workers' complaints. I have seen these complaint- and suggestion-boards a hundred feet long outside large factories.

And here was the commune *ta tzebao*, in three large sections, covered with gaily coloured paper fluttering a little in the warm air. One entire section, my interpreter told me, was the commune 'writing-board'. Here were posted poems and stories which the peasants had written. I had already seen such boards at factories, but was fascinated to learn what the country people would be writing.

'Do please copy a dozen or so of the shorter poems,' I said.

*

I later added many other samples from the *ta tzebaos* of other communes, and back in Peking I asked a friend to translate them — but with no 'improvements'. Here are a few of them:

> Outside the village, peach blossom
> opens out; now at this time
> commune members work their hardest.
> Furrows with the sod turning over
> like waves breaking along a beach.
> Then in the paddy fields, rows of wheat
> being planted out like long arrows,
> so swiftly. An eighty-year-old man
> insists on coming to work, standing

at night in the middle of the field
holding the light for all to work by.

———

Lad and lass with two hearts
as one, treading together
at the windlass that brought up water
from the well below. At times
he pushes faster and then she
keeps pace — always the two
in harmony, the water flowing out
in a bright stream of silver.
And they in their day walking
together so many miles, yet never
leaving the place an inch. The water
in the well stays as deep as ever
but not so deep as their love
for each other.

———

Don't hurry little sister.
A great round moon, bathing
our village in its light,
and by her window, little sister
doing up her hair. So I ask
just where is she going, knowing well
it is off to night school.
Then asking her not to hurry
but to wait for me while I go home
to change, so that we two
may walk to class together,
perhaps on the road helping each other
to write a poem for our village
newspaper.

———

So lovely was she, standing there
under the trees, flowers all over her.
Though we have grown up together,
today, for the first time I seem

to really understand her; and though
I would speak to her, and try a thousand
times, yet somehow the words do not come
from my lips — simple words that say
'When will you marry me?' Any others
I say easily enough but somehow
only these I do not dare to ask.

———

Drought? but we have
plenty of sweat to spend.
Steep hills? but then
we have lithe legs.
Water too distant? See
how strong are our shoulders.
You old Weather-God,
what can you do to us?

And Above All, Hope

On the basis of studies made in fifteen communes in various parts of
China, it seems to me that the general plan of organization, the pattern
of daily life as I saw it in the Chengchow commune in Honan province,
is typical of the entire movement.

I visited other communes which were much more prosperous. For
example in the dining-halls of communes near Peking, and near
Shanghai, meat and fish were being served once a week instead of six
times a year. I observed a menu in one of these dining-rooms which
offered a choice of fourteen different dishes. These were communes
with more fertile soil, better climate, and favourable locations close
to large urban markets. I saw communes with modern, excellently
equipped hospitals and laboratories. Buildings, housing, schools, the
variety of goods available in the commune shops — everything on a
higher level. In Chengchow, to summarize the picture by one comparison, average accumulated savings per family amounted to only six
yuan; in some communes, savings per family were almost a hundred
yuan.

The average level of rural existence in China lies somewhere between these two limits. The fact is that China's peasants are lifting themselves by their own bootstraps out of an abyss inconceivable to our imagination. It is clear that conditions have improved. Life is tough; life is austere; yet I found it often lighted by gaiety and bubbling enthusiasm, and above all by *hope for the future*. Along with the facts and figures I set down, let me quote several notes from my journal, which may be more revealing than any statistics.

Hopei Province

Met a teacher at one of the nurseries. The children were all out in the yard helping to wash down their little chairs in preparation for the October 1st festival. The walls had been newly whitewashed. This young girl — she looked twenty-two but was probably older — turned out to be a graduate nurse from Peking Medical College. She was doing her stint 'in the country' — originally for four months, but this has been extended and she doesn't know how long it will be. She said she was enjoying the work with the children, and looked as if she meant it. She was definitely not of peasant background.

Liaoning Province

Had a long talk at the pig-breeding station about artificial insemination, which they now prefer to natural. They showed me the two hogs from which they obtained semen once daily; this they keep (in refrigerators) to inseminate any pig coming into heat. The precision is now such that they can count on 100 per cent conception.

Kirin Province

We visited the old people's home. It is usually depressing to see people at the end of their usefulness just waiting their time out. But not here. Watched the men playing chess. The oldest is ninety. They seemed a cheerful enough bunch of old fellows. One of them whom I spoke to told me that in the old days he had owned one mu of land (one-sixth of an acre). He never married. He had lived with his nephew until the nephew died three months ago.

'What would you be doing today,' I asked, 'if you didn't have this home to come to?'

'Me?' he cried. 'I wouldn't even be *here* on this earth!'

Honan Province

They showed me their 'radio station' — a small bedroom in which three people slept, but which could also be used as a studio. This station is linked by land-line to all seventy-five villages in the commune. They use it for announcements, news bulletins, and music. Also they have 'radio conferences' in which the six brigade-leaders can confer without having to come in from their districts. Sometimes the commune committee meets in this room and the proceedings are broadcast.

Hupeh Province

Another 'Home to Honour the Aged', described this time in a letter I sent to Elena.

I asked to be introduced to the oldest man in the home and they called him from his bedroom. A wrinkled, stooped old fellow of eighty-five. We sat at the table and talked while the others stood around listening and joining in with comments and sometimes jokes which I couldn't understand. I asked this old fellow where he had lived before the communes were set up. 'Nowhere,' he said. 'But you must have lived somewhere.' 'No, I didn't have anywhere,' he said. 'But where did you *sleep*?' 'I had a light hand-cart on wheels,' he said, 'and at night I would tip it over and lean it against a wall, and sleep under it.'

Kiangsu Province

Each production-brigade represents a village, and in this commune there are six. I was taken to visit a fruit-picking brigade — they were picking things that looked like English medlars. When we arrived, the group was not working and we found them under a lean-to to keep out of the sun, singing. A young girl led the song by pointing out the words written in large black characters on sheets of newspaper. They all sang with gusto, paying no attention to me. 'What's the song about?' I asked. The three marvels, I was told: the commune system, the mass line, and the great leap forward! When I photographed the song leader, for some reason they all thought this terribly funny and the song broke down because of the laughter.

China Kaleidoscope 2
NOTES FROM MY JOURNAL AND LETTERS

Patterns of Thinking

PATTERNS of thinking are not easy to shake. The prevailing Chinese image of the United States is that of a country controlled by a few rich capitalists grinding down the poor. They refuse to listen when I try to correct that image and when I tell them that American society is far more varied, far more complex, far livelier than they imagine, and that whatever fraudulence and exploitation does exist is more subtle, more hidden than their image would suggest.

When I tell the Chinese something that conflicts with their preconceived idea, they are bewildered but are too polite to tell me that they think I'm shooting a line.

Examples of things they have had a hard time swallowing: that the negro girl who comes once a week to help my wife with the housework comes in a car better than our own (negroes are the most crushed of all the American poor); that I take the garbage to the rubbish dump and help with the washing-up (a capitalist like myself, rich enough to travel, would have poor people working for him); that the unemployed are not lining up in the streets in New York waiting for the soup-kitchens to open, and that they often have enough funds to keep running their cars for a while.

The Czech football team had a big party on the top floor of the hotel a few nights ago, celebrating a victory. There was much singing and drinking — an outburst like this hadn't been seen at the Hsin Chiao for many a year. This completely floored the Chinese. They watched in amazement. Americans get drunk and become boisterous, but not Communist friends!

Three years ago the Indians had a magnificent exhibition here in Peking and I went along with my guide to see it. The Indian guides and

I got talking (they all spoke perfect English), and they invited me and my interpreter to have lunch. My interpreter declined. Afterwards when I rejoined him I could see that something was disturbing him. 'Mr Greene,' he finally said, 'how is it possible that these Indians could invite you, an Englishman, to lunch?' 'Why on earth not?' I asked. 'But you represent the cruel colonial power that has been crushing India for years!' My lunching with them just didn't fit the image!

Cables on Credit

I've noted many times indications of the trust that runs through Chinese relationships with each other. Yen, my interpreter, has a monthly ticket for the Peking bus and trolley-bus service — it's a reduced-rate card that's valid for unlimited travel. On leaving the bus I give up my ticket to the girl who stands at the door, but I have noticed that Yen merely says 'Monthly ticket', and she accepts this and has never, while I've been with him, asked to see it.

Another example took place at the Central Telegraph Office. Sending cables from China is fiendishly expensive, and on this occasion I was cabling the B.B.C. in London, C.B.C. in Toronto, and N.B.C. in New York. The messages were all very long.

When the girl totted the total up it came to more than 350 yuan (£52). I only had half the amount, and so I told her I would go back to my hotel to fetch some more. 'Pay tomorrow, or when you come this way again,' the girl said.

'I can't do that,' I replied, 'these cables have to go immediately.'

'Oh, we'll send them right away, but pay us when you come by next time.'

There are those who will say, 'They know where every foreigner lives, they would quickly catch up with him if he tried to get away without paying.' And that is quite true. But I don't think this went through the girl's mind at all. Here, they go on the assumption that people are *not* cheats.

Censorship, Chinese Style

I recorded a fourteen-minute news commentary for the Canadian Broadcasting Corporation today at Radio Peking. Studios, wood-panelled and air-conditioned; equipment, first-rate. Studio rather more 'live' than we have ours. Two technicians, a man and a girl, took charge and afterwards made duplicate tapes for me to send to the New Zealand radio network and the United States. The correspondents here had told me there was no censorship bureau — they file their cables through the ordinary telegraph office and they shoot right through.

I took my tapes to the Central Post Office to airmail them, wondering whether this freedom would apply to news tapes too, or whether they would hold them up to check them. The girl asked me for my press card (which I showed her), and then, having unwrapped one of the tapes, to my alarm, she brought out a pair of scissors. From the end of it she snipped about an inch, tested it with a match to see if I was using safety tape or inflammable (it was safety), wrapped up the parcel for me again, and accepted them all without demur.

Letter to Elena. *July 20th*

The Chinese have a characteristic which is both charming and puzzling, a knack of making the simplest situation an *event* (and therefore complicated). Everything must yield its last ounce of amusement or drama or intrigue. At home, ordering a taxi, arranging a dinner, or buying a railway ticket can be settled in a few moments by phone. But how dull! Here nothing like this is simple; it is developed into an 'occasion', requiring talk, discussion, planning. There are always undertones, nuances, even intrigues, which baffle the newcomer. And if an element of *secrecy* can be worked in, so much the better. It lends colour and an exciting uncertainty to life. (Or am I reading all this into situations because I do not speak the language?)

I have watched Western businessmen come bustling into Peking. 'Everything is set—just came to sign things up. Be back in London by Monday.' Three weeks later they are still here. 'Business' to the Chinese is more than signing an agreement. I sometimes feel it is really an excuse for something much more important — the real interplay of personalities.

These thoughts come to me as a result of an encounter with an old man on a bus today. As always, someone had stood up for the foreigner when I could find no seat; but then farther along the way an old, bent, weather-beaten man climbed on to the bus. I was sitting near the door. No one had apparently noticed the old man, so I got up and offered him my seat. His clothes were dirty, his face lined, and his hands were clutching a small parcel. He was so stooped that he had to look up sideways at me, and when he saw that it was a foreigner who had offered him a seat, he looked utterly astonished. He then gave me a broad grin and, with a small bow as dignified as that of any *grand seigneur*, he took the seat. It was perfect. Part real, part a superb bit of ironic acting. So much richer an encounter than if he had mumbled something about me keeping my seat.

This kind of wry, humorous interplay I notice everywhere. The Chinese make the most out of a situation. For us, to stand in line for half an hour waiting for a bus is a tedious waste of time. Not for the Chinese. They don't allow it to become a boring interlude with chilly strangers. They make contact, they acknowledge each other's presence, they are in touch with one another. They are never anonymous, never unresponsive. They may (rarely) be angry; they may be friendly; they may argue; but they are never indifferent or aloof.

I go about by bus whenever I can, rather than by taxi. Not only to save money. And not to be 'close to the masses', as my interpreter says. Or rather, not in the way he means. I go by bus because something always *happens*, some oblique exchange between people who are themselves strangers, some humorous incident which makes us all laugh, and very often tiny acts of marvellous kindness. I feel I am among a large family who are communicating at a number of levels.

Hsinhua

We are quite cut off here from Western papers — you can't just go down to a paper-stall and buy *Newsweek* or the air edition of the *New York Times*. Thanks to Clare McDermott I see Reuters' copy of *The Times* — which if it connects with the jet from Moscow gets here within two days. But by-and-large it's the English edition of *Hsinhua* (the official China news agency) that I have to digest with my breakfast every morning.

Hsinhua is both interesting and maddening. Interesting, because reading it you look at the world through quite a different kind of telescope and read things which you would never see in a Western newspaper. But the style is excruciatingly bad. It is bombastic, boastful, repetitive, and boorish — in fact, all the things that the Chinese are *not*. It breaks every rule of competent journalism. As a result, you could read *Hsinhua* a thousand years and never know that the Chinese are a highly perceptive people, of subtle and sensitive intelligence. To this extent, and in this way, *Hsinhua* does China a notable disservice. It would be a pity if *Hsinhua* ever became just another Western-type news-service; it would be wonderful if it could become really Chinese.

Wages

It is impossible to make any worthwhile comparison between the wages here and in the United States. Some Intourist interpreters, for instance, earn the equivalent of nine pounds a month, which seems little enough. But then, Mr Ku, who is one of them, tells me he only pays one yuan (three shillings) a month rent for his two-roomed flat.

I could, with immense and tedious effort, draw up a chart showing how many hours a man would have to work in China and America respectively to earn enough to buy this, that, or the other. And all this would show would be something we know already without the help of charts — that the American working man is prodigiously better off than his Chinese counterpart.

To the Chinese the only meaningful chart is one comparing today with ten years ago, and this year with last.

Grasshopper in a Hospital

In Chengchow I went to one of the hospitals to have my foot dressed. It was built in 1953, I was told. It was much less crowded than the P.U.M.C. Hospital in Peking and had an even more informal atmosphere.

I was taken at once to the out-patient surgical department; a young doctor (with slender, capable hands and the look of an intellectual) showed me into a room, where I lay on a surgical bed. Everything very neat and trim. The door was open and several people wandered in to see what was going on. They were just friendly and curious. The doctor was quite at home with these people and didn't shoo them out, as I was afraid he might.

While the doctor and nurse, both in surgical masks, were attending to my foot, I tried to chat with some of the people, but they couldn't understand my Chinese and just giggled. A ragged boy of about ten came and stood quite close, staring at me. His hands were cupped. After a few moments he opened them so that I could see what he was holding — it was a bright-green grasshopper. It was his pet, I think, for he looked at it affectionately and stroked it from time to time. Then he handed me the grasshopper to hold. I held it by the hind leg and stroked it too, and then gave it back to the boy. He went off smiling.

Passion for Improvement

The train yesterday taking me to Wuhan from Loyang was a long-distance one — it had started several days earlier from the far North-west. I had Chin with me, so I was able to talk with the girl who sweeps out the sleeper and brings the incessant rounds of tea. I asked her if she would have a few days off before her next trip.

'Yes,' she said, 'but first we must have our meeting.'

I thought she meant a political study meeting, but she said no, it was a meeting to discuss the journey. Apparently after these long-distance trains reach their destination the entire train crew get together to see what went wrong, and how they can do things better next time. It's also a way of airing any complaints. If there wasn't enough bed-linen or if the beer ran out — these are the sort of things that come up.

'Also,' the girl said, 'if we have complaints against each other, we discuss them at these meetings. For instance, if the engine driver should stop too quickly and things in the dining-car get spilled, the dining-car attendants will ask him about this and he will either explain why he had to brake so fast, or he might apologize and say it was a mistake. In ways like this we can learn how to run our trains better.'

'A Deeply Disappointed Man'

For the people, life is not all production quotas, political meetings, and slogans. I feel that I am in a country breaking through on all fronts into a new world.

Last night I had tickets for a concert in a big semi-open-air theatre that has been built in one of Peking's parks. The entrance fee is a few fen. I arrived early and sat on the grass near a rose garden watching the audience as they drifted in. Old men and women, students, soldiers, youngsters of ten and eleven, even of five and six, young men and their girls.

Not far away I could see the coloured lights above the dance area and hear the orchestra tuning up for those who wanted to dance in Western style. A small moon was coming up through the trees.

Sitting there, among these lively unhurried people all having a good time, a phrase from a supposedly profound analysis of China in the *Atlantic Monthly* flashed through my mind. Envisioning his country today, Mao Tse-tung, said the writer, 'is probably a deeply disappointed man'.

And *that*, I think, must be the silliest remark in the history of highbrow journalism.

Diplomatic Gallup Poll

In the past few weeks I have been invited to most of the West European and Asian embassies. I have taken the opportunity of conducting a one-man poll. I have been posing a hypothetical question: 'If the people of China could, entirely freely and secretly, record their approval or disapproval of the present regime, how many would record their approval?'

The *lowest* figure that anyone has yet given me is 80 per cent. Some have put it higher than 90 per cent.

Tonight I was again at one of the embassies. Someone had brought along a copy of a Hong Kong paper which had quoted General Wedemeyer's letter to the Washington *Star* of June 24th. The General was incensed at Montgomery's remarks at the banquet here in Peking. 'Obviously he is unaware,' the General wrote, 'of ample evidence concerning the massive famine in China of recent date and the official police action required to crush ruthlessly the dissident elements rioting for food.... ' And ' ... Naively Lord Montgomery accepted Mao Tsetung's statement that there is widespread hatred of the United States throughout China.... '

When part of this letter was read aloud there was a kind of embarrassed laughter. Someone said, 'If that's representative of the information about China in Washington, then Lord help us all!'

The Psychological Revolution

The longer I'm here, the more fundamental do the changes that are taking place appear to me. The new developments in education, the advances in medicine and industry, are only the outward manifestations of inner, psychological changes, and it is *these* which in the end may be more important than anything else. The changes going on inside people really intrigue me more than production statistics.

For example, the relationship to possessions. The Chinese, it appears to me, are significantly changing their attitude to property, to ownership. Men's activities in the past have very largely been dominated by a search for security, and to possess things is one way to secure a small foothold on a life full of uncertainties. But this drive to possess seems always to run to excess. Above our basic biological necessities we in the West have constructed an immense and ever-expanding pyramid of supposed necessities which are not necessities at all, but psychological wants, or luxuries.

The Chinese recognize that every human being needs an adequate standard of food, shelter, and clothing. But they are aware, I think, that ownership above these minimal real needs leads to competitiveness and rivalry, and that everything above the simplest personal possessions can much more happily be held in common. The result is that the element of *personal* acquisitiveness here appears to be reduced almost to vanishing point. This is no 'me first' economy; it is a 'we' economy that is growing here. They are *really* not interested in making more money for themselves.

I wonder whether this isn't too good to last. Perhaps the personal-possessiveness drive is inherent in human nature and will eventually emerge here as it has elsewhere. It may be that China is like a country at war which must for sheer survival bury individual rivalry until the crisis is over. Of course China needs to raise its general level of life, and will want to go on raising it. But will she avoid falling into the same old trap that the rest of us have been caught in — I mean making the 'standard of living' the end-all and be-all of life, with everyone wanting to possess more and more of everything, regardless of whether it makes us happier or not?

No one can tell. They seem to be *aware* of the problem and that's half the battle. Economically, they are already looking to the day (though it is still a long way off) when the working week will be very greatly reduced, and they are in a thousand different ways encouraging the development of personal creativeness. But on a deeper level the Chinese have long been aware (without expressing it in psychological or religious terms) that personal rivalry and personal protectiveness both lead to individual alienation. The Chinese appear to be finding their basic psychological security not in the search for personal possessions, but in the quality of their relationship with each other, and the implications of this are enormous.

```
**************************
*                        *
*      PART FIVE         *
*                        *
**************************
```

XVIII

On Chinese Law

AT whatever level one views the China scene today, one sees a nation on the move, in a state of flux. Law in China is no exception.

The nation has many laws, but no codification of laws. It is impossible in China to refer to any legal abstracts or résumés. Even the structure of the courts, the definition of crimes, the procedures of handling criminal and civil cases, are changing almost from day to day. Chinese law is in a trial-and-error period.

'A time of rapid social change is not the time to codify laws,' I was told by one of China's top legal authorities, Mr Wu Teh-peng, vice-president of the Chinese Political Science and Law Association, and a member of the Committee of Judiciary of the National People's Congress. 'We are now in a period of transition from one kind of society to another, moving towards socialism,' Mr Wu said. 'Law is the armour of the social system and it must change as the system changes. If, for example, laws pertaining to property had been codified during the co-operative stage of agriculture, they would now be quite out of date, since the commune movement has altered the whole basis of ownership.' Mr Wu, vigorous, with a bristly moustache, was, I felt, a very able scholar-politician. He looked at me over his glasses. 'Besides,' he added, 'we prefer a gradually evolving system. Law must always remain in harmony with the realities of human nature....'

*

This last comment struck me as being very much in the Chinese tradition. It reminded me of all that I had read of earlier Chinese legal procedures; it would have been a remark, I feel sure, that would have been approved of by Kuan Tzu in the sixth century B.C.

We tend to forget, sometimes, that China has had a long and remarkable legal tradition, though based on principles quite different from our own. As Dr Joseph Needham has reminded us, as early as the sixteenth century Portuguese travellers were bringing back accounts of the care which was taken by Chinese magistrates to see that the people's rights were protected; and they reported that life was held much less cheap in China than it was in the Europe of those days.[1]

The Chinese mind has never thought comfortably in terms of absolutes. Just as the sense of 'sin' (the breaking of extra-human, divine rules) never played much part in their religious life, so in their law the sense of an abstract right and wrong was largely missing. The Chinese never considered that an illegal act could be judged just on its own; it must always be seen in the light of the circumstances which surrounded it. To prescribe a fixed punishment for a given crime would, in their eyes, lead more often than not to injustice. In civil law, disputes were not seen so much in terms of one party being right and the other wrong, as in terms of a disharmony that needed to be resolved. The Chinese have always been a pragmatic, unsentimental people, and they recognized that there are two sides to every question, that human motives are always mixed and often dubious.

Abstract law appeared to the Chinese mind as too rigid, not sufficiently in harmony with the ebb and flow of human nature, and therefore likely to be destructive of human relationships. Professional legal sophistry was avoided, for the aim was not to see that the niceties of justice were imposed but that equity was achieved. It was tradition, rather than 'respect for law', that held Chinese society together through the centuries.

Criminal law was the only law that concerned the state, and it was often severe and cruel. It applied only to the common people, for the scholars and the aristocracy (except where treason to the throne was concerned) were usually unrestricted by any law at all. For the ordinary

[1] 'The Dialogue of Europe and Asia', *Eastern Horizon*, Hong Kong, July 1960.

people all other disputes — civil, commercial, religious — were discussed by the elders of a village or the leaders of the guilds and associations of which a citizen might be a member. It was by discussion that the real balance was found and harmony was restored — and always, if possible, without one side or the other feeling injured or resentful. Such discussions were usually held in public, so that friends and neighbours could follow and see that neither side was unfairly treated; and they would participate too. Problems were talked over, and neighbours helped to build a bridge between opponents.

But a system of behaviour enforced by tradition is highly vulnerable at moments when tradition itself is foundering. With the disruption of Chinese society that began with the 'opening-up' of China by the Western powers, ancient rules and unwritten restraints broke down. In the final agonizing decades the ordinary Chinese learned that he had neither custom nor law to look to for his protection.

All this passed through my mind as I sat with Mr Wu Teh-peng, who was telling me about the new legal structure that was being built in China today....

'We are attempting,' Mr Wu said, 'to develop a system of law that can serve the needs of a modern industrial society and yet remain in harmony with the best of our ancient Chinese precepts.' He went on to explain that they want their law to 'grow' out of actual practice and real needs, 'just as your English common law has grown,' he said. 'But we expect it to grow much more rapidly because the rate of social change is much more rapid.'

Despite this emphasis by the Chinese on *experimentation* and *movement*, it is clear that the broad lines of a legal apparatus have already been marked out. There are at present some three thousand civil and criminal statutes adopted by the National People's Congress. As China is a *unified* rather than a *federated* state, these laws have nation-wide application (with certain exceptions in the cases of autonomous nationalities), and this is true also of the hierarchy of courts.

The court system comprises three main levels: The Supreme People's Court, Special People's Courts, and Basic People's Courts. The last-named are courts of first instance. Article 19 of the 'Organic Law of the People's Courts', adopted in 1954, states that in addition to trying cases, these courts will 'settle civil disputes and minor criminal cases which do not need a trial'; and 'direct the work of people's conciliation committees'. Higher courts can act either as courts of first instance or of appeal. Judges in China are appointed by the legislative bodies corresponding to the level of the courts and may be removed by the same bodies. There are thirty thousand of them.

But the number of cases that come into court is small, Mr Wu told me; and the number reaching trial smaller yet. (This was confirmed everywhere I went.) This is partly because property of a personal kind plays a far smaller part in the life of the Chinese today than it does in ours; and this is especially true since the development of the co-operatives (and later the communes) in which property is held in common. A very high percentage of the cases that come before the U.S. courts are concerned, in one way or another, with property rights. Many minor disputes (which would otherwise come to court) are disposed of by the Conciliation Committees described later in this chapter.

In all China today there are, according to Mr Wu, only two thousand lawyers, and these are so under-employed that it causes the government serious concern. The government is anxious to maintain law as a subject of study, and is recruiting students to enter the several law colleges. Lawyers frequently take jobs as teachers. As for the judges, most of whom do not have enough court cases to occupy their full time, and who are not permitted to accept other employment, the government encourages them to help in legal educational work — teaching the background and the importance of law through lectures and seminars in communes, factories, and colleges.

One reason for the small number of lawyers is that China is what could be described as a non-legalistic country. 'Contracts' play only a small role in Chinese business relationships; the given word is still a binding sanction. Even insurance is often a matter of a verbal promise rather than a contract requiring lawyers. Basically one might say that the Chinese developed as a highly homogeneous population whose closely-knit social life had to depend on a mutual trust.

I asked Mr Wu whether the death penalty was still applied in China. He said, 'Yes — for murder; rape causing the death of another person; for rape of a girl under fourteen years of age; and for certain anti-revolutionary crimes. But the law requires that all death sentences be reviewed by a higher court, whether there is an appeal or not; and, further, that the penalty in every case be suspended for two years before it is carried out. Some Westerners have told us they think this a cruel provision. We think of it otherwise. Our aim is to get a man to reform during those two years — and what chance does a man have to reform if we kill him? Only on very rare occasions do we now carry out the death sentence.'

When I asked Mr Wu how many executions there were in a year, he said that he was unable to give me the number, as it was a state secret. 'We are Marxist-Leninists,' Mr Wu continued, 'we do not believe a *class* can ever be reformed; but we think *individuals* can be. In the ten years since liberation there have been a number of people condemned to death who are now living useful and productive lives.'

Like the European systems based upon the Napoleonic Code, Chinese law makes no provision for trial by jury. However, a somewhat analogous function is performed by the People's Assessors. Trial courts at first-instance level are composed of one judge and two assessors who serve, in a sense, as lay representatives of the public interest. Assessors must be citizens, twenty-three or older, and are elected, Mr Wu said, by popular vote for a term of two years. Judges, in all cases, are persons who have had several years' legal training. People's Assessors receive some legal training while serving their terms of office; and they may be re-elected.

Discussing the role of the assessors, Mr Wu continued, 'There are usually forty to a hundred assessors elected in each county. When a case comes into a district, the county is asked to send two assessors. They are paid only the equivalent of their loss in salary plus a modest travel and expense account. In court they share equal rights with the judge. Two assessors can outvote the judge.

'Assessors are not used in appeals, since these usually revolve around legal points. The *facts* are presumed to have been determined in the indictment and trial of first instance. Appeals are heard before three judges.

'At a level below the regular courts we have what we call the Neighbourhood People's Conciliation Committee,' Mr Wu went on. 'These committees are composed of residents in a local community who are well liked and trusted by the people, and their function is to try to settle personal disputes, minor infringements, and domestic conflicts. Parties in a dispute come before their neighbourhood committee only if they wish to — it is entirely voluntary. The committee cannot compel anyone to appear — citizens can take their grievance to a formal court if they prefer. The findings of the conciliation committee are not binding, although the public gives them its moral support and they manage to settle a great number of small grievances which would otherwise have to be heard by the courts. As in the old days,' Mr Wu continued, 'the neighbours and friends are present and take part in meetings of the conciliation committees.'

*

So much for Mr Wu's outline of the general structure of the courts. I was, of course, particularly interested to find out what protections are provided by law for the rights of accused persons. I was glad to have made available to me a report by a Canadian attorney, Mr Kenneth Woodsworth, entitled *Notes on the Legal System of the People's Republic of China*, which he prepared after his return from China in 1960.

Mr Woodsworth reported:

... There seems to be a considerable degree of protection against arbitrary arrest and imprisonment, and the impression is that the direction is towards greater safeguards in this respect.... Before a person may be arrested on suspicion of a crime, a full investigation must be made and evidence sufficient to satisfy the court (i.e., judge and people's assessors) must be submitted in advance.... After charges are laid, the arrest must be made publicly, in daytime, and witnessed by neighbours, and the family must be notified. No inducement or compulsion may be used to secure a confession. The accused must be shown the full evidence at least three days before trial and he may choose his own counsel, or ask that counsel be appointed for him. Trials must be in public, except in cases involving public security. If a case is not heard and dealt with within one month of the time when charges were laid, the delay must be explained and approved by the court of next instance. After conviction, the court must explain to the prisoner his right of appeal....

Mr Woodsworth attended not only several criminal trials but also meetings of the conciliation committees. Discussing the work of the committees, Mr Woodsworth wrote that he 'was very much impressed with the judiciousness and common-sense conduct'. Mr Woodsworth concluded his general discussion of Chinese law with these words: 'The nation appears to have left behind it the comparative chaos of the immediate post-civil-war period. It would seem that a permanent structure of law is emerging that is providing certainty in the administration of justice. I was favourably impressed with the general appearance of public order everywhere and with the conduct of legal processes, as I had opportunity to see them.'

In 1956 an outstanding British barrister and Member of Parliament, Mr F. Elwyn Jones, Q.C., visited China to observe several major criminal trials. In a report over the B.B.C. on his return (included in *The Listener*, July 19th, 1956), Mr Jones said:

My impression is that the stage has been reached where more attention is being given to the rights of the individual citizen. I felt a real concern for justice among the lawyers I met, and a desire to create an effective independent court system.

The difficulty I found in seeking to assess the quality of their justice is that their basic approach is different from ours. In our own history we have found that the independence of our judges from the Government and from political control is a vital safeguard of the liberty of the citizen. The Communist doctrine does not accept this. They claim that the government is the people and that the people does not need to be protected from itself.

I attended two criminal trials. The first was in the High Court at Peking. The accused, a peasant, was charged with murder and with being a Japanese agent in 1942. He was tried by a judge sitting with two 'lay assessors', as they are called. There is no system of trial by jury in China. The accused was represented by a defending lawyer. Each year they are training more lawyers in the law schools.... I was glad to find that the Chinese accepted the principle that it is essential to the administration of justice that accused persons on serious charges should be represented by a professionally qualified lawyer.

The Peking trial ended in the conviction of the accused and a sentence of three years' imprisonment. The trial was conducted with dignity and simplicity. There were no wigs or robes. But there was a real sense of the gravity of the occasion. The accused in this case pleaded guilty and he had previously made a full confession of his guilt. After the trial was over, I asked his lawyer whether he had satisfied himself that there was independent proof of the accused's guilt apart from his confession. He assured me that he had. This prisoner had been in prison for four months before his trial. It appears that since 1951 the period of waiting between arrest and trial has been cut down a good deal.

In the second trial I attended, at Nanking, the accused was an electrician charged with causing malicious damage in a factory. The prosecution alleged that the accused had become bitter because the management had promoted someone junior over him, and this had led him to commit the crime. The electrician denied the charges vigorously, as did his defending lawyer. I did not discover the result of this trial because it was adjourned for the calling of further evidence. I saw no press reporters in this or indeed any court I went to, and there is little, if any, crime reporting in the Chinese press. But there were relatives of the prisoner, students, and members of the public in all the courts I attended....

The most interesting case I heard was an appeal in the Shanghai High Court of a prisoner who had been sentenced to death on a charge that he was a colonel in Chiang Kai-shek's army, who had been landed secretly from Formosa in 1954 in order to organize a counter-revolutionary group in the Shanghai area. He too had a lawyer to represent him. His appeal was successful and his death sentence was varied to one of eight years' imprisonment.

These accounts (so largely favourable) by visiting experts do not mean justice is all-triumphant in China. China's civil conflict is not yet over it is a nation still at war. And as in every country at moments of danger so today in China normal legal procedures are subject to the overriding imperatives of survival. Civil war and extensive borders make it easy for spies and saboteurs to infiltrate. Chiang Kai-shek talks openly o the spies who are parachuted on to the mainland or put ashore from boats. And there must be many of the formerly privileged who, while outwardly co-operating with the present regime because they have to, are still bitterly resentful and antagonistic.

There are no signs of terror in China today and no sense of fear; but there is intense vigilance. With those who are accessible to discussion, to persuasion, the Chinese are often remarkably patient; but little mercy would be shown to those who remain determined to throw obstacles in the path of the social progress that is being attempted. I rather think appeal to abstract 'legal rights' would be of little help to them.

XIX

A Divorce Trial

DURING a tour of a heavy machinery plant in Shenyang, word reached me that a municipal court would be in session at eleven o'clock. As I had not yet had a chance to see a court in action, I at once called off the factory visit and drove back into the city with Mr Chang Ming-lun, one of the most efficient interpreters I ever met. His ability to give an instantaneous, running translation of the court proceedings enabled me to transcribe them almost verbatim.

We arrived at the court early. I looked around. The court-room was a small, rather drab chamber, filled almost to capacity by about thirty women. The wooden floor had been recently scrubbed. Between the benches for the public and the judge's platform was a long table covered with a bright-red table-cloth. This was the only splash of colour in the room. No flags, no slogans, no pictures, not even of Mao Tse-tung. While we waited for the judge to appear, I learned from the court secretary that the case to be heard was a divorce action, and the presiding judge would be one of the youngest on the bench — only twenty-three. This particular court, he told me, heard thirty or forty such suits a year, and a smaller number of criminal cases. To divulge the exact number was not permitted. There were only six municipal courts of this kind in Shenyang, a city of nearly three million. He told me the court was called in session only when there was a case to be heard, usually only every ten days or so.

A woman, whom my interpreter told me was the court recorder, entered through a door behind the judge's table and loudly summoned the public to rise. As we did so, the judge and the two assessors took their seats on the platform. One assessor was an elderly, bespectacled man who might have been a shopkeeper or small businessman: The

190

other was a buxom woman, a housewife perhaps, with white ribbons binding her black hair. The judge himself, in his freshly-pressed cotton work-suit, looked even younger than twenty-three. I should have taken him for a student. His face was serious. From the moment he stepped into the court this young man was in complete control of the proceedings. He looked at us for a moment and then said:

'Please, everyone sit down.'

He remained standing.

'Before this hearing begins,' he said, 'I wish to tell the members of the public what the regulations are. They are simple and I wish them to be strictly obeyed. There is to be no smoking. Do not clap or shout. Do not fidget. If any members of the public have questions to ask or suggestions to make, please do so at the end of the case. Do not interrupt during the hearing.'

In addition to the judge, the two assessors, and the court recorder, another woman had taken a seat on the far side of the dais. She was to be a witness, I was told.

The judge then said, 'Let the man and woman be brought in.'

A young couple entered, side by side, and stood facing the judge, their backs to the public. On a gesture from the judge they sat down in two chairs which had been placed there for them, and remained seated throughout. The judge asked each in turn for name, age, occupation. The woman was a teacher, twenty-four years old, her 'cultural level' that of non-graduate teacher. The man was a doctor, twenty-seven, and a university graduate.

The judge then told them:

JUDGE: My name is Tao Wan-yi; the people's assessor on my right is Lui Shi-ying and on my left Li Shu-lan. The recorder's name is Chiang Ming-chin and the name of the woman's representative is Yie Rung-chin. She is the principal of the primary school where Chang Wen-hung works. Your rights are these: you can put forward your reason, Chang Wen-hung, for wanting to divorce this man; and then Chang Wei-man will have the right to tell this court why he opposes divorce. You have the right to call evidence and you have the right to appeal to the higher court if you are not satisfied. You have the right to call any friends you wish to speak for you. You have the right to have a lawyer if you wish to have one. You also have the right to read the record of today's hearing at any time during the next four days, and any members of the public can read it also. If either of you two have any reason not to be satisfied with this court, either as to myself or the two people's assessors, you have the right to withdraw the case now and take it before another judge and assessors. Have you listened carefully to what I have said?

(*All three say* 'Yes.')

Have any of you any question as to the membership of this court? ('No.')

We will then proceed. According to this woman's depositions she says she wants to divorce this man because there is no harmony in the home, that they often quarrel over quite minor things; that they have different temperaments and tastes; and because he has a very bad temper. He says in his deposition that she pays too much attention to her family and not enough to him, that she is not tender and very rarely has a good word for him. He also admits that he has a bad temper but is trying to correct that. But he opposes the divorce because he still feels there is a basis of a good relationship.

That, briefly, is the situation. The law says that when two people agree on a divorce it is to be granted, provided adequate provision is made for the protection of the children's interests. If either party disagrees, then a hearing must take place before a people's court. That is the position today.

JUDGE (*to the woman*): When did you first get to know your husband?

WOMAN: In 1955.

JUDGE: When did you get married?

WOMAN: In May 1956.

JUDGE: How long did you love him before getting married?

WOMAN: For a year. But I didn't get to know him very well. He talked very well and pretended to be a good man. He often asked me to go to the park with him or to the cinema, and kept asking me to marry him.

JUDGE: How about your feelings after you got married?

WOMAN: Not very good. He began to be rude and my state of mind about him became clearer and clearer. Since 1958 I have helped him with his work, so that though the feeling wasn't very good between us it was still possible. But his temper got worse and worse, and he often beat me. I often spoke to him but it had no effect. We didn't seem to be the same family — we began to have nothing but quarrels and fights.

WOMAN ASSESSOR: Did he beat you?

WOMAN: Yes, and I couldn't stand his rude ways with me. His mother always supported him and that made things worse. We would often quarrel in the middle of the night. His mother didn't help at all, only made things worse.

MAN ASSESSOR: Why do you want a divorce now?

WOMAN: The work at my school is very heavy; I just cannot stand the strain any longer. If ever I come in late from school he says, 'Where have you been? What have you been up to?' For a long time I felt that though he beat me and slapped me, things would improve. While he was a medical student at Shenyang Medical College I helped him with money and other things and gave him as much as I could.

MAN ASSESSOR: How did he treat you while you were helping him?

WOMAN: Not always very well but much better. His attitude wasn't always patient. But I decided to go on just as long as I thought the relationship had a chance of improving. I tried to discuss things with him, especially about the children, and all he would say was, 'You gave birth to them, they aren't my responsibility!' How can one bear it when one's husband says that about his children?

JUDGE: What does he do with the money he earns?

WOMAN: Usually spends it on himself or on his mother, so I use my money to keep the children and for food and so on. I sometimes need books too, so there is often no money to hand over to him, though he thinks there should be.

JUDGE: What resources do his parents have?

WOMAN: They have enough to manage on — there's no need for him to spend money on them.

MAN ASSESSOR: Do you ever have a discussion with him about how to spend the family money and how to arrange the economy of the family?

WOMAN: Oh, yes. Before he graduated we had many discussions as to how we would budget our money. But after he graduated these talks annoyed him. Sometimes when he saw what the children needed he would buy them something, but usually he left that to me and paid no attention to the children.

JUDGE: How did the quarrels begin? Who started them?

WOMAN: Sometimes he did, sometimes I did by trying to correct him.

JUDGE: Did you ever strike him?

WOMAN: No.

JUDGE: What did he strike you with?

WOMAN: His hands. Sometimes he would come home at midnight — a normal man doesn't come back at that time.

JUDGE: Do you often try to correct him?

WOMAN: Yes, and I asked friends to intervene.... Sometimes quarrels would last until midnight and neighbours would complain.

JUDGE: He said in his deposition that you often swear and curse at him — is that true?

WOMAN: (*Part of this reply couldn't be heard.*) ... I was treated just like a stranger by his mother, who would also call me names.

JUDGE: Who did the housework?

WOMAN: His mother mostly, because I had to go to school; but I did all the children's laundry.

JUDGE: Who looked after the children's expenses?

WOMAN: I did.

JUDGE: How many children have you?

WOMAN: Two. One three years old; one, one year.

JUDGE: Are you pregnant now?

WOMAN: No.

JUDGE (*turning to the man*): What about your feelings towards your wife?

MAN: After our marriage it was very good. We often did things together, cooked together, and we paid much care to each other.

JUDGE: Was this because she was supporting you while you were at college?

MAN: Yes.

JUDGE: How did you treat her?

MAN: Very well. I tried to study well.

JUDGE: Did you put your feelings of kindness into actions?

MAN: I wasn't much good at looking after the children. At that time

I was living at the college and we would see each other on Saturdays and Sundays.

JUDGE: Why, after two years, did it get worse?

MAN: I think the trouble was largely because she wasn't on good terms with my mother. She had a weakness, too, in that she couldn't stand anything that would distress her, anything unpleasant. Also we are very different temperamentally. She likes to lead a quiet life, I like to be active.

JUDGE: She says you often beat her — is that true?

MAN: We had frequent quarrels, but I didn't beat her frequently.

JUDGE: Why did you quarrel so often?

MAN: My irritation and temper. Also she looked down on me. I'm a doctor, but she would always know best.

JUDGE: Do you feel superior to her culturally?

MAN: Yes.

JUDGE (*bearing down on him*): Don't you know there's a law that says couples should help each other? If you thought her cultural level was low you should have helped her to improve it. You think you are her cultural superior — is that a right way of thinking?

MAN: I think my thinking was wrong. I relied on her for money and help, but when I got near to graduation I began to think 'I'm better than a mere primary-school teacher' — that, I admit, was wrong.

JUDGE: Who do you think is responsible for the quarrels?

MAN: I think I am, because I asked too much of her.

JUDGE: Has she tried to help you to overcome your rudeness?

MAN: She has tried to improve me lots of times!

JUDGE: Why didn't you take her help and advice?

MAN: Because of loss of face; I couldn't admit my weak points.

WOMAN ASSESSOR: Why do you think you would lose face by accepting her advice?

MAN: Mainly because I looked down on her culturally and couldn't accept her as an equal.

JUDGE: Why did this all happen only after your graduation?

MAN: Because then I could support myself.

JUDGE: Is it your lack of feeling for her or her lack of feeling for you that is the real problem? When she paid such tender care for you, why were you unable to respond in the same way?

MAN: Because of my lack of knowledge of how to look after a family and a wife.

JUDGE: Do you know the marriage law?

MAN: Yes.

JUDGE: Since you know the marriage law you should know the husband's obligations towards his wife and children.

WOMAN ASSESSOR: Was it because you had different opinions that you fought with your wife?

MAN: No. But because in the past, before liberation, I often saw my father beat my mother and I was brought up to think that men should be superior.

JUDGE: When did your father beat your mother?

MAN: In the old society.

JUDGE: And what does the present law say?

MAN: That men and women are equal. But I still think the wife should obey the husband.

JUDGE: But don't you know the law?

MAN: I don't think it matters if a man beats his wife — but he mustn't beat others. In the family it's all right.

JUDGE: What law allows the husband to beat the wife?

MAN: No law.

JUDGE: What was the reason you beat her the last time?

(*Court-room throughout all this very still. Everyone listening intently. No interruptions at all.*)

MAN: Because she took the children to her mother's without consulting me. I also loved the children and my mother did too, and we didn't want them to be taken away.

JUDGE: But isn't it fair for her to see her parents and take the children there too? Who else did you beat?

MAN: I hit her mother once, but that was quite accidental — a slip of my hand. It happened in a struggle ... and also I had had some wine.

JUDGE: On what have you been spending your own wages?

MAN: Sometimes on myself. I bought a bicycle.

JUDGE: Do you agree to the divorce?

MAN: I think it's been my fault and I think it's quite reasonable of her to ask for a divorce. But I hope she gives me a chance to correct myself. I'll try my best. If later on I again fail, then I won't object to the divorce.

JUDGE: What is your plan for the future?

MAN: I will certainly pay more attention to my wife and family.

JUDGE (*to the woman's representative, the principal of the school where the teacher worked*): Do you want to say anything?

REPRESENTATIVE: I have made a thorough study of the case and all its aspects and made many inquiries. Though love was there at the start, there was never any real basis of a good relationship. He used fine words to start with.

You cannot see the realities of this marriage on the surface. The marriage on this basis cannot be consolidated. I believe the main trouble has been the man. The law says that marriage should be based on free-will and equality. Everyone has the right to freedom and to social life and a mutual life of shared obligations, and the shared duty to look after the children. But instead this man beat her — even when she was pregnant. As a doctor he should know very well that is a time when special care should be taken — and that is why she began to lose her health.

Bad treatment — those are the grounds for this application for divorce. This man has no real feelings for this woman and his actions show it. He has often promised to change, but hasn't. He often apologized but never changed. It is his feudal background that makes him treat his wife as an object to be possessed — it is a bourgeois view to look down on a wife as he has done. While he was dependent on her help, he never showed his real nature, but when he became independent his real attitude showed itself — a university graduate looking down on a mere primary-school teacher! No real relationship can ever be built on another's pains. When he says he doesn't know how to look after children he's only lying. Fancy! a doctor saying he doesn't know how to look after children! And the only reason why he doesn't want a divorce now is because of public opinion!

JUDGE: Anything more?

WOMAN: No.

JUDGE: Anything more?

MAN: No.

JUDGE: Have any of you anything to say about the representative's statement? (*to the woman*) Just now your husband said he would like to correct himself and pay tender regard for you and the children. What do you say to this?

WOMAN: It is not the first time he has said this. He will be quite different as soon as he gets back home. One moment he says that he looks down on me, the next he says he will be kind to me. I am firm. My mind is made up. If this court does not grant me a divorce, I will take it to a higher court.

JUDGE (*to the man*): What do you say to that?

The man was struggling to find words. The judge leaned forward, waiting. Finally the man began to speak. He was looking straight ahead, over the head of the judge, but seemed really to be addressing his wife.

MAN: I know the basis of our life has not been good. I have not been a good husband, nor a good father. But many people have educated me and today I have really woken up. I know in the past I have heard all these things, but I didn't ever realize them as I do today. I have loved you, but I have neglected you. I have really loved you. We have two children and I now really commit myself to look after you and our two children. I know I have said this before, but today it is true.

This is the last time, and in front of so many people, I tell you that you can trust me and I am asking you to give me one more opportunity. Let us try once more to make a happy home and in this way to contribute to our society. I still believe we can make a happy home for ourselves and the children. I will take tender care of you. I will never again think, as I have done in my bourgeois way, that the man is more important than the woman. I now see that is nothing but a feudal attitude which I have not shed from my past.

JUDGE (*to the woman*): What do you think of giving him another opportunity?

WOMAN: It's not true that our relationship was ever all right. He has said all this before. He so often goes back on his words....

MAN (*breaking in, his eyes still straight ahead*): Please ... please.

The room was absolutely silent and all eyes were fixed upon the woman. We could not see her face, but from the set of her shoulders, and the bitterness of her previous words, I felt certain her answer would be no. The judge also had been watching her closely and at the very moment she started to speak, he rose to his feet, interrupting her. A superb piece of timing. He said, 'There will be a recess for fifteen minutes for this man and woman to talk things over in private. Then I ask that they come to see me personally. The court is adjourned.'

We waited for half an hour or forty minutes. Some of the people went out to smoke and talk on the steps. The court secretary, as before, announced the court's reassembly. The judge, the assessors, the secretary, the woman's representative came in; then the man and woman. The woman had been crying and was twisting her handkerchief in her hand.

JUDGE (*standing*): Please sit down. The court is again in session.

Chang Wen-hung, schoolteacher, and Chang Wei-man, doctor, have had an opportunity to talk together while the court was adjourned and they have informed us of their discussion.

Chang Wei-man has declared several times this morning his determination to improve his behaviour towards his wife, and she has told us that she agrees to give this marriage one more chance, but only on one condition. The condition is that if she finds that his behaviour does not improve and that she feels it necessary to apply for a divorce again, her husband will not oppose her. In that case the divorce would be granted without a court hearing. The court will now make its declaration.

As the judge said this, the two assessors and the court recorder also rose and stood while the judge gave the finding of the court.

This court declares that since Chang Wei-man has criticized himself in public here today and since his wife is ready to give him another chance, her application for a divorce should be considered withdrawn on the condition she has made. The two people should now try to make every effort to consolidate their relationship in affection and understanding.

MAN: I should like to thank the judge and the assessors and all the comrades present who have consistently advised me.

JUDGE (*to the man*): The court wishes to address these words to you. I think you have many problems which you must think over, many difficulties you have with your own character, especially your bad temper. You have shown a bourgeois attitude and this you must do your best to eradicate. You are hereby formally reprimanded by this court. We charge you to do your utmost to correct your behaviour and erroneous attitudes and we charge you to see that you carry out in your actions what you have promised here in open court this morning. (*more gently*) You are a doctor. As a doctor in a socialist state you have a great responsibility. Try in future to conduct yourself so that you can lead a happy family life with your wife and two children, and this will also help your country and comrades. While we reprimand you, we want you to know that we understand how difficult it is to shed old attitudes. Our whole country is in the process of changing from one set of values to another. That is a very difficult task. Changes of attitude can only come when we consciously become aware of the old values which have to be eradicated. We understand the difficulties, and ask you to do your best. (*to all of us*) The court is now over. After we have left we wish the public to remain seated until Chang Wei-man and Chang Wen-hung have left the court-room.

The man and woman, without looking at anyone, the man with slightly averted face, left by the public door. The audience rose and we drifted slowly outside.

As I went through the outer hall to the street I saw the judge, a policeman, and some of the people who had been watching in the court-room, lighting cigarettes and chatting together.

XX

Prisons: Bad and Good

A T the culminating end of any system of law stands the system of retribution or of reform. In the West both these ideas, retribution and reform, have become intertwined. We frequently call our prisons reformatories; we often declare that our aim is to rehabilitate the transgressor and send him out again as a functioning member of society. In practice, however, we still demand of the law that it exact revenge. The criminal must 'pay his debt to society'; the violator must be made to suffer. The result, since retribution and reform are nearly always mutually exclusive, is that our penal institutions customarily fail in both aims.

I have always been deeply concerned with prison reform. I was for years a member of the Howard League for Penal Reform in England. I have visited prisons all over the world, lectured *in* prisons and *about* prisons. In general, my conviction has been that caging people can never cure them. There will always be some who are psychologically so injured that they must be kept out of society. But the vast majority of those we put behind bars should not be there. And when they are released, far from having been reformed, they are usually less capable of fitting into society, and more bent upon beating or outwitting society, than they were when they went in.

I was, therefore, keenly interested in learning how China approached this problem.

*

In theory, or at the verbal level, the main stress appears to be on *reform* rather than retribution.

Mr Wu Teh-peng, the vice-president of the Chinese Political Science and Law Association, and member of what would correspond in the United States to the House Committee on Judiciary, had said to me, 'The essence and spirit of our laws is not solely to punish the criminal or to give society powers of reprisal. Our aim is to prevent the criminal from continuing in his criminal ways and to transform him, if amenable to education. Generally criminals are put in prison. Certain crimes are punishable by death, but even in these cases we give opportunity for reform.'

Prison sentences, Mr Wu told me, ranged from six months to twenty or twenty-five years. Six months is the minimum sentence. Misdemeanours and minor crimes are not punished by imprisonment. Sentences are always subject to reduction for good behaviour, and by parole, and so forth.

Thus, with the exception of the two-year delay between imposition and execution of a death-sentence, there appears to be no great difference, at the theoretical level, between the Chinese and Western penal systems. When it came to actually visiting prisons, however, I found some striking differences, and also some notable similarities.

I was able to inspect two prisons, one a 'good' prison in Peking, and the other a very 'bad' one, not only in my view, but in the opinion of the Chinese as well, in Shanghai.

Let me start with the bad one.

My visit came about in a rather curious way. I had heard talk in Peking of the Nanking prison as being one of their very best — the most advanced, the 'freest', the model which best illustrated their new attitude. In Peking I had been assured that I should be able to visit the Nanking prison; and on my way to Shanghai from Wuhan I left the river-boat which was taking me down the Yangtze River at Nanking, largely for the sake of that visit. There, however, I learned that my visit to the prison would 'not be convenient'. They were very sorry. The governor was away. I said I didn't care whether the governor was there or not, I was more interested in the prisoners and the prison than I was in the governor. But in this I made no progress. It was clear they were saying 'No'.

Later I was told that there is considerable local autonomy in these matters, and probably a certain guarding of prerogatives. Local officials don't like to feel themselves pushed by Peking; and perhaps if I had arrived in Nanking without any prior word from the capital, they might have been delighted to show me their prison. But who can tell?

Arriving in Shanghai the following morning, I mentioned my interest in prisons and my disappointment of the previous day. They immediately invited me to visit the Shanghai prison. This I had already heard of as being one of their very worst.

The Shanghai prison was of the fortress type, built, I am sorry but not surprised to say, by the British, sometime between 1913 and 1925 (the Kuomintang had lost the records). Known as the Ward Road Jail, it had been modelled, quite obviously, on late-nineteenth-century prisons in London. As we drove up, we came to an immense iron gate, guarded by a soldier with a tommy-gun. The gate was opened, the car moved forward to an inner portcullis. Above us loomed a row of frightful brick structures, four storeys high, with rows of barred windows.

The chief warden, however, seemed curiously out of place in this sinister pile. He was a young fellow, wearing a white short-sleeved shirt with open collar. An open face, firm but likeable. They certainly *use* young people. His name was Wang Chi-hu.

The style of the prison, he told me, made it difficult to adapt to the new system of reform through labour. But they were not planning to build another prison because they thought that within a few years there would be no need for anything as large as this. The prison population has been steadily diminishing. They now have 2,400 inmates. (According to the Department of Correction, the prison population of New York City on March 1st, 1961, was 9,574.) The prison is less than half occupied. Several of the huge cell-blocks are being used for storage, a fact I was able to confirm by my own observation, though I was not able to confirm Mr Wang's even more interesting statement that this was the only prison in Shanghai, a city with a population of more than six million.

With respect to vital statistics and the general routine of this sombre institution, Warden Wang gave me the following facts:

They have one hundred guards.

The guards are all armed.

There are no escapes.

Families normally visit once a month, but may come at any time if there is some special reason. Mail is unlimited, but letters in and out are censored. Visitors are separated from the prisoners by barred grilles.

Prisoners have the same rations as the people outside, in winter they eat meat here three times a week, fish more frequently in summer. There is a big library, unlimited reading material is permitted. Prisoners work eight hours a day in workshops: at printing, shoe-making, and other light industries. A large part of the cost of the prison is met by the profits made out of the production.

There is a spare-time programme which offers classes in reading and writing and various technical skills, as well as current events and inter-national relations. Films are frequently shown, and there are lectures by people brought in from factories, communes, and steel mills. The pur-pose is to keep the inmates informed of the progress of their country, to make them want to get out and take part.

Every prisoner receives a very thorough medical examination on entrance, and regular check-ups. Mr Wang said there had been no new case of venereal disease during the past three years. At the time of my visit the only cases were two men over fifty. The TB rate was fairly high, but he would not specify. A separate section of the prison is reserved as a sanatorium for tubercular prisoners.

Six months was the shortest sentence, Mr Wang said; the longest was life. This did not exactly tally with the statement made to me by Mr Wu Teh-peng, to the effect that the maximum sentence in China was twenty to twenty-five years. Perhaps, however, as in other countries, 'life sentences' are all commuted after a prolonged imprisonment.

I inquired what percentage of prisoners were second offenders.

'None,' said Mr Wang.

I record the remainder of this conversation exactly as I noted it down.

I asked, 'What happens to the family of a prisoner if he had been the only wage-earner?'

'Since the family has committed no crime it should not be punished. The family receives an allowance from the state.'

Commonest crime, both for men and women, is theft. When I asked about prostitution, he said no, a girl arrested for prostitution would not be sent here; in fact, would probably not be arrested at all, but would be referred for medical care and rehabilitation. At the time of liberation, he told me, Shanghai had many thousands of prostitutes; these were rounded up and sent to special centres for treatment and education.

'What are the means of rehabilitating, or reforming, prisoners?'

'Confession must be the first step. The prisoner must realize and fully accept that he has done wrong, or rehabilitation is impossible.'

'Are life sentences ever remitted?'

'Many. The policy is to remit sentences for good behaviour and upon evidence of a desire to take part in the country's efforts. The prisoner is then more useful outside than in. Some life-termers are released after only a few years.' Paroles were not allowed for harvest work, he told me, as they frequently are in Russia; but in case of family illness or bereavement a prisoner could go and visit his family.

'Do you have many prisoners,' I inquired, 'who were under death sentence and are now serving out commuted sentences?'

'Several dozen.'

'Prisoners sentenced to death,' I said, 'pending this two-year stay of execution — would you think the majority give satisfactory indications of reform?'

'There are exceptionally few who do not reform before the expiration of the stay.'

That I could readily believe.

'What about society's attitude towards the ex-prisoner?' I inquired, 'Does this make a problem in rehabilitation?'

He said he thought there were no such difficulties.

That night I wrote in my journal:

Prisons are appalling places; symbols of society's failure, or, more accurately, symbols of ignorance. Future generations will one day look back on our prisons — Shanghai, London, Alcatraz — with shocked wonder at our insensibility, just as we look back to the days (not so long ago) when children could be publicly flogged for stealing a penny or men could be hanged for stealing a sheep.

It was lunch-time as we passed through the great main cell-block — the men were back from the workshops, locked in their cells. They sat on their haunches, hardly looking up as we went by, apathetic, lost. How it reminded me of those English jails — the locking and unlocking of every door as we passed through from one section to another! England has left a really bad part of her here in Shanghai as a legacy!

They must, of course, have been up against a far tougher type of prisoner here in this one-time 'wickedest city in the world', than in any other part of China — this city which was a kind of Mecca for every pimp, drug-trafficker, and gangster in Asia.

But the most startling and, I should like to think, the most hopeful of today's impressions was the contrast between the old laggards, the left-overs, and the young chief warden. And the most impressive thing about him was not his level-headed, unsentimental approach to his job, or even his youth, but that to him these wretched creatures behind the bars were still men.

Peking prison stands at the end of Self-Renewal Street.

It too is an old structure, built about the turn of the century. The prevailing impression is one of drabness: old grey buildings, dusty courtyards, vegetable patches heavy with dust, and a few trees with drooping leaves in the inner courts. But compared with Shanghai, this prison is a gem. There are no guards in sight except a soldier at the gate with a rifle and another on a distant tower. Inside, I saw that the guards were unarmed and the doors unlocked. In fact, the old iron doors had been taken from the cells and replaced by glass doors, and there were casement windows, many standing wide open, where obviously, at some earlier date, had been barred windows.

Even I could have escaped from this prison.

Over tea and cigarettes with Mr Wang Chien, the vice-warden, I learned there were 1,800 prisoners, 100 of whom were women. This, he said, was the only prison in the municipal area of Peking, which now includes seven and a half million people.

Commonest crime for both men and women is 'corruption', which is defined as 'converting public property to private use', and the familiar crimes against persons. Forty per cent are in for counter-revolutionary crimes (espionage, assassination, sabotage, etc.), but these prisoners are not regarded or treated differently from the others. 'Counter-revolutionary,' Wang explained, would mean those who have performed definite acts against the state. For those who have merely spoken against the state, there is no punishment, though such people may be recommended for some sessions of political instruction. But an overt act is necessary before opposition becomes a criminal matter. Incitement of others *is* considered an overt act; but apart from this, voicing hostile views is not a matter for punishment. (Here is a subtle distinction upon which the United States Supreme Court has expended a good many hundreds of pages of argumentation.) I did not press the point with Mr Wang, but went on, as I had in Shanghai, to the problems of rehabilitation.

Here, too, confession, the inner recognition of fault, was emphasized as the necessary first step.

'The prisoner must realize the dangers to his country resulting from his criminal action, and must understand that his punishment is deserved. This lays the foundation for the prisoner to accept reform as a conscious process.

'The prisoner is educated in current affairs so that he can understand the significance of national and international developments, so that he can realize the strength of the socialist state. To help him to perceive the great advances being made, to enable him to compare the old with the new, he is taken on field trips to communes and factories, he hears discussions by leaders and workers from outside.

'The purpose of this stage is to make the prisoner realize that labour is a glorious matter and can create a national wealth which he should be sharing, and in the building of which he should be taking part.' Here Mr Wang quoted Article 4 of the Labour Reform Code: ' "*To carry out a policy combining punishment and surveillance with ideological reform and to integrate productive labour with political education.*" '

He went on to explain that the prison routine, which requires each inmate to put in eight hours a day in one of the prison workshops, not only inculcates regular work-habits, but guarantees that the prisoner, when he gets out, will have acquired some useful skill. Afterwards there would be no problem of his getting employment. And because there was a general understanding of the policy of reform through labour, there would be no special stigma attached to his having been in prison. The manager of the factory or commune where he went to work would be informed of the prison term, but it would be up to the individual whether or not he informed his fellow-workers. Most do, Mr Wang thought. The prison keeps in touch with the progress of discharged prisoners.

'Not to look down on criminals is highly important,' the vice-warden declared. 'Reform is absolutely impossible if there is an atmosphere of moral condemnation and disapproval. It would only make it much more likely that he will become a criminal again.'

*

The general routine here was similar to that of the Shanghai prison, but much more relaxed, much fuller. There are radios in the workshops and living-quarters. The daily schedule for inmates would run something like this: eight hours' work, eight hours' sleep, two hours' study, one hour for cultural activities and recreation, five hours for meals, washing, resting, letter-writing, etc. There are arrangements for spare-time hobbies, as well as spare-time education. The prisoners have an amateur theatrical group. Women are allowed to mix with men at evening socials, which may be dances, performances by the theatre group, or films.

Prisoners have one complete day off every two weeks, which they can use in any way they wish.

Good behaviour is rewarded by a bonus in money, or a present of some kind, or by a citation on the good-behaviour notice-board. And, of course, parole or reduction of sentence by the court would be based on the behaviour record.

Bad behaviour may be punished by warnings or a citation on the bad-behaviour notice-board. Genuine wrongdoers may be sent to 'meditate on their misdeeds' in solitary for a few hours, or for as long as a week. No physical punishment is permitted.

Mr Wang said, 'We only very rarely meet here cases of prisoners who do not respond to education and reform. We can recommend to the courts that the sentences of such prisoners be lengthened. But this almost never occurs.

'After the confession stage,' he continued, 'and the understanding of the need to reform, they hardly ever try to escape. Those who do — well, nearly always they will be sent back by their own families.'

I noted in my journal at the end of that day:

Given the ideological framework, and the emphasis on 're-education and reform through proper understanding of Marx-Leninism', the prison apparently is doing its job, with a real attempt at humane treatment. Obviously the thing to do if convicted is to *go along*, to become a model student and get the hell out. And perhaps this *going along*, even though begun for an ulterior motive, is the way they catch the individual within the collective assumptions on which everything is based. There would be tremendous relief, particularly for certain types of neurotics, in abandoning themselves to authority, as in the army. But what of those whose neurosis drives them to separateness, whose satisfactions derive from the need to be in rebellion? There must be a hard core of *unreformables*. What becomes of them?

And what about this 'confession' business? It seems absurdly unreal to me (just ask an American or British prisoner to 'confess' and hear him tell you where to put yourself!). What methods do they use to secure them? I'm probably falling into that old, old error of trying to understand the inner processes of another people in terms of my own. If my theory is right, that the greatest psychological pain for a Chinese is to feel himself outside the group, then 'confession' perhaps is the door that is offered to reacceptance, reinclusion, an end to an intolerable isolation. Who knows?

So many questions remain unanswered.... Still, it is ironic, particularly for one who formerly put in as many hours as I did over the years agitating, with so many others, and with such notable lack of success, for the humane treatment of prisoners, for the removal of the moral stigma of imprisonment as a pre-condition for rehabilitation — ironic to find these very principles being extolled, and to some extent practised, by prison authorities under the 'inhumane' regime of Red China.

XXI

The Mass Line in Education

WITHIN its boundaries, China includes one-quarter of the human race, probably more than a quarter of the world's children, and certainly more than a quarter of the educational problems of the world.

Consider the China of eleven years ago. A population of over half a billion people, 80 per cent or more illiterate; a land predominantly agricultural, but with almost no schools in its rural areas; a nation with virtually no industry, little technological or managerial experience; with skilled labour, teachers, professional people in desperately short supply. Consider further that this nation had been devastated by a prolonged civil war and a seven-year military occupation by Japan. Consider a country in which disease and illness were rampant, in which the number of trained doctors was so few that there was only one for every 25,000 people, and where a province, Sinkiang, twice as big as France, had only fifteen; consider a people so close to starvation that (according to foreign estimates) 20,000 bodies were picked up each year from the streets of Shanghai alone — adults and children who had gone under, who had succumbed in the relentless struggle for survival.

And consider, finally, the determination of this country to shed this nightmare past and thrust forward, swiftly, into the twentieth century.

That, in brief, was China's educational problem.

The segments of the problem interlocked. To support an expanding educational programme, a higher national output was needed. But increasing national output depended on 'raising the level', with respect to skills and technical training, of the labour force. And raising the level of the labour force depended on teaching workers to read and write. Here was a veritable Chinese puzzle.

The first segment of this closed circle against which the new regime launched a massive attack was, as might have been expected, illiteracy. Actually this campaign began in the North-west and the border regions several years before the Communists captured Peking. By 1960, the year of my second visit to China, the spare-time schools for adults, tens of thousands of them, and the new network of schools for children were showing results. The Ministry of Education expected 130 million people (10 million more than the population of the United States in 1940!) to pass literacy tests during 1960; and estimated that by the end of that year illiteracy would be down to just over 30 per cent (mostly people too old to learn).

A factory manager in Harbin told me, with a sense of pride, and before he mentioned productivity figures or quality of his output, that his factory would be able to 'liquidate illiteracy' among its employees that very month.

On hundreds of factory and commune notice-boards I saw posted the poems and letters of men and women who had just passed their literacy tests.

I met a commune manager in the Yellow River Valley, running an enterprise which involved seventy-five hundred families and millions of dollars' worth of plant and equipment, who had himself learned to read and write only a few years previously at the age of thirty-two.

All this, of course, is at an elementary level. The literacy test, for urban areas, is generally based on knowledge of two thousand characters; for rural regions it varies between twelve hundred and fifteen hundred. With twelve hundred characters it is possible to read simple newspapers.

Literacy, the means of communication, is the essential tool which the people of China, or of any other country in the world, need for their advancement. With it, change is possible; without it, almost nothing is possible. China today can no longer be classed among the illiterate nations of the world. I noticed that even the pedicab drivers of Peking, formerly among the most ignorant people, today invariably were able to read instructions or directions I had had written out for me.

Next to 'liquidation of illiteracy', in order of importance, comes the provision of universal primary-school education. Target date, according to Mr Shiu Fang-chien of the Ministry of Education, with whom I spent a long evening going over these matters, is 1962; and he thinks they will achieve it. The target date for universal secondary education (that is, to college-entrance level) is 1967; and he rather doubts whether they can achieve that. 'But if we don't get there by 1967,' he said, 'we will get there soon afterwards.'

I learned from Mr Shiu that the total enrolment of primary-school pupils in the best year prior to 1950 was slightly more than twenty-three and a half million. Enrolment in 1960 was ninety-one million, an increase of almost 300 per cent. Secondary-school population during the same period has increased from something less than two million to thirteen and a half million (a 575 per cent increase). In spite of this advance, grammar-school education in China is still a privilege reserved for the more fortunate; but the 'fortune' hinges not at all on financial affluence, but on ability and on geographical location. A large percentage of city children go to grammar school, but a very small percentage of rural children do, because of lack of teachers and schools. And as for enrolment in institutions of higher learning, it has risen from 110,000 to 810,000 — 636 per cent increase. It is no longer one Chinese out of nine thousand, as it was fifteen years ago, who has the opportunity to go to college or university, but one in eight hundred. This figure is still very low. Entrance is determined by ability alone. Competition is usually stiff and the eagerness and quality of the students is correspondingly high.

It is probable that no country in the world is devoting so high a proportion of its national revenue to education as China. In 1960, 8,620 million yuan (£1,293 million), or 12·3 per cent of the national budget, was allocated to education and health, and of this 6,400 million yuan was for education. The proportion of the national budget in 1960 spent on education and health was 48 per cent *more* than that spent on China's military expenditure. And this is only *national* expenditure. More schools are run and paid for by local communities, communes, and factories than by the Ministry of Education.

My own observations tended to confirm this. In almost every factory I visited I went through factory schools, which would be offering classes for adults all the way from ABC and first-form arithmetic to college-level engineering. The same was even more true in the communes, though here the schools were generally of primary or secondary level. In

Honan Province I visited a large but quite poor commune, all of whose children were going to primary school. Sixteen of the schools were national; twenty-eight were run by the commune — and this meant providing the buildings and paying the teachers. Like others I met, the chairman told me he had learned to read and write only a few years ago.

'We believe that communes have a three-fold purpose: to develop agriculture, to develop industry, and to develop education. We have accepted education as part of our purpose.'

What about the quality of education? Undoubtedly this varies enormously and is much more advanced in the cities than in the country. The primary schools I saw were lively, gay, and apparently a source of great enjoyment both for the children and for the teachers. Some of the secondary schools I visited, however, seemed to me rather stricter in their discipline than we should expect to see in America, and more on a par with English schools. In grammar-school science classes I saw in Peking and elsewhere the laboratory equipment and the quality of the experiments and demonstrations being conducted were also comparable to their English counterparts.

There is a strong trend towards science and technology. But at least one foreign language, and some art and literature, are required of secondary students. Most grammar schools offer both Russian and English as a foreign language, and the child is free to make his own choice. I was told the proportion learning English a few years ago was higher than it is now, but that it is still about the same as the number learning Russian. The Chinese fully realize that their language is a difficult one for foreigners, and the authorities hope that one day all Chinese children will be bilingual.

The standard grammar-school-level curriculum includes thirty-six weeks a year of class-work, four weeks for revision and examination, and three weeks on some work-project. There are eight weeks set aside for holidays. And one week is kept free — it may be granted as holiday or used for special study. The six-day week itself is divided into six or seven fifty-minute daily periods. Chinese school officials believe that children should not spend more than eight hours a day studying, and this includes homework.

From secondary level on, military training is included. All boys are taught drill and marksmanship. Propaganda and patriotism probably occupy a larger share of the school day than they do in the United States or Western Europe. In an earlier chapter I have described a kindergarten where the teachers discussed American imperialism with their four-year-olds. And Dr T. F. Fox, in his article in *The Lancet* (see Part Seven, Chapter 27), expressed doubt as to the wisdom, for internes and doctors, of devoting as many hours a week to political studies as he found them doing.

It is not only a question of taking time away from other studies. The danger, it seems to me, is that an undue emphasis on patriotism, on understanding and adhering to the correct political line, will create an atmosphere where conformity will become more important than originality or independence.

This, I think, may constitute a serious danger for Chinese education, particularly in the years ahead.

On the other hand, it would be impossible to mistake the intellectual renaissance taking place today in China. It is nothing less than a cultural explosion. One of the problems I heard alluded to by every educator I talked with was that students, particularly at college level, studied too hard. They were not allowing time enough for sports and recreation, and this, in the view of school authorities, will hamper all-round development, and would, in the long run, lower intellectual achievement as well.

At Peking University the head librarian told me they were considering closing the library on Sundays in an effort to get the students out of doors. While it may be difficult for Americans to view this very seriously, the problem itself is intensely revealing. School for the Chinese does not mean football, or flirting in the park, or ski-trips. It means a chance to catch a grip on life. They throw themselves with passion into the business of learning. And this is not propaganda from the Ministry of Education: I have watched it myself.

It is difficult for most of us to imagine even remotely the *hunger* that exists for education in countries in which, until recently, educational opportunities for most people were denied. This is not only true of China, but of Asia, Africa, and Latin America. Education, to millions of people, is the tool, the magic key that opens new worlds, new and undreamed-of opportunities. For an adult to learn to read is, as one

Chinese said to me, 'like a blind man being granted sight'. The government of China, by providing the organization and leadership to make this expansion of education possible, has, in this respect alone, won the allegiance of tens of millions of people in China.

*

One aspect of China's educational programme is the emphasis on productive work as part of the learning process. This applies at every level. On my visits to the communes I several times ran into classes of small children, with their teachers, busily engaged in 'assisting' the communal farmers. These were children from city schools, having a go at pig-raising or poultry-breeding. Many secondary schools have established their own workshops which produce and market such things as fabrics, machine parts, condensers, preserved fruit.

Peking University is humming with such enterprises. In addition, the students are sent out for regular stints on the farms or in industry. At the Conservatory of Music I was told that these work-periods provide an essential link between the art of the young musicians and the needs of the peasants and workers. When I visited an Academy of Folk-Opera in Kiangsu province, the director assured me that some of their richest discoveries in folk-music were being made by students at work in remote country communes.

The concept of work-in-learning and learning-through-work is the present 'mass line' of Chinese education.

It is not, it seems, a line that was easily arrived at. During the early 'fifties there took place a debate of long duration and considerable asperity among pedagogues and government officials over the general direction of education. One group favoured a crash programme which would turn out specialized technicians through cram courses (similar to the classes developed in England and the United States during the war, in which, for example, a student completely innocent of trigonometry, might learn the principles of air navigation in a couple of weeks). The other group favoured a longer-range programme aimed at 'all-round' development of versatile individuals, capable (in the words of Engels) 'of going over in sequence from one branch of production to another, depending on the requirements of society'. According to this view, the student must not only learn how to wind the armature, but must understand Ohm's law and the theory of electro-magnetic force.

By 1958, the 'year of the great leap forward', the second group had carried the field, and their position was made official in a report by Vice-Premier Lu Ting-yi, entitled, appropriately enough, 'Education Must Be Combined with Productive Labour'.

'We maintain,' said the Vice-Premier, 'that workers should be versatile in industrial production and peasants should be versatile in agricultural production; moreover, that workers should at the same time be peasants and peasants should be workers. We maintain that civilians should take up military service and retired military men should go back to production. We maintain that cadres should participate in physical labour and productive workers in administration. All these propositions are already being put into practice gradually. Measures such as these which involve both the division of labour and change of work conform to the needs of society. They are more reasonable than the division of labour under the capitalist system. They not only increase production, but enable the state to carry out reasonable readjustment of the productive forces when this becomes socially necessary, without causing social upheaval.'

*

We can catch a glimpse here of the virtuosity with which Chinese leadership has adapted a rather abstract programme (that of Engels), formulated a hundred years ago in Western Europe, to the needs of China in 1960.

The 'mass line', however, offers even greater advantages than mobility of personnel. It points a road, through education, to national unity.

For many centuries the curse of China has been its dual division, by geography and by caste. The geographic division separated north from south, east from west, rural from urban. The caste division separated the scholar from the landowner and the merchant, with their satellite bureaucracies, and both from the vast majority of the Chinese people, the peasants. But above all, it separated the hand from the brain.

Intellectual activity was the privilege of the upper caste. Work was the burden of the lower. Thus for a scholar to pick up a wrench or a screw-driver was to demean himself; for a peasant to pick up a book was to overstep the laws of nature. Every feudal society has generated such a separation. The relics of it may still be found in Latin America, even in Western Europe. But in China the separation had acquired the rigidity of centuries.

When one bears this background in mind, the 'mass line' in education acquires a new perspective. A great deal of criticism has been directed by Western writers to this mixing of education and physical work. Stanley Rich, an American Broadcasting Company correspondent in Hong Kong, for instance, wrote with horror of the Chinese attempts to wipe out the distinctions between mental and manual work, between peasants and intellectuals. Mr Rich (in the *New Republic*, January 5th, 1959) draws the conclusion that 'the worker ... is stripped of his technical identity. He may be a teacher one day, a farmer the next, a steel-smelter the next.'

But this, surely, is precisely what Western sociologists have so often called for, a move away from the increasing and deadening specialization of our way of life, which tends to limit human beings to an ever narrower range of experience.

Dr Joseph Needham, of Cambridge University (in a letter to the *New Statesman*, January 31st, 1959), takes a different view after seeing Chinese education for himself:

In China in the olden days there was a great traditional aloofness of the scholars ... from manual work – perhaps nowhere in the world was this more marked. Now the Chinese people are deter-mined to overcome it. There may be exaggerations in particular times and places due to excessive enthusiasm, but the movement is fundamentally sound.

All cultures and civilizations have suffered from this divorce of theory and practice. But the greatest thinkers, experimenters, and artists have always seen that only when the manual and the mental (or the intellectual) are combined in one individual's experience can mankind reach its highest stature. The combination not only brings true knowledge of Nature but also deeper sympathy with

217

those members of society whose contribution must still for some time be primarily manual.... To think of manual work as a humiliating punishment is to misunderstand utterly what the Chinese are doing.

XXII

Peking University

PROFESSOR WANG SHÊ-CHEN, vice-dean of Peking University, and I were sitting in one of the smaller houses on the campus. The room smelled faintly of incense, and the light filtered through the green foliage of the bamboo outside the window.

Founded in 1898, the university was, for many years, a hotbed of radical activity. It was sparks from the campus that kindled the revolutionary fervour just after the First World War. Mao Tse-tung was an assistant in the library. Founders of the Chinese Communist Party studied and taught here, and Lu Hsun, later known as the Chinese Gorky, was a professor of literature during the early 'twenties.

Since 1952, Peking has been producing more graduates in technology and science than any other university in China. There is a liberal-arts school, but more than 70 per cent of the nearly 11,000 students are reading basic and theoretical science. The college of medicine and the department of agriculture were transferred to Peking Medical College and Peking Agricultural College after the nation-wide amalgamation in 1952.

The average age of students at entrance has gone down to eighteen, with the increase in secondary-school attendance. Students of the arts take a five-year course, science students a six-year one; those who show special ability can stay on for three years of research.

Women make up 20 per cent of the student body, a lower percentage than in teacher-training and medical colleges. There are three hundred foreign students from thirty countries.

Tuition, rooms, books, and medical care are free. Those who are able to afford it pay 12 yuan (£1 16s.) a month for food, those unable to do so receive a subsidy. Sixty per cent of the students get grants for food and clothing. The library they showed me contained over two million books but it is too small, and a new library is about to be completed.

The top salary for lecturers and professors is more than that of the general manager of a steel mill. Depending on seniority, salaries range from 62 to more than 300 yuan a month; the average is about 200 (£30).

There is a two-month stint at 'putting theory into practice' for students. Those reading chemistry, for example, spend their time at a chemical plant; a physics student will work in metallurgy or electronics. The second month can be spread out over the academic year, a few days at a time, depending on the student's schedule. Professors go for one month, the ailing or aged being excused.

I talked to a number of students as I wandered with Professor Wang around the campus, into the workshops, through the dormitories, and into the dining-hall. We were joined by a young student who was reading English — he had studied it since secondary school and now he had a chance to make use of it.

In one of the women's dormitories I found four girls having a late lunch. Their room was extremely simple: four stacked bunks, one chair, and one table by the window. It was neat and clean. There were a few pictures, one of a film star, and on the table some bright artificial flowers. The girls were in their second year, studying Chinese language and literature. In another room a girl wearing glasses was reading at a table. She told me she usually got up at half-past five, had her first lecture an hour later, and went to bed by half-past ten. She put in eight hours a day in lectures and study.

As we were on our way to one of the workshops, a volley ball bounced out across the path. My young friend knocked it over to me and I volleyed it back across the net. This seemed an enormous joke and they were still laughing about it when we walked on.

There were twenty large precision lathes all in operation in the workshop. One of the lathe operators, quite the prettiest girl I had seen in China, told me she was nineteen and not a student. She was a factory worker who, as she put it, helped to teach new students who had never done any mechanical work.

Strains of un-Chinese music grew louder as we went on. A band was tuning up in a wooden shack not far from the workshops. It was a terrific row: everyone seemed to be playing something different. When I appeared in the doorway everyone stopped except the bugler who, with his back to me, played lustily on. They told me they were practising a number called 'The Young Commune Worker'. In answer to my query about American jazz, they said emphatically, 'Never!'

Loudspeakers blared a message over the campus. It was a report on the accomplishments of students who had gone to work on a commune. I noticed a few couples strolling along hand in hand. Only the other night I had read an account by a recent Canadian visitor who declared that young Chinese regard such displays as 'decadent'.

As we passed the water-tower — built like a sham pagoda temple — and circled the lake in the late afternoon sunlight, I raised the question of freedom with Professor Wang. I told him that one of the things I was concerned about in China was the unanimity of thought: everyone thinking alike, talking alike. Any healthy society must make room for disagreement, and dissent should not be construed as disloyalty.

He hesitated before speaking. 'Our society makes room for the man who disagrees as long as he doesn't attack socialism and the government.'

'But that's just the point,' I said. 'There must be some people who disagree; why can't they express themselves?'

'Because this government is what the majority wants.'

'Majorities can be wrong. All advance comes from a few who don't like things as they are. After all, *your* revolution was led by dissenters.'

'You don't understand. You cannot realize what great changes and improvements have come to us. We know we are being led by those who have our interests at heart. Why should we want to attack them?'

'I don't say you should attack them. But you must acquire the habit of criticizing them. Your leaders today may be wise. But one day they will no longer be living. As you know, unwise people can attain leadership. What if you can't dissent then? This happened in Russia: no one was allowed to criticize Stalin, not even Khrushchev, until after Stalin was dead, and many terrible mistakes had been made. Why were people not allowed to point them out?'

'What about America?' he asked. 'What about Senator McCarth
and loyalty oaths? Isn't there hypocrisy in all the talk about freedom
in the United States?'

So it went on, round and round, alongside the lovely lake in the quiet
sunlight — not angry or defensive, but our minds never meeting be
cause our terms of reference and our vocabulary and concepts were so
different. And above all, I did not have behind me the spectre o
previous degradation, oppression, and hunger. Success brings its own
persuasion; and against the enormous fact of China's emergence into
self-respect and health and vigour I could see how my talk about
intellectual freedoms must appear to these young men as so much
chatter, an idle and rather profitless verbal game.

'Come and see China again in a few years' time,' Professor Wang told
me as he said goodbye, and added with a smile, 'perhaps you will be
convinced then that our system works.'

*

My visit to the university and my discussions there left me with some
mixed feelings. But what I did come away with was the picture of those
students' faces. This remained more vivid in my mind than anything
else. These were faces of happy people.

Never mind the buildings and the surroundings. Look at the human
material. There is a vitality and enthusiasm, as if life isn't long enough
for all that has to be done. Stand in the huge dining-hall, like an over
grown armoury, without tables or chairs, and watch the crowded little
knots standing and eating from bowls which will be rinsed under a tap
outside. Forget the drabness and look at these young people, and you
will begin to understand China.

'What are you studying, what do you want to be?'

Physics, language teacher, hydro-electric engineer, geologist ... the
answers would come quickly, all stated proudly and directly. How
many of them are sons and daughters of peasants, I wonder?

'Where do you want to work?' The answer, in different words, i
always the same: 'Wherever my country needs me most.'

At first this seemed to me naive and even perhaps a little insincere
But when I heard it many times I began to believe that they really

meant it. Again the desire for collective advance rather than personal gratification.

I did not know then that I would, before many months, hear another young voice, in a very different country: 'Ask not what your country can do for you, but what you can do for your country.'

XXIII

Long Live the Dancers

THERE is for me a ponderous, heavy-footed quality to the slogan 'mass line in education'. One thinks of an army moving over difficult terrain; gradually, by sheer force of numbers and determination, overwhelming the opposition. But China is a land in which there is always another surprise waiting. I thought I had understood the national education policies fairly well and had neatly enclosed them in my notes, until I visited the Conservatory of Music and the Peking Dance School.

This was like coming across a poem of Keats in the middle of a fifteen-hundred-page census report.

The discovery occurred purely by accident. No one had told me about either of these institutions beforehand.

One evening I happened to go to a performance of *Giselle* at a Peking theatre. While the dancing was good but relatively undistinguished, the music was exquisite. I could not see the players in the orchestra pit, but kept wondering who they were, whether some group of French or Czech or Russian musicians might be in town whom I had not heard about. I asked a friend sitting by me, and he said, 'Go and have a look.' And during the interval I did. Not only were the players Chinese, they were all teenagers! We always think Chinese children younger than they actually are; and these looked like twelve- or thirteen-year-olds, boys in neat white shirts and girls with ribbons in their hair. And here they were, re-creating that dated, stylized nineteenth-century French mood as if they had all just stepped off the Boulevard Saint-Michel.

I learned that they were students from the middle school attached to the Peking Conservatory of Music. And I made arrangements as soon as possible to visit it.

*

Miss Yi, a quiet, rather prim young woman (my first female interpreter), opened the magic casements for me one morning and we
stepped through a multi-coloured gate into the courtyard of the
Conservatory. At once we heard a variety of different instruments,
tuning up like a forestful of tropical birds at sunrise. The director met
us, led us about the buildings. The place was alive with music, swarm-
ing with youngsters. We opened doors at random, saw eager-faced girls
plucking hesitant notes from their violins or hard at work on piano-
fingering exercises. Everywhere groups were practising together — a
string quartet in the corridor, an orchestral section on the stair landing; even on the balcony of the auditorium the woodwinds were having
a practice session, while the cast of an opera got ready for a dress rehearsal
on the stage down below.

We stood at the back of the auditorium (brand-new, still not completely finished), watching the youngsters on stage. This opera, the
director told me, was one the students had composed themselves, and
were producing collectively, for their examinations. Girls were splash-
ing paint on stage-sets, an amateur electrician kept fussing with the
lights, they were raising and lowering the back-drop, just like any college
theatre in the States. A boy in dark shorts, apparently one of the com-
posers, was making vehement last-minute suggestions to several of the
young ladies of the cast.

The title of the opera, I learned, was *The Song of Youth*.

*

Even Calliope must have her facts and figures; and I sat down, after
our tour of the premises, with the director.

The study of Western music was practically non-existent in China;
the Conservatory is new since the change of government in 1949. They
now have 370 students in the Conservatory and 470 in an attached
middle school (grammar school). There is also a primary school under
the Conservatory's direction. These two lower schools, which are open
to children with special aptitude, provide, in addition to the regular
school curriculum, a musical training which prepares them for entrance
into the Conservatory.

As for the Conservatory itself, it has seven major departments:

Composition, Symphony, Conducting, Vocal, Theory and History, Piano, Folk and Chinese Classical Music.

Regardless of the field of specialization, every student spends a considerable amount of time on the folk and Chinese classical studies. There are also requirements in their school curriculum in literature, language, history, science, and the humanities.

Political instruction, the director told me, is considered an important part of the curriculum here, as in all other schools of China. Each pupil puts in six hours a week. How political instruction fits into the training of a musician, the director explained as follows:

In these courses a young person learns how to be a good servant of the people and not to work just for himself. This determination to use one's gifts for the benefit of others is further strengthened by trips made by the students to the factories and communes. They give performances and also share in the work. What kind of work they do would be governed by common sense: piano- and violin-players are not expected to ruin their hands by heavy work. It is generally considered that music itself is their contribution. Through close contact with workers and peasants, the students learn what kinds of music appeal to the masses. They themselves hear the local folk-music. Sometimes students and peasants compete with each other in singing contests. The students also help with musical instruction in local spare-time schools. Sometimes, in this way, fine new talents are discovered.

The visits are reciprocal. Groups of peasants or factory-workers are frequently invited to the Conservatory, to attend classes or performances or to give performances themselves.

All the students in the Conservatory (and almost 80 per cent of those in the middle school) are boarders. And they come from all over China. Entrance requirements are extremely high and competition is stiff. There is no charge for room or tuition. There is a payment of 12 yuan a month (£1 16s.) for food, but this is covered by the school if the student or his family cannot pay. Ability to pay is not a factor either in selection or retention of students at the Conservatory.

The director agreed with my criticism that the buildings, much older than the school, were not altogether suitable. They are making alterations and additions as rapidly as they can. Equipment seemed to me ample. They have more than three hundred pianos, a large number of these being imported, and several thousand musical instruments, both Western and traditional. What impressed me particularly was their library, which contains 80,000 volumes dealing with music, both theory and history; also 70,000 recordings of music from all over the world. Some 10,000 of these are European or American; but China is now producing its own L.P.s.

In its ten years of operation this Conservatory has already shown some notable results. (There are two other similar schools: one in Shanghai, one in Tientsin.) I mentioned earlier that on the night of my arrival in Peking I heard a throughly professional rendition of several selections of Western classical music by a full symphony orchestra. At the Russian Tchaikovsky Competition several years ago the pianist who was placed second to the American Van Cliburn was a nineteen-year-old graduate of the Peking Conservatory, Liu Shih-kun. I heard him here in Peking as soloist in the Schumann Memorial Concert, and there is no question of his excellence.

*

Even newer than the Conservatory of Music is the Peking School of Dance.

They have three hundred students, equally divided between boys and girls, housed (in this case) in a brand-new building, designed especially for the school. Organization and general curriculum are very similar to those of the Conservatory. Here, too, the pupils are selected by rigorous standards, including local recommendation and examinations. Some 80 per cent of the student body come from families of workers or peasants. Dance students receive substantial extra privileges. Their food rations are almost double the ordinary. Vacation trips home are paid for by the school, and parents visiting from distant areas are put up at the school. Tickets to musical and dance events are free. The rigorous competition makes it fairly certain that the students, once admitted, almost always prove satisfactory and complete their training; and this is highly fortunate, because they told me it costs the state thirteen times as much to train a dancer as it does to train an engineer!

Like the Conservatory, the dance school gives instruction both in Western and Chinese disciplines. One department of the school covers

Chinese folk-dancing, acrobatics, and theatre. The other includes Western ballet, foreign folk-dances, and the Chinese *ballet de deux*, which is based on Western classical dance.

I learned from the director that there are schools similar to this one in several cities.

During vacations, he told me, teachers and pupils both disperse to the mountains and villages of remote regions, to find stories and dances of the local people which haven't come to light before. 'We are rediscovering our national inheritance in folk-art,' he said, 'and adapting it to the new conditions. But we are anxious to draw from all sources, from our own traditions and from the dance-forms of other countries.'

As an example of the adaptation of folk-material, the director told me of a dance-drama just completed, *The Lotus Lantern*. This was based on an old story, common, with slight variations, to many different regions of China. But it had never before been danced. They worked out a choreography based on the traditional patterns of Hopei Province, took the main story line as told in Fukien Province, but incorporated anecdotes special to other districts. So the old folk-story, on the way to being forgotten, becomes a new national property.

After graduation most of the students go directly into performers' groups. But they also continue to teach. And the teachers continue to perform. They would consider it harmful to allow a separation between these two functions.

A dancer when just beginning draws a monthly salary of one hundred yuan, whether he is in a show or not. The wage goes up when he marries and has a family.

'Do experienced dancers earn a great deal more?' I asked.

Laughing, the director replied, 'We are only six years old so we haven't any dancers as experienced as that. The difference in pay is not very great.'

*

I spent many evenings, while I was in China, at performances of all kinds. China is bursting with theatrical, dance, and musical developments, and almost every city has its 'experimental' drama or dance group. There are more than four hundred and fifty opera schools scattered across the country, teaching traditional opera; and students in all these schools, as in the Conservatory and the School of Dance in Peking, receive room and tuition free.

Generally I found straight dramatic performances quite difficult because of language; and for traditional opera, which is the most popular form of entertainment, I have not been able to acquire much taste. But the new developments in ballet, and especially the dance-dramas, I have found very exciting. These are usually based on Chinese folk-stories, and the performers are learning to combine classical Chinese and Western ballet techniques, together with singing, in an extremely interesting way. One particular piece, *Maiden of the Sea*, seemed to me a superb work of art.

For a professional appraisal, however, of Chinese progress in the dance, I turn to an interview in *The Times* of March 6th, 1961, with Miss Mary Skeaping, English director of the Royal Swedish Ballet, which had just completed a Chinese tour.

'One of the nicest things for me personally,' said Miss Skeaping, 'was to meet Tai Ai-lien, whom I had not seen since she studied ballet and modern dance in London during the 'thirties.... Today she is Director of the Peking Dance School and a Deputy to the National People's Congress, which means (imagine!) that the dance has representation in Parliament!

'The Peking Dance School began in 1954 with Russian teachers. Now they have their own Chinese staff.... The course lasts for seven years. The ballet dancers have achieved a high standard of technique in the short time since they began. They have assumed the Russian school of dancing completely and it seems to suit them very well. The girls have beautiful, easy back and arm movements and high extensions. The boys perform the showy demi-character type steps brilliantly. Their *pas-de-deux* work is also very good. Among the ballets in the company repertoire is a full-length *Swan Lake* and *Le Corsair* which they dance to their own symphony orchestra.... Music and dance is very active and interesting in China.

'I saw a beautiful, completely successful, full-length ballet ... called *The Woodcutters*, produced by the Tientsin Light Opera Theatre. It had Western-type scenery with a Chinese flavour.... The costumes were entirely Chinese and very beautiful. The music combined Western and Chinese instruments in the way they are developing everywhere with great success.

'A fair scene in this ballet included a Chinese circus which was superb, with delightful folk-dances. They have wonderful folk-dances, and are doing fine work collecting them. Indeed, they are basing much of their new musical development on this rich folk-tradition and seem likely to reap a big reward before long.'

*

I wrote in my journal, after returning from the visit to the dance school:

One of the most delightful experiences I have had in Peking! It gave me the same *lift* as the Conservatory. Here were children, eager, healthy, intensely interested, being given what seemed first-class training.... I was particularly struck by a group of teen-age girls going through their basic skills. They had had about five years' training. The control, the grace, the 'projection' seemed superb. They work very hard. The eagerness and a kind of innocent fresh-ness of these girls was delightful. I asked one girl of twelve to pose for a photograph, which she did with neither coyness nor shyness. They carried themselves already like experienced artists, and as a matter of fact had frequently danced in choruses for performances of the Peking Ballet.

But perhaps the most remarkable sight I saw this morning was a group of boys and girls studying Spanish dances. What gripped my attention at once was the young instructor; he was twenty-two, Chinese, but Russian-trained. I would have sworn he was Spanish, and he *was* Spanish in this classroom. By sheer volatility of feeling, he communicated the Spanishness of these steps to his group of young Chinese. It was an extraordinary and quite wonderful ex-perience to see this man live within these traditional movements, and from *inside*, not just by technique.

The students had not yet quite caught it — perhaps they never would — so alien, so extravagantly extrovert (for them). But it was scarcely possible to watch them while the teacher was on stage — this was an outstanding dancer in any language....

LONG LIVE THE DANCERS

I felt that here, as at the Conservatory, I had seen something of the very best of the new China, for me more immediately moving than the march of tractors off the assembly line. Numerically, of course, these two schools are small. But the standards are high; their zest infectious. And the Chinese authorities say that their aim is eventually to provide the chance of a musical education for every child in China who shows a gift for it.... So, long live the dancers and singers, on both sides of the great wall!

XXIV

Polonius and the Organization Man

'FROM now on your pen will be your weapon. Take as good care of it as a soldier does of his gun. See that your gun is always aimed at the enemy; take care that it never hurts your own comrades.' This piece of advice (according to an article in the *Peking Review* for January 13th, 1961) had been offered by the party organizer of a Shanghai steel mill to a young steelworker, who, having shown promise as a writer, was about to embark upon the high seas of literature. This was several years ago, and the young man took the advice to heart and is now one of China's best-selling novelists. His name is Hu Wan-chun, and I had a long talk with him while I was in Shanghai. But before we come to that, let me note that several centuries earlier another piece of advice was offered to a young man about to set forth on an equally perilous journey: 'To thine own self bè true,' said Polonius to Laertes, 'and it must follow, as the night the day, thou canst not then be false to any man.'

Here, in few words, is a central precept of the Renaissance, which became in turn the ethic of the man-of-letters of the Protestant Reformation, and of the 'enlightened' revolutions of the eighteenth and nineteenth centuries. Thomas Jefferson would have subscribed to this, and so would Walt Whitman; and probably the majority of writers in the Western world of 1961 would be willing to claim it as their own.

It stands in apparently direct opposition to the ethic stated by the Communist organizer.

For Polonius, truth can only be discovered by the individual. There can be no vicar. That which is right is what *my* conscience tells me; that which is true is what *my* reason recognizes. It would be impossible for Polonius to say, 'Take care that your pen never hurts your comrades,' because he foresees that it may be necessary to deny his comrades. He may be obliged to go to the stake declaring that (in his judgment) the earth does *not* stand at the centre of the universe and the Pope, after all, is fallible.

On the other hand, it would have been equally impossible for the Communist organizer to have said to the young writer, Hu Wan-chun, 'To thine own self be true ... ' because he does not believe that truth is to be found within 'thine own self'. A truth, and the discovery of truth, does not come from reliance on dubious, subjective feelings, but from a study of objective facts.

The same issue of the *Peking Review* attributes the following comment to Hu Wan-chun himself:

> Many people have asked me what I have done to improve my writing techniques and what is the 'secret' of my creative writing. I have always answered: technique is important; but what is more important is a proletarian world-outlook and mastery of the ideological weapon of Marxism-Leninism.

This sounds forbiddingly sloganistic and dogmatic. We must remember, however, that by *Marxism-Leninism* the Chinese Communist would understand something like '*a scientific view of man's existence and history*'. Thus truth is to be approached through a study of history and man's response to his environment, which, by definition, can never be complete, and which will always appear as the culmination of the efforts of many generations. It cannot be determined individually; but it can be understood and *acknowledged* by the individual. Once he has grasped the driving force and recognized the necessary direction — classless society emerging at last from millennia of class struggle — then he can achieve his own freedom through affiliation; through labouring to speed the advent of the coming synthesis. Here is a purported reconciliation of two generally irreconcilable elements: freedom for the individual, *plus* a theory of historical development, a process which can be delayed but never reversed. In this combination of history determined by law, and the notion of revolutionary activity in which the individual can participate, lies a large part of the enormous world-appeal of Marxism. Dimitrov, on trial, virtually certain of his own execution, could still yell triumphantly from the dock, 'The wheel of history slowly moves on to the ultimate, inevitable goal of communism! That certainly transcends and justifies his fate as an individual. He, too, can go to the stake, if need be; that is unimportant; but, unlike Polonius, he can never deny his comrades without destroying the meaning of his own existence.

*

To return now to Mr Hu Wan-chun.

If we take the trouble to recast his words into more familiar terms, deleting the (for us) highly-charged adjective *proletarian*, we arrive at this rather formidable statement:

'In creative writing, technique is important; but what is more important is a world-outlook based upon a scientific view of man's existence and history.'

Even this would scarcely appeal to Polonius, who would defend *individual conscience* against any scientific theory of history; and might even deny the notion of a direction in history altogether. Before we applaud too loudly, however, it will be well to note that modern Westerners may find themselves, in practice, closer to the position of Hu Wan-chun than to that of Polonius. *To thine own self be true* epitomizes what David Riesman describes as the *inner-directed* man; but Riesman, and many contemporary scholars, regard the *inner-directed* man as a vanishing species, in the United States at least. He is being replaced, they tell us, by the *other-directed*, the *organization*, man.

Mr Hu Wan-chun, as I can testify from my talk with him, is also an organization man.

*

I met Hu Wan-chun at the headquarters of the Writers' Association in Shanghai. This was a palatial building with panelled rooms, wide staircases, spacious gardens. It had been, I learned, the private home of a Shanghai capitalist. Did the Writers' Association confiscate the building? I asked. Far from it. They were renting it from the capitalist himself, for sixteen hundred yuan a month.

As for Mr Hu, he is clearly one of the rising stars among writers. At thirty-one he is rich by Chinese standards. He wears silk shirts, fine new shoes, speaks humbly in an assured sort of way. Mr Hu's is a veritable Jack London story of success.

Son of a steamboat-hand and a maidservant, he went to work when he was thirteen as a labourer in the steel mills. By the time he was twenty-one he was still illiterate, could barely read the daily newspaper. But as an activist in the Shanghai Number 2 steel mill, he was appointed press correspondent, a job which he could carry out only by filing his dispatches verbally with the newspaper reporters. This aroused his determination to master reading and writing.

He began sending out short stories, finally selling one entitled *Repairs at the Rolling Mill*, an account of some workers who gave up their New Year's holiday to get a damaged rolling mill back in operation ahead of schedule. Mr Hu's fellow-workers liked this story, which inspired them to work still harder for socialism. The party organization now pushed Hu Wan-chun forward. He was sent to special cadre-training classes. He was put in touch with established writers. Other stories rolled from his pen, bearing such titles as *The Man Who Works for an Ideal*, *On the Way to Work*, and *Red Flag*.

'His work is hugely popular,' says the *Peking Review*, 'not least because of the sure touch in the way he deals with everyday reality.... All of Hu's stories have been closely linked with the current political battle. *Key*, which deals with the unmasking of a counter-revolutionary, was written during the campaign to weed out under-cover counter-revolutionary elements. *Youth* tells about the dedication of a man's youthful years to the service of his country: it was written to educate our young people in communist ideals. This topicality has trained Hu to be a rapid writer. During the big leap forward which began in 1958, life in China moved with exceptional rapidity, and many activities kept Hu busy; nevertheless, he has squeezed out the time to write eighty-five pieces ... totalling some 400,000 words. Hu lives the life of his time with an infectious zest. The more stirring life is, the more prolific is his pen.'

Mr Hu told me that he is attached now, as a writer, to the steel mill where he once worked as a labourer. There has been an immense upsurge of writing in China, he said. Nearly every factory has its writing group. Many publish their own magazines. His job (apart from writing about steelworkers himself) is to help the younger writers, to participate

with them in discussions and writers' circles, and to criticize thei
material.

He is paid, he explained, by the Shanghai Writers' Association. Eacl
member draws a monthly salary of one hundred yuan, more if th
family needs it. The money is not regarded as an advance. For a filn
scenario dealing with three generations of a steelworker's family, h
received thirty-five hundred yuan, which he offered to return to th
Writers' Association. They refused it.

This struck me as an extremely interesting organization.

'How does one become a member?' I asked.

'By election,' Mr Hu said.

'Election by whom?'

'By the Secretary's Department of the Association.'

'And what makes a person eligible?'

'Any writer who has had a piece published is eligible. Membership i
not open to amateurs or beginners. But if you publish just one article
provided it has a sound influence on the readers, then you would b
acceptable. Some publish as many as two or three books and neve
become members of the Association.'

'I see,' I said. 'And what if a writer, after he has become a member
writes a book which does not have a sound influence on the readers –
is he thrown out?'

Mr Hu said he was not. No one could be dismissed from the Associa
tion. 'Some members,' he added, 'have written only one good piec
and nothing of value since, but they are still members. No writer ca
always be good.'

I inquired about royalties and learned that this system is based partl
on word-count, partly on sales. He cited, by way of example, one of hi
own novels that ran to 180,000 words. First edition was 20,000 copies
for which he received three thousand yuan. The second printing wa
60,000 copies and he received two thousand yuan. The book is stil
earning royalties. Average first printing, he told me, is 20,000. But th
Song of Youth (one of China's best-sellers) started with a first run o
400,000 copies.

I asked if it were not true that writers were enormously better off tha
steelworkers.

He agreed that they were.

'There is a move on to reduce the royalty given to writers,' he said. One author recently earned 140,000 yuan for a single novel; it is now thought that writers ought to lower their scale somewhat. The purpose of writing,' he stated, 'is not to make money, but to help the people understand what they are working for.'

*

I spent another afternoon with a general secretary of a chapter of the Writers' Union, who came to my hotel in Wuhan. (In some towns they are called 'Associations', in others 'Unions'.) The official, Mr Han Pei-chun, was a somewhat nervous individual who chain-smoked and kept his foot jogging at high speed throughout our two-and-a-half-hour talk. He fanned himself with compulsive haste. I gathered that his job entailed a good deal of pressure.

'There's so much going on in China,' said Mr Han, 'no matter how many writers we had, we couldn't cover it all. There is absolutely no dearth of material, it is bursting all around us every day. We pay the expenses of any member who wants to travel to get local material. Our books are read by workers and peasants and what we write must sound real to them. We must live with the workers and peasants to feel their life and to get the true story, otherwise they would reject what we write.

'Of course, writers have to do their share of political study, too. Before a writer is accepted into the Wuhan Writers' Union, he must have shown himself ready to reflect the ideals of China in his writing. For this, personal experience is not enough. All writers must study Marxism-Leninism and the works of Mao Tse-tung, and must raise the level of their political understanding. Only thus,' he said, 'can they write with more sensation.' ('Sensation' was the rendering of the interpreter.)

'Writers must also learn from our culture of old. Everything they write must be acceptable to Chinese readers, must reflect China and the Chinese style. But neither must they neglect their knowledge of other countries.'

'What foreign authors do they generally read?'

'Shakespeare,' said Mr Han. 'They read a great deal of Shakespeare. And Schiller, Ibsen, Gorky, Turgenev.'

'Any contemporary English or American writers?'

'Certainly. Many different ones. Of course, many of our writers have been to college and have studied world literature.'

As it was clear that Mr Han was not too well informed about modern Western writing, I offered a question on Chinese folk-traditions, which he more readily took up.

'The Writers' Union,' he said, 'is encouraging our members to go out and discover these traditions for themselves. We want them to scatter into all parts of the country to discover not only the old stories, but the living poets and story-tellers of those distant regions. Sometimes members of the Musicians' Union go with the writers. The musicians transcribe the tunes, and the writers record the words. In this way thousands of ancient songs and ballads are being preserved. We are rediscovering traditional opera, too; that's a most important branch of our work. The people love to see performances of these old operas. But the Kuomintang paid no attention to all this,' he added. 'Many wonderful things have been lost.'

*

My discussion with Mr Han ended, I am sorry to record, on a note of disharmony.

I raised the question of the writer's freedom to write as he wished without being bound by the tenets of an official philosophy. Some of the greatest writing, I pointed out, had been in protest against existing conditions. Writers are the conscience of the people and must be free to criticize.

Mr Han responded at great length, and to start with, at least, we both exercised considerable restraint. His answer, in general terms, went as follows:

'It is difficult for Marxists and non-Marxists to find common ground on this subject. You have your world view, we have ours. Ours is that writers must deal with the world as it is, they must reflect the realities of our time. We in China have come through a vast revolution. The job of writers is to help to root out remnants of old ways of thinking. It isn't a question of freedom to "write as one pleases", it is a question of expressing the national desire to build a society in which there will be equality between people and in which everyone works for the benefit of all, rather than for himself alone. Such a change cannot take place easily. We have many who still hanker for the old, exploitive days. But if you had known the horror of life in pre-liberation China, you would not now be speaking as you do of "freedom". There was no freedom of any kind then. Today there is the freedom to live. And our writers are free to write what they feel, provided they accept the basic concepts of our new society. Why, if you told members of our Writers' Union that they were not free, they would laugh in your face! This is something bourgeois writers cannot understand! The fundamental question remains: *Is their work loved by the masses?*'

I thought I had him there.

'Many great writers were not *popular*,' I said. 'What of Marx himself? His works were not even read or understood by the masses, let alone loved.'

'It is true that Marx was ahead of his time,' Mr Han replied, 'but if the masses had been sufficiently educated to read him, they would have understood and loved his works.... '

'What suffocates me,' I burst out, 'is the universal approval, the monolithic unanimity with which everyone talks and thinks in China today. Surely it is the duty of writers to raise the level of intellectual exchange, to inquire, to dissent, to disapprove if need be, not always to speak the acceptable words.... '

Our argument continued for a long while, each of us repeating himself, neither one really meeting the thought of the other. It thus ceased to be a discussion, and I will close my account of it here, allowing myself (naturally) the last word.

Mr Han, to me, personified the weakness of the writers' position in China today. In many ways writers are being encouraged. They are urged to step forward out of the ranks of industrial and commune workers. They are offered financial security, prestige, opportunity for study, even considerable freedom in choice of material. But always the proviso remains in the background: their work must have that certain 'sound influence on the readers'. And who is to judge the influence? And who is to turn thumbs up or thumbs down when it comes to 'electing' new members into this marvellous club which is the Writers' Union? If I were a Chinese writer, I think I would not care to have Mr

Han as arbiter of my destiny. This, despite the fact that I felt him to be honest, devoted to his work, thoroughly efficient — only a little too official, too humourless. And perhaps, like some of the writers Mr Hu Wan-chun had spoken of, a bit too well paid, at least by contrast with the mass of China's peasants and workers. What he was doing wasn't as *good* as that; it couldn't have been....

I accompanied the general secretary down to the front door — at least I could say goodbye politely — and he climbed into a new, copper-green, chauffeur-driven Austin which was waiting at the kerb. We shook hands, but between us there was a wide gulf of non-understanding.

*

Mr Han was a bureaucrat, and these are to be found on both sides of the great wall. In his presentation of the writer's role he was faithfully reflecting the official outlook of the government and Communist Party. Thus at the Third Congress of Chinese Literary and Art Workers, held in July when I was in China, the vice-chairman of the All-China Federation of Literature and Art Circles, Chou Yang, set forth the task of artists and writers as follows:

> Literary and art workers, in their role as drummers of the times, are using every form of literature and art to give a sharp and prompt reflection of our people's struggle against imperialism, and in defence of our motherland and world peace, and the new people and new things which are constantly appearing on all fronts of construction in our motherland, enthusiastically depicting the growth of the new in the midst of struggles, showing the positive role played by literature and art in close co-ordination with politics....

In a later portion of the same report, Mr Chou Yang discussed the famous policy set forth by Communist Party Chairman Mao Tse-tung, several years earlier, of letting 'a hundred flowers blossom and a hundred schools of thought contend'. This had apparently led to certain misunderstandings, which Mr Chou clarified as follows:

> Regarding style, form, genre, and subject-matter in art, however, we are for greater variety and encourage originality, while opposing

monotony, rigidity, and narrowness. Our principle is the integration of uniformity in political orientation and variety in artistic styles.

And further:

When we let a hundred flowers blossom, poisonous weeds may appear in the guise of fragrant flowers. Therefore, letting a hundred flowers blossom and a hundred schools of thought contend necessarily involves two opposite and interrelated aspects: letting a hundred flowers blossom and eradicating the poisonous weeds.

One of the characteristics of Chinese Communists is that they say exactly what they mean.

*

No human activity can be judged outside its historical context. The writers of America, England, and France would, I feel sure, find the intellectual atmosphere of China today far too uniform, and unbearably suffocating. But their historical moment is not ours.

Here is a nation emerging from illiteracy; a vast awakened population hungry to find itself in art, writing and drama, setting out upon a forced march of essential construction. Everything is urgent and must be treated urgently. Action takes top priority. If the dikes are not built, the dams not completed this autumn, a million people may die in the floods next spring and the drought next summer. This is a stirring period for the Chinese, an epic era; and a war of immense proportions is being fought against poverty, disease, and ignorance. Will the writer pitch in or won't he? He will. He will sit down in the back of his jeep to write the exploits of construction heroes and commune brigade-leaders, just as Tom Paine once sat down at a drum-head to write, 'These are the times that try men's souls.... '

Particularly in such times it is well to give credit where credit is due. More classics of Western literature are being read at present in China than at any previous period in history. These are not smuggled in. They are pushed by the government, the school system, the Writers' Union. As Mr Han himself told me, Chinese writers are reading nineteenth-century European playwrights and novelists. And Shakespeare. 'A great deal of Shakespeare,' he had said. A list of recent translations from English reveals twelve editions of William Shakespeare, including both sonnets and plays.

Polonius will thus have a chance to speak his piece directly. He may rise up at a conference of the Chinese Writers' Union some day, after the urgency of their crash construction programme has eased off a little, to discuss the problems of truth in literature and the writer's responsibility to mankind. Whether he will be welcomed there with the same courteous and impartial attention which we would expect for him at an assembly of, shall we say, the Commercial TV Writers' and Directors' Syndicate of Madison Avenue, is a question which had best be set aside as, for the time being, unanswerable.

China Kaleidoscope 3

NOTES FROM MY JOURNAL AND LETTERS

Letter to Elena. August 10th

The Chinese are extraordinarily unself-conscious with each other.
(I have told you this before.)

Yesterday on the train — it was very hot — the two men who were
sharing my compartment took off their trousers and sat comfortably in
their underpants, and I did the same. Very sensible and comfortable.
I had a momentary shudder thinking of what would happen to me if I
took my trousers off while travelling on the Southern Pacific! This
morning I shared the washroom with a young woman. We smiled
good-morning to each other and went on with our respective tooth-
brushings and washing without concern.

This sense of being among a family has its sad side, too. I feel, however friendly they are, that I am still on the *outside*. As when staying
with a large and affectionate family, they can do everything to make one
feel at home, but one is never one of them. I think a Westerner could
be in China for years, perhaps all his life, but would never escape the
sense that he is suspended between two worlds, never able really to
enter and become part of the stream of Chinese life.

The Sad Story of Lizzy

One Sunday afternoon in Shenyang I wandered to the sports ground
and watched a local track meet, the athletes of Shenyang against a neighbouring city. I sat down for a while next to a schoolboy of about twelve
or fourteen, with a Red Pioneer scarf round his neck. After a few
moments he summoned up enough courage to ask me in very hesitant
words, 'You speak the English?' I said yes, and we got on fine. He was

in his second year of English at secondary school.. He had a pile of his schoolbooks with him and he fished out his English-language textbook, and later I bought a copy of the same book from a local bookseller.

I studied the book. I expected to find a tirade against the wicked imperialists. But that word isn't mentioned. It takes the children through the months, the seasons, the days of the week, and has several simple and harmless little stories about ping-pong matches; catching sparrows; and the new Yangtze bridge. This was too good to last. Towards the end of the book (Lesson 35) comes the story of Lizzy. Lizzy was a poor English girl of twelve who lived in a big city in the north of England. Lizzy led a sad life:

> Every morning Lizzy went to work in a cotton factory. The workshop was dark and noisy. The air was hot. Little Lizzy was afraid of the big machines. And noise and the hot smell of the room made her ill.
>
> In the afternoon Lizzy went to school. Miss Brown, the schoolteacher, did not like her because she was poor. Very often Miss Brown punished her and made her stand in class. She did not know how hard Lizzie studied. She did not understand how tired Lizzy felt. She did not help her.
>
> Lizzy loved to work, but she hated the factory. She loved to study, but she hated the school and Miss Brown.
>
> Today many children in capitalist countries are like Lizzy. They are poor and miserable.

Quite good, but about eighty years out of date.

Enemies and Friends

The Chinese, Pearl Buck once said, make the finest of friends and the most terrible of enemies.

I think she is right; and this says so much.

Égalité

Assumptions of our superiority lie deep. Today, Yen and I were talking together in the hotel entrance and a visitor, rather upper class and just out from Europe, came up. 'I wonder,' he said, 'whether your man could help me a moment?' I felt Yen stiffen. He was not 'my man', he was Yen Chao-hua, citizen of the new China. I caught his eye and winked, and he relaxed.

This is an *egalitarian* society. You feel it everywhere. I watched some soldiers at drill one hot day. They were smart as could be, officers barking orders. Then drill ended, and all, officers and men, raced each other to the tubs of fruit juice. No priorities.

Every foreign country here entertains on its 'national day', and last week one of these receptions was held in this hotel. I was standing near Chou En-lai and I watched while a waitress with a large tray of drinks came up and offered one to the Prime Minister. They stood chatting together as easily and naturally as could be, the girl without a trace of shyness or servility. With respect, of course; but the respect, I felt, was both ways.

It was probably easier to maintain this sense of equality and comradeship when they were guerrillas in the mountains; more difficult now as this country becomes an elaborately organized modern state. But they are trying. It is a pretty well-established rule that everyone in authority must spend at least one month a year in the lowest rank of the organization of which he might be the head. The director of the steel company I visited told me he had just finished a month's work as a puddler. All officers, generals, even the chief of staff, spend one month a year in the ranks as ordinary privates. I asked about this; it struck me as being a little theoretical and phony, and that the other privates would probably make it pretty easy for him. Not a bit, I was told. No special privileges. The point being that it gives the privates a chance to see whether the general running their show is the kind of man they can trust. *They* are inspecting *him* for a change!

The other day I was with Yen in a taxi, and the driver seemed puzzled about the way, and I didn't think he was driving very well either. I asked Yen whether he was a new driver. 'No,' Yen said, 'he isn't ordinarily a taxi-driver. He's in the taxi administration office.' This was one of the bosses, doing his month's stint.

Cultural Shock

I talked with an English businessman today in the hotel. He had just arrived and he was very unhappy. Never having been to China before, he was suffering from what I believe psychologists call 'cultural shock'. Many Westerners feel this when they first come to China, especially the lone traveller.

I remember, on my first trip in 1957, feeling for several days painfully bewildered, disorientated, unmoored; all I wanted to do was to run away. A Swiss radio man I met in Hong Kong told me he was driven nearly mad with loneliness and misery when he first arrived in China. The disorientation comes, I believe, from suddenly finding oneself in a totally alien environment, with no point of contact with anything in one's normal life.

Added to this is the sense of being precipitated into complete illiteracy. Between you and the swirling crowds around you there is a total gap in communication. Street signs mean nothing. You cannot ask for the simplest necessities. Even the name of your hotel (if you can remember it at all) is beyond your ability to pronounce in a way that would be recognizable to anyone else. I remember being reassured (while in this state of initial bewilderment) by absurdly irrelevant things: a half-obscured sign above a shop written in *English*; a bath fixture with an American trademark. Even a French clock in a shop window, I recall, gave me an obscure comfort.

So I didn't deride this Englishman's misery. Instead I took him for a walk and showed him the Imperial Palace. But he wasn't very interested. In the park we sat on the ground sipping tea, and he told me about Huddersfield, where he was born, and how he didn't think much of this Chinese tea; it wasn't nearly as good as the tea they have in Huddersfield.

The Inside Change

Today, Ku (my interpreter) and I were having lunch together at the Shung Lung restaurant near the Tungan Market. We talked about some of the changes that have taken place in China — I was thinking especially of the disappearance of tipping, begging, stealing.

The absence of beggars, Ku told me, was easy to explain: everyone now has work so there's no need to beg. Those who are sick and cannot work are looked after. As for tipping, this is now a country that tries to share everything, he said. (The British would call it a 'fair-shares-for-all' country.) The slices may not be very large, but everyone believes he's getting a more or less equal share of the pie. So there are no longer rich people who can buy extra attention or flattery by tipping. And apart from this, though Ku did not put it into these words, accepting hand-outs would injure their pride.

But the lack of stealing? That puzzles me. Like everyone else who comes to China, I have grown careless about my possessions. I come back to my room to find I left money strewn over the desk; I never bother to lock my door, though in this hotel there are keys, which is more than can be said of the place I stayed in three years ago. The wife of one of the British Embassy officials told me the other day how she had some jewellery stolen on a visit to Hong Kong because she had forgotten that people elsewhere lock up valuables. I asked Ku how the regime established this moral sense, what fearful penalties are imposed on those who do steal.

He hesitated. He was obviously puzzled as to how he was going to explain it. 'I don't think these changes have come because of laws,' he said. 'You can't change people by passing laws. We have laws, of course, against stealing, and so does every country. And don't think stealing doesn't happen, because it does, although not very often. I think your question shows that you haven't really understood the Chinese revolution. The change inside people that now makes stealing rare — well, that change *is* the revolution; that is what the revolution is, and what it did to us. We can't think of stealing from others any more than we would steal from our own family.' And then Ku made a little gesture with his hands which conveyed much more vividly than any words how impossible it was to explain this to someone who had not been through it.

Nobody loves me!

(A poem found on a factory wall notice-board)

> The leadership is too careless
> of my well-being; comrades
> are not in the least polite to me.
> In my work-group all

simply criticize me! Who then
can I say is close to me?

Letter to Elena. July 11th

This evening I've been to Wu's house — I mentioned him to you some time ago. He's the chap who studied in England and then went to the University of Chicago. His family was rather upper crust before the Communists came and he must have had quite a time adjusting himself.

I've seen Wu once or twice since I first met him and have always enjoyed meeting him. He's youngish — under forty is my guess — very learned, and is something important in one of the government departments, though what he actually does he never lets on. They asked me to dinner, but I wasn't sure how much this would strain their food situation (this reminded me of war-time England), so I had dinner at the hotel and went after, taking along a bottle of *mao tai* for good cheer.

It was a lovely evening, though still very hot. We sat on wicker chairs in their little courtyard, shelling peanuts and sipping *mao tai* and fanning ourselves. Mrs Wu called to the two girls to come out of the house to greet me, which they did very demurely — I almost expected them to curtsy as in a Victorian drawing-room — and then they went off to bed and Mrs Wu left with them. Wu and I didn't talk much, just sat fanning ourselves and helping ourselves to the *mao tai*. I was glad. I've been talking too much lately, and been too much talked to.

All I wanted to do this evening was to sit and watch the great lazy moon creep over Peking. Wu is companionable and sensitive. He has a thin, intense face, the face of a scholar, serious in repose but quickly responsive. The Chinese are comfortable to be silent with — they don't feel they have to talk. I was quite content to watch the silhouette of the curved roof with its little goblins perched along the rim as the moon rose behind it. The courtyard, the graceful roof-line, the golden moon, the *mao tai* — it was almost too Chinese. But then Wu spoiled it all. He began about America. The same old record. I have heard it a thousand times already. Why does America do this? Why does America do that? American imperialism.... He went on and on. The thought of America *preys* on the Chinese so.

Wu disappointed me. I expected something a little more perceptive from him. He has a subtle and sophisticated intelligence and I usually find I can really *communicate* with him. He's lived in the West long enough to know our idiom of thinking. But here he was giving me the same old rehash, like any junior Party member who had never been outside his village.

'Oh, for God's sake, Wu!' I said, 'you talk and talk about America but you know you aren't really saying anything. You people seem to know only what's wrong with America. You know the latest crime statistics down to the last child-murderer. You probably know exactly how many drunks there are in Los Angeles. You know all about our juvenile crime and how we cheat each other and all about Little Rock....' I spoke sharply.

I told him what he was saying might all be true, but add it all up and it still doesn't spell America. And it was my turn to go on and on, partly out of irritation and disappointment, partly out of a sudden ache of nostalgia. And a homesickness for you and our young Anne was mixed up in this too.

When I finished Wu didn't say anything for a while, and then he said, 'I don't think you realize why we feel as we do; and I think you should.'

I felt we should get into a deeper and even more self-defeating wrangle, so I didn't go on with it and in a little while I left. Wu wanted to walk with me to Wang Fu Street where I could catch the trolley bus back to Hatamen, near the hotel, but I said I'd rather walk by myself, which was unkind. He came to the doorway to say goodbye. He is rather slender, and he stood there blinking through his glasses. He suddenly seemed touching and vulnerable. I felt (as I always feel when I have been cross with a Chinese) that I had been crude and something of a bully. I wanted to say something to put it right, but didn't know how, so I said goodbye and went off. I found my way through the maze of *hutungs*. Quite deserted now, all the children indoors and asleep. I didn't take the trolley but walked home. There was a line from *Family Reunion* that kept running through my head (I may not have it right): 'Something important should have come of this conversation.' And it should, but it didn't.

PS. Next Morning

I've just sent a note round to Wu's house. 'I am sorry about last night. I was defensive and irritable. Sometimes one needs to talk; sometimes for the sake of one's sanity one needs to be silent. Our needs last night just didn't coincide! I shall be leaving Peking soon. Can we meet again before I go?'

*

I never had an answer to my note.

But during the next few days one sentence of Wu's kept recurring to me: 'I don't think you realize why we feel as we do and I think you should.'

He was right. Wu tried to tell me something and I shut him off. If I was to try to understand China I should be less argumentative, more ready to listen. Though I did not see Wu again (I learned he had left Peking), there were others. From then on I kept notes. I made a file of the newspaper articles and clippings (mostly American) that were sometimes thrust into my hands. Those who (like Wu) had been educated in America, and Chinese historians, were especially anxious to explain the Chinese position; and sensing that I was willing to listen, they often spoke at great length. Some were passionately angry, some were legalistic, as if they were speaking from a lawyer's brief, some were jeering, and some spoke with dignity and restraint; and further comments came to me in letters after I returned to America. From this mass of material I have written what might be called 'The Chinese Case'. I have tried to represent as clearly as I can what the Chinese feel about America, and why. And this case forms the next part of this book.

```
***************************
*                         *
*        PART SIX         *
*                         *
***************************
```

XXV

The Chinese Case

WE believe, Mr Greene, that you came to our country in order to understand us. Many come already convinced that anything to do with communism is evil. They see what they want to see. They are appalled at our poverty, our backwardness, and all that is ugly and mean in our country. They are quick to notice our mistakes. They will carry back with them what they came with, for where in the world cannot a visitor find unpleasant and unworthy things if that is what he is looking for? And others, thoughtless people, idealists, come disposed to see only what is good. They have an idealized picture of the new China in their minds, and they are in some ways more difficult to deal with than the others, for when they can no longer pretend to themselves that everything in China is wonderful, they turn on us bitterly and reject everything because we disappointed them.

We want neither to be prejudged nor idealized. We should like to be seen as we are — a people trying, and with great effort, to lift ourselves from a state of poverty and feudalism into a modern nation with equal opportunities for all.

The lines of communication between China and America are now so tenuous that they hardly exist at all. We read with amazement what is said about us by writers living in Hong Kong who have never been here — never, at least, to the new China, which bears so little resemblance to the old — or by China 'experts' sitting in New York or Washington. We do not think that any writer can comment with understanding upon a gigantic social revolution such as ours without seeing it himself. That is why our government offered visas to American correspondents a few years ago and invited them to come and see for themselves what we are trying to do. But what happened? Your State Department immediately announced that they would not be allowed to come. And since then many eminent American citizens and some of their most trusted political leaders, even the wife of one of America's greatest presidents, were told they must not travel to China. Why this reluctance on the part of the American government to allow its citizens to see for themselves? Is it possibly a fear that some of the myths about us might be dispelled?

All we ask of our visitors is that they come ready to report honestly whatever they find. Is that so much to ask? But let these writers always bear in mind that no country can be understood except within the context of its own historical development. They will not find parallels here for many of the social or political institutions that you have developed in America or England, but that does not mean that those we have developed are not better for our own needs.

The improvement of relations between China and the United States is essential if there is to be a way for all of us to continue to live peacefully on this earth. And it is for this reason that we here in China feel it necessary to expose to the world the real nature of American policy, which prevents this necessary improvement. This policy in its most belligerent form has been in existence since the day we formed our government in 1949. But it was, long before that, based on exploitation and assumptions of superiority which deeply wounded the self-respect of our people.

We have read reports of a television programme broadcast in London by the B.B.C. This was the interview you had with Premier Chou En-lai. As you must know, in England this interview was followed by a discussion in which an American correspondent took part. Presumably he was invited to present the 'American view'. He appeared puzzled as to why China should feel unfriendly to the United States.

'We never tried so hard to help another country as we did China,' he told the British audience, 'and therefore, when China suddenly turns against us and becomes hostile to us, we find it a little difficult to understand.'

When Americans say, as they often do, with a look of innocence, 'We haven't done anything to China,' we can only answer, *'Look at history.*

252

Let us recall that when the West 'opened up' China (as your historians say), Chinese society was the oldest in the world. It was a feudal society, and as such an oppressive one, but it is quite wrong to think, as many Westerners do, that through the centuries China was constantly in turmoil, always being pulled apart by factions, war-lords, and civil wars. Cut off from other countries, China enjoyed long periods of peace. Isolated by poor communications, most of the local needs were met by local craftsmen. There was little money and there was little need for it, and among the people there was a general dedication to a humane regard for the needs of others. Confucianism influenced our people greatly, and though it arrested needed reforms, it taught them a universal sense of mutual responsibility. From across the years our poets and artists speak to us of our culture moving from generation to generation, from century to century.

Change, it is true, had to come to China; it was long overdue. But the change should have been our change, accomplished our way, not yours. To our people, for purposes of commercial plunder, with an unbounded certainty of its moral superiority, the West brought strife and great misery.

When your Western traders first came to China it was not at our invitation. The government of the time was not eager for it, but was prepared to engage in foreign trade if your merchants would obey our laws. In our commerce with the West at this time we were the suppliers of tea, silk ... and fine porcelains, but there was little that China required from the outside world, and the Europeans had to pay in silver for what they bought. The British, however, found something else to make up for their not inexhaustible supplies of silver. From their recently subjugated colony of India, they brought in opium, a drug banned by the Emperor in 1729 and which, since then, was little known in China.

British shipments of opium from India began arriving in 1781, and it was not long before this trade had become highly lucrative. By 1800 our Emperor attempted to reinforce the prohibition, and penalties for its importation were increased. However, profits now were so great that it became impossible to prevent corruption and smuggling at all levels; the trade continued to grow. In 1800, 280,000 pounds of opium were imported into China. By 1838 this had risen to 5,600,000 pounds.

Although the bulk of the opium trade was in British hands, Americans were also involved. Turkish opium was carried to China in American vessels, and, just as in the case of the British, the profits made in opium served as the foundation for some of the large American trading organizations that later dominated the foreign commerce of China.

By 1839 the Chinese government, aghast at the physical and economic effects of the opium trade on the people, made another desperate effort to suppress the trade. An Imperial Commissioner, Lin Tse-hsu, was sent to Canton. By this time even the British superintendent of trade in China, Captain Elliot, had written to his fellow-countrymen in Canton saying that 'this course of traffic was rapidly staining the British character with deep disgrace'. On June 3rd, more than 20,000 chests of opium, on orders of the Imperial Commissioner, were publicly destroyed in Canton. This led to aggression, and in 1840 the British declared war. Thus began the first Opium War, which lasted for two years.

The result of this war, which ended in a Chinese defeat, was the humiliating Treaty of Nanking. Under its terms the Chinese government had to pay a large indemnity for the opium seized; the cities of Canton, Foochow, Amoy, Ningpo, and Shanghai, occupied by foreign troops, were to be opened to British trade, and residents were exempted from Chinese law. We had to give up our island of Hong Kong. This was the first of the humiliating 'Unequal Treaties', imposing conditions which no country would ever have dared to offer a vanquished European nation.

Perhaps the cruellest of all the conditions imposed on us by this treaty was that the Chinese government was prevented from ever levying more than a 5 per cent import tax on foreign goods. This opened up our country to a flood of cheap manufactured articles and prevented the development of our own industries. Countless thousands of our artisans and small traders were brought to ruin and starvation by this decree.

This, then, was our introduction to a century of exploitation by the 'civilized' and 'Christian' nations of the West. We submitted because we had to, for we were not a military power. But do you not suppose that our sense of justice was outraged?

China, still embittered after this defeat by the British, was forced to cede even wider extra-territorial privileges to America under the Treaty of Wanghsia and additional special rights for American ships on China's internal waterways. But the British were not to be outdone. Under the 'most-favoured-nation clause' they immediately claimed the extra benefits extorted by the Americans.

In 1853 the British, Americans, and French took over control of the Chinese customs. In 1856 a dispute about a flag (a dispute in which we still think we were in the right) was made the excuse by the British and the French to declare war on us again. Once more we were defeated; once more we were required to pay a war indemnity. Under the Tientsin Treaties which followed, both the opium trade and missionary activities were legalized and the foreign control of our customs was made perpetual. Under this treaty foreign powers were permitted to export our very people to their colonial territories for use as cheap labour. When the Chinese Court, shocked by the harshness of the conditions, delayed ratification, the war was resumed and Western forces occupied Peking, looting and burning the famous Yuan Ming Yuan Summer Palace and committing barbarous outrages against our defenceless people. As the nineteenth century drew to a close, the Western powers grabbed further territorial footholds. It became a veritable scramble. In 1897 Germany seized the naval port of Tsingtao; in 1898 she took the Shantung peninsula. Three weeks after this treaty was signed, Tsarist Russia forced a lease on the naval base of Port Arthur and the commercial port of Dairen. Within five days Britain appropriated the naval base of Weihaiwei, and a few weeks after that France seized the South China bay of Kwangchowan. 'Spheres of influence' were assumed by each of the powers.

And what about America? Did she protest? Did she attempt to curb the rapacity of her allies? Did she condemn the wanton sacking of Peking? No protests, no condemnations. In 1899 she pronounced the famous 'Open Door' policy. This policy did not in any way dispute the advantages wrested from China by the others; all that it required was that the commerce within each 'sphere of influence' be equally open to all. While able to assume a pose of 'not wanting any of China's territory', America was able to reap all the financial and commercial advantages gained by the other nations by force. 'Hitch-hiking imperialism', one of your writers has called it!

How readily some Americans see themselves playing the heroic and magnanimous role in history — how rarely do they know the real facts! When our people, provoked beyond endurance, rose up in what is known to you as the 'Boxer Rebellion' in 1901, a further infamous treaty was imposed upon us; foreign troops (including United States Marines) were stationed in our capital, the Chinese were excluded from parts of the city, and another huge indemnity was levied on our people.

But if there was even a small amount of good will that survived the exploitation of a century, it was finally dissipated by the support by successive American governments of Chiang Kai-shek. Do Americans not realize with what hatred we recall those last dreadful years of Chiang's regime? Do they not know of the countless thousands killed or tortured by Chiang's secret police? Or of the fortunes made by his politicians while our people everywhere were starving? Can they not realize that this persistent support of a man who was inflicting the most gross injuries on his own people convinced us that American policy was designed in no way for our benefit, but to prevent us from controlling our own country? In spite of countless official reports, articles by reputable American reporters, eye-witness accounts, documented proof of his cruelty and corruption, Washington has persisted to this day in giving Chiang money, arms, and all the moral support that she can muster.

*

The first and central issue which divides the United States and China and prevents any lasting settlement is the issue of Taiwan. Over this the United States government has thrown a cloud of confusion and complexity. Finding themselves in a politically hopeless and embarrassing position, politicians and writers jumble facts, raise political issues which are irrelevant, rewrite history, and hide their own previous statements from public view. But the facts themselves are quite simple. Let us outline them without feeling. Let us segregate the myths from reality.

The Myth: Taiwan was never part of China.

The Reality:

> A.D. 607 (1,354 years ago). The Sui-dynasty Emperor sent an official to administer Taiwan.

1360. During the Yuan dynasty Taiwan was governed as part of Fukien Province.

1624. The Dutch (and for a while the Portuguese) occupied portions of the island.

1662. The Dutch were driven out by the Chinese.

1684. Taiwan's status was raised to that of Prefecture.

1885. Taiwan became a province.

1895. Taiwan was ceded to Japan after China's defeat in the Sino-Japanese war.

1943. In the Cairo Declaration, Britain and the United States agreed that 'all territories Japan has stolen from the Chinese such as Manchuria, Formosa and the Pescadores shall be restored to the Republic of China'.

1945 (July 26th). The Potsdam Declaration confirmed that 'the terms of the Cairo Declaration shall be carried out'.

1945 (August 30th). The Chinese government proclaimed Chinese sovereignty over Taiwan.

1945 (October 25th). The Japanese Governor formally handed back Taiwan to China.

The Myth: That the Taiwanese are 'not really Chinese'.

The Reality: More than 90 per cent of the eight-million-odd people who were residents of Taiwan are Hans (Chinese). In addition there are about 200,000 Kaoshan people living in Taiwan. Like the forty or more other national minorities on the mainland, the Kaoshans are members of China's big family of nationalities. To say that the residents of Taiwan are not Chinese is as absurd as to say that the residents of the United States are not Americans because the Indians were the original inhabitants!

The Myth: That the Taiwan people 'never really wanted to rejoin the mainland'.

The Reality: In an official memorandum (April 18th, 1947) the United States ambassador, Dr Leighton Stuart, had this to say:

The Formosan Chinese greeted the surrender of Japanese authority to the Chinese with immense enthusiasm on October

25th, 1945. After fifty years under Japanese control ... they welcomed a return to China, which they had idealized as the Mother Country.

and again:

Japanese rule had sharpened their sense of Chinese nationality and race.... Formosans have been ambitious to see Taiwan become a model province of China ... proud of their race and nationality, proud to be taking part in the National Reconstruction.

The Myth: That the United States has never conceded that Taiwan was a province of China.

The Reality: On January 5th, 1950, the United States Secretary of State announced:

The Chinese have administered Formosa for four years. Neither the United States nor any other ally ever questioned the authority of that occupation. When Formosa was made a province of China nobody raised any lawyer's doubts about that. That was regarded as in accordance with the commitments. The United States is not going to quibble about the integrity of the position. That is where we stand.

The Myth: That the United States never promised not to interfere in the Chinese civil war.

The Reality: On January 5th, 1950, President Truman said:

The United States has no predatory designs on Formosa or any other Chinese territory. The United States has no desire to obtain special rights or privileges or to establish military bases on Formosa. ... The United States Government will not pursue a course which will lead to involvement in the civil conflict in China. Similarly, the United States will not provide military aid and advice to the Chinese forces on Formosa.

The Myth: That the existence of a Communist government on the mainland gives the United States moral right to disregard previous pledges.

The Reality: The United States Secretary of State on January 6th 1950, declared (after the establishment of the Communist government)

The world must believe that we stand for principle and that we are honourable and decent people and that we do not put forward words, as propagandists do in other countries, to serve their advantage, only to throw them overboard when some change in events makes the position difficult for us.

and again, five weeks later (February 9th, 1950):

Taiwan has been included into China as a province since 1945. For the United States Government at this date to seek to establish a non-Chinese administration on Formosa, either through SCAP [Supreme Command Allied Powers] or a United Nations or Far East Commission-sponsored plebiscite, would be almost universally interpreted throughout Asia as an attempt by this Government to separate Formosa from China in violation of its pledges and contrary to its long-standing policy of respecting the territorial integrity of China.

The Myth: That to allow Taiwan to fall into the hands of the Communists would seriously endanger the military security of the United States.

The Reality: In a State Department Policy Information Paper, written in 1949 and presented to the Senate Committee on Armed Services and the Committee on Foreign Relations in June 1951, it was stated categorically:

Formosa has no special military significance. It is only approximately 100 miles off the China coast.... China has never been a sea power and the island has no special strategic advantage to the Communist armed forces.

In other words, the return of Taiwan is a *political*, not a *military* issue.

The Myth: That Chiang Kai-shek still plans to launch a successful return to the mainland from Taiwan.

The Reality: No one really believes this any more, not even Chiang's own people. As early as October 5th, 1958, a Taiwan military spokesman reported to the *Observer:*

We haven't seriously considered invading the mainland for at

259

least five years now. We have to keep up the pretence, of course, largely for domestic consumption — a matter of morale and discipline.

We wonder whether the taxpayers of the United States realize how much it costs to keep up this pretence. In the authoritative *Foreign Affairs Review* of Washington of April 1958 (with which Allen W. Dulles, the head of the Central Intelligence Agency, is connected as a member of the Editorial Advisory Board), a report from Taiwan stated:

Chiang Kai-shek maintains about 800 generals and admirals on full pay waiting for commands, a skeleton officialdom for the provinces, and the Central Government of China.

And all to 'keep up morale and discipline'!

The Myth: That the United States government is seeking only a 'peaceful solution' to the problems in the Far East.

The Reality: The scene: the subcommittee of the Committee on Appropriations, House of Representatives, Washington. The date: January 26th, 1954, seven months after the end of the Korean War.

Representative Frederick R. Coudert: 'Did I correctly understand you to say that the heart of the present policy towards China and Formosa is that there is to be kept alive a constant threat of military action vis-à-vis Red China in the hope that at some point there will be an internal breakdown?'

Mr Walter S. Robertson, Assistant Secretary of State for Far Eastern Affairs: 'Yes, sir; that is my conception.'

Coudert: 'In other words, a cold war waged under the leadership of the United States, with constant threat of attack against Red China, led by Formosa and other Far Eastern groups, and militarily backed by the United States?'

Robertson: 'Yes ... '

Coudert: 'Fundamentally, does that not mean that the United States is undertaking to maintain for an indefinite period of years American dominance in the Far East?'

Robertson: 'Yes. Exactly.'

*

We have referred to the State Department Policy Information Paper of 1949. It is a very remarkable document. It is worth careful study. One of the most interesting parts of the document is where the State Department argues excellently against the very policy that was subsequently pursued, and forecasts what the consequences of following such a policy must be.

'... Sending in troops [into Formosa] supplying arms, dispatching naval units or taking similar action would:

'(a) Accomplish no material good for China or its Nationalist regime;

'(b) Involve the United States in a long-term venture producing at best a bristling stalemate, and at worst possible involvement in open warfare;

'(c) Subject the United States to a violent propaganda barrage and to reaction against our "militarism, imperialism and interference" even from friendly peoples, and particularly from Chinese, who would be turned against us anew;

'(d) Eminently suit the purposes of the U.S.S.R. which would like to see us "substantiate" its propaganda, dissipate our energies and weaken effectiveness of our policies generally by such action.'

*

What sort of regime on Taiwan is it that the U.S. government is supporting? A well-documented characterization of the Kuomintang may be found in another publication by the State Department, which we believe is not widely known to the American public. We refer to the report by Ambassador Leighton Stuart on massacres of Taiwanese by Kuomintang forces, contained in the White Paper on United States Relations with China published in 1949.

Taiwan had greeted its reunion with mainland China after Japanese surrender with 'immense enthusiasm'. The islanders were, however, quickly disillusioned. They found themselves virtually excluded from all government posts. These were awarded to Chiang's friends from the mainland. Once again it was the old Kuomintang story of nepotism and corruption. Smuggling and official black-marketeering were

widespread. The economy declined. Health services broke down.
Cholera epidemics occurred for the first time in thirty years.

Resentment against Chiang's regime became more and more intense.
On February 27th, 1947, a crowd of some two thousand Taiwanese, in
protest at the fatal beating of a woman cigarette-vendor by Chiang's
police (for selling 'untaxed cigarettes'), marched in orderly fashion to
the Governor's office, where they wished to submit a petition. Without
warning a machine-gun opened fire on the crowd and a number of the
people were killed. This unprovoked shooting was the signal for a city-
wide outburst of anger. American officials on Taiwan reported that
though there was rioting and protesting, the people refrained from looting. Nor were they armed. The next few days there was general disorder. Buses filled with squads of government troops armed with
machine-guns swept through the streets firing indiscriminately. The
military were evidently trying to frighten the public into obedience. In
one incident observed by American officials a long burst of machine-gun
fire swept a crowd without warning, felling at least 123.

On March 8th, General Chang Wu-tao made the following categorical
statement: 'The demands for political reform are very proper. The
Central Government [Chiang's government] will not dispatch troops to
Taiwan. I can risk my life to guarantee that the Central Government
will not take any military actions against Taiwan.' This statement was
made when the speaker must have known that Kuomintang troops in
great numbers were about to land. After dark that same night Chiang's
troops began to disembark and for the next nine days troops poured in
from the mainland to Taiwan.

'Beginning March 9th,' continues the United States White Paper,
'there was widespread and indiscriminate killing. Soldiers were seen
bayoneting coolies with no apparent provocation ... soldiers were seen
to rob passers-by. An old man protesting at the removal of a woman
from his house was cut down ... anyone thought to be trying to hide or
run was shot down. Looting began wherever the soldiers saw something desirable ... a systematic search for middle school (high school)
students was begun ... students were beheaded.... Many bodies began
to float into the inner harbour at Keelung.... In rural areas ... mounted
machine-gun patrols were observed shooting at random in village
streets. Man-hunts were observed being conducted through the hills.'

Established critics of the government, middle-school students, teachers, lawyers were seized and executed. 'The continuing presence of fresh bodies in Keelung Harbour and other evidence indicate that the eliminating of the informed opposition is continuing.... It is reported at Tapai that although shots and screams in the night have become less frequent they continue.... '

We have given this brief account of the terrible massacre in Taiwan because we think that you and others in America have never realized the real nature of Chiang Kai-shek's government. The sequence of events in Taiwan, first the bleeding of the economy by Chiang's officials, and then the mass executions of those who dared to rise up in protest, came as no surprise at all to the millions who for years suffered under his terrible regime on the mainland, a regime sustained and supported by the American government. When America supports the Chiang Kai-shek regime as representing 'free China', it discredits her name throughout Asia.

Even the most naive of Chiang's followers must today realize that no amount of money, guns, or planes will ever set Chiang back on the mainland into a position of power. The accumulated hatred of more than six hundred million Chinese has swept this tiny remnant from the stage of history. This remnant is irrelevant. It is on the mainland, and not in Taiwan, that history is being written and lived, and the little gang on Taiwan will one day be as completely forgotten as the band of Royalist refugees who fled from America to Canada at the time of your revolution.

When some Americans ask how many people the Communists in China have 'executed', do they ever show any curiosity about the millions of dead, wounded, and murdered in the civil war on the mainland, the direct result of American aid to Chiang? Does anybody wonder how long the fighting was prolonged after VJ Day because of the billions of dollars in aid, military and civil, which were handed to the Kuomintang? A few voices were raised from time to time about the American taxpayers' pouring money down a rat-hole; but has there been one public figure of first stature who has asked how many Chinese were killed because of the shipments of guns, of planes, of tanks that Washington sent to China between 1945 and 1949?

Even now the aid continues. American planes piloted by Kuomintang officers have bombed our cities from Taiwan, from which, but for this aid, Chiang Kai-shek would have long since been removed. Your government may have succeeded in keeping 'free China' in the United Nations, but it has at the same time succeeded in earning the contempt and hatred of the Chinese people.

*

The 'Taiwan problem' is a problem of America's own making. If wiser decisions reached earlier regarding 'non-interference' in China's civil war had been adhered to, Taiwan would now be peacefully and happily a part of the mainland of China. By sending the Seventh Fleet to intervene in our civil war, American policies have kept alive political problems which would have found their natural historical solution. There would now be no embarrassing pretence that Chiang Kai-shek's clique 'represents' China at the United Nations. The United States would not today be committed to a lost cause. By financing and arming the remnants of Chiang's discredited regime America has only multiplied her own difficulties and ensured her own future humiliation. The Seventh Fleet is still today enabling Chiang to harass our coastal shipping, interfere with peaceful commerce, and even sink our civilian ships. And for what compensating advantages?

Your Mr O. E. Clubb, who served for twenty years as an official in the United States Foreign Service in Asia, was Consul-General in Peking, and later became the head of the office of Chinese Affairs in your State Department, had this to say in an article (*The Progressive*, November 1958):

> The United States' political position on 'the China question' is crumbling, for it was built on sand.... Through our own policy ... we have been entrapped and isolated on the China coast. Never before in our history have we joined vital interests to so barren and ill-omened a cause as that of Generalissimo Chiang Kai-shek. Our China policy has poisoned our Asian relations for years; now we discover that it has brought us to a position vis-à-vis China from which we can neither advance nor retreat with profit.

We believe that when the American people learn the facts they will insist that past errors be corrected and that steps be taken to bring their government's policy into line with realities. As long as your leaders and your public opinion veto any gesture of reconciliation, any correction of historic error, no settlement between us seems likely. But we are a patient people and time is on our side. We are willing to wait until some new generation of Americans are prepared to sit down with us as equals. We will not talk with those who try to 'negotiate from strength', or attempt to intimidate us with guns of their fleet. Do not expect us to talk under the shadow of missiles trained on our cities from a dozen bases. Do not speak to us in tones which imply that you are very nearly perfect and that we are almost wholly malevolent. But we are ready to sit down with you at any time as equals and discuss our problems like men.

*

While the Western press has been almost silent on the background of the Taiwanese dispute, there has been a great deal written about 'Chinese aggression' — first in Korea, more recently in Tibet, India, and Laos.

With respect to Korea, the facts, as we Chinese record them, are the following: Fighting in Korea started on June 25th, 1950. No Chinese forces were involved at the time. Indeed, the Indian ambassador to Peking, Mr K. N. Pannikar, reported in his book *In Two Chinas*, 'that United Nations intervention in Korea caused no particular reaction in China.... During the first three months of the Korean War, there was hardly any noticeable military activity.... '

Upon the outbreak of hostilities in Korea that June, the American Seventh Fleet was ordered to 'protect' Taiwan, and has been so engaged ever since, thus providing Chiang Kai-shek with a shield from the shelter of which he has carried on an endless series of raids and nuisance attacks against coastal shipping and against the mainland. Deployment of the Seventh Fleet constituted a direct intervention by the United States in the Chinese civil war. Had it not been for this intervention, the civil war might have ended in that summer of 1950 — with the removal of Chiang from his last foothold on Chinese soil. This in turn would have terminated Chiang's claim to a seat in the United Nations.

In October 1950, American forces began their drive north to the 38th Parallel, which had been established by the Allies after Japan's surrender as the dividing line between North and South Korea. Certain American generals spoke publicly of going all the way to the 'Manchurian border'.

On October 2nd, Premier Chou En-lai called in the Indian Ambassador to inform him that 'if the Americans crossed the 38th Parallel, China would be forced to intervene in Korea'. Mr Pannikar records how he then asked Premier Chou whether China would intervene if only the South Koreans crossed. The Premier was emphatic: the South Koreans did not matter, but American intrusion into North Korea would encounter Chinese resistance.

This warning was passed on to the British Minister in Peking, and was relayed to Washington. It was ignored. There were many who believed the Chinese government was bluffing. The 38th Parallel was crossed, and a week later Chinese troops entered North Korea.

We do not believe that any other nation could have stood by and watched the encroachment of an obviously hostile army — whose government was supporting our chief enemy on Taiwan — to its very border.

For ten years the Western nations in the U.N. refused to discuss China's credentials because (so went the argument) the People's Republic of China had been an aggressor in the Korean War and was therefore not eligible for the U.N.

That myth has now been shattered by a report prepared by the Rand Corporation, who were commissioned by the United States Air Force to make a dispassionate examination of the reasons why China entered the Korean war.

The Toronto *Globe and Mail* on February 22nd, 1961, commented editorially on the Rand Corporation report: 'General of the United States Army Douglas MacArthur ... Far East commander of the United Nations forces ... wanted to cross the Yalu into China and crush the Communist armies.... This week the general once more bewailed the cruel fate that stopped him.... It [the Rand Corporation report] claims that China neither participated in planning the initial North Korean aggression nor intervened later as the result of Russian pressure, but was "rationally motivated" when it moved its armies into Korea after apparently ignoring the first three months of war there. The Rand Corporation study concludes that the Korean war provides an instruc-

tive warning on the dangers of a limited war exploding into a thermo-
nuclear war.... China intervened because it assumed from belligerent
statements issuing from General MacArthur's headquarters in Tokyo
that he intended to invade China.... General MacArthur this week
reaffirmed that this was his intention and that it remains an unfulfilled
ambition.'

So much for China's 'aggression' in the Korean War!

*

Regarding Tibet, it ought to be made clear, first of all, that Tibet has
been, until very recently, one of the most isolated and backward regions
of the world. A system of serfdom of an appallingly repressive nature
actually prevailed there until it was abolished by the Chinese government in 1959. The so-called 'Tibetan independence movement' was in
fact a counter-revolutionary action, led by groups of feudal landlords
and religious aristocrats, with assistance from outside. Even Western
sources never estimated that more than 20,000 were involved. Out of a
total population of 1,200,000 living in Tibet itself (there are almost three
million Tibetans living in other parts of China), this does not sound like
mass support.

Let us also add this: one of the first acts of the Chinese government
after the liberation of Tibet in 1951 was to prohibit *mutilation*: it was
still the custom there to gouge out eyes, cut off ears, and employ similar
brutal punishments. The only hospitals in Tibet are those that have
been built by the People's Republic, the only secular schools were begun
after liberation, and peonage and the medieval system of land-tenure
were abolished, as reported by *The Times* of June 28th, 1958.

As in the case of Taiwan, no question about Tibet being part of China
was ever raised officially until recently. Until it became convenient to
charge China with 'foreign aggression' it had been accepted both by
international law and by immemorial custom that Tibet was part of
China. From as long ago as the thirteenth century we have records
showing that Kublai Khan appointed the Grand Lama of Tibet; the
British recognized Chinese suzerainty in 1792; and during Chiang Kai-
shek's rule Washington refused to admit a trade delegation from Tibet
until it had obtained visas from the Kuomintang government. It is

significant that when the Dalai Lama, after his 'flight' to India, appealed to the great powers to bring the case of Chinese 'aggression' before the United Nations, no great power would take the initiative. The reason? That under international law there was no case of aggression.

*

We have been accused, too, of aggression in Laos. In the summer of 1959 the United States, in apparently great alarm, called an emergency session of the United Nations Security Council to consider the 'foreign aggression' against this small country. The United Nations sent an international commission to investigate the charges on the spot. The Commission reported no evidence of aggression; that no foreign troops had crossed the border. In 1960 the same wild charges were repeated, and again quietly dropped for lack of evidence. There never has been any proof of Chinese soldiers in Laos because there never were any. However, a report in the New York *Herald Tribune* from Vientianne on October 5th, 1960, revealed that American soldiers disguised as civilians were secretly training the Royal Laotian army.

*

As for India,[1] it is true that our relations are not as cordial as they were some years ago. But we do not feel that we are to blame for this. Premier Chou En-lai discussed this matter with you [see pp. 363 ff. for a description of the author's TV interview with Chou En-lai], as he did with Edgar Snow [*Look* magazine, January 31st, 1961]. We know that we have been called 'aggressive' and 'intransigent' in connection with this border dispute, yet we are sitting down with the Indian government and attempting to negotiate the demarcation of a border some thousands of miles in length which has never been precisely agreed upon in the long and peaceful history of China and India. In a similar situation we reached an amicable solution with the Burmese government. We are confident that in the course of time a just settlement for both India and ourselves can be found.[2]

[1] 'The Chinese Case' was written in 1961. Since then large-scale fighting has taken place along the Sino-Indian border. The significance of this is more fully discussed in Appendix 6.
[2] In the course of a conversation I had with Mr Nehru in 1959 I gained the impression that he felt the issue had been exaggerated for political reasons and

We who are so frequently accused of 'aggression' have often been victims of it ourselves. We believe we know it when we see it. We know that American planes at the disposal of Chiang Kai-shek bombed our cities after liberation and continued to fly arms to remnants of the Kuomintang forces on the mainland. We know that American U-2s have flown over our land. We know that weapons have been dropped to counter-revolutionary forces in Tibet.

On December 15th, 1960, the *Christian Science Monitor*'s correspondent in New Delhi reported that Prime Minister Nehru 'has expressed the belief that some of the air violations of India's north-east frontier about which India has made several protests to Communist China may be due to overflights by United States planes.... New Indian radar devices have been plotting the course of marauders at a height of more than 60,000 feet and as far as New Delhi knows, Communist China lacks aircraft flying at such heights.' The same correspondent also stated: 'The fact that several incoming Tibetan refugees have been found to carry United States arms leads to the supposition that some United States planes may have been engaged in dropping arms to help the still simmering Tibetan revolt against Chinese overlordship.... Unless doubts are cleared up, both Peking and Indian Communists have another perfect opportunity to make U-2 type of propaganda.' [This interview, needless to say, was not reported by the rest of the American press.]

*

Which brings us to the question: Is it China or the United States that is the aggressive country?

Item: How many military bases is America maintaining on foreign soil? Hundreds. And China? Not one.

Item: America has a navy larger than all the other navies of the world combined. China's navy? Negligible.

that a settlement with China was possible. This attitude was confirmed by L. M. Morris of the *Christian Science Monitor*, who in an article on January 28th, 1961, reported that Mr Nehru '... surprisingly dismissed the Communist China invasion of India's borders by first saying he felt it had petered out, and secondly by stating that "up there" there are only mountains and a couple of small villages' — F. G.

Item: America today spends six million dollars *every hour* on military armaments. America spends in just sixteen days what China spends on her military requirements in the whole year.

Item: America has a stockpile of H-bombs with an explosive force of 96,000 megatons, or *45 million times the force that was exploded at Hiroshima.* Mr Leo Goodman, who is the atomic adviser to the United Automobile Workers, gave this figure to the Annual Conference of the American Association of the United Nations in March 1960. Dr David Inglis, physicist at the U.S. government's Argonne Laboratory, who was present, said, 'I think you are 30 per cent low.' Taking this lower figure, what does this mean in terms that are more imaginable? That the United States today has stockpiled in its arsenals the equivalent of 32 one-ton bombs of high-explosive T.N.T. *for every man, woman, and child in the entire world.*

Item: America spends 56·4 per cent of its national budget on current military expenses, *excluding* the billions of dollars she gives to arm her allies. The Chinese spend 8·3 per cent.

Item: In dollar equivalents America spends $47 billion; China spends $2·3 billion. For every man, woman, and child America spends $260 annually on current military expenses; China spends $3·50.

Item: The proportion of America's national budget that she spends on military expenditures increases year by year. In China the proportion *decreases* year by year. The average annual expenditure on military defence during China's first five-year plan was 17 per cent. In 1960 it was down to 8·3 per cent.

Item: Ten times more money is spent in America on its current military expenditures than for the combined expenditures on social security, education, health, and welfare. China spends 50 per cent *more* on these items than on military expenditures.

Item: It was agreed at the armistice that both sides would withdraw their troops from Korea. Today (and your leaders have acknowledged this) not a single Chinese soldier remains on Korean soil. The American troops have not been withdrawn from South Korea. Today they number tens of thousands, and the airfields in South Korea have recently been enlarged.

With these facts before us, which would appear the more 'war-like'?

*

Americans do not like being an 'imperialist' power. They believe we are stretching words beyond their accepted meaning. 'Point out to us,' your leaders say, 'a single people that America is ruling as a colonial power; show us one country that America is threatening to seize.'

In our view colonialism is only one aspect of imperialism, and though the United States may not 'rule' as a colonial power, she nevertheless effectively dominates and controls other countries by her financial and commercial power. Americans should understand that we use the word *imperialism* as a symbol, a kind of shorthand description, of the control of one power by another. Let us not split hairs over words, let us look at the facts. European colonialism, deeply damaging though it was, was at least open, it was admitted, even gloried in. The worst feature of American imperialism is its *secrecy*. Its actions throughout the world are flagrant, but they are largely hidden from the ordinary people at home. American commercial imperialism operates without public control or check. It is politically irresponsible.

A dozen or twenty men may meet in New York and their decision can mean that 10,000 workers in Bolivia or Venezuela or in the Philippines are thrown out of work and their families starve. But how can they seek redress? Who in America speaks for them? Who even knows? How can these workers, many of whom cannot even read, understand the intricacies of finance and world markets, the return on invested capital, and the many subtle considerations that led to their predicament? Who can explain to them how a few men five thousand miles away can exercise such a terrible power over their simple lives? Who in American public life, in Congress or out, feels called upon to challenge decisions based on exclusive commercial interests?

The American government, far from challenging these unrestricted powers, feels that its duty lies in protecting them. Without the American people being aware of it, the full weight of American diplomacy is directed towards propping up in these backward countries the men who can best serve American financial interests. Look at the leaders whom your government has supported! Why else has it supported them? Why Franco? Why Syngman Rhee? Why Batista? Why Chiang? Why Perez Jimenez in Venezuela? Why Boun Oum in Laos? Why Pinilla in Colombia? All dictators. All your men. All 'good' men from the point of view of your commercial interests, but all hated as oppressors by their own people.

The recent revolution in Cuba sent a wave of apprehension through financial and government circles in the United States. Reaction was harsh. Diplomatic relations were cut off. An American-equipped and financed invasion of Cuba was attempted. How many Americans realized why there was a revolution? How many Americans knew, before Castro shouted it from the roof-tops, that 40 per cent of Cuba's productive land was held by American interests? And 90 per cent of her electricity supply? Almost all her oil resources? Fifty per cent of her railways? Eighty per cent of her telephone system? How many Americans knew that the American government was supplying the arms and the bombs and the aeroplanes with which Batista murdered his own people? Your government told you that he was 'against communism' and therefore must be a good man! And because those in financial power were behind him, he was recognized by your government after a blatantly corrupt election, within eleven days!

Are you so naive as to imagine this is not taking place elsewhere? And not only in the backward countries! An intricate network of commercial and financial control has been spread across the world. What name would you have us give to American actions other than imperialism? Being kept so much in ignorance of what is done in their name, it naturally comes as a shock to most Americans to hear that their country is thought of as imperialist even by their allies. As the *Observer*, a paper by no means unfriendly to the United States, wrote on July 10th, 1960:

> The crisis in the relations between Cuba and the United States underlines a paradox which pains and surprises most Americans: that the United States, which sees itself as the precursor of colonial freedom, is widely regarded abroad as an imperialist, even a colonial, power....

In Latin America it has too often behaved as an Imperialist Power itself. The Monroe Doctrine ... was obviously motivated by anti-colonial altruism, but it did not stop the United States from feeling free to intervene itself in Latin-American affairs. This intervention started in Mexico with the occupation of Texas, formerly a State of the Mexican Union, and continued with the foundation of the Republic of Panama, formerly a province of Colombia; the invasion of Mexico shortly before the outbreak of World War One; the occupation by the U.S. Marines during the war of Nicaragua, the Dominican Republic, Cuba, and Haiti; and finally the overthrow of an elected Guatemalan government in 1954.

Though officially Cubans have been free from colonial domination for nearly sixty years, in fact they have been tied to the United States as Iraq and Egypt were to Britain. And their pride very naturally resents this....

Britain, over Suez, learned the hard way that being tough with proud people no longer pays.

America, it seems, still has that lesson to learn.

For the past twelve years China has lived under constant military threat. A network of installations keeps American planes, missiles and rockets zeroed-in twenty-four hours a day on our major population centres. Quemoy is almost as close to our shores as Alcatraz is to the Golden Gate. Almost within shouting distance. How would the people of San Francisco and the leaders in Washington react if on that island were guns and missiles in hostile hands? In Japan, in Okinawa, in South Korea, in Taiwan (in Laos, too, if she had her way), America has huge military establishments. Riding close to our shores as a constant harassment and interference to our coastal shipping is the Seventh Fleet, armed with nuclear weapons. Your ships encroach on our waters and your planes fly over our territory.

Can you not, just for a moment, make the effort of imagination to reverse our roles? When the Russians offered to assist Cuba with arms, there was immediate talk in your press about a 'Soviet base' being established in Cuba. Did we hear you respond in 'measured tones'? What happened then to the 'temperance' of language which you demand of us under infinitely greater provocation? You yourselves have a powerful naval base in Cuba, but a wave of indignation and fear swept your country at the thought of the Soviet Union having one there too, 'within a hundred miles' of America! If a mere rumour of a Russian base in Cuba can so excite and enrage your public, how would they respond, we wonder, if a hostile power held bases in Mexico, in Canada, in Hawaii, in Bermuda? If a hostile navy encroached constantly on your coastal waters and hostile planes were flying over your cities?

Your leaders, of course, tell you that your huge array of armaments are needed to preserve your 'way of life'. Americans believe that their country stands for tolerance and decency and for the essential equality of all men; they see themselves as the supporters of the under-dog against the arbitrary powers of wealth and prestige. Your way of life apparently is so precious that the future of mankind must be jeopardized to protect it. But who in his right senses can now think of America as standing for the under-privileged? Where does she uphold the weak against the strong? America stands for power and wealth. Instead of fighting privilege, she protects it. Is it to America that the ordinary people of Africa, of Latin America, of Asia look for help in their struggle against tyrants? How can they, when more often than not it is America that supplies weapons to their oppressors?

That something is profoundly ailing in your society you yourselves know. Deep in the national consciousness there appears to be a growing conviction that America has lost her way. Your lawlessness has gone beyond all bounds; your jails are full, your courts are overworked; from your own records we learn that 5,500 of your juveniles are arrested by the police every twenty-four hours; 55 per cent of your hospital beds are used for the mentally ill; your syphilis rate (according to your own medical reports) has increased by 200 per cent in the past two years — and half the new cases are young people between the ages of fifteen and nineteen. A country that spends more on drink than education, more on advertising than on health, must indeed ask itself: *What has gone wrong?*

The speeches and writing of your more thoughtful men are full of serious self-searching. 'I am concerned, desperately concerned,' said your Mr Adlai Stevenson in a speech in 1959, 'about our mainspring. That it has run down, we know. But is it broken beyond repair?'

We can give Mr Stevenson an unexpectedly reassuring answer. No nation's 'mainspring' is broken beyond repair. We do not believe that history is just a jumble of accidents. We think the rise and fall of nations, the health and sickness of societies, are susceptible to rational understanding and improvement if the laws that govern these changes are understood. The basic direction of American society can be reversed as soon as the real reasons for your country's predicament are understood by the masses of the people.

To us it seems self-evident that your competitive economic system (the system you so greatly extol) was bound eventually to bring about precisely the social results you now deplore. It is a self-destroying system. By the force of its own inner logic the system becomes a jungle in which every man is compelled to seek his own gain even if it be at the expense of his fellows — or of society as a whole. One analysis that Marx makes and which you reject (usually, we suspect, without ever really reading it) is that when once commodity production for personal gain becomes the central focus of man's existence, all other preoccupations will be subordinated to it. Marx makes sense to us because we see his general laws working out in history. You, for instance, have become a 'business-obsessed' society.

That your system has produced enormous wealth we cannot and do not wish to deny. But at what cost of suffering to others? With what exploitation of people in a less advanced stage? With what a ruthless plundering of your own resources? And in your own society, it is wealth that has been achieved by denying other values which we hold too dear to sacrifice. With you the individual is the unit. With us it is the group, the family, the village, the co-operative, the association of friends working together for a common end. Without this sense of interrelatedness and comradeship we believe there can be no happiness, only a restless striving for personal success. Where there are no stable human relationships, where there is no reverence for the past, no respect for excellence, no discipline, no deep, feeling contact with the great rhythms of nature, but only an insatiable desire to exploit nature for financial profit — there, we think, there can be no true harmony. Within the terms of your competitive system you measure the degree of civilization by material wealth; we measure civilization by the quality of our relationship with our fellow-men. It is relationship and not the possession of things which in the end provides all that is most dear and precious in life.

And hating so much in their own life but unable to express it, caught within a system which compels them to deny so much in themselves that is tender and trusting, it surely isn't surprising that many Americans have to express their hatred elsewhere, outside of themselves — against 'communism', against 'China'. Is it really communism they hate? Is it China? For indeed what do they know of China? They see China and communism only through the distorting lenses of their own frustrations. As long as people assume that their system is fundamentally sound, while every day there is mounting evidence that something is very wrong with it, it is utterly unavoidable that they will continue to find an external enemy that must be the cause of their predicaments.

We in China look across the oceans and see people in different stages of their historical development. We see some still in feudal conditions, or as colonial subjects. We see some societies suffering (as America is suffering) from the contradictions of advanced capitalism. But with the people in these countries we feel a sense of common humanity. When we shout our defiance at American imperialist policies in Asia, it is not the people of America we shout at. We cannot any more 'reject' the people of America than we could 'reject' ourselves — though we reject with all that is in us the corrupting influence of their public philosophies.

This has led some of your writers to suggest that we are trying to 'divide' the American people from their government. We are not so naive as they suppose. What seems to us clear is that American imperialist policies abroad and the inner decay of American life at home are part of a single process. They are problems related to this specific period of American history, they are developments following historic imperatives, but they are not rooted in the particular 'character' of the American people. Historic processes can be retarded or hastened. We shall continue to shout our defiance at America's imperialist policies, and we shall continue to feel a democratic relatedness to the people of America. And in this we see no contradiction at all.

*

The rest of the world, we can assure you, has grown weary of America's moral admonitions, her holier-than-thou attitude. Standing far above the pressures of hunger and poverty, she preaches to the world as to how we should all behave. We watch the creeping degradation of American life and listen to her sermons. The nation with the highest crime rate in the world talks to us about 'respect for law'; the nation with one of the highest rates of drunkenness tells us to be sober; the nation with the highest divorce rate preaches to the world about 'sanctity of the home'; the nation that has the largest navy the world has ever seen, and has piled up the equivalent of 32 tons of high explosives for every man, woman and child on earth, talks to us about not being 'warlike'; the nation which is in perpetual racial crisis with its negro population, and a hundred years after the abolition of slavery has still not found it in its heart to deal with coloured peoples on a basis of equality, talks tirelessly to the world on the virtues of democracy; a nation renowned for the extent of corruption among its public officials gives us homilies about good citizenship! It is enough to make a cat laugh!

Wake up, Americans! Come off your moral high horse and join the people of the world. You are no better than the rest of us. All of us are part good, part bad; part self-seeking, part generous. China has foolish, passionate, bigoted people just as you have. We are not saints. We make mistakes. But we are trying not to pretend to ourselves, so that here in China today it isn't any longer considered undignified to say, 'We made a mistake — let's try something else.' And if some of us do pretend, and in our enthusiasm give larger figures of production than are true (as we did two years ago with our grain figures), we publicly correct the figures when we find this out. But you, in your ivory tower, encased in your moral rectitude and your poses and pretences, you feel you dare not admit mistakes, or the whole sham front will collapse. You make an historical error as you did with Taiwan, and though you know it's an error and is leading you every year into greater and greater difficulties, you cannot say (as the British have learned to do), 'It is time for our withdrawal,' and do it with dignity and good feeling. You cling to your false positions and your false allies, just as you cling to your H-bombs and missiles, because that's all the 'security' you know. You cling to an economic system that is inwardly and outwardly bringing you to ruin because you dare not make a change. You cling to your super highways and super cars and super kitchen gadgets and super tranquillizer pills and tell yourselves, 'This is the life!' because you cannot face the full extent of your inner impoverishment. Wake up, Americans, before you do yourselves and all of us irreparable harm.

In China we are extremely poor compared with you, but we are enjoying life. We are enjoying ourselves as we have never enjoyed ourselves before! We work hard, perhaps too hard. We get tired, we don't have much to eat, though no one starves, and when we have bad harvests we get even less — but we are as excited as schoolchildren. And we are busy — as your pioneers were busy — not making money, but building colleges and schools and hospitals; we volunteer by thousands at weekends or holiday times to help farmers make dams and bridges and new irrigation ditches. We are learning something new every day; millions of us are learning how to read and write for the first time in our lives; we are studying to be doctors and physicists and geologists and engineers and dancers and poets.

We are the oldest country in the world, but we are much younger than you are. We are like you were when you started America, still able to thrill to new ideas. And we are not alone. We feel we are moving with history. Africa is waking up, Latin America is waking up, Asia is waking up — and we are all working harder and with greater zest than we have ever done before. But you do not *thrill* any more, you Americans! You have lost your capacity to believe. What visions stir your hearts? What new horizons move your children? And how will history judge between us? We who are trying to bring health and education and morality and cleanliness and joy to our old country — and you who stand on the sidelines and sneer?

China Kaleidoscope 4
NOTES FROM MY JOURNAL AND LETTERS

Continuity

In 1958 Mao Tse-tung said, 'China's six hundred million people are first of all poor, and secondly, "blank". That may seem like a bad thing, but it is really a good thing. Poor people want change, want to do things, want revolution. A clean sheet of paper has no blotches, and so the newest and most beautiful words can be written on it, the newest and most beautiful pictures can be painted on it.'

Almost 2,500 years ago, Lao-tzu, speaking of Tao, the 'Way', said, 'The Way is like an empty vessel....' And, 'We turn clay to make a vessel, but it is on the space where there is nothing that the usefulness of the vessel depends.... Just as we take advantage of what is, we should recognize the usefulness of what is not.'

Peking, Taipei, and Quemoy

Chinese are Chinese, whether they are on Taiwan or the mainland. Their civil war is imposed upon a much older and deeper conflict, against the foreign powers. Chiang accepts U.S. help, not because he has the slightest sympathy with American democracy, but because he has to.

Mao's government and Chiang's are agreed on two things: that Tibet is part, and has always been a part, of China; and that Taiwan must never, under any circumstances, be detached from China. The United States would like to solve her Taiwan predicament by encouraging a 'Two Chinas' policy; the great stumbling-block in her way is that this policy is rejected by *all* Chinese, Nationalists and Communists alike.

In June 1960 Lei Chen, a newspaperman on Taiwan, announced that he was forming an opposition party; Chiang Kai-shek responded by promptly putting him into jail for sedition. Those familiar with the ways of Chiang saw it as just one of his old methods of handling opponents. And, of course, it was partly that. But my reading of the incident is this: Chiang jailed Lei Chen not so much as a political opponent, but because he suspected that Lei was being groomed by the U.S. State Department as a possible leader who would be amenable to the Two Chinas policy. To Chiang, this was an immediate threat; once this policy was openly formulated and received the full weight of American official support, it could mean an end to his rule.

I sometimes suspect that on this question of two Chinas, however bitterly they distrust each other on other issues, there is more understanding between the Chiang group and the Peking government than we realize. We look on, utterly baffled, by the on-again, off-again shelling of Quemoy from the mainland, often with loud-speaker announcements to inform the islanders where the next day's shells will be aimed so that they can get out of the way. This is *not*, we feel, the way to fight a serious civil war!

The clue to this puzzle can again be found in the essential unity of the two Chinese groups on the question of two Chinas. The United States has, it is generally understood, for a long time been urging Chiang to withdraw the very heavy military contingents he has been holding in Quemoy and Matsu. Both Chiang and the Peking government probably consider that a withdrawal of these troops might well be the first step in a compromise which Washington would welcome — the evacuation of Quemoy and Matsu (as being of 'no military significance') in return for an 'independent Formosa'. This neither side will allow. So Quemoy and Matsu must be made to appear by no means of military insignificance. And, anyhow, how could Chiang be expected to withdraw under fire? Would that not be interpreted everywhere as defeat? So the shelling on alternate days goes on; the Chinese chess game is played, and Washington remains bewildered and frustrated!

Letter to Elena. August 16th

... This is an uncomfortable country to be in in some ways. I find I am constantly confronted with *myself*. Krishnamurti once said the real value of relationships is that they can act as a mirror to oneself. This whole country is a mirror. When I get annoyed here the Chinese never respond with annoyance, they respond by being solicitous and helpful which makes one feel as if one had acted like a little child. They have a rare gift for letting one sit with one's anger, and I am always left feeling rather ashamed of myself and boorish. Another thing I notice, especially when I am tired and am not getting my way about something, that my voice takes on that damned supercilious English tone, the voice of some-one who unconsciously feels he should be specially treated. Other things I notice here about myself that I wouldn't even *see* at home. I find myself automatically leaving my heaviest bag, knowing it will be carried by someone else. This comes from years of expecting someone to be around to do the donkey work. I think if I lived here I should have a hell of a job rooting some of this superior-status assumption out of me.

And perhaps *that's* at the bottom of this self-criticism business. China was confronted, even to a greater degree than England, with people who were extraordinarily conscious of their *status*. An upper-class Chinese must at first have found it inordinately difficult to adjust himself to a society that was deliberately and consciously setting out to be egalitarian. I hate to think of the criticism meetings I should have had to go through! And perhaps the Chinese are right that it can only be done through constant reminders by interested, friendly and deter-mined comrades.

Though the Chinese I meet never respond to anger with anger, this doesn't mean that their feelings are not hurt. I had a good example of this with Yen at the time he was taking me to the hospital to have my foot dressed. I was in pain and hadn't slept; and I was irritated that he and the doctor were having a conversation which Yen was not translat-ing. I asked three times, but they just went on talking. I finally said, very irritably, 'For God's sake, Yen, the whole point of your being here is to translate for me...' and so on, in a very who's-paying-you-anyway tone of voice.

Yen didn't say anything, but I could feel that he was hurt. The next day he didn't turn up — they sent someone else to interpret for me — or the *next* day. The third day he came but was rather aloof. I said, 'Yen, let me practise a little self-criticism. I was annoyed and spoke im-patiently to you the other day and I think now it was without cause. I wish to apologize.'

From that moment we got on fine again.

I am coming to see what they are trying to say when they talk about getting rid of the 'last vestiges of feudalism'. That phrase can hit close to home.

Do-It-Yourself Country

For a people with no technical background, the Chinese peasants seem to be taking to mechanics like ducks to water. They are extraordinarily confident that they can do *anything*. This has led to some heartbreaks. At one commune they showed me where they had originally placed a dam for a water catchment, but the water seeped underneath and washed the whole thing away. Thousands of man-hours wasted. But they went to work immediately and put it in another place which held.

I came across a typical example of this readiness to make anything, in a rural commune in Hopei Province. I found one workshop in the commune turning out transformers, the kind you see slung on high-tension poles. This seemed such an unlikely product for a rural commune to be making that I asked how it all started.

It seemed a long-distance power line was built across the commune land; and the management committee, all excited, bought electric pumps, saws, grinders, etc. But when they asked the linesmen to hook them up, they learned there were no transformers available. The commune would have to wait its turn, six months or more. The committee didn't think much of this, particularly in the year of the great leap forward. So they sent one of their members into town to borrow an electrical handbook from a technical library. For nights they poured over this manual, trying to understand how a transformer works; then they went ahead and made one, using old wire and pipes and odds and ends they picked up or bought second-hand. The power engineers came out to see it. (Inspectors aren't as fussy in China as ours would be, and do-it-yourself efforts like this one are thoroughly approved of.) It didn't look like much of a transformer, but they hooked it up, and it worked. When the story got around, a number of neighbouring communes in the same fix put in orders. By this time the Party, having got word of this example of local initiative, sent down a man with blue-prints. From then on, the commune was in the transformer-making business. And there I saw their previous week's output awaiting shipment, stacked up in the yard with ducks and chickens pecking around them.

Cost of Entertainments

I have gone a great deal to concerts, drama, and ballet here in Peking. Tickets are cheap and very much in demand. One yuan (3s.) will usually buy the best seat in the house. I have gone to performances in the park concert-halls for as little as fifteen fen (5d.). Today I looked in at an exhibition of contemporary painting. The ticket was three fen (1¼d.) for the public and two fen (¾d.) for students. I asked the girl selling tickets what would happen if a student who couldn't afford even two fen came. She said, 'I'd pay for him myself!'

The Militia

The women's militia brigade of this hotel has a drill in the quiet side-street outside my window at six in the morning, twice a week. Each woman has a rifle, and a man is trying to train them in the rudiments of close-order drill. They are dressed in ordinary work-trousers. At first they were a pretty ragged group, and quite giggly.

'*Yi! Er! San! Sih!*' (One! Two! Three! Four!), the instructor would yell, but they couldn't keep step at all. And the rifles slung over their shoulders got mixed up too. That was some weeks ago. But what a difference today! Smart; no giggles. They fling themselves to the ground, up again, down again; and their marching is precise.

All over China young men and women are training in the militia, millions and millions of them. I have seen them outside factories, in the fields, at colleges — everywhere. It makes me think a little of what America must have been like after the revolution, when the citizens insisted on a constitutional guarantee of the right to bear arms.

The *Sunday Times* of June 12th came in from London a few days ago with Montgomery's article, and I was interested to read what he made of all this militia training. This is what he wrote:

All fit persons between the ages of 18 and 25 have to serve. These militia units are the 'Ming-Bing', the people's soldiers.

I inspected the militia unit of a factory in Canton which made electric torches. It was an amazing parade of men *and* women, all armed with rifles or tommy-guns; there was an anti-aircraft section manned entirely by women; a signal section of men and women; and a medical section.

This militia organization covers the country, and in the event of a foreign invasion of China the invading army would have a very poor time, indeed it would be engulfed by the Ming-Bing. I have always said that the *second* rule of war is not to go fighting with your land armies in China, and what I saw of the Ming-Bing proves the correctness of that rule. I was once asked what is the *first* rule of war, and I replied without any hesitation, 'Don't march on Moscow.'

These are armies of civilians — a Home Guard, we should call them in England. I have seen the peasants in the communes drilling or at target practice in the evening after work; each man and woman drills twice a week, I think, but this probably varies. Sometimes I have seen the peasants strolling home after drill carrying their rifles with them.

For years we have read in the Western press that China's people are 'slaves' awaiting the opportunity to revolt. But here they are being armed by their government! It is unlikely, I think, that a regime which was uncertain of popular support would set about arming its peasants and workers.

Foreign Aid

A dispatch from Delhi today reported that the Planning Commission there had announced that steel and grain targets for India's second Five-Year Plan (April 1956–March 1961) will not be realized. The target for finished steel was 4·3 million tons, but the government now expects production to reach only 2·6 million; grain was set for 80·ₓ million tons; this now is expected to be 75 million. The same dispatch quotes the *Times of India* as saying that agriculture 'has remained almost stagnant'.

These are *low* figures. India has almost two-thirds the population of China but is producing proportionately far less. Chinese steel production in 1960 was over seven times the production of steel in India

China's grain production (in spite of the climatic disasters) was two-and-a-half times greater than India's. China's rate of industrial growth is much steeper than India's.

I know the attitude in the West is that India is going slower because she is accomplishing her revolution through a politically democratic process, more gradually, more humanely. But when we move from political theory to the mathematics of human survival, we face the fact that a Chinese child today has better health, better food, better work-prospects, more education, and greater security than an Indian child, despite the fact that Britain left India with a more advanced industrial base and more extensive communications than China had when the present regime took over.

Walter Lippmann, whose judgment I often greatly respect, has stated (in *The Communist World and Ours*):

> The Communists are expanding in Asia because they are demonstrating a way, at present the only obviously effective way, of raising quickly the power and standard of living of a backward people. The only convincing answer to that must be a demonstration by the non-communist nations that there is another and more humane way of overcoming the immemorial poverty and weakness of the Asian peoples.
>
> This demonstration can best be made in India, and there is little doubt in my mind that if we and our Western partners would underwrite and assure the success of India's development it would make a world of difference.... India is the key country.... To make a show-place of a small island like Formosa ... is a good thing to do. But it is not very convincing.... If there is any other way of meeting the communist challenge in Asia, I have not heard of it.

I think, however, that Lippman has missed a crucially important point: aid by itself can do very little to help a country if other conditions are not present as well. Let us look at the simple arithmetic of aid to India. Not long ago three eminent bankers, members of the World Bank, were asked to report on the needs of India and Pakistan. They suggested that these two nations required about 8,500 million dollars in aid from the West to carry them through their next five-year development plans. Per head of population, this amounts to scarcely more than a penny a day. I do not believe that aid on this scale — or any scale, for that matter — is really getting to the heart of the matter.

Chinese advances have *not* been dependent on foreign assistance, nor on coercion, for that doesn't work either. Russian aid (almost all of which was paid for by China) has amounted to less than one-tenth of a cent a day per capita of population. The vital factor is not money from abroad, but the *latent labour power in the people themselves*.

It appears to me that if backward countries rely on programmes that are Western-inspired and which do not come out of the genius and will of the indigenous people themselves, they are certain to fail. India's problems will be solved only when she discovers ways of releasing the tremendous creative powers of her people that are at present lying unused. It seems to me that India's real revolution lies before her. She is hanging on precariously to political and economic concepts which are more Western than Indian; she should not look to Russia or China any more than she should look to the West. She must look to *herself*, discover the sources of her own energies within herself, find an *Indian* political and economic system that makes sense to the Indian people — then, and only then, I think, will foreign money and technical assistance really help her on her way.

Reflex

At the Swiss National Day reception, Chou En-lai made an unexpected pronouncement. It was generally thought that a Central Committee meeting was in progress at the time. Chou arrived well after the reception had started. He made a speech in which he brought up once again the Chinese suggestion of a Pacific peace plan, to include the United States and all countries bordering the Pacific Ocean, the purpose of which would be to make the Pacific a zone free of all nuclear tests. It was a dramatic proposal.

Clare McDermott was the only Western correspondent present; Ullmann of Agence France Presse was away; Hsinhua was unprepared and it took them some hours to get the story on the wires. McDermott rushed immediately to the Central Telegraph Office and filed his story to London, a clear beat of several hours for Reuters.

Within minutes the message must have been relayed to the United

States. Only an hour or two later the 'Voice of America' announced the official response. A spokesman for the State Department had already dismissed Chou's proposal as 'nothing but propaganda'.

Who made this evaluation? Who sat down and pondered what was behind the suggestion? What its implications were? How sincerely or otherwise it was put forward? It was a Chinese proposal, and therefore automatically had to be rejected.

Some European governments huffed and puffed a little at the rapidity of Washington's rejection of a suggestion that might have had some interesting nuances. But the damage was done. Those here who have been advocating a hard line against the United States have been given more ammunition.

Callisthenics

On long train journeys, at the first stop in the mornings (usually between six and eight o'clock), some of the passengers tumble out for their morning exercises on the platform. From loud-speakers strung along the light poles come music and instructions. I usually join in.

We sometimes make a motley display; portly businessmen from Shanghai, professors thin and bespectacled, students, the girls from the train crew, soldiers, children — there we all are. 'Bend *down*, one, two, three, four; swing *sideways*, one, two, three, four; stretch hands above the head, one, two, three, four,' comes the voice above the music.

Farther down the platform there are usually some older men who scorn these newfangled Swedish callisthenics. They, with deliberate slow-motion movements, with rapt and inward concentration, go slowly, beautifully, through motions of *tai chi chwan*, the traditional Chinese form of physical and mental training. No one looks at them. It is a very common sight, in towns, in the park, out on the streets in the early morning, to see these older men (and sometimes younger ones, too) performing these ritual movements. If I were here longer I should take instructions.

As for the Swedish drill, I'm for that too. After a fitful night on the train it limbers up the old joints.

```
**************************
* *************************
* PART SEVEN *
* *
**************************
```

XXVI

Public Health and the Mass Line

THERE cannot be the slightest doubt that China, during the past eleven years, has achieved enormous advances in public health. As early as 1957 nine distinguished British doctors visited China. They reported that while some formidable problems still remain to be conquered, the Chinese claim many outstanding achievements:

Item: 'Between 1949 and 1957, 860 new hospitals were built (averaging 350 beds)', i.e., one hospital was completed somewhere in China every *three-and-a-half days*.

Report by F. Avery Jones, M.D., F.R.C.P., *British Medical Journal*, November 9th, 1957

Item: On the care of the mother: 'In some ways, of course, the Chinese are giving a lead.... Five to seven ante-natal examinations are done.... Maternal mortality in 1956 was said to be only 0·3 per 1,000 live births in this district [Peking] and 0·28 in Shanghai ... the rate in England and Wales in 1955 was 0·54.'

Report by T. F. Fox, M.A., M.D., F.R.C.P., *The Lancet*, November 9th, 16th, and 23rd, 1957

Item: Since 1957 the maternal mortality rate in Peking has been still further lowered to 0·26 per 1,000.

Reported to me by Madame Li Teh-chuan, Chinese Minister of Health, August 1960

Item: The Child: 'Infant mortality is said to have fallen in Peking from 117 per 1,000 births in 1949 to 37 in 1956.... In one area where work has been intense it has come down to 22.... Shanghai figures were 31 in 1956 — not so much higher than the English figure of about 25.'

Reported by Dr Fox

Item: 'China has apparently been free of cholera since 1949 and from smallpox since 1950. In Peking relapsing fever has disappeared and typhus has almost done so.... This epidemiological transformation of huge Eastern cities ... required intelligent organization of medical resources ... and no small scientific competence.'

Reported by Dr Fox

Item: 'In some of the more densely populated areas considerable success has already been achieved in the control of gastro-intestinal diseases such as typhoid and bacillary and amoebic dysentery, together with many of the common worm infections.... The standard of hygiene reached already is ... most impressive.'

Reported by Professor Brian Maegraith, Dean of the Liverpool School of Tropical Medicine and formerly Dean of the Faculty of Medicine at Oxford, in *The New Scientist*, December 5th, 1957

I am not a doctor nor an authority on public health, and for this reason I am quoting extensively from the reports by the British doctors who went to China specifically to study medical developments. I myself visited many hospitals in China — I received treatment in some of them — and I cannot but record the astonishing contrast between these hospitals in China and those I have seen in other parts of Asia, the Middle East, Latin America, and Africa.

The findings by men eminently qualified to form judgments confirm and validate the conditions I myself saw in China.

'The cleanliness was impressive, with complete absence of litter and filth, and practically no flies,' wrote Dr F. Avery Jones of the Central Middlesex Hospital. 'Many litter-boxes were to be seen, particularly in the parks. Even the mules had dung sacks under their tails to prevent them soiling the streets. The eradication of flies had been the result of a national campaign and had proved an important contribution towards the public health.'

Professor Brian Maegraith reported:

The successful control of flies, the litterless streets, and fanatical household cleanliness are having a profound effect on the spread of gastro-intestinal infections, especially in children, in whom, we were told, bacillary dysentery is much less common than it was.

How has this been done? How, for instance, can a notoriously dirty city be tidied up? The answer lies in the will of the people, who must be persuaded that it is worth while making their dwelling-places clean and keeping them that way. The public co-operation demanded in such an exercise is immense, and the government has been remarkably successful in achieving it. This may have been easier in a totalitarian state than elsewhere, and there was probably some element of compulsion needed to persuade the population to clear away hundreds of thousands of tons of dirt and litter from the streets and to swat flies and trench maggots until the insect population was brought under control. Nevertheless, the Chinese man-in-the-street is essentially practical, and no amount of cajoling without a good leavening of common sense and social persuasion could have given him his present passionate belief in hygiene.

... In vast rural districts ... interim measures leading to conservation of night-soil are already in operation and are helping considerably to limit further the spread of intestinal diseases. Perhaps this is nowhere more important than in communities like those living huddled together in sampans along the banks of the Pearl River, for even the casual stranger to Canton must be impressed with the early morning parade of decorated family pots awaiting collection of night-soil, which, not so long ago, would have been cast freely into the swirling yellow waters.

While the doctors of this British group naturally concentrated each on his own speciality, they expressed general agreement in their reports that the major advances have been achieved through broadscale campaigns involving the people at a grass-roots level.

Dr T. F. Fox, editor of *The Lancet*, had this to say about a 'street committee' which he visited in Shanghai:

... I want to introduce you to the chairman of a street committee. He is a small, worn man in early middle-age — a pedicab driver.... His committee looks after a section of a district, and it is the representative body for about a thousand families — say 5,000 people. Its three functions are (1) to administer welfare services, (2) to explain the policy of the government, and (3) to reflect and transmit the opinion of the residents. The chairman, at any rate, seems to think of himself as chiefly representing his people, rather than authority. If the dustbins of his area are not cleared as usual at 5–6 a.m., the city office responsible will hear of it very soon.

As the medical authorities see it, the main function of the health group of a street committee is to 'carry out the directives' of the city health office as regards sanitation, immunization, and health propaganda generally. Having such close contact with people in their homes, they are in the front line of the patriotic health campaign; and in Shanghai, the health office has in the past few years given no fewer than 50,000 such voluntary workers the elementary training they need as campaigners.

The slum we visited was pretty frightful ... but it was under hygienic control....

An example of such a grass-roots campaign in the rural areas was presented by Professor Maegraith, the tropical-diseases specialist, in his description of the drive to 'liquidate' schistosomiasis, a hideous tropical parasitic infection, for centuries a scourge of South China:

It is endemic in twelve of the major food-producing provinces irrigated by the waters of the Yangtze and the rivers to the south. A recent survey disclosed that something over 11 million of the inhabitants of this great granary are suffering from the crippling physical and economic effects of the disease. Transmission ... depends on contamination of water with human faeces containing the eggs of the worm. Active larvae hatch from the eggs and invade certain snails, and from these other larvae are eventually discharged, which in turn infect the farmer by penetrating his skin when he is exposed to the water of the canals, creeks and irrigation ditches in which he spends his working life. [Symptoms of the infection in human beings include debilitation and enormous swelling of the abdomen.] The chain of transmission could be broken by preventing contamination of water by faeces ... by destroying the larval forms, or by killing the host snails. In theory, control sounds easy. In practice it is extremely difficult, and requires exceptional organization and the all-out co-operation of the people exposed to risk. The Chinese have achieved both.

A lay committee was formed directly under the Communist Party to co-ordinate the attack, and each province was provided with its own central organization below which subsidiary units for the districts, towns and villages are now being formed. All methods of control, from treatment of infected persons to destruction of snails, are carried out by these units, in which approximately 70,000 workers are already engaged.

To ensure the co-operation of the mass of the people concerned, intensive propaganda is being directed at the farmers with the intention of making them appreciate the economic and social dangers of the disease.... Village news-sheets, posters, cinemas, radio talks, group meetings and discussions are all being used to this end. Since the disease is the vital concern of the whole community, it has been decided that the community should help as much as possible in its control, and this principle is being brought into effect everywhere. For instance, the practical business of killing snails is not executed, as in other countries, by experts from outside, but by teams selected from the local farmers, who ... take over the work in their own villages and paddy fields.

I saw this scheme working in the outskirts of Shanghai. The banks of the canals and streams in the villages were being slowly scorched by flame-throwers. Beyond the villages, the ditches and paddy fields were being cleared by arsenical spraying. These simple procedures were estimated to kill about 80 per cent of the snails during the summer.

In the winter, the surviving snails burrow into the mud near the water line. Ditching this mud and packing it in the fields above kills most of them in a few months....

One further method of control which goes on all the time, illustrates the degree of general co-operation obtained. Until artificial fertilizers can be developed on a big enough scale, human excreta remains the cheapest and most valuable manure. Fortunately the dangerous schistosome eggs do not live long if left in faeces without contact with water. Storage thus renders the material non-infective. Thanks to skilful propaganda, this essential conservation of night-soil is becoming an economic and social fact. Each family now has its own privy, a portable, gaily-coloured pot. Every morning, the contents are poured into large communal earthenware containers, which are sealed when full and left for the appropriate time necessary for the ammonia generated to kill the eggs, after which the faeces are safe for use in the fields. The collection of family night-soil is assured by paying the family for it *pro-rata*, so many cents a day per person, according to age. This scheme is also being used for the control of water-pollution by fishermen, for each boat now has its own collecting pot, which is regarded as a regular source of income.

The reports by these medical people graphically describe what might be called the 'First Five-Year Plan' approach to public health. The pace has not slowed since 1957, when these positive accounts were made. For example, Dr Jones reported 860 new hospitals, averaging 350 beds, between 1949 and 1957. By 1960 another 161 hospitals, each with several medical departments and qualified doctors and nurses in attendance, had been added. This over-all figure of 1,021 new hospitals since 1949, of course, does not include the thousands of small hospitals, clinics and maternity homes that have been introduced throughout the countryside.

Lacking doctors, lacking hospitals and clinics, lacking many of the more complicated medications which are easily available in the Western world, the Chinese Government carried out nation-wide immunization programmes and selected those diseases which can be effectively attacked by simple methods of sanitation and prevention, upon which to concentrate its first efforts. This was sensible in any case, because these diseases happen to be the great mass killers and debilitators — gastro-intestinal infections, parasitic infections, malaria, venereal disease, and the common diseases of children.

Regarding the plans to combat malaria, Professor Maegraith wrote: 'The general campaign is similar in many respects to that in operation against schistosomiasis.... The magnitude of the social problems it presents can be judged by the population at risk, which is estimated at somewhere between 300 and 350 million. The ultimate aim is eradication.... This is to be achieved in 1969.'

With respect to schistosomiasis, considerable progress had been made by the summer of 1960, according to information I received from health officials in South China, but the disease was a long way from being 'liquidated'. However, farther north in communes I visited in the Yangtze valley, in an area where schistosomiasis had previously been fairly common, I learned that no new cases had been diagnosed during the past two years.

Perhaps one of the most spectacular public-health victories achieved by the new regime has been the virtual wiping-out of venereal disease. I visited, in all, ten hospitals in China — city and country, old and new. In each one I asked about the incidence of syphilis. In each it drew a similar response: 'None for two years', 'None for a long time', etc. Wassermann tests are required from both partners before a marriage certificate is granted.

I met, while I was in Peking, a most remarkable man, an American of Syrian descent, Dr George Hatem, who came to China in the early 'thirties — a resident, in fact, of such long standing that he is usually known here by his Chinese name, Ma Hai-teh. He is one of the few Westerners to have lived with the Communist Eighth Route Army during their years in Yenan.

Dr Ma works at the Research Institute of the Academy of Medicine in Peking, specializing in skin and venereal diseases. I found him vigorous and highly informed, still with a trace of the accent of North Carolina, where he had lived as a young man.

We had dinner together one day before I left Peking for the Northeast, but it was from others that I learned about Dr Ma's remarkable medical achievements, and these were confirmed from various sources. It appears that in the past five years only four fresh cases of syphilis have been diagnosed in Peking, a city of four million people. Two of the four cases involved a man and his wife who had come in from an outlying province. One was a baby, born to a woman previously infected, who had neglected her pregnancy blood-test. Thus only one of the four represented an actual new case in Peking. At a 1960 conference of venereologists from the large cities, all cases reported for Peking,

Shanghai, Tientsin, Shenyang, Hankow, Sian, Chungking, and Canton totalled only twenty-eight. 'The problem of fresh cases in the cities is finished,' Dr Ma said in a recent report.

Most venereal-disease work is now in distant areas, among the national minorities. The doctors go out to clean up localities where there still remains some infection — and to obtain specimens for slides at medical schools. At the Research Insitute in Peking, most graduates during the past five years have never seen an active case of syphilis or gonorrhoea. Dr Ma reported that in his last three trips to Inner Mongolia, which used to be a sink-hole of venereal disease, he had not found a single case.

He attributes these seemingly extraordinary results to the following:

The end of the Kuomintang armies with their camp-followers and their bevies of officers' concubines.

The closing down in 1950 of all houses of prostitution. Organized prostitution is today non-existent.

And finally, *health education* — the fact that the vast masses of the Chinese population had become involved in the national health campaigns.

The methods which had been used in the rural areas in the fight against venereal disease were described to me. A check list of symptoms was drawn up and posted in every village shop, every co-operative headquarters, every community centre, throughout the country. 'If you remember you ever had any of these symptoms,' the posters announced, 'go to the clinic and get a blood-test.' And the slogan was: 'We don't want to take syphilis into communism. Let's get rid of it now!'

Peasants know their fellow-villagers very well. And there was probably many a case of someone who didn't quite wish to remember, being jogged by a friend or neighbour: 'Didn't you have this trouble when you used to go around with so-and-so; or when you used to visit the whorehouse?'

Later, I was told, as facilities improved, doctors were able to provide blood-tests for every suspected case. The great thing was to get the people to understand the problem, then give them the techniques. That's really what is meant by the 'mass line' that one always hears about in China.

On my return to the United States I related this account of the virtual elimination of venereal disease in China to a doctor of some eminence in California, expecting a snort of disbelief. Instead, he said, 'We in America could do the same in six months if we really applied our knowledge and resources to it.' [1]

[1] I was under the erroneous impression that with the arrival of the antibiotics, venereal disease was virtually eliminated in the United States, until I read an editorial in the December 1960 issue of *Today's Health*, published by the American Medical Association. Here I learned that the U.S. Public Health Service reported that one million new gonorrhoea cases are developing every year; that syphilis has increased over 200 per cent in a period of three years; that there is an appalling increase in syphilis in the larger cities — New Orleans showing an increase of 818 per cent since 1955, San Francisco 591 per cent, Washington, D.C., 280 per cent — and that teen-agers are among the primary victims of the resurgence of venereal disease. More than half of the new V.D. cases are in the fifteen- to twenty-four-year group. The Communicable Disease Centre also found, the editorial states, that more females are being infected today at school-leaving age than at any other age.

XXVII

Madame Minister

'TAKE your jacket off,' she said, 'feel at home — as your countrymen made me feel at home in England!'

This was how my interview with Madame Li Teh-chuan started. Madame Li is Minister of Health, in charge of the national medical programme since 1949.

In my hotel immediately afterwards I wrote the following account of the interview in my journal:

I have just returned from the most enjoyable, confusing, lively, frustrating interview I have had in China.

An official was waiting for me at the entrance of the Ministry of Health and took me across a garden court to the main building. On the second floor at the top of the stairs were standing Madame Li and a Vice-Minister of Health whose name I never recorded. She greeted me warmly in very fair English and took me to a pleasant reception room, flowers on the table, sun pouring through the windows.

After the tea was poured I waited for Madame Li to give me the accustomed 'briefing', but she said, 'Go ahead, go ahead — ask me some questions.'

I began by asking her to give me a picture of the over-all development of medical services that had taken place in China.

Madame Li: 'The total number of hospital beds available in 1949 was 60,000 in 171 hospitals; today our latest figures are 467,000 beds in about 1,200 hospitals. Still far too few. But I'm talking now only of well-equipped hospitals with various departments, fully trained doctors, and a trained nursing staff. In addition we have hospitals and maternity homes at the county level — 6,000 of them; and at a still lower level we have 200,000 health clinics in the rural communes.'

F. G.: 'How many doctors are you training today?'
Madame Li: 'I'll have those figures immediately.'

She sent out one of the young aides, who returned with a list as follows:

1. *Higher Medical Colleges*

Total qualified in twenty years before liberation	9,499
Number qualified in 1949	1,314
Number qualified in 1959	14,849
Total qualified in ten years	48,474

This is 510 per cent more than the number qualified in twenty pre-liberation years.

2. *'Secondary' Medical Schools*

(Doctors receive four-year course but are not fully qualified.)

Total trained in twenty years before liberation	41,435
Number trained in 1949	3,803
Number trained in 1959	50,157
Number trained in ten years	181,263

This is 437·4 per cent higher than the number trained in twenty pre-liberation years.

I next asked Madame Li about infant mortality.

She was off! Speaking fast, sometimes in English, more often than not in Chinese, with Yen trying his best to keep up....

Madame Li as she spoke was leaning forward, hands on knees. She has black hair, swept back; glasses; she wore a blue skirt, white blouse, strong shoes. Her hands are those of a peasant, strong and capable. She reminded me of some of the vital pioneering women of the West — Elizabeth Fry in England, Jane Addams of Hull House in America. Jane Addams and Madame Li would, I think, have understood each other perfectly.

'The greatest causes of infant mortality in the past were tetanus infection and old-fashioned methods. Another reason was that in the minds of the women there was something shameful about pregnancy, and they attempted to hide their condition. Also there was a measure of shame attached to having their babies delivered by a man doctor.'

She had, she told me, a very special, personal interest in this question of infant birth and care. She had spent a great deal of time in the countryside. She had seen and talked to the midwives, and found them eager to learn new methods.

The state today, she went on to tell me, makes every effort to see that mothers are delivered in a hospital or maternity centre. She feels the psychological state of a mother is as important as the actual medical care. Good equipment is important, of course, but the attitude of a mother towards childbirth is equally so. She is now studying very hard to get a real insight into the current psychological attitudes prevailing among the people in the country.

In the cities maternal mortality is low; in the countryside — especially in the remote regions of Inner Mongolia, Sinkiang — where communications are bad, it is higher. She estimated the national average rate of maternal mortality as ·26 per thousand.

We then had a lively discussion about the causes of mental ill-health. I said it was the number-one socio-medical problem in the United States; that the incidence in China was undoubtedly lower, but that we had heard of some developments here, especially regarding a new treatment for schizophrenia.

The Minister replied that mental health was largely dependent upon the relationships between human beings. She had visited the United States for two years: 'There was far too much that was overstimulating there; night and day it would go on — crash, crash, noise and pressure — no tranquillity is possible there. Living is insecure, which leads to anxiety. Undoubtedly in China there are some mental cases handed down from the old society, and a few cases that are new for a variety of reasons. But our society is paying the greatest possible care to the security of livelihood of everyone and the healthy relationship between people.'

The Vice-Minister then broke in and said, 'Mental ill-health is a social disease often brought on by economic insecurity. A number of people get mentally ill through anxiety. Who is it that gets mentally ill? Stockholders, speculators, and so on — this anxiety is an important factor in causing mental illness. We are not in a position to say there is no mental illness, but as our economy expands and we move ever closer to real socialism, we shall eliminate even the little we have.'

F. G.: 'There are surely factors more important than economic anxiety. We have learned, for instance, that the primary cause of mental illness is the lack of real affection which a child receives in his early life, but which might reveal itself only many years later.... '

Madame Li (breaking in): 'I want to tell you an experience of my own during the anti-Japanese war, when I worked with the Children's Health Protection Committee. Many fathers were killed in this war and their children had become beggars, because the mothers were unable to look after them, having to go to work to earn. This was in 1938. We took 20,000 of these children and took care of them in institutions and public-welfare centres, and I haven't heard of a single case of mental illness in any one of them. Other people can take the place of mothers and fathers.'

Vice-Minister: 'Consideration and love are important to children and so are physical and mental care; and these are closely connected with the child's education. We think it is very important to give children humane care, adequate nourishment, and plenty of physical exercise. Some in your Western countries who have no economic insecurity have mental illness, so we agree there are other causes than that.'

Madame Li: 'I will tell you something of my own experience. During these last few years I have been very happy — I wish I were a child again so that I could go on enjoying life longer, and have the fun the children get now....'

This account is far more orderly than it really was. I interjected here with a question about population increase. What was the official figure? I had heard estimates ranging between 2 per cent and 3·5 per cent.

Even a simple factual question like this gave rise to a flood of talk, sometimes both Ministers talking at once, one often breaking in again before the first translation had been completed; often the Minister would turn and talk to me in English while Yen was still translating — utter confusion. That is why this interview was both enjoyable and frustrating; enjoyable because here were two highly competent, humorous, extroverted, jovial, and friendly people. But frustrating because here, at the very pinnacle of the public-health programme, were two people who had it in their power to give me all the statistics I required, but not doing so. *Not* because they were hiding anything from me — why should they? — but because statistics are so boring compared with the vivid stories of improvement, personal anecdotes, chit-chat, enthusiastic references to the Chinese recovery, etc. They were too human, too spontaneous to think that *figures* could be of interest. I felt over and over again during this interview that by bringing the conversation back to a factual, statistical level I was a little boorish. They must have felt as one would telling an exciting adventure story to someone who kept asking about the blood-pressure of the young man or the calorie-intake of the heroine.

But it was exciting to see their excitement. The health story of China is one of fantastic success. Children who ten years ago were scratching for food on rubbish-heaps, eating grass, dying by tens of thousands through malnutrition, are now among the healthiest children in Asia. Smallpox licked, tetanus licked, venereal disease licked, cholera licked, maternal mortality down to Western levels; schistosomiasis, a terrible scourge in China, being tackled, the streets cleaned up; a public highly health-conscious, universal immunization programmes, flies 'liquidated', slums cleaned up and under hygienic control, hospitals built by the hundred; streets, hotels, trains, public buildings, schools, as clean as our own. The greatest transformation, probably, in the history of public health!

And realizing I was not getting an answer to my question on population increase, I tried another tack and asked the Minister about the official birth-control policy.

'We have no *moral* objection to birth control. To women in a weak condition, women who shouldn't have any more children or who do not want any more children, we give birth-control advice. Otherwise, people who want children have as many as they want. It is entirely and absolutely up to the family. There are two main considerations: the protection of the women's health and the health of the children.'

Turning to me suddenly, Madame Li asked, 'How many children have you?'

'One,' I said.

'Pooh, shame on you. I have five, the Vice-Minister has four. I wish I had more.'

Again it is the *personal*, the immediate, that matters.

I tried once more to get the figure on population increase.

Vice-Minister: 'Yes, yes, we will try and find the figure. Somewhere around 10,000,000 a year, more or less.' (Again the non-interest in the population growth as a problem. Here, just as in the agricultural department, the figures that we know and worry about are just not known off-hand, and are not considered very important.)

F. G.: 'Are there any signs of exhaustion among your population? They work harder than any people I have ever seen. I notice they sleep in buses coming back from work. I have seen men lie down on the pavement, put their caps under their cheeks for a pillow, and go to sleep. Are you not pushing your people too hard?'

Madame Li: 'Yes, there were periods when we worked too hard and there are still some cases of exhaustion. We have given this quite special attention. The national policy now is no workday to be longer than eight hours, six days a week. There may be exceptions such as during harvest-time, but these are quite temporary and unavoidable, as all farmers know. The general rule today is an eight-hour maximum day, two hours of study, eight hours of sleep — and six hours for recreation, doing nothing or whatever one wants. We are very aware of this problem. We are encouraging wherever we can the development of reading-circles, drama-groups, individual creativity through painting and music, and in this way people can learn while they are also relaxing.'

Vice-Minister: 'Our problem is really one of urging people not to work too hard, rather than of urging them to work harder. That is difficult for Westerners to believe, but it happens to be true. The collective socialist enthusiasm for getting on with all the things that need doing, the socialist construction of the country, has been so great that we have had to devise ways through propaganda to teach people not to overdo it, but to give themselves plenty of time to relax and sleep.'

I asked two questions about fall-out. First, are tests made to see to what extent food and milk are being contaminated in China through fall-out of strontium 90, etc.? Second, sooner or later China will have her own bomb, and what are those who have opposed all tests to say to China when she contributes *her* share of contamination?

This started another avalanche of talk from both at once, more confusion. I finally got the general drift: that this country is opposed to all nuclear weapons (no mention was made of possible Chinese weapons), that they are very conscious of the genetic consequences of excessive radiation dosage, that it is less dangerous to small children here as milk is not part of the Chinese diet.

Madame Li: 'Our children, all of them above ten years old, know very well about the bombs on Hiroshima and Nagasaki and the horrors of war. They sing little songs about it. So from the youngest children to adults we are *all* against H- and A-bomb tests.'

F. G.: 'What is the Chinese suicide rate?' (A guffaw from the Minister.)

Madame Li: 'What should *we* want to commit suicide for?'

I press this. Another flood of talk. (I *like* this, I'm dealing with people, not calculating machines, but it is difficult for me as a reporter!)

Vice-Minister: 'We are now "walking on two legs". That means we are using both skilled and less-skilled doctors; full education and spare-time education. We are using all our human resources. This means that we are trying to eliminate unhappiness. Of course, there is some. But this is a socialist country and the relationship between our people is a good one. There is great *hope* in this country and a great sense of *purpose*, and those are not conditions that lead to a high suicide rate. I think the number of suicides must be infinitesimal, certainly far too small ever to appear on any of the returns we compile here.'

F. G.: 'What is the expenditure from the national budget that is devoted to public health?'

Madame Li: 'We will look that up for you. It is the second highest of the social expenditures, it comes after the expenditure on education.'

(I received this figure later: 1,600 million yuan (£229 million) was spent by the state for medical purposes in 1960. This does not include provincial or local expenditures.)

Vice-Minister: 'Expenditure on public health falls into two sections: 1) the facilities provided by the Department of Health, and 2) the facilities provided by the factories and other enterprises. When any factory is built now, a clinic and a hospital *must* be built as an integral part of that factory, though it needn't be right at the same site. This is for the factories above county level. In rural areas each residential district must set up a clinic; the size varies according to the need, but it must provide hospital care and an out-patient department. This means that virtually every Chinese is covered by some medical service wherever he may live.'

F. G.: 'Madame Li, you were once closely associated with the Christian Church. Are you still a Christian?'

Madame Li: 'That's a very good question and I want to answer it. I was born of very poor peasant parents, neither of them could read or write. They were ignorant, but they were Christian. I was baptized when I was three months old. My parents couldn't afford to send me to school but they did send me to a missionary school. Missionary schools were divided, there was one kind for the richer people and another kind for the poorer. I went to the poorer one. The food was very bad. We used to sing' (and here the Minister sang lustily) 'do re mi ... mi re do.'

'The work at this poor school was done by the pupils — part work, part study. I washed clothes, my own and others'. I cleaned up the yard, too, and that sort of thing.

'Then I went to college at the expense of the mission school; they would pay for some of us on condition we would pay it back. After I left college I worked for five years getting the equivalent of twenty-four yuan a month, and half of this I paid back to the mission school until it was all paid off. I paid back not only the tuition but the interest on the loan as well.

'At that time I believed in Jesus, because he was the son of a carpenter. "There is a nest for the birds, a lair for the wolves, but the son of man hath nowhere to lay his head." ... I may not have got that right, but you know the quotation. That's why I loved Jesus. As you may know, my late husband, Feng Yu-hsiang, was known abroad as the "Christian general". At that time I loved Christianity. Later on I got an understanding of Marx and Lenin. I saw the U.S.S.R. I wanted to help improve the conditions of the people, but everywhere I saw the way in which the landlords were making improvement impossible. I saw that it was the Party that seemed really concerned with the welfare of the ordinary people.'

*

The discussion having lasted over two hours, and knowing how busy these Ministers must be, I felt it was time for me to leave. They insisted on coming down to the street to see me to the car. We walked through the gardens — part of the Ministry had been a private house belonging to the uncle of Henry Pu-yi, the last Emperor — and I climbed into my car. The two Ministers remained standing in the road, waving as I drove off.

A remarkable interview with a remarkable woman.

XXVIII

'Walking on Two Legs'

ONE sip is worth ten thousand words.

Somehow I had picked up a nasty variety of foot-infection while I was in Peking, and found myself, one disenchanted morning, in company with my interpreter headed for the hospital, not as a V.I.P., but as a rather anxious patient. For ten days I had been on antibiotics and sleeping pills. Today, my foot being twice its normal size, they were to decide what further action was called for.

My journal for that day reads as follows:

I sat for half an hour in line downstairs outside the clinic surgery. It reminded me of some of the older London hospitals, the cracked paint, the exposed pipes everywhere, the people crowding the benches waiting their turn.

Alongside me was a Young Pioneer, red scarf round his neck, short pants, keen-looking. Little by little in the hot passage his head drooped, and finally I felt it resting against my arm.

On another bench a father with a small girl and younger boy waited while the wife was being attended to inside. I watched the endless delight he seemed to take in his children as he played with them, letting them thump him playfully on the chest, letting the boy go through his pockets. No one took much notice of their antics; I think they would have been 'hushed' in England or America. The little fellow, perhaps he was about three, crawled under the bench and tugged away at a loose bracket. But no one minded.

Down the line was a young tough whose injured forearms were bandaged together to keep him from moving them too much; and an old lady with bound feet, with that wise and patient look so many elderly Chinese have. Then, a mother who held an infant and showed

307

her neighbours where the child had a skin-disease which was causing his wailing. To comfort him she lifted her blouse and fed him. A woman, with a four- or five-year-old, paced up and down the corridor. She wore a pretty skirt and matching red shoes, carried a neat shopping-bag. She was unmistakably middle-class. I looked at her a moment wondering whether she really was Chinese. I made room for her beside me and we spoke in English for a few minutes before she was called in. She reminded me so much of the ladies one sees nowadays in England waiting in line at a public hospital who find everything quite awful, wishing they could afford a private doctor and not mix with the *hoi polloi*.

There is no aura of 'authority' about doctors in China. They don't appear to be much different from their clients and there is a definite lack of putting on airs. But I learned from Yen that doctors enjoy high social respect, which is not necessarily translated into their pay cheques. He doubted whether many doctors earned more than 150 yuan a month, a senior surgeon perhaps as much as 200. 'But they have a great opportunity to serve the people,' Mr Yen said.

My foot ached outrageously and I agreed with him.

My turn having come round, I was ushered into the examining room.

Dr Wang, after some careful probing, decided that minor surgery was necessary. He got on the telephone, told me there would be another short wait because an emergency had just come in, but it would not take long. Meanwhile I was sent off in a wheel-chair to a dressing-room where I was given a quite attractive pair of blue pyjama trousers and a striped institutional-type top. I am a tall man and must have appeared rather ridiculous in a pair of pyjamas made for the average Chinese.

The fourth floor was in great contrast to the sub-basement. No little boys peeking through dividing screens, no babies crying. Everything quiet. Orderlies were moving anaesthetic equipment about. The nurses wore masks and close-fitting white caps.

Dr Wang turned me over to the surgeon, Dr Wu, slight and young-looking, but, as I learned later, one of their most experienced surgeons. He spoke English well. He and his assistant wheeled me into an operating room. I should think this one is chiefly used for small affairs like mine, although it had all the lights, instruments in cases, and other gadgets in case they were required.

Lying on the operating table, I could see through the window the sloping roofs of the hospital, one of the eaves leaning so close to the window that the little animals on the green glazed tile seemed almost to be looking in.

Dr Wu and his assistant examined the foot with great care. They discussed it, checked my pain reactions. Dr Wu then told me they would freeze the foot, make an incision, and clear the abscess. He didn't know how deep he would have to go. I should feel some pain, he told me, but not for long; then I should notice an immediate diminishing of the pressure which had caused so much discomfort. He was in no hurry. Sterile instruments were brought in under a steaming cloth. Two nurses in masks stood by. Dr Wu's hands were delicate and deft and I felt completely confident of his skill.

I felt a number of jabs, and I am sorry to say emitted a few groans and ouches, all the while telling myself that it was incumbent on me to set a good example of Western fortitude. However, I was sweating like a Turk in a steam bath before the doctor finally said, 'That's all. It's all over.'

I should have asked Dr Wu a few professional questions: How long had he been practising? Did he specialize within the field of surgery? Was he a member of the Chinese Medical Association? Where was he trained? Instead, I just watched him swab and bandage. What I wanted most was to get back to the hotel and lie down with a good shot of Chinese brandy.

The inquiring reporter could wait for another day.

*

The field of medicine in China has had its share of ideological struggle since 1949. At first there was a tendency to discard completely traditional practices as feudal and non-scientific. Then there were other 'theoreticians' who insisted that Western medicine was 'capitalistic' and urged strict adherence to 'socialist' (Russian) medical practice and theory.

While this 'great debate' raged, however, emphasis in training much-needed medical personnel continued to be on Western methodology, 'capitalist' and 'socialist'. In 1956, though, the whistle was blown and both sides stopped short. All aspects of Western medicine were to be considered. In an address to a group of intellectuals, Lu Ting-yi, head of the propaganda department of the Central Committee, suggested that in general 'we borrow everything worthwhile the capitalists have devised in the field of science and technology'. At the same time the need to incorporate the best features of traditional medicine was stressed.

Although the bulk of China's new doctors are being trained in Western methods, the present trend indicates an integration of the traditional and the Western. Thus, traditional practitioners are urged to acquire some Western learning, and vice versa.

For us in the West, one of the peculiarities of Chinese medicine is this dual acceptance of Western and traditional practice.

The traditional includes a bewildering variety of herbs and medications; muscular massage; control of pain through induced relaxation; and acupuncture, a technique which allegedly relieves pain and other symptoms by means of a fine needle thrust deeply into the tissue.

The position of the Chinese Western-trained doctors is that since traditional methods unquestionably cure patients, there must be something good in them and therefore they merit study. They point out that many drugs on the shelves of a modern pharmacy have been included for centuries in the traditional Chinese pharmacopoeia. Ephedrine (derived from the Chinese herb *ma-huang*) is only one of the most recent examples.

In all the hospitals and clinics I visited, both in the cities and in the communes, I was told that Western and traditional doctors work closely together. A patient may choose either variety he wishes; and one school of physicians frequently refers patients to the other school. In my own case, for example, when I returned on the day after surgery to have the dressings changed, I complained of muscular cramps in the calf and thigh, and was sent over by Dr Wu to the 'traditional' department.

There I received a good old traditional Swedish massage, and very comforting it was, too. On another occasion, when I was visiting a hospital in Chengchow, I asked one of the traditional doctors to try an acupuncture on my arm, which he did readily enough. Since I was not feeling any pain to begin with, I could scarcely determine how much it might have cured. But at least it didn't cause any pain. And the insertion of an inch or two of needle into the flesh provided an experience sufficiently dramatic for me to feel confident it would take my mind off whatever anxieties might be troubling me.

Written records show that acupuncture dates back to the Sung Dynasty, A.D. 1000. The needles are manufactured from a silver-steel alloy and range in length from three-eighths of an inch to three and a half inches.

The general theory seems to be that the stimulation of key nerve-centres, often some distance from the area of ailment, can result in a partial or complete cure of certain types of disorders, chiefly motor and digestive. Treatment of deaf mutes is traditionally done in this manner.

How effective, or ineffective, all this is I am unable to say. It continues to be practised and tried out by both styles of doctors in China. They believe it has merit.

There was, apparently, sufficient evidence that Chinese traditional medicine obtains, under certain conditions, striking therapeutic results, for the government to set up an institute for a full-scale investigation to determine what scientific basis for it there might be. This is a long-term inquiry and its reports are not expected for some time.

Here in Peking, as well as in some of the commune clinics I visited, Western doctors tried to convince me that appendicitis was now being treated by traditional methods. When I pressed for chapter and verse, it turned out that persistent or acute cases are still being sent for surgery just as they would be in Chicago or London.

Dr Fox, in his article in *The Lancet*, writes: 'How much importance Chinese "modern" doctors really attach to traditional medicine is not quite clear. Co-operation has been ordained and it is easily made to sound sensible....

'The more cynical among us [he is referring to the visiting group of English doctors] could not but note the convenience of being able to refer one's less-rewarding patients to an alternative system of medicine, which makes full use of the scientific arts.'

There are other, and I think even more compelling, reasons.

China had in 1960 a little more than 200,000 doctors trained in Western medicine — this included those with 'secondary' training — in a population of 700 million inhabitants. But there were 400,000 traditional doctors, more or less. Obviously the vast majority of Chinese, particularly those out in the country, if they ever received a doctor's care at all, would have to receive it from one of the traditionalists.

Had the government attacked this group, it would only have created widespread opposition. To include them, to grant them acceptance and status, thus bringing them into co-operation with, and to some extent under the direction of, the Western doctors, was a thoroughly sensible compromise. I learned that traditional doctors in many areas were being taught sterile techniques and were carrying out government programmes of vaccination and immunization.

I remember, as I remembered a good many times during my trip through China, what the Vice-Minister of Health had said to me on the occasion of my visit to the Health Ministry: 'We are now "walking on two legs". That means we are using both skilled and less skilled doctors; full education and spare-time education. We are using all our human resources.'

XXIX

The Misfits

IT takes two sides to make a revolution, any revolution, and one side loses. Thus every revolutionary upheaval must leave behind masses of uprooted and disorientated persons. From these come the forces of active opposition if there is to be any. And from these come the inevitable *émigrés*, loyalists, refugees. The Chinese civil war was a bitter thirty-year struggle, combined with seven years of a war of national liberation against the Japanese. The residue of social dislocation is correspondingly vast. The *losers* of China's revolution could be divided into three categories:

1. Top leaders of the Kuomintang, many of whom had amassed huge fortunes. Some of these — for example, the Chiangs, Kungs, Soongs, Chens — left China even before the communists had completed their victory. The wealth they took with them ran into hundreds of millions. The Associated Press, on August 13th, 1949, reported that the United States had frozen 500 million dollars deposited by Chinese citizens in American banks to prevent the new Peking government from getting its hands on it. The amount of similar funds in Europe and South America has never been made public.

2. A second major group among the losers were the landlords. It has been estimated that there were twenty million landlords in China. (This figure includes their families.) With the coming to power of Mao Tse-tung, they lost all their holdings, except a plot of land for each one to work himself. Many of these were 'rich' only in relation to the poverty of the bulk of the population. They could not have fled even if they had wished. During the first years they probably thought communist rule was only a passing phase; and that the Kuomintang forces would return, as they had done in the 'thirties in sections of South China.

313

Besides the loss of most of their land, many landlords suffered more severe penalties. Probably thousands were tried for various crimes, particularly in connection with the Japanese war, when landowners frequently sided with the invaders and were used by the Japanese. And there were those who had taken advantage of periods of calamity to extort the last remaining plots of ground, tools, and even children from peasants made desperate by starvation. How many were tried and condemned, and whether justly or unjustly, and how many were killed without trial it would be impossible to estimate. But the price was not always death. All were deprived of the rights of citizenship for several years; some were denied admittance to the developing co-operatives or communes.

3. The third group among the losers were those elements of the middle-class professions, businessmen, and intellectuals who were not able to come to terms with the new regime. These groups, for the most part, were not among those who had fought actively on the side of Chiang Kai-shek. They had been caught in between, unable to identify themselves with either side. They had shared neither the misery of the peasants nor the age-old privileges of the wealthy. Many, particularly young people, as the Kuomintang disintegrated during its final years through corruption and chaos, had thrown in their lot with the revolution. These were writers, actors, students, teachers, and some Christians.

But others remained on the fence. They could neither support the revolution nor reject it. Living largely in the coastal cities, they had developed a sense of inferiority about their country and its people. They felt that progress could only be *Western* progress, and above all, American. They would display a certain esteem for China's ancient culture; but for anything of contemporary China, they felt only shame.

These groups from among the intellectuals and the middle class, during the ten years since the end of the revolution, have fared considerably better than the ex-landlords. Opportunities on a scale never before dreamed of have opened up for their children. Still, there remain, I am sure, considerable numbers of the older ones who have not become adjusted and probably never will. How many, I have no way of telling; but I would not be surprised if there were several million, perhaps 1 or 2 per cent of the population. With the exception of the handful who may find their way out of China to Taiwan or to over-crowded Hong Kong, for the most part these people are living out their lives as outsiders in their own land, misfits in a world they are no longer able to comprehend.

Their lot is a deeply tragic one; history has left them stranded. They are not likely to play any very effective role, either in China or outside of it.

I ran across a few of them, altogether by accident, during my travels. A glimpse of their stories is revealing.

There was a young man I sat beside at a concert one night in Shenyang. He spoke English and we chatted. As we were parting, I said, 'Look in and see me if you have time.' Which, unexpectedly, he did. For an hour we sat in my room and talked. He said he was a Christian. He hoped I would write objectively about China; and added, 'I mean *really*, not just what they tell you.' I pricked up my ears. 'How much do the people believe of what they say?' I asked.

'Most believe every word. Some only some. Some none at all. We conform. It's no good spoiling your career before you've begun.'

He was eager to talk. During that discussion we covered many topics: the monolithic similarity of all public speeches; the food situation, which was very tight in the cities then; the Party committee in control of every undertaking; the question of dissent.

'The real penalty of being named a rightist,' he said, 'is public ostracism. Sometimes even to the point where shopkeepers will not sell to such a person.' He estimated that in a free election only 50 per cent of the people would approve the new regime.

I asked him about sexual codes.

He said there was some sexual relationship among unmarried young people and this was not morally disapproved of. Extra-marital relations were not held against a man if it were known, unless his political views happened to be suspect as well. 'The correct political attitude is more important than your sexual morals.'

A wife might complain of her husband's political outlook at a Party meeting (or vice versa) but this would be largely for outside consumption. Their relationship at home would not be changed. He thought a good deal of this was political hypocrisy.

He seemed to me an earnest, intelligent individual, rather Western, rather liberal, still attempting to respond within the framework of his religious conditioning. He would be more at home in Europe than in China, and is hungering for a greater degree of individualism. Not caught up by the collective *élan*, he finds himself an outsider, and that must be painful indeed. But he was by no means a counter-revolutionary.

I asked him, 'What do you think is the alternative to the present regime?'

Here he paused. This clearly was the crux of his predicament. In his answer lay the tragedy of his life.

'I don't think there is one. This regime, historically, was inevitable.'

'What is your personal hope?'

'That it may change in time. Russia has changed. That's my only hope.'

There was another man, thirty-five I should say, who started a conversation with me as I sat on a park bench in Shanghai. Our first meeting was brief. We talked about a number of things, none of them particularly interesting. I didn't take to him too much; I felt that at any minute he was going to try to sell me something. When he asked whether he could come to my hotel to see me again, I hesitated, but I said 'all right', and we fixed a time.

At the second meeting we talked quite a long time. For what it's worth, I record the gist of our conversation.

I started by asking him how freely people could travel in China today.

'Foreign travel is out, of course. Even if I saved up my money for ten years, I shouldn't have enough. And if I did, I shouldn't be allowed. Before, Chinese of my family's status often went abroad; now there's no chance. But I think it's important that young people should see the world and so be able to judge things for themselves. For a while I had a chance of seeing foreign magazines; this gave me a picture of what the outside world is.'

'What restrictions on travel *inside* China?'

'No actual restrictions, no travel permits or anything like that, but there are many difficulties which make travel complicated. And of course, there's always the money problem.'

'What sort of difficulties?'

'You have to arrange your rations; and immediately you arrive at a place you have to notify the street committee where you are to be. And the authorities can come and ask you how long you are to be there, what you are planning to do, why you came, and even suggest that you return to your own town sooner than you had wanted to. Accommodation is a difficulty, too. There are so few hotels or small inns.'

'Tell me about the political meetings you have to attend.'

'There are two kinds. First, the regular meetings held once or twice a week for political discussion. I have to go twice a week, and the meetings last from two to four hours. We read sections of Mao's writings and discuss them under the tutorship of a Party member.'

'Is it a *real* discussion?'

'No one would be foolish enough to *question* anything fundamentally. We might ask for some passage to be explained technically, or say we don't quite understand how this fits in with that ... not as a criticism but merely for enlightenment. It's very boring, but I have to do it. The other kind are the criticism and self-criticism meetings. They are held more rarely and are much more drastic. During the anti-rightist campaign they were held frequently, but now my group doesn't have more than one every month or even two months. What happens is that if in your group of four or five it has been determined that you are the one that they will concentrate on, the others are told beforehand. When the meeting starts everyone says some of the things that they have done wrong, but when this has gone round the circle they will then come back to you and concentrate on *you*. It is very important for everyone to be able to say something bad about you, so you hear all the things that everyone can think up to say. You cannot get out of it by just admitting it, even if you *mean* it and quite genuinely see that what they are saying is right; you are still made to think it over and discuss it further and go over it.'

'What is the purpose of this criticism?'

'To eradicate any of the old feelings, especially in those of us who had money and family position. It is one way in which the Party controls opposition. They don't have to discipline you, your associates do. It saves the Party a great deal of trouble.'

'What is the result of this criticism on the one who is being criticized?'

'It is humiliating, of course, and very painful; and it makes you feel that the only way to get on is to lose your old courteous ways and begin criticizing others, and in this way you might avoid being the target yourself.'

'Have you ever been the target?'

'No, but I have to join in and criticize the others.'

'Don't you all begin to feel that it's something of a game, a play that you have to go through but that doesn't mean very much?'

'That might be true of some, but most people believe in the system and the Party enough for these criticisms to be taken very seriously.'

'What do you think the system should be?'

'I don't know, but I think this country is more restrictive than Russia was twenty years ago. And things are tightening. We used to see a few Western films, but we hardly ever see them now. We used to be able to read translations of contemporary American and British authors, but we hardly ever see them on the shelves any more. Formerly we could read foreign books, criticize and praise them; now it seems that almost *all* Western books are bad; *all* Western films are bad. We are more cut off from the world than we used to be.'

'Do you believe one reason might be that this government genuinely fears there is a likelihood of invasion, and that it is preparing the people for it?'

'Yes, I believe that is true. The government is more militant, more all-the-time denouncing America. I think it is preparing to meet what it considers an inevitable conflict between East and West. We see reports about America strengthening her forces in Asia, especially around China, and what can we think?'

'Should America get out of Taiwan?'

'Of course. The Kuomintang was very bad. Even intellectuals, non-communists, were so disgusted that they felt *anything* would be better than that. The Kuomintang is responsible for everything. It was their rottenness that made this government inevitable. You would not believe what I have seen in my youth, the disregard for the people, the cruelty and arrogance of that gang. Chiang Kai-shek is responsible for millions of deaths, people who starved because his officials were too corrupt, people he had shot.

'I wish that many young Americans could come here and that many

318

of us could go there. I think it's very important for us to know America. But that can't happen until everything is changed.'

'What are you going to do?'

'Do? There's nothing to do but go along with it.'

*

From an acquaintance who was not at all an opponent, but a supporter of the regime, I gained a picture of the difficulties in adjustment encountered by a Chinese intellectual acclimatized to Western ways.

Tsu Shou-cheng had returned to Shanghai from ten years in the United States only eight months previously. The authorities, he said, had been understanding of his problems. Realizing he was accustomed to a high living-standard (he had been earning nearly £300 a month in Chicago), they first put him up in a hotel, then found him a pleasant four-room flat. They also paid his fare from San Francisco. He is now engaged in research in the ceramics industry, he was a ceramics engineer in America. He doesn't want to go back. The country is basically on the right lines, he believes; and as for the talk about freedom or lack of freedom, he feels that is all meaningless until a society can really stand on its own feet, until people are secure in their basic wants.

He said, 'Whether a man coming back to China after ten years in America can adjust himself here depends on what he really wants from life. As you advance towards middle age, you realize that your time on earth is limited. So what do you wish to do with it? If your aims are merely personal, then it would be best to stay in America. If you want to feel you are part of a great movement that is trying to do something for the good of others, then return to China.'

He has periods of nostalgia, he told me, for the easygoing life of America; but feels his place is here with his own people. He insisted that living in China today calls for a fundamental readjustment of values, a drastic re-examination of one's own motives.

'The real revolution,' he said, 'is in the people.' But he had had a rough time finding the key to all this. He felt the easiest way to grasp what was going on was to consider it as a 'religious' movement, directed not towards personal salvation, but towards a common advance. The results of this, the improvements he found in China after ten years away, were staggering.

Let me conclude this chapter with a word on Hong Kong refugees.

The picture that has been painted in Western reports is of a stream of desperate people, fleeing under cover of darkness, at the risk of their lives, across a heavily fortified frontier, from slavery to freedom. The theme has been embroidered endlessly in news dispatches on 'mass executions' and 'slave-labour communes', date-lined Hong Kong.

Actually the facts are rather different.

Certainly there are refugees in Hong Kong, large numbers of them, who come from one or another of the various groups of losers discussed above. But it is important to place the refugee problem in the context of a realistic picture of Hong Kong and its relation to the mainland.

First of all, there is little necessity for people to sneak across the border 'at the risk of their lives' because the frontier is practically open. Trains to the border run frequently; small boats ply back and forth; there is a constant flow of people from China to Hong Kong and from Hong Kong to China. For example, in February of this year, a C.B.S.-TV news report quoted a British border official as saying that 'a thousand to fifteen hundred Chinese a day go to China [*from* Hong Kong] to visit relatives: they pass quite freely; their papers are accepted by Red China'.

Second, it is important to remember that Hong Kong is a *Chinese* city. It is ruled by the British, and 99 per cent of the population are Chinese. And Hong Kong bears the same relationship to adjacent areas of mainland China that a metropolis always bears to the agricultural hinterland. The city imports food from the country and the country people migrate to the city looking for jobs, just as young people from 'downstate' go to Chicago to work in the factories. This has been true for centuries, except that before 1949 they were called *migrants* or *temporary residents*, rather than refugees. The Chinese in Hong Kong even today do not call the newcomers 'refugees'.

Finally, it is important to keep the size of this migration in proportion. China has a population close on 700 million, some of whom were obviously the losers in the revolution. Many of them suffered deeply and wanted to get out, just as there were considerable numbers of

Empire Royalists, the losers in the American Revolution, who became 'refugees' in Canada.

For the Chinese losers Hong Kong constitutes virtually the only port of exit; and for most of them it is a route that leads to no other place. Once in Hong Kong they must stay there or return, as many do. A few reach America or Taiwan. Long before 1949 there was a steady migration from both China and other parts of Asia to Hong Kong. The population of Hong Kong today is, roughly, three million. In 1949 it was 1,700,000. In eleven years, therefore, the island's population has increased by 1,300,000. But Hong Kong, like every other place, has a *natural* increase of population which in 1960 was estimated as no less than 60,000 per year.

When all these facts are balanced out, it appears that there has been an average influx into Hong Kong *from all countries* of about 70,000 a year, which represents *one-hundredth of one per cent* of the Chinese population.

Across the border, as I have said, stream many hundreds every day in both directions, and accurate figures are difficult to come by. Even the estimates of the numbers going into China every day for visits to relatives and friends vary considerably. Among those who come to Hong Kong from China there are undoubtedly many genuine refugees: those who have either detested the life there and find it too restrictive, active counter-revolutionaries, or those who are being sought, perhaps for non-political crimes, by the Chinese police. But the figures, in popular imagination, have, I think, been greatly exaggerated.

No one would want to minimize the hardship or the extent of the human suffering implied by this migration to Hong Kong, nor the acute problem that it created for the tiny island which had to find accommodation for these newcomers. But from an account by the Hong Kong Government we can see another and more hopeful side of the picture:

At first the endless lines of immigrants were regarded with pardonable misgiving. Overcrowded Hong Kong could well do without people who obviously would become a burden on its already strained resources.

These fears were quickly proved unfounded, however. Many of

the Chinese were not refugees in the accepted sense. They had capital and they brought it with them. The rest showed traditional Chinese characteristics — a strong desire to find work, make money and be independent of everybody.

XXX

The Wealthy and the Wise

THERE is a widespread belief in the West that all the rich people of China, the former owners of businesses, for instance, as well as the intellectuals and scholars, even if they outwardly support it, must be secretly opposed to the Peking regime. I think this is a mistaken conception.

I had talks with several intellectuals — professors, heads of university departments, elderly scholars engaged in historical research — and I am convinced that their support of the government is genuine and not a clever bit of acting. They might on this aspect or that express sharp criticism, but their basic acceptance and the reasons they gave for it appeared to me full-hearted and honest. And that seems to be true, also, of the middle class, although I met only a very few of these. There was one extended talk, however, that I had with a man who had once owned a large textile mill in Shanghai.

I was staying in Hangchow and was planning to leave the following day by train for Canton; this involved an overnight journey. I wanted, at the last minute, to bring my journey forward by a day. A train was due shortly — it was coming from Shanghai and had already left there — and I was told there were no tickets available for this train. But I took a chance and went with my bags to the station, hoping that the guard would be able to find me, if not a sleeper, at least a seat on the train. As it turned out, there was one place available in a sleeping compartment which I shared with a Mr Wang.

I relate these circumstances of my catching the train because others since have said that 'quite obviously' Mr Wang (whose conversation I am about to relate) was planted on the train specifically so that he could fill me with propaganda. This was quite impossible, for he had already boarded the train in Shanghai before I decided to catch it at Hangchow.

Mr Wang spoke English fluently. He was on his way to Hong Kong for a two-week holiday. He was clearly a man of wealth. His shirts were of silk, and he had cuff-links of star sapphires; his clothes were probably Hong Kong made. We had this long journey together, and enjoyed each other's company and had a good many congenial beers.

I asked him to tell me what happened when the Communists took over Shanghai, and this in outline was his story:

Shanghai suffered total demoralization during the last few months of Chiang's regime. Business had virtually come to a stop. Inflation made money valueless. So almost everyone was in favour of change — anything, they felt, was better than what was going on. The strong 'defence' of Shanghai — before Chiang himself left for Canton he had ordered the city to 'fight to the last man' — simply petered out. The few pill-boxes the army had built round the city were soon overrun, and large segments of the army deserted to the Communists, including many officers. Everyone knew by that time that the game was up, so why lose one's life in a hopeless cause?

'But what happened to you, I mean those of you who owned large undertakings?'

'Nothing at first. The Communists supported us. They confiscated immediately the holdings of the key Kuomintang officials, but as for us, they needed us, they wanted the mills and factories to keep going and they helped us do it. A political party was formed and sponsored by the Communists, the capitalist party. This was all written into the constitution; it says there that the positive sides of capitalist industry which are beneficial should be retained. But, of course, from the beginning it was made clear to us that this was just temporary, that sooner or later the government would take over our enterprises.[1]

[1] Article 10 of the Constitution reads in part: 'The state protects the right of capitalists to own means of production and other capital according to law.

'The policy of the state towards capitalist industry and commerce is to use, restrict, and transform them. The state makes use of the positive sides of capitalist industry and commerce which are beneficial to national welfare and the people's livelihood, encourages and guides their transformation into various forms of state-capitalist economy, gradually replacing capitalist ownership with ownership by the whole people.'

'We worked, of course, under strict regulation,' Mr Wang continued, 'and eventually the state decided step by step to take over legal ownership of our undertakings. The transfer was gradual, but the plans were precise. There was no room for argument.'

'What was their deal?'

'It was this. The capital value of our undertakings would be mutually agreed upon. They were prepared to pay us 5 per cent of this value each year up to ten years. It was simple and forthright; and it was also a take-it-or-leave-it proposition. Most of us took it, there seemed to be nothing else to do. Some wouldn't, they left for Hong Kong or Taiwan, where probably they had salted away some funds earlier. I stayed.'

'How has it worked out?'

'For me? Fine. They will pay me the final instalment in a few years. I invested the money — it comes to a great deal — in the People's Bank and am drawing good interest on it. In addition I earn four hundred yuan a month as manager of the factory I once owned. In my life it has made very little difference. I even live in the same flat as I did before. I don't have the worries I used to have!'

'And what happens to the money in the bank when you die?'

'Oh, my family get it. Under the constitution there is the right to inherit family property.'

'One last question,' I said. 'What do you call yourself?'

He laughed cheerfully. 'Do you know what we call ourselves? We call ourselves "Communist capitalists"!'

And that, I thought, was as good a description as any.

*

Here was self-interest at work. It was a straight business deal that the Communists offered, more sensible than running these men out of town or executing them. It was a no-nonsense plan that benefited both sides. They had clearly learned something from the Russians, who were left after their revolution with no people of managerial skill and had to start painfully from scratch.

But the intellectuals?

There is a general impression in the West that the scholars and intellectuals have suffered greatly under the new regime. Forgotten are the executions and assassinations of writers and professors by Chiang Kai-shek in the 'thirties and 'forties. The assassination of Professor Wen Yi-tuo in Kunming in 1946 was one that received some note in the Western press at the time; the full list, running into hundreds, has always been known in China. In the final desperate years many intellectuals were forced underground, others fled to Hong Kong. In the latter case there were wholesale returns following Chiang's defeat in 1949.

With the exception of a handful, the leading writers, artists, scholars, poets, scientists, philosophers, and religious leaders not only welcomed the new government, they have continued actively to support it. A number who had been living abroad returned to China after the government was already entrenched. Lao Sheh, author of the best-selling novel *Rickshaw Boy*, came back from America, where he had been a guest of the United States Information Service.

A few have had their difficulties, some have been dismissed from their positions. Two well-known members of China's literati, Hu Feng and Ting Ling, are examples of intellectuals who were dismissed from the Writers' Union for political reasons. Hu Feng is a well-known literary critic and Ting Ling a famous woman novelist. Submitted to severe public criticism, both fell out of favour, but neither was imprisoned.

In the case of Hu Feng, in 1955 his two-hundred-page protest, calling for the abolition of the Writers' Union and pleading for the removal of cultural affairs from the hands of the government, was published as a supplement to China's leading literary magazine, *Literature and Art*, but neither Ting Ling nor Hu Feng is getting any stories or articles published.

It would be quite wrong, I believe, to assume that the intellectuals of China just go along. They continue to play a vital role in the life of the nation. Dr Joseph Needham, whose reputation as a Sinologist and student of Chinese science is second to none in the West, and who was a personal friend of innumerable scholars in China before 1949, reported after his 1958 visit how much less ideological pressures were influencing their work or lives than he had expected.

The names of the intellectuals who remained in China and are wholeheartedly supporting the regime read almost like a roll of honour: Feng Yu-lan, philosopher; Fei Shiao-tung, sociologist; Mao Tun, Tsao Yu, and Pa Chin, novelists; Kuo Mo-jo, historian and academician; Ai Ching, poet; Mei Lan-fang, Peking opera; Li Ssu-kuan, head of the Ministry of Geology; Tao Meng-ho, President of the Academia Sinica; Y. T. Wu and T. C. Chao, leaders of the Protestant Church.

The list of eminent intellectuals — scholars and scientists — could be extended almost indefinitely. With rare exceptions, such as Dr Hu Shih, who left China before the Kuomintang debacle, there is scarcely a single intellectual of world reputation who has not found a useful place for himself in China.

Professor C. P. Fitzgerald addresses himself to this point in his book, *Revolution in China*, which when it appeared was described by *The Times* as 'the most important contribution that has so far appeared on the nature and behaviour of the Chinese People's Republic'. This is what Professor Fitzgerald says:

It is difficult for the West to believe that the Chinese people can have voluntarily accepted Communism. It is hard to credit the free support given to a regime which denies freedom to some and only hands out a very qualified freedom to others. And yet there is no real doubt that the new system has obtained the support of the people, has satisfied the aspirations of the literates, and has won to itself the devotion of the men of religious temperament.

The military success of the Communists would have been in itself insufficient to secure the new regime had it not been accompanied by a conversion which has aligned the great majority of intellectuals behind the Communist movement.

Nevertheless it is probable that the initial alliance between the Communist Party and non-Marxist intellectuals soon became a somewhat cautious one on both sides. The intellectuals were thankful that Chiang Kai-shek's repressive measures and his indiscriminate purges in the universities had come to an end, and they were ready to give the new regime full support in its agricultural and industrial reforms, but they must have looked with some dismay on the retention of political power by a single party — with all the restrictions on freedom that that would imply. To the Communists, on the other hand, the non-Marxist intellectuals must have appeared too deeply conditioned by bourgeois ideas of 'individualism' to be fully trusted.

Pressure on the intellectuals to become aware of their 'mistaken attitudes' continued until 1956. They were expected to undergo intensive political study to overcome their 'ideological inferiority'. The Communist Party undoubtedly hoped that a sincere change of outlook, a sort of religious conversion, would bring the intellectuals wholeheartedly to their side.

In 1956 Mr Chou En-lai called for more support for intellectuals and less suspicion of them. And this was followed up in 1957 by Mao's famous 'Hundred Flowers' speech in which he declared that ideological differences could not be expected to disappear all at once, and that they could only be resolved by free discussion. Mao invited the people of China to criticize the Communist Party's conduct of the revolution. There was an overwhelming response. The freedom to criticize lasted just one month.

It became clear that some of China's intellectuals refused to limit themselves to a criticism of the working of the system, but condemned the system itself. They were accused of rightism, and some were sent to the country to work among the peasants to learn the real meaning of the revolution at first hand.

It was immediately assumed in the West that the 'Hundred Flowers' speech had been merely a trick to catch the discontented ones. I, personally, do not believe that this was so; and nor do others who have followed this episode closely. A most interesting analysis of the speech and its consequences by Mr John Gray was broadcast by the B.B.C. and subsequently printed in *The Listener* of March 9th, 1961. Mr Gray is a lecturer at the School of Asian Studies at London University. This in part, is what he said:

It is widely believed in the West that the whole 'Hundred Flowers' movement was simply a stratagem for flushing out heretics ... in my view this explanation is untenable. For one thing, the movement grew out of an admitted practical need for more freedom of expression. For another thing, it is impossible to suppose that the theory of contradictions among the people — probably the most significant addition to Marxist doctrine since the death of Lenin — was produced merely to justify a very brief and very mild purge. The alternative explanation, that Mr Mao Tse-tung's request for criticism was sincere, is much more plausible. It would be consistent with the whole of his political philosophy, which has always clearly reflected his belief that bureaucracy and not reaction is the enemy from which Communism has most to fear, at least in China. In this context the 'Hundred Flowers' movement can be regarded as one of a series of attempts to keep open the channels of communication between Party and people which Mr Mao has been making since 1942. The reaction in which it ended is more than adequately accounted for by the fact that the criticisms were unexpectedly radical, that the critics clearly had Hungary in mind, that they showed that they had forgotten none of their western bourgeois prejudices, and, finally, that the revision-ism which they represented had become — as a result of events in Eastern Europe — a threat to the unity of the Communist bloc ... The only surprising thing about that reaction was its mildness; a year later, most of the principal victims were at liberty and had been restored to some, though not all, of their positions. Indeed, in theory the 'Hundred Flowers' still bloom. The emphasis, however, is no longer on the recognition of 'long-term coexistence' between the Party and non-communist intellectuals, but on discussion as the best means to secure unanimity under the formula 'unity-criticism-unity'.

Mr Gray proceeds to put forward a most interesting and provocative hypothesis — that the criticisms revealed during the 'Hundred Flowers' period and the creation of the communes may have been related.

... One followed hard on the other, and one may have been the answer to the other. The motives for the creation of the rural communes were partly technological and economic, but in their political aspect, involving for a Communist state a most remarkable and courageous degree of decentralization, they may have been an attempt to get rid of the evils of the bureaucracy which was the main target of criticism — not in the way proposed by the critics, that is the relinquishment by the Communists of their monopoly of power, but by short-circuiting the bureaucracy and putting affairs in the hands of the local communities and their elected leaders, under the supervision of local Communist Party members.

Mr Gray finished his lecture with a very timely warning:

The Chinese revolution is so complex, and in many respects so novel, that we must approach it with an open mind and with a certain humility, and we must not expect to understand this or any other aspect of it unless we are prepared to provide for twenty times the amount of research on it which is at present being carried on in this country. We must at least avoid falling into the assumption that all criticisms of Communist policies made by the Chinese liberals are automatically correct. We must remember that it is the Communists and not the liberal intellectuals who have been responsible for the success and verve of the revolution.

The French writer and poet Claude Roy, who was also seeking clues as to why China's intellectuals had in such large measure given their allegiance to the Communists, records the following interview in his book, *Into China*:

Professor Feng Yu-lan [author of *A History of Chinese Philosophy*, which is regarded by American and European scholars as the definitive work on Chinese philosophy] is an old Chinese gentleman of between 60 and 70, with long, thin, classic goatee and extraordinarily fine and expressive hands.

'Have you spent all your life at the Tsing Hua University in Peking?' I asked.

'No, I took my philosophy degree in 1924 at Columbia University and my doctorate at Princeton in 1946. I taught Chinese philosophy in the States.... I was offered a permanent chair but preferred to return to China in spite of the civil war.'

'Were you interfered with or persecuted by the Kuomintang government?'

'No. Like many intellectuals I adopted a passive but rather distant attitude towards the Kuomintang. I felt that I was keeping aloof from politics....'

'Weren't you tempted to leave China after the liberation?'

'No, but I prepared to follow the course of events with all my powers of criticism. Out of curiosity I asked permission to participate in the land reform in the country districts and in this way I made contact with the people as I had never done before. I was extremely impressed by the technique of criticism and self-criticism practised by my Marxist colleagues. Before leaving for the front, two of my students, both Communists, discussed their ideas with me for two days. When they left, I was so interested by all I had seen and heard that I wrote an essay on self-criticism from the philosophical point of view. One of my friends then pointed out that I was trying to lecture academically on self-criticism but not to practise it myself. I was forced to admit that was right....

'I am definitely convinced today that the goal of philosophy should be the modification of men and the world. I have resumed the study of Chinese philosophy in the light of this principle and on the basis of a total union between practice and theory, between thought and action. I have just finished a work in which I outline the epistemological evolution of Chinese thought through Confucius, the Moists, Taoist idealism and the School of Laws down to modern times.'

[After speaking of this work] Professor Feng took a book from his shelves and read me a few lines of Wang Yang-ming (a philosopher of the Ming dynasty, who lived from 1472 to 1528): 'It is not necessarily difficult to know but it is certainly difficult to act. The most difficult then should be our preliminary preoccupation, and this same preoccupation will be difficult at the outset. Knowledge depends on action for its fruits, but action does not necessarily depend on knowledge to be effective. Action, however, always leads to knowledge, whereas knowledge does not necessarily lead to action.'

'Philosophers like ... Wang Yang-ming were misunderstood or unknown even in China. I think that it would be of the greatest interest both here and in the West to rediscover them and to see their ideas being realized at last in contemporary Marxism,' and Professor Feng added: 'Tell my friends and colleagues in America and in the West that there is no mystery about my intellectual evolution. There is a Christian saying: "For the tree is known by its fruit." I have tasted the fruit of the New China and I wanted to know the roots of the tree which produced it. That is the entire story of my "self-criticism".'

*

I recall, too, an evening I spent in Peking with a historian, a man educated at Oxford who came from a wealthy and distinguished family. He was a scholar to his fingertips.

I had arrived at his house a little earlier than he. His wife greeted me and he appeared a few moments later, looking rather drawn and tired. We sat for a while quietly sipping tea and eating small cakes.

I asked him if he was ever involved in any of the political meetings I had heard so much about.

'Oh yes,' he said, 'we have meetings every week. We are all, whatever our work, members of some group. We meet and exchange ideas about our work.'

'Aren't these meetings a fearful *bore*?'

He smiled. 'It depends on who you *are*. A pedicab driver, I think, will look forward with real eagerness to his political meetings. After all, reading is still difficult for most of them; it's a chance to be read to and meet and talk. It's an occasion for them, a weekly social gathering. And they learn a good deal about the society they are living in.'

'And you?'

'Well, yes, it often becomes tedious for us; and I find it especially aggravating when I am in the middle of some intensive work. But more often than not, the discussion is what we make it. If we are dull, the meeting is dull. And of course, some of these meetings are self-criticism or mutual criticism and they are never dull!'

'Tell me about them.'

'I do not think you can understand the workings of this new society unless you realize the profound effect these criticism meetings have had on the people, on all of us. From the earlier days these meetings have been an integral part of the Communist technique for the remoulding of this country. Tonight — that's why I was late — we had a criticism meeting; it's part of a campaign that my research group is involved in just now to rectify mistakes in our work. Sometimes during these campaigns we might have to meet almost every night. What's happening in this campaign is that we are going through and evaluating both our research and our teaching work. We are attached to a university and we bring up mistakes that we think the university is making; they might bring up mistakes they think we are making. It's like an elaborate post-mortem. Every mistake is discussed very seriously. [He looked across

332

t me and smiled.] Oh, we are very, very solemn about all this; and we
usually find that the mistake was because of some error of thinking by
ome person who will then have to be helped to reach an understanding
f the failings that led to the mistake.'

'Would he ever get fired?'

'No. Dismissal is very rare. It's the last, most drastic step, and we
onsider it a collective failure. Now, it is a little different in a university,
ut if I were in a bank, shall we say, and I were constantly making
aistakes, or always in disputes with my colleagues, I should first be
eprimanded by my immediate superior. If that didn't help, I should
e asked to attend a mutual-criticism meeting. One or two other people
a my group (mutual-criticism meetings are usually not larger than five
r six, never more than ten) would have prepared suggestions as to how
could be helped. A whole evening might be spent in discussing my
ifficulties. You must remember that criticism today is considered
elping. We do not regard it as hostile, as you might. And if the meeting
properly conducted, I should be made to *feel* that the motive was
eally to help me, and not by any means to injure me or to lower my
elf-respect. Of course, there are some who resist even so; and then a
ig criticism meeting would be called, and that would be a very gruelling
xperience. But only after these successive steps had been taken, and
nly if they had failed to improve the situation, would dismissal or
ansfer be felt justified.'

'To me,' I said, 'all this sounds frightful! I would rather be fired.'

'I can understand that. I felt at first as you do. I suffered intensely.
erhaps I was too Westernized, too remote and aloof. But do you know,
have come to believe that they are on the right track. The end-result
f these criticism meetings is therapeutic. They break down the wall of
retensions and defences we build around ourselves. You cannot go on
retending and putting up a bluff after you have been through two or
aree of these meetings with your immediate associates! And we are
ever really very hard on the "victim", for we've been through it all
urselves.'

'They sound like group-therapy sessions to me,' I said.

'Not really, but they have some of the same effects, and go through
ae same cycles. At first when a group meets, the members are strangers
nd distrustful; and then as these meetings progress the members bring

up all kinds of hidden hostilities that they have for each other. But that stage passes, too. And at the end of it all you find you are working among people who really know each other and have become a group of intimate friends. The meetings are a conscious attempt to break down our pretences and protectiveness. When I look back on my life I am not sorry that things have turned out as they have. We work too hard, and we often are too tired; and if you looked into our kitchen you would see how little there really is to eat. We both nearly always eat at work, you see, except on special occasions. But I think I am being honest when I tell you I am really *happier* now than I was before. I get twinges, of course. There was much in the old life that was more comfortable, and we were greatly respected and looked up to ... but the fact is that I go to work every day quite happily because I am going to be among friends, real friends, not just professional colleagues.

'There are others, of course, who haven't really gone along with things; they resist this whole idea; they never will break down the shell of ego-defensiveness; they do their work, they join in, but never really feel one with the group, because basically they want to feel superior to the group; and anyone who wants to feel superior to a group in China today is a very lonely person.'

XXXI

Food and Famine

CHINA has long been known as the 'land of famine'. Before 1949, Americans were all too familiar with appeals for Chinese famine relief. For centuries the twin plagues of flood and drought wreaked havoc upon the Chinese people; in the public mind this and a huge population were the sole causes of recurring famine in China.

Scarcely, if at all, was it recognized that the nature of Chinese society was the main contributing factor. Feudal and backward, China lacked the necessary machinery to subdue the ravages of nature in such a huge area. A completely inadequate transport system prevented the movement of food to stricken areas, even though a surplus might exist elsewhere.

Under the Kuomintang, corruption and war-lordism were further contributing factors. Detailed accounts have been published in the West of relief supplies and funds from abroad finding their way to the black market and into official pockets, while hundreds of thousands were reduced to eating bark and grass. It will be recalled that the former Mayor of New York, Fiorello La Guardia, resigned his post as China UNRRA director in 1947 for precisely this reason.

One of the monumental changes which have come to China under the new government has been the launching of the huge complex of flood-control, water-conservation, and afforestation projects, which, helped by the extension of railways and highways, has diminished the hazards of flood and drought. Measures previously unheard of, such as transporting flood-evicted peasants to areas where planting can be done while inundated lands are drained, have been carried out.

*

335

While I was travelling in China during 1960, I saw many signs both of the excessive rainfall and the extreme drought which had afflicted the country during the first half of the year. In some areas there had been no rain for more than two hundred days, in others there were disastrous summer typhoons — eighteen hit the north-east coast alone. Westerners who had known China in the old days told me that 1960's drought, following the poor harvest of the previous year, at one time would have meant death for millions.

By the end of 1960, after my return to the United States, reports of the agricultural disaster in China were familiar headlines. *The Times* of December 30th described weather conditions in China as 'something not merely worse than in any year since the present government came to power in 1949 but worse possibly than anything China had experienced in this century. Certainly the succession of rainless days in north China last winter and spring was longer than that which led to China's last major famine in Honan Province in 1943 ... [when] it is estimated two million people perished.... ' (The 1942 famine carried over into 1943.)

Despite sensational headlines in our press of 'famine', 'bungling', 'mismanagement', there was no documentation of mass starvation, or of hordes of refugees and beggars as in former times. In my opinion there will be no repetition of the famine of 1942, and this belief was shared by Western observers with whom I spoke while I was in Peking. The work already done on flood-control and water-conservation has enormously cushioned the impact of adverse weather conditions. Beyond that, the Chinese will do exactly what the Americans do when the Missouri River floods — send in relief supplies from outside. And the government, for the first time in Chinese history, is capable of doing so. It has the railways and the lorries. Due to its immensely strengthened international trading position it has the foreign exchange. During the autumn and winter of 1960–1, the commercial pages of Western newspapers were reporting large Chinese purchases of grain from Australia, Canada, France, the Sudan, and Burma. And these were not charity hand-outs to aid the 'starving Chinese'. They were paid for in cash.

Any assessment of the adverse weather conditions of 1959 and 1960 on China's economy must differentiate between short-term changes of emphasis and long-term policies. The greater emphasis placed on agriculture in 1961 does not mean that the nation's basic objectives — the simultaneous and proportionate development of agriculture and light, medium, and heavy industry — have been abandoned; as the Chinese put it, they intend to 'walk on two legs'.

When the Communists came to power in 1949 both industry and agriculture were appallingly backward; industry made up a minute proportion of the national economy. The new government felt it necessary to plan for a more rapid growth of industry than agriculture in order to form the necessary base for the development of the entire economy. But the Chinese envisaged an eventual narrowing of the gap between the two, not by slowing down industrial expansion but by speeding up agricultural growth.

In 1958 Chinese economists were explaining the importance of agricultural growth as a vital cog in a rapid and proportionate economic advance. The importance of agriculture in supplying industry with raw materials is now being emphasized, as is the fact that China's peasantry offers industry the largest home market in the world. For some time to come agriculture will continue to be a major source of capital accumulation, as well as an important means of obtaining foreign exchange.

China's unprecedented high rate of economic growth has been possible, according to the Chinese, because agricultural development was carried out simultaneously with the swift expansion of industry. Statistics reveal a highly significant fact: the yearly increase in industrial production has been influenced by the preceding year's agricultural output. For example, in 1952 the agricultural rise was 15·3 per cent, and in 1953 the industrial rise was 30·2 per cent. After the great leap forward in 1958, the ratio was 25 per cent and 66 per cent. In 1959 agricultural production rose 16·7 per cent and industry followed with a 39·3 per cent increase.

Contrary to reports common in the United States, the communes, which originally grew out of the nation-wide movement for irrigation and land-reclamation, and the development of industry in the countryside, have not only proved their ability to meet the natural disasters of 1960, but are said by Peking to be the key factor in the drive to expand agricultural production in 1961, to help overcome the losses of 1960.

Nevertheless, there are enormous problems facing Chinese agriculture. This was acknowledged by the authorities while I was in China, and still is. They are written about and talked about in the press and on the radio, and discussed in meetings on a national scale. These problems are:

1. The immense demands of Chinese agriculture on industrial resources. The Chinese estimate that to fulfil their agricultural programme several million tractors will be required. In 1960 there were only about 100,000; these were being turned out at about 20,000 annually. It is estimated that millions of tons of industrially-produced fertilizer are needed annually, while output in 1959 was less than one and a half million.

2. A statistical system which is insufficiently developed to enable production and distribution to be competently planned and carried out.

3. Lack of adequate storage facilities. Although there have been years of abundant crops in the past ten years, food supplies have been lost through deterioration. Also, refrigeration in China is far from sufficient.

4. The general increase in the standard of living, which has enormously enhanced the pressure of demand on agriculture. This is not Peking propaganda. Anyone who has ever seen or read about the China of ten years ago knows this to be a fact as far as more than 90 per cent of the people are concerned — this is especially true of the nation's 500 million peasants, who consume a greater share of what they produce than at any time in China's history. I am, after seeing records and talking to peasants in many parts of the country, fully convinced that this is so.

With perhaps only half of her land-potential being used and still in the first stages of mechanized agriculture, China's food production and consumption have shown a steep increase in the last decade. The Chinese view their food difficulties in late 1960 and early 1961 as a temporary setback. While the government was alerting the population to the need for temporary over-all belt-tightening, preparations on an immense scale were being made to ensure an adequate harvest for 1961. If the 1961 harvest again fails, the Chinese people will indeed be in the most serious difficulties.

It is commonly held that China, with its 700 million people, is tremendously over-populated. The annual birth-rate of about 2 per cent is often cited as conclusive evidence of the impossibility of China's ever supplying its people with enough to eat. The Chinese do not agree. In fact, on this subject they seem curiously unperturbed; the bogy of Malthus and his contemporaries holds no terrors.

Some years ago William Vogt, a widely read writer, stated in his book *Road to Survival*: 'There is little hope that the world will escape the horror of extensive famines in China during the next few years. But from the world point of view, these may be not only desirable, but indispensable.'

One of the more knowledgeable and wiser of the prophets of doom is Aldous Huxley. When he looks to the future he speaks in tones of almost unmitigated despair:

Human numbers are now increasing more rapidly than at any time in the history of the species ... every four years mankind adds to its numbers the equivalent of the present population of the United States, every eight-and-a-half the equivalent of the present population of India.... It took sixteen centuries for the population of the earth to double. At the present rate it will double in less than half a century.... In parts of Asia and in most of Central and South America populations are increasing so fast that they will double themselves in little more than twenty years.... Over-population leads to economic insecurity and social unrest.... It is a pretty safe bet that, twenty years from now, all the world's over-populated and under-developed countries will be under some form of totalitarian rule.... If over-population should drive the under-developed countries into totalitarianism, and if these new dictatorships should ally themselves with Russia, then the military position of the United States would become less secure and the preparation for defence and retaliation would have to be intensified. But liberty, as we all know, cannot flourish in a country that is permanently on a war footing, or even a near-war footing. Permanent crisis justifies permanent control of everybody and everything by the agencies of the central government. And permanent crisis is what we have to expect in a world in which over-population is producing a state of things in which dictatorship under Communist auspices becomes almost inevitable.

And what, when I presented this view to Chinese agricultural experts and economists, was the general tenor of their reply? It could, I think, be fairly summarized this way:

1. The world is confronted with a staggering paradox. The peasant countries — where nearly everyone is engaged in growing food — are the hungry countries. The *industrial* countries — in which only 10 or 20 per cent of the population are occupied in growing food — have ample food. The United States has a rate of population increase greater than that of India; it is the greatest industrial nation; and it has on its hands an agricultural explosion and a food surplus so great that it doesn't know what to do with it. In some non-industrialized countries it takes ten men growing food to feed one non-food-growing man. In countries where agriculture is highly advanced, one man growing food can feed forty who are not growing food.

2. For thousands of years, with sickle and wooden ploughs, the average time needed to produce one hundred pounds of wheat was three hours. Today, with modern equipment, it takes less than two minutes, including the time taken to make the ploughs and harvesters. At the end of the Middle Ages a cow produced eighty-eight gallons of milk a year; today in a modern agricultural country a cow produces nearly eight hundred and eighty gallons. Indian cows today still produce only one-tenth of the European average.

3. Seventy per cent of the world's food-growing families are still using wooden ploughs or hoes — and this alone is a cause of primal poverty. Only 2 per cent of the agricultural families of the world possess tractors or motor ploughs. It is this handful that have caused the agricultural revolution.

4. The present-day world average of agricultural land is approximately 3·3 billion acres. This could, by irrigation, forest clearance, and drainage, readily be doubled. With modern farming techniques the world's food production could be increased by five to seven times. This with our present knowledge. And what new discoveries lie in store for mankind?

5. As for Huxley's fear that over-population will lead to an intensification of war preparations, the Chinese would say this: That he is still thinking in terms of the nineteenth century. The greatest obstacles to

the full development of food production in the under-developed countries are the superstitions, the religious taboos, the dull passivity, the lack of hope, and, above all, the class exploitation that is present in feudal or colonial territories. No real advance can be made without a fundamental change in a social system. There can be no significant release of human energies without such a change. And, as this would inevitably be one towards a socialist, planned economy, this makes archaic the notions of international rivalries envisaged by Huxley. He assumes military rivalry because he is still thinking in terms of mutually exploiting, mutually competitive capitalistic nationalities.[1]

*

As far as the Chinese are concerned, I found no agricultural expert or economist who did not talk to me in terms of *optimism* about their agricultural potential, and they never question its ability to take care of a much larger population than the country at present is sustaining.

China today is still using less than one-half of the 900 million acres of her potentially cultivatable land.

In the past ten years, while the average rate of population increase has been about 2 per cent, the rate of increase of grain has been well over four times this rate. The peak year for grain production prior to the new regime was in 1936, when 150 million tons were produced. When the new government came to power in 1949 this had sunk to 113 million tons. By the beginning of the First Five-Year Plan in 1953, production was 167 million tons; by 1958, production had risen to 250 million tons (final corrected figures), and despite the climatic calamities the 1960 production was probably not much less than that of 1957. India, with a population nearly two-thirds that of China, is expecting a 1961 grain production of less than 75 million tons.

I have travelled I don't know how many thousands of miles across China, north and south and to its centre, by land and air. I have seen something of this vast country. Most of us have a picture of a China teeming with people. Like many of the images we have it is based on a partial truth. Not many of us realize, I think, that at least half of this

[1] *Die Weltwoche*, Zürich, of September 6th, 1958, carried a most interesting analysis of the world food prospects, to which I am much indebted.

huge land has less than thirty-nine persons to the square mile — a 'rich' country like Holland has over eight hundred! Or that west of Lanchow (the equivalent of Chicago on the map of the United States) there is no city with even half a million people. Much of this empty western space could be used if modern techniques of water-conservation and irrigation were applied.

I did not, until I travelled in China, fully appreciate the tremendously wide disparities in population densities that exist, even in the Yangtze Valley, China's traditional 'Rice Bowl'. I came away from China with the powerful impression that much of China is waiting to be settled and developed just as was the American West a century ago. And that given a rational and planned approach, the solution of the abnormal distribution of China's population lies in something more than trying to persuade 500 million peasants to practise birth-control.

One official in the Ministry of Agriculture with whom I discussed population and food-production was confident that new, and as yet unimagined, methods of producing food would make the anxiety shown by Westerners seem quite foolish. He showed me a copy of an editorial which had appeared in the London *Daily Mail* on September 2nd, about three weeks before our meeting. The editorial was a comment on a conference of British agricultural experts in Cardiff, and this man obviously shared its sentiments:

Traditional methods of food-production are still far from being fully exploited. Beyond them are newer methods, and after them again are the miracles wrought by biochemistry. To begin with our own small island: there are still seventeen million acres of completely undeveloped countryside lying on the hills. Think of the immensities there must be elsewhere. Outside the West, most agriculture is primitive, inefficient, and on the wrong lines. Fertilizers and other techniques could double food production in less than a generation. But it would not stop there. Many countries have recorded individual yields of five tons of food an acre. This should be possible nearly everywhere. The human race is in sight of a very high standard of living and unlimited leisure. Unless we all go mad the best is yet to be.

The arguments put forward by this official and others I found attractive and compelling; they spring from an essentially optimistic outlook on life itself. But I must admit that some doubts remain. As I brought up in my discussion later with Premier Chou En-lai, I still feel that eventually there is a limit to the amount of food that any country can grow, and when that limit is reached, for sheer survival, population will have to be curtailed or other territories be plundered. Even this, to me unanswerable, logic does not dismay them. As one Chinese said to me, 'The time when we exhaust the possibilities of increasing our food supply is very far distant and we needn't worry about that yet. When the time comes that the population of China should be stabilized, we shall by then have learnt new ways.... '

XXXII

China through the Eyes of Others

EXCEPT in Peking one is not likely to run across many foreigners in China today. However, in the nation's capital, almost every country in the world is represented, except of course, America: official delegations and advisers from the Soviet bloc, European, Asian, African and Cuban diplomats and businessmen, 'peace delegates' from all parts of the globe, students from several score of countries, and a handful of resident Westerners who work for the Chinese Government.

These people have opinions, ranging from high optimism to crushing pessimism, on what is taking place in China. I have met a fair sampling of them; I've chatted with some and engaged in extended talks with others. Most of my contacts were with foreigners (Europeans and Asians) who have been here for at least a year or more, either on business or in the service of their governments.

The following are some of the thoughts and observations they expressed to me, as I recorded them in my notebook:

Englishman: The leaders, especially Mao, are not motivated by desire for personal glory. They are basically modest men. The cult of Mao does not spring from a growing self-importance on his part. The government remains, as always, a group government; the policy of establishing Mao as the father-figure of the nation was probably a consciously arrived-at, politically sophisticated decision taken collectively by the Politburo for reasons of sound necessity. The Chinese have traditionally looked to a man as a leader, rather than an impersonal 'government'.

Indian: 'China's attitude towards India underwent a change in the summer and autumn of 1958, at the time of the great leap for-

344

ward. The Chinese, filled with self-confidence, saw themselves playing a new role in international affairs, achieving great-power status under their own steam. Also, they felt the Indian Government was drifting to the right, and saw Nehru in his declining years more and more a prisoner of the right.

'As to the border dispute, China genuinely believes she has a legal case. We, of course, feel we have a case too. The reality probably lies somewhere between. The border has never been settled between our two countries and we are trying to sit down and reach an agreement. The Chinese demands are such that, even if our government were willing, it would not be acceptable in terms of Indian public opinion.'

Wife of European Diplomat: This is the only country she has ever been to where she leaves her jewellery lying on her dressing-table, and never even thinks of it.

Another wife: 'I hate these people. They stare at me so. I feel their silence and curiosity express hostility. I hate going out of the compound. I try to go out as seldom as possible. When I have to go to the hairdresser I drive out and rush back as quickly as possible.'

Five minutes later she was telling me, 'You people who come here for just a few months, how can you expect to get to know these people? You need to live here as we do.'

Burmese: 'The most impressive thing about China is her self-reliance. She is a nation pulling herself up through her own efforts. She wants to reach the time when she is not dependent on any outside help.'

Indonesian: 'The Chinese government is making a real effort to settle its dispute with Indonesia on the question of the Overseas Chinese and their dual nationality. This is partly because China cannot afford to have too many disputes with Asian countries.'

East European (oil expert): Gave the Chinese credit for a remarkable industrial development, but he personally was finding life here difficult; the Chinese were very much lacking in initiative, too reliant on the foreign expert, too ready to copy. Until 1959, he said, they were extremely anxious about their lack of petroleum resources. However, within the past year vast and hitherto un-suspected oil-fields have been uncovered. He now believes China will be one of the great petroleum-producing countries of the world.

West European (recently returned from trip to hinterlands): He listed his outstanding impressions: Massive unity of the people. Self-confidence of the government, which knows it has the allegiance of the people. Improved material conditions. The enthusiastic youth are the base of the society. A real danger of China's withdrawing from the world, excluding the world, revert-ing to her traditional isolation; at heart disliking other peoples. A tremendous desire to become independent of everyone. Pride of a strong nation, which doesn't want charity, even from the Russians. A nation where people are in great ignorance of the outside world they shun; they have stereotyped images of the West, particularly the United States, while the leaders themselves are very highly informed.

Pole: China was, in some ways, fortunate to have a hard time in 1960 on a number of fronts, especially with her crops. This has helped to correct various mistakes and to bring their agricultural planning back to a basis of reality. Mao has said that they must 'turn calamity into good fortune and disaster into luck'.

All this has tested the durability of the commune, which basically, this man feels convinced, is the best system for China. As a result of the setbacks, a new approach to the communes was being taken. The trend will be towards more individual freedom and initiative. Mao's 1959 tour of the communes and his analysis have been largely responsible for this shift.

There is very little individual decision-making even at the high-est level. Mao himself invariably seeks the opinions of many before making his pronouncements.[1]

[1] One of China's leading writers has confirmed this to another Western cor-respondent. Weeks before Mao makes an important pronouncement, he said, copies were circulated to several dozen people in the Government and Party. Those receiving these drafts (this writer was one) are expected to give their criticisms and comments absolutely freely. A second draft is sometimes circulated. Mao's formal declarations and speeches are thus the product of collective thinking.

There is a strange contrast to be found in the Chinese Government's dealings at home and abroad. At home they have shown an extraordinarily keen sense of what their people want, how to talk to them; they really understand their own people and how to handle them. Here they have shown wisdom and flexibility. In their dealings with other countries they sometimes lose this 'feel', sometimes act clumsily and with a very un-Chinese lack of deftness. He thought they had shown cleverness in dealing with the United States, however; they had refused to be provoked into military action against American forces around Quemoy and Taiwan. The Chinese had allowed America to stew in its own predicament without giving any excuse for military retaliation. The Indian dispute they had handled badly and had lost far more friends in Asia than they need have done.

The Chinese, after years of suffering from the arrogance of foreigners, are touchy. They won't let themselves feel humiliated by American policies re the U.N., etc., but they have built up an 'over-compensation'. A single word of criticism in an otherwise friendly article by a foreigner will sometimes damn the writer as not understanding and objective. This is not an intellectual reaction, but an emotional one.

Although they do not show it outwardly, the Chinese become exasperated with what they call Western obtuseness and the tendency to talk in meaningless clichés. For example, in the middle of an explanation of the details of benefits for women workers — leave with pay during pregnancy, and so on — a Western visitor will say, 'That's all very fine, but what about *freedom*?'

Russian (While I was in China, reports in the American and European papers of a Sino-Soviet split were becoming frequent. More and more talk was being heard in Western circles in Peking. The Chinese and the Russians were saying nothing. On one of my trips I had an English-speaking Soviet technician for a train companion. This man had been in China once before, in 1956. From all I could gather, because of the nature of his work and his contacts, this man seemed well qualified to deal with the range of subjects we discussed.):

On the split: 'We are aware of the rumours about Chinese and Soviet differences of approach and emphasis towards the Western powers. It should be clear that both the Chinese and ourselves are united in our fundamental hostility to the foreign policies of the Western bloc led by the United States; we are agreed that the United States is the greatest single barrier to world peace and progress.

'As to differences, they are not as serious as the West likes to make out. If we don't have differences we are said to be rigid and monolithic, if we do we are said to be splitting.

'The conditions confronting China and the Soviet Union vis-à-vis the United States are not the same. The Americans have had to accept the Soviet Union as an equal power, while they do not yet have to do so with China. For example, the United States is actually occupying Chinese territory in Taiwan. This is an act it could not attempt with regard to us. China's only recourse is to be outspoken and militant in speech.

'If there is one single piece of advice I would give Americans it is that China should be dealt with on a basis of equality. The greatest mistake in American foreign policy is her treatment of the Chinese as a lesser power.' (He was very emphatic about this.)

Taiwan: 'This is the outstanding issue preventing any normalization of Sino-American relations. There are two possibilities for resolving the impasse, internal revolt against Chiang Kai-shek, or American withdrawal. The former is unlikely, although it would be well to bear in mind the violent expression of anti-American feeling during the riots in Taipei two years ago.

'The answer for the United States is to face reality and withdraw, leaving the Chinese to settle the civil war. This would not necessarily be brought about militarily. By making such a move the United States position in the eyes of Asians, who do not look at Chiang as a symbol of freedom, would be improved. Moreover, it would avoid ultimate mortification for the United States.

'On the matter of Taiwan, there is complete agreement with the Chinese, as Premier Khrushchev has often stated. This means 100-per-cent military support in the event of any American military action against China over the island.' (Would the U.S.S.R., I wondered, risk a major war and possible obliteration for Formosa? I doubted it.)

Technicians: 'Recent accounts of a sudden mass withdrawal of our technical experts from China are highly exaggerated. The governments concerned did not make any statement about the matter so as not to give it undue importance.

'The total number of Russian technicians who have come from Russia to China since 1950 is only something over ten thousand. The peak was between 1955 and 1958, when there were more than five thousand. At present there are less than one thousand, which is about the average for the ten years. As perhaps is natural, there have been some purely technical disputes, and some of our engineers feel the equipment we have supplied is sometimes over-worked. But this has no political significance. The Chinese are now taking over all of the normal engineering functions. It is only in very advanced techniques that China still needs our help, which we are very ready to give.'

Nuclear Physics: 'In the field of nuclear physics we have helped to set up the Chinese Institute. We have also helped in construct-ing a cyclotron. China now has four. Many Chinese are studying in the Soviet Institute of Nuclear Physics, and the Vice-Director there is a Chinese.' [1]

Uneasiness: 'Regarding speculation in some quarters about Soviet uneasiness over the unexpected rapidity of China's indus-trial advance, this is Western wishful thinking. The Russians, far from being apprehensive, welcome it. The stronger the socialist world becomes the better domestically and in terms of world peace.

'The Chinese are the first to admit that they have learned much from us. Unlike the Soviet Union, they have not had to build their industrial base without friends.'

Recognition: 'We have always felt that it is only a matter of time

[1] According to Dr Robert T. Beyer of Brown University, reporting to the American Association for the Advancement of Science, one-third of the scientific papers originating at the Russian nuclear research centre near Moscow have Chinese names attached to them. (See chapter XI.)

before China obtains her seat in the United Nations. Each year brings it closer.

'As for American recognition, it took sixteen years in our case and the delay did us no harm. The Chinese are in no hurry, and it is not harming them, either.'

```
*******************************
*                             *
*         PART EIGHT          *
*                             *
*******************************
```

XXXIII

'Water in Our Hands'

ALL China is intensely conscious of the problem of water, because on water depends both the industrial and the agricultural future of the country. The use of water power is understood by *everyone*, from schoolchildren who make model dams, and commune brigades which back up small streams in order to drive their home-made generators, to the engineers planning vast hydro-electric and river-control projects, comparable in scale to America's Tennessee Valley Authority.

China has too much water in the south (though in the past most of it was lost through flood run-off) and too little in the north, particularly the north-west. The planners are talking of long-range schemes for diverting some of the great rivers, or channelling part of their flow, into the semi-arid northern regions. But that is for the future. The most immediate problem was to check the floods which for centuries had ravaged China's two greatest food-producing areas, the Yellow and Yangtze basins; and at the same time, to realize the potential hydro-electric power for mechanization of their farms and for general industrial development.

I selected the Sanmen Gorge Dam in Honan Province for a visit, not because it was the largest, but because its construction was furthest advanced of all the really big projects.

*

It was late at night when I arrived at Hui Shin Station, closest point on the railway to Sanmen Gorge. It had been raining heavily. The sky was black, starless; and the station building, which showed half-finished

351

concrete walls, was surrounded by wallows of mud and pools of water in which the lighted windows of the train appeared in fragmentary reflection between gusts of wind. Beyond the station there was no light to be seen in any direction. I was glad someone from the hotel had come down to meet me.

We piled into a Russian-built jeep, gunned out axle-deep in mud, slewing half sideways down a steep hill.

To my surprise, we came out on a hard-surfaced road where an ordinary saloon was waiting, into which we transferred for the rest of the ride to the hotel. The hotel, like the station, was only half finished; everything here was brand-new. My room had a bathroom, but most of the plumbing apparatus was lying outside in the hallway, not yet installed.

In the morning when I woke, the sun was shining.

We set off at 7.30 sharp in a Russian car for the twenty-two-mile trip to Sanmen Gorge. As we drove out to the highway, I saw there was a good deal more to the town than I had perceived the night before. Rows of new buildings, cinemas, theatres, offices, playgrounds. Originally a village of three thousand, the chauffeur told me, it had grown since the project began in 1957 to sixty thousand.

The road to Sanmen Dam had taken six months to build; and as we rolled up over the long, well-constructed road, I saw that it was taking us into some of the most remarkable country I had seen in China. The green hills climbed higher and higher. There were no rocks, almost no trees. The soil appeared to be a mixture of sand and yellow clay, and everywhere the hills had been terraced, step by step, up these enormously steep slopes; in some places the terrace walls had to be higher than the breadth of the terraces they supported.

Now and again, coming suddenly over a high ridge, we would catch a glimpse of the hills stretching off far into the distance, endlessly looped and contoured by those terrace walls. What labour! It was the work of centuries. And the terraces, as far as the eye could see, bright green with young wheat.

'Look there!' The driver pointed.

Far below us I caught a glimpse, deep among those tumbled hills, of the bend of a great river. It was yellow-brown like the earth and looked peaceful and sluggish enough at that distance. And all this under a

352

China-blue sky with clouds driving on the wind and their shadows racing across the terraced landscapes.

It was only when we reached the dam itself that I saw there was nothing sluggish about the Yellow River. The main body of the river came thundering out through the spillway in roils of brown foam.

*

There is always, for me, an intense excitement in the sight of a great engineering work. I have felt this at Grand Coulee and at Boulder, and I felt it now as we stepped from the car by the engineers' shanties, looking out over the Sanmen Dam. The construction seemed largely complete. Crews were still at work along the top, finishing the floodgates and the roadway. Containers of concrete sailed out by high cable line from a mixing plant on the opposite bank. These were taken off by huge cranes along the top of the dam and dumped into the square section forms. It was an impressive sight.

A senior engineer, Mr Jiou Yi-ning, stepped out of his shanty to greet me. He would give me a general outline of the project from this viewpoint, and later one of the junior engineers could take me on a tour of the work.

'The Yellow River,' said Mr Jiou, 'follows a course from Ching-Hai Province and flows through nine provinces till it reaches the ocean above Shanghai. Its total length is three thousand miles. The drainage basin is arid country with an average rainfall of only 1·57 inches per year. But these rains are concentrated into a very short period, and consequently there is a great variation in the rate of flow. The yearly average varies from 35,200 to 292,600 gallons per second. But in some years it falls lower, or rises much higher. An absolute maximum,' Mr Jiou continued, 'which has perhaps occurred only once or twice in history, would be 7,810,000 gallons per second. This is the figure we have reckoned with in our construction of the Sanmen Gorge Dam.

'Here at Sanmen is where the stream comes down from the high country and runs out into the coastal plains, which are wide, but low. Over the centuries, silt carried from the hills has raised the level of the river bottom till for long stretches it is higher than the surrounding country. The people, to protect themselves, have been constantly

M 353

building dikes, so that now the Yellow River flows through a raised trough across some of the most heavily populated sections of China. There are eighty million people who live in the floodlands of the Yellow River. When very heavy rains have fallen in the hills, the river has broken its dikes; and our historical records show that this has occurred fifteen hundred times during the past three thousand years. The river actually has changed its course twenty-six times. This river,' said Mr Jiou, 'has been the scourge of China. But we have tamed it at last.

'The worst disaster of recent times was in 1938, when the Kuomintang broke the dikes in an attempt to halt the Japanese advance. Insufficient warning was given to the peasants and there were no plans for evacuation. The area flooded was greater than the engineers had anticipated. The result was that twelve and a half million people were made homeless and 890,000 lost their lives.'

'By whose estimate was that?' I asked.

'By the estimate of the Kuomintang, made immediately afterwards.

'For thousands of years,' Mr Jiou went on, 'our people have been struggling against this river. But they had no proper means. Later, under the Kuomintang, the social system made any fundamental planning impossible. It was only after liberation that plans could be made and carried through. The first stage was that of strengthening the dikes on the lower course. During the past ten years there has been no flood damage downstream. But even so, an unusual run-off might have broken the dikes, and this remained always a danger until the second stage could be put into effect.

'The second stage,' he concluded, 'is the Sanmen Dam.' He waved his hand across the view before us.

'When will it be finished?' I asked.

'We closed the gates last spring. To this extent, it is already complete so far as controlling the river is concerned. The generators which still need to be installed will be in operation by the end of the year. That is a year ahead of our schedule.'

(He was wrong. The generators were being made in Russia with delivery timed to the original schedule. For a year the dam remained complete but for generators.)

Then he turned me over to one of his assistants and I spent the morning touring the project. We visited the concrete plant and the

354

gravel quarry; had a look into the interior galleries; descended long sets of ladders through a forest of bamboo staging to see the partially completed power-house and the enormous pipes, each one twenty-two feet in diameter. The eight turbine generators will have a capacity of 6,000 million kilowatt hours, which will make possible the industrialization of the central Yellow River Valley. Minimum flow required to keep these generators turning will be 250 cubic metres per second for each one. The lake already filling up behind the dam will have storage capacity of 35,400 million cubic metres, and this water will be put to work not only for power-generation, but for irrigation as well. The great basin of the Yellow River has suffered almost as grievously from drought as from flood. The dam, with its storage lake, will regularize the flow, making possible effective irrigation of some 40 million mu (6,667,000 acres) of potentially rich agricultural land lower down. The young engineer added that it will also be feasible, then, to maintain a predetermined channel depth below the dam, so that ships of 500-tons displacement will be able to come inland as far as Sanmen. In addition, they anticipate raising fine harvests of fish (he was not speaking of sports-fishing) in the new reservoir.

*

In anybody's language Sanmen is a big project. Its height of 348 feet compares with 550 feet for Grand Coulee. (Both are gravity dams, therefore comparable.) Sanmen has a base of 312 feet, while Grand Coulee has a base of 500 feet, but Sanmen will hold more water than Grand Coulee and Boulder combined. Grand Coulee took slightly less than eight years to build. Sanmen will be completed in a little less than four.

Perhaps an American foreman might not be satisfied with the finish of the concrete. The form panels were of rough planking rather than plywood, and the junction lines did not run true. Obviously they considered this a minor matter. I saw the compressed-air vibrators they were using, and noticed that no aggregate was exposed on the surface. Safety precautions were minimal. The stagings were all of wooden poles lashed with cord, and the ramps and cat-walks were frequently innocent of any guard rails. Very, very few accidents, the assistant engineer assured me, but I could not get any figures. Heavy construction everywhere has its accident rate; I can offer no comparison.

It seemed to me that with the tremendous burden of sand and topsoil carried by the stream, the consequent silting up of the storage lake must eventually become a problem. All this, I was told, had been taken into consideration. The master plan calls for one other large dam comparable to Sanmen, and for forty-six smaller reservoirs on the headwaters which will convert the fall of the river into a series of controlled steps. They call it the 'step-ladder' plan. Much of the silt will thus settle out hundreds of miles upstream. This, combined with afforestation and erosion control, will reduce silting of the power-dam lakes to a negligible factor. The same difficulties exist, undoubtedly, for all river-development projects. I have heard the problem of silt discussed in the United States, particularly in relation to the Colorado River and Boulder Dam.

*

I imagine Mr Jiou's assistant would have hurried me back and forth, his hand under my elbow, pointing and explaining, all that day and the next day, too. But I had to be back at Hui-Shin station by mid-afternoon to catch the train which would take me down the valley to Chengchow and Wuhan.

As we returned to the car at the engineer's shanty, Mr Jiou himself came out to bid me farewell.

'Whatever they tell you there downstream,' he said laughing, 'remember you have seen here at Sanmen the key to the Yellow River Basin. From here we shall check the floods. From here we shall send water for irrigation. From here will come the electric power for lights and workshops. And this is only the beginning. They have already started some projects on the Yangtze River which will make this one look like a toy....'

I stopped the car to take some last photographs from above, where the road enters the project area. An archway spans the road just here, and on it were characters written boldly. I asked my interpreter what they said.

> Conquer the Yellow River!
> Command it to make way
> And the mountains shall bow to us.
> Harness the river to rock
> And we shall hold the water in our hands!

XXXIV

A Quick Look at Shanghai

My hotel in Shanghai caters chiefly for Overseas Chinese who are visiting China, or coming home to stay. For the latter this hotel serves as a '*pied-à-terre*' until they find permanent quarters in Shanghai or move on to jobs elsewhere. Most of the guests are from South-east Asia, but some come from Europe, and I am told that several have returned from the United States.

The building is in the Western style, with large rooms and excellent service. Meals are Chinese or European. From my seventh-storey window I look out over an expanse of lawns, trees, flowers; and off to the right is the Museum of Natural History. All this was once the famous Shanghai Race-course. Now it is the People's Park.

Nanking Road, where my hotel is, remains Shanghai's most thriving shopping district. Night and day, Nanking Road is crowded with people, bicycles, and buses; and already some of the tiny new two-horsepower, four-seater taxiettes — it is hoped they will in time replace the pedicabs — are beginning to appear. About a mile south from the hotel is the Bund, the famous quayside along the muddy Hwangpu River. Just this way from the bridge across Soochow Creek, opposite the British Consulate compound, is Garden Park, where, so my interpreter hastened to inform me, used to be posted the never-to-be-forgotten, never-to-be-forgiven sign: 'No dogs or Chinamen admitted.'

*

Shanghai, when I came here three years ago, had seemed stagnant and drab. But on the present trip, nowhere was I so struck by the rapid change as here in this city. Shanghai is booming; her streets are

357

crowded, her shops bustling. New 'satellite towns' in the surrounding countryside have made possible the demolition of slum sections which, as I can well believe from what I saw myself, used to be among the most terrible in the world.

Shanghai, in 1960, has again become one of the world's great ports, her docks are handling more cargo than ever before in the city's history.

Compared with Paris, Rome, or Peking, this is not an ancient city. Marco Polo, on his travels, would never have heard of it, since it was no more than a fishing village at the time. By the end of the Ming dynasty, as a result of the construction of the Grand Canal, which linked the city to Peking, and its network of smaller canals, Shanghai was becoming the trade centre for the lower Yangtze Valley. But the city's period of rapid growth came after 1842, when it was designated a 'treaty' port following China's defeat in the Opium War. Concessions and rights of 'extra-territoriality' were granted to the victorious Europeans. Shanghai became the main 'open door' for the West into China.

The city grew during the following century into a commercial and industrial centre. Nearly 80 per cent of its industries (chiefly textiles) were foreign-owned. The hungry, overpopulated countryside of the Yangtze Valley fed Shanghai's mills and factories. By the time of the First World War, Shanghai was China's largest city. Its working class supported the revolution initiated by Sun Yat-sen. When, in 1927, two years after Sun's death, the revolutionary armies under Chiang Kai-shek approached Shanghai in the great 'northern drive' to unify China, Shanghai's workers, then under Communist leadership, seized the city and opened the gates to Chiang's forces — as André Malraux has vividly described in his novel *Man's Estate*.

It was at this point, immediately after the occupation of Shanghai, that Chiang broke with the Communists. Shanghai trade unions were dissolved, twelve thousand workers, supposedly Communists, were executed in three weeks, and another fifty thousand imprisoned or put to death within the year. By a curious stroke of fate Chou En-lai, who had helped to plan the rising of the workers, was one of the few Communist leaders to escape from Shanghai.

For the next ten years Shanghai (the Chinese, not the foreign, section of the city) was ruled by the Kuomintang government of China. In 1937 it was taken by the Japanese, who held it till the end of the

Second World War. Then, for a brief period, once more under Kuomintang control, Shanghai regained its old position as the financial centre of China, and as the 'wickedest city in the world'. It was also called the 'least Chinese of cities', and on the surface this was true. The great hotels, the waterfront skyscrapers along the Bund, which housed the Hong Kong-Shanghai Bank, Butterfield and Swire, Jardine's, the American-owned telephone and power companies, and a host of other American or European firms, all gave it the appearance of a Western metropolis. Every public utility in this largest of Chinese cities was foreign-owned.

By 1949 the wheel of fortune had turned full circle. The victorious Communist armies of General Chen Yi (now Foreign Minister), amply supplied with American lorries and material, marched into Shanghai.

*

That was eleven years ago; yet something of the Western atmosphere still remains. Shanghai is the only city in China today where one sees advertisements for cosmetics. The lift girls in the hotels wear lipstick, the waitresses have their hair waved. Women here are more style-conscious than anywhere else in China. They show off their hair-do's, flowered jackets, and contour-fitted slacks; and for a visiting Westerner, at least, they are a true delight to look at. Some of the big shops even have fashion parades! At a cosmetics counter on Nanking Road I counted thirty-eight brands of perfume, twenty-eight toilet soaps, ten different shades of lipstick.

Nevertheless, the atmosphere of the new China — the sense of the importance of being earnest, the emphasis on study and production — is dominant. And one sees the same contrasts of old and new as in other Chinese cities: the housing project rising from the ancient slum; human beings dragging overloaded carts, and fleets of modern diesel lorries; ramshackle sheds serving as factories, and up-to-date plants that cover acres of ground.

*

In Shanghai, a city in the past notorious for its filth and its slums, I asked to visit the worst slum in the city. The worst, they told me, had been torn down several years before; but there were still some nearly as bad.

What the *worst* must have been like in the old days I dread to imagine. The one I did visit was like the bad parts of Marseilles or Mexico City, except that here it was a *clean* slum. The hovels, the lean-to sheds were miserable enough, there were dark corners and narrow lanes; but no stench, no refuse lying about. And the people were not badly dressed. It was drizzling, but in spite of the rain a crowd of curious children followed wherever I went; every one of them looked adequately nourished. (Nowhere in China did I see signs of undernourishment in children.) From the appearance of these people it was apparent that they were not here because they were poorer than others in the city, or because they were out of work. Actually they were employed at the same kinds of jobs as those who live in the brand-new housing estates. But Shanghai was not built in a day, and its reconstruction will not be done in a day either. The people were waiting their turn. It was, if I may put it this way, a *hopeful* slum, and this was something entirely new in my experience.

I later met the chairman of the neighbourhood committee, who told me there were twenty thousand people living in this district. Bad as it looked now, it had, apparently, been far worse. During the last years of the Kuomintang the people had suffered terribly from unemployment and inflation. Most of them were pedicab drivers or pedlars, existing at best on the very margin.

Next to starvation, their great fears were: *Rain.* The area had no drainage. A heavy rain flooded the houses and converted the streets and house-floors into mud which took weeks to dry. *Fire.* Roofs were almost all of thatch. No one had electricity. If they used lights or cooking-stoves at all, these were fuelled with paraffin. Between 1942 and 1946 three disastrous fires swept the neighbourhood, causing many deaths. *Wind.* Summer wind-storms, occasional typhoons, would carry away roofs, flip up the flimsy walls like card-houses.

There was, then, no sanitation of any kind. There were no latrines, no running water. Drinking-water came from roadside ditches and in these were washed everything, from cooking pots to night-soil containers. Cholera, typhoid, dysentery, TB were perennial killers.

Ninety per cent of the population had been illiterate.

That was the situation as it had been. Since 1949 there had been improvements, many improvements, the committee chairman told me. He pointed proudly to the fresh-water taps which stood at intervals along the narrow alleys. Rubbish collection and disposal of night soil are now carried out daily. But by far the greatest improvement, the chairman said, was in the economic conditions. Some of the people still are pedicab drivers; the others now held regular jobs in the new factories and workshops. No one went hungry. There was no fear of inflation. 'Every family in this neighbourhood can now afford to eat,' the chairman said.

Health, and the level of education, too, had risen since the old days. Cholera, typhoid, dysentery, were virtually gone. There was a hospital in the neighbourhood, several clinics. All children received immunization injections. And the children were going to school. As for the adults, the chairman estimated that 90 per cent had now passed their literacy tests, not including the people who were too old to learn.

At the end of my visit, as I was taking my leave of the chairman and the various others who had come with us to the neighbourhood committee room, an old man stepped forward, gave me a toothless grin, and spoke a few words. My interpreter told me, 'This old man says they all hope you will come again and see for yourself how things have changed here, the next time you are in Shanghai.'

I told him I certainly intended to.

I had also intended to visit some of the urban developments already completed — the *satellite* cities on the outskirts, where self-contained communities are being constructed, with their own markets, schools, theatres, their own industries, and their own sources of food supply from the rural communes near by.

But my stay in Shanghai was cut short.

Upon my return to the hotel after my visit to the slum neighbourhood I found a message from the local office of the Ministry of Foreign Affairs that they must see me at once 'on a very serious matter'. I was alarmed. Certain that I was in trouble of some sort, I racked my brain trying to imagine what I had done wrong. I must have stepped on somebody's toes without realizing it. The Writers' Union man in Wuhan, with whom I had the argument over freedom of conscience? Had he reported me? It seemed quite possible.

So be it. I shrugged my shoulders and went over to the Ministry. A bright-eyed young woman at the reception desk greeted me, 'Oh, Mr Greene, we are so glad to see you!' Then a higher official hurried out, grasped me by the hand.

'Mr Greene,' he said, 'we have a message for you from Premier Chou En-lai. He wishes you to know that if you care to return to Peking, he will be glad to see you for an extended talk, and that, if you wish, part of the interview can be filmed for television. It would be best, I think, to return to Peking as soon as possible.'

The Foreign Office man was very enthusiastic. He shook my hand several times, repeating, 'Congratulations, Mr Greene, congratulations!'

'Will you send word to the Premier,' I asked, 'that I will catch the next train to Peking?'

XXXV

An Interview with Chou En-lai

I HAD prepared my questions on the train, and on arrival in Peking, hurried to the Information Department. The Shanghai message was confirmed. Mr Kang Mao-chao, Deputy Director, told me the rules. Mr Chou En-lai wished to see the questions in advance. Part of the interview could be filmed for TV; the remainder would be an impromptu and private discussion afterwards. I was free to submit any questions I liked, but the Premier would prefer me not to ask personal questions. He would be speaking officially, not personally. Further, I must agree that the interview, whenever released, would be broadcast in its entirety, without cuts. I agreed to this.

I gave Mr Kang my list of questions. They were, I thought, the key issues that any thoughtful Westerner would have liked to raise regarding China's policies. Many implied a critical attitude. Mr Kang, after reading them with close attention, suggested there were too many to be properly answered in a half-hour TV interview. If I would choose eleven or twelve which I considered particularly suitable for an international audience, the others could be taken up during the non-filmed portion of the discussion.

I did so. He then asked what technical arrangements I would propose. This was the first TV interview with a top official ever photographed in China. They wished it to be of technical excellence. My requests were simple: three cameras with first-class cameramen. A beautiful, and typical, Chinese setting. An experienced sound engineer, and a top-notch interpreter. None of these presented any problem. I stopped at the cable office on my way back to the hotel and sent off messages to England, Canada, and the United States.

Then nothing happened. One week passed, then another. I phoned the Ministry. No news. I decided that the project was off. The Premier had changed his mind; they didn't like the questions. The Indian ambassador tried to cheer me up: 'If they said you were going to have an interview, you will have one.' I didn't believe him. In fact, I was on the point of making arrangements for my departure when, at a reception in the Great Hall of the People, I had my first official re-assurance, and this came from the Premier himself. He walked across to speak to me. Chou En-lai speaks very little English and for once he had no English interpreter with him. I had no interpreter either. We stumbled, both of us, trying to cross a no-man's land of non-com-munication. Then at last I made out the words: 'Excuse delay — few days, few days.... '

So it was on again — the great Felix Greene scoop. I was elated; and I sat out another seven-day week with no word.

Almost three weeks after I had rushed back breathless from Shanghai, I received a phone call one morning at 8.15. It was Mr Kang, who told me he had heard from the Premier at four o'clock that very morning, instructing him to schedule the interview for noon. What about technical arrangements? I asked. Everything had been in readiness for many days. I put on my best suit and waited for the car from the Ministry to call for me.

*

The cause of the long delay was, I believe, the gravity with which the Chinese Government viewed the occasion. No such interview had ever before been granted in China. Here was an official pronouncement to be made, by one of their highest officials, which would be heard by people in many countries of the world. (The TV interview was later broadcast in England by the B.B.C., in U.S.A., Western Germany, Mexico, Sweden and a number of other countries.) The questions I had offered touched all the most sensitive points of Chinese foreign relations.

At a quarter to twelve, guided by Mrs Chen of the Ministry of Information, I entered the Great Hall of the People. One of the recep-tion rooms — the Kiangsu Room, she told me — had been equipped as a TV studio. Mrs Chen and I waited in an adjacent chamber where a young woman brought us tea and damp towels, softly scented. Precisely at noon I was ushered down wide, carpeted passages to the Kiangsu

Room. The doors stood open, and as we approached I could see the cameras, and camera tracks laid over the carpets, a profusion of wires and brilliant lights.

There Madame Kung Peng was waiting. While she greeted me, I heard the cameras begin to whirr; saw them follow us as we walked together across the wide hall to where Mr Chou En-lai was seated. He rose, shook hands, beckoned me to a seat beside him. Then, without pause, without opportunity, for rehearsal or voice-balance or light-meter check, the interview was on. I thanked the Premier for agreeing to see me and answer my questions. As I had many questions, could I begin at once?

'*Shih*' (yes), he said.

During the long translations of Premier Chou's replies (they were afterwards dubbed over his voice) I had ample opportunity to look around me. This was the most orderly, and certainly the most beautiful, 'studio' I had ever had the luck to work in. It was a vast, high-ceilinged room, at least eighty feet long. A single carpet covered the entire floor, magnificent, with a central floral design, though this was now inter-twined and partially obscured by tracks and electric wires.

Two cameramen stood beside each camera, the sound engineer sat at his controls; a still photographer from *Hsinhua* moved silently over the thick carpeting; and beyond the batteries of lights, motionless around the room, sat the top officials of the Prime Minister's office, the Ministry of Foreign Affairs.

It was all enormously impressive.

As TV shows go, however, the interview, I am afraid, left much to be desired. It was neither lively nor brisk. It was far too formal. I had hoped the Premier's wit and warmth, which are immediately apparent in any personal exchange, would come through. But the occasion was too serious. Despite my previous request that he speak without notes, this was not done. He was reading his answers, which was under-standable, for the issues were important, but it was unfortunate.

All in all it went smoothly. The technical quality — sound, photo-graphy, interpretation, and later, the dubbing — was excellent.

After the televised portion of the interview we shook hands again while flashlights popped, then moved into another magnificent hall where armchairs upholstered in blue silk were drawn up to a tea-table.

The Premier glanced at the chairs and said he didn't care for that kind, I suppose because of their being the type one sinks half a yard into, like a very soft bed. When I suggested we bring up another chair, he smiled, and waved me to a seat.

We proceeded with the remainder of the list. I was able to question some of the answers the Premier had given in the filmed part of my interview. I had other questions on communes, questions on intellectual freedom, questions on their plans for increasing the supply of consumer goods. All of these the Premier answered at great length, though he had not previously seen these questions.

Only at the end, as we were saying goodbye, did our exchange slip into a less formal pattern, and we stood for quite a while chatting together. We had been talking about the endless, and rather fruitless, Warsaw discussions, then (and still) going on from time to time between American and Chinese ambassadors in Poland.

'Why are you so worried?' Premier Chou En-lai said to me, smiling. 'All your questions are *worried* questions. These Warsaw talks are proceeding, things move forward little by little. There have been over a hundred talks at Warsaw.'

'Yes, but what's been accomplished?' I asked.

'They are going on, *that's* the main point. Just as the Korean armistice talks went on, for over two years, and they accomplished the armistice in the end.' And as this was being translated, he broke in, in English. 'How old are you?' he asked.

'Fifty-one,' I told him.

'Well [slipping back into Chinese], I'm much older than that and I'm not worried. So why should you be?'

I said that perhaps we are more impatient, that we need quicker results than the Chinese.

'No, no,' he said, 'you live in the United States but you are British — the British have a long historical perspective too.'

'But even the British haven't four thousand years of history behind them,' I said. And Chou En-lai laughed and held out his hand and we said goodbye again.

*

It had often occurred to me while in China that the confidence in the future that one senses everywhere among her people springs from a consciousness of age, of having met wars and invasions and disasters of all kinds through many centuries and survived them all. China has the confidence of immortality.

And Chou En-lai, I felt, having delivered the official views of his government, was taking this opportunity for a personal word, through me, to those whom I would speak to in the West: *'What are you all so worried about?* China has been here four thousand years, and China will be here a great many years longer. That is the reality you are dealing with. You and I, as individuals, are of no great importance.'

Postscript

No one can come away from a visit to China today without being impressed, even overwhelmed, by the experience. It is impossible not to feel while one is there that one is witnessing one of the great episodes of history and that all our futures are bound to be influenced by it.

Throughout my stay in China, as during my visit there in 1957, I had an extraordinary impression that China was drawing on resources latent within her for a long time and was moving forward very rapidly to a great future. With her vast manpower, the industriousness and intelligence of her people, and the aptitude they are showing for advanced technological processes, it is quite possible that our children, or theirs, may see China regain the position of world leadership that she held before for so many centuries.

The advances achieved by the Chinese people in the past eleven years have been too well documented to be denied. But questions at once come to mind. The material advances may have been great, but at what human cost have they been achieved? At what loss of human dignity? With what denial of human freedom?

But on whose standards are we to judge and make an answer?

If China's advances are well documented, so are the conditions of the past.

'I knew Shanghai when it was the gayest city in the Far East — ' wrote Richard Hughes of the *Sunday Times* — 'gay, that is, if you were a foreigner or a Chinese millionaire. But there were corpses in the street every night, 20,000 died a year from hunger, cold and exposure. And there were swarms of beggars. And the childish street-walkers. And the sweating rickshaw coolies, with a professional life-expectancy of eight years if they didn't smoke too much opium....

'Now no one goes hungry in Shanghai....

'So arises the dilemma. Who can strike the balance between freedom from starvation for the majority against freedom of thought for the minority? The comparison, one must keep repeating, is not the China of today with the Western world of today, but the China of today with the China of yesterday.'

A French correspondent, Robert Guillain, though a sharp critic of life in China today, gives us the same reminder: 'Before, it was appalling — that truth predominated over every other. Poverty, corruption, inefficiency, misery, contempt for the people and for the commonweal, these were the elements which made up the most wretched nation on earth. And I knew China then.'

*

It is difficult for us who stand so far above the corroding effects of poverty to understand that some peoples' conception of human dignity is very different from our own. Not much dignity is possible when life is dominated by the most basic and elemental anxieties. The values of free thought seem remote and irrelevant to those whose history is being written in the language of sheer physical survival.

When a Chinese worker or peasant says he is freer today than he has ever been in his life, he means it. And he sounds as if he means it. Perhaps he doesn't mean it in our way, for he has never known the particular forms of political and social freedom which have been the product of our own historical past and which are the fruit of our relative physical security.

A Chinese uses the word 'freedom' in a very personal, down-to-earth, non-theoretical sense. He is not talking about abstractions but experience. He means that he is at last free to eat, and not to starve; he is free of the landlord and money-lender; he is free to learn to read and write; he is free to develop skills and to exercise talents which would otherwise have remained hidden; he is free to send his children to school, and when they are ill there is a doctor who can help to make them well; he is free to look at the future with hope and not with despair. For him these are all *new* freedoms. And it's not such a bad list!

As for dignity, I think it is very probable that the forty million people of minority races in China who for the first time are enjoying complete political and social equality with all others, would say their dignity has been enhanced, not lessened. The Marriage Law, which is described in the Appendix, released the women of China from the miseries of a very degrading feudal system. I should like to see someone ask one of the young women of China today if she feels her human dignity has been infringed!

*

This book is about China, but by implication, it is also about America. I cannot promise that on one point or another some error may not be found, and cannot be sure, of course, though my checking was careful, that on this fact or that I may not have been deliberately misled. But I do not believe you can fake a whole country, and I think in all significant respects this book presents a fair and honest account of what is going on in China today. If this is so, or if only half the facts that I have presented are true, then it becomes clear that the American people have been most seriously misinformed. I have in one chapter shown the contrast between the reports about the communes as presented to American readers and the reports which appeared in the press of other Western nations. If that is the case with respect to the communes, it is equally the case in regard to most other Chinese developments.

A nation which allows itself to be deluded to this extent is on a dangerous path.

It is not that true reports about China never appear in the American press. They do, along with many untrue ones. But by selection, even true reports may convey a false impression. Ugly and brutal things happen in all human communities and I am not suggesting that they do not happen in China too. But think for a moment what a distorted image of American life readers in another country would receive if the only news they ever heard about America was what was discreditable, if they read only accounts of the crime, the corruption, the juvenile murders, the racial segregation.

What is happening in China today is far livelier, far richer in content, far more *successful*, than Americans have been permitted to learn. It is inconceivable to me that ordinary Americans would not welcome and support the vast improvements that have been made, in the health of children, in education, in the general level of cleanliness and morality, in the care of old people; or the devoted restoration of historical buildings, the encouragement given to artists, the support of traditional handicrafts, the new developments in drama, dance, and music. Of all this they know virtually nothing.

To this extent at least, this book may help to redress a balance.

Nor is it realized, I think, the extent to which the Chinese people support their present leadership. The Chinese Communist revolution was not a sudden one. It did not flare up; it burned slowly, as a peat fire burns, and the source of the flame was always deep in the Chinese soil. For this reason, it was unquenchable.

America's ignorance of what is going on in China has its counterpart in her political attitudes, her decision to have nothing to do with China, and her determination to perpetuate the fantasy that Chiang Kai-shek is the real leader of the Chinese people. America's present China policy is ripe for debate, for discussion on the widest possible scale. Both political parties are involved in her present policy, both have supported it in the past, but there is, I believe, a growing sense that it is a policy which no longer serves America's best interests, for it is essentially based on unrealities.

' ... We have wandered lonely in a cloud of self-deception and wishful thinking [wrote C. R. Sulzberger, foreign affairs expert of the *New York Times*, in his book *What's Wrong with U.S. Foreign Policy?*]. Contrary to our own diplomatic traditions and all good sense we have refused to recognize the Peiping regime.... We imposed an embargo and an economic blockade.... The only consequence of this was to force the Chinese more closely into Moscow's arms.'

Mr Walter Lippmann, of the New York *Herald Tribune*, has repeatedly criticized a China policy based on the 'untruth that the real government of China is in Formosa'. He described U.S. relations with Chiang Kai-shek as: 'a classic example — the most far-reaching in our history — of an entangling alliance. Far from it being, as the official apologists say, indispensable to our prestige and influence, this entangling alliance is an enormous liability which, if it does not entangle us in war, is losing us surely and steadily the respect and confidence of our friends.'

I share this view. I believe America's present policy of hostility towards China and friendship towards Chiang Kai-shek is a mistaken and detrimental one. It has brought her to an impasse which permits her no initiative for action, and offers no compensating advantages. Rarely has history afforded such an example of a nation of first magnitude self-entrapped into a predicament where it can do nothing but wait upon events. It is very easy, I know, to be wise after the event, and I claim no special gift of insight, but looking back from today's perspective it is surely possible to trace with increasing clarity the mistakes which, one by one, led the United States to this dead end.

The refusal by the State Department in 1956 to allow correspondents into China when the Chinese Government offered them visas without conditions was, I think, possibly one of the most tragic of many diplomatic errors, for it has ever since clouded the issue of the exchange of correspondents and so contributed to the present prevailing ignorance about China. Now, when America may want to send her correspondents, she may find it impossible, for China now says that more fundamental issues must be settled first.

United States relations with China have too often been irrational and clouded by emotion. Like the unfolding of a Greek tragedy, initial errors led to others and were then still further compounded; indefensible positions were rationalized and made the basis of 'moral obligations'; myths took the place of reality; until today America finds herself with no strategic alternative to a policy of military opposition and economic boycott towards 700 million Asian people.

The easing of the present tension between the United States and China is surely essential if the peace of our world is to be preserved. I do not believe that this tragically bitter enmity is likely to be resolved by any sudden 'bright' solution; and still less will it disappear as a result of clever manoeuvres aimed at putting the other side to disadvantage in debate. No single measure will substantially alter the situation — the exchange of correspondents, for example, or relaxing the trade embargo — though both of these would appear to me sensible steps. And least of all is a solution likely to be found through the much-discussed 'Two Chinas' policy, which would attempt to make Taiwan an independent country. For the Chinese consider (and with compelling historical reason) that Taiwan is part of China; any such 'solution' would only further embitter the Chinese people, and would only consolidate and in no way ease the tensions that exist at present.

I believe that America's relations with China can no longer be seen as an issue by itself, in isolation. For it is, at bottom, the consequence of America's world policy. At some future time the United States and China must once again enter into practical and common-sense relations. That is bound to be. But before this can occur, America will, I think, have to undertake a deep and searching examination of what her world policy *is*, and when all is said and done she must make up her mind what kind of a world she wishes it to be. The grand language of military threat and moral crusade on which she relies so heavily today may turn out to be irrelevant to her necessities and to the world's hopes.

Understanding starts with a wish to understand. It is difficult to assess what is happening in China today and easy to be deluded by fears and prejudices; China must be understood within the context of China's history. Understanding, sanity, and perhaps human survival itself, can be sought only by looking at facts, not by ignoring them.

Appendix 1
LANGUAGE REFORM

AMONG the real problems confronting the Chinese people as they move into the modern world is the complexity of their language written and spoken.

Unlike our own language, Chinese has no alphabet. Written Chinese was originally ideographs, or pictures, of the object denoted; and though these ideographs, known as characters, today are no longer recognizable as such, they are a cumbersome way of expression.

With our alphabet of twenty-six symbols we can make tens of thousands of words with comparative ease; in Chinese each word requires its own character to be laboriously memorized. Many of them are highly complex. The word for 'I' in Chinese requires seven strokes. 'Salt' calls for no less than twenty-four.

I

Salt
(Traditional)

Salt
(Simplified)

The Chinese have estimated, for example, that it takes a child at least two years longer to master the rudiments of reading and writing in China than it does his counterpart in a country where an alphabet is used.

The handicaps of written Chinese are obvious. Typewriters in China — there are very few — need several hundred keys; typesetting of books, magazines and newspapers is enormously complicated; telegrams have to be encoded and decoded, with each character given a four-number code; and the work required to learn even a minimum of one thousand to fifteen hundred characters — enough to be able to read a newspaper — is extremely arduous. A scholar is required to know characters in the thousands. Experts are divided on the total number of characters in the language — between forty and fifty thousand.

Another complication that confronts the Chinese is the great variety of their dialects. Although more than 70 per cent of the people speak various forms of *pu tong hua* (known in the West as Mandarin), the remainder speak dialects quite different from this, as well as different from each other. While the written language is the same throughout the country, the dialects often are so different that people from one area cannot understand those from another. For example, Mandarin pronunciation for cabbage, *bai tsai*, is pronounced *bak choi* in Cantonese. Wu dialect, which is spoken in and around Chekiang province and Shanghai, pronounces the word for foreigner *na ge ning*; in Mandarin it is *wai gwo ren*.

Many urban Chinese speak Mandarin and one other dialect, and it is not uncommon to hear a conversation going on between two people in two 'languages'. It is also not uncommon, as I have witnessed, to see men from different areas trying to communicate by writing out a word in mid-air, or one dipping a chopstick into the soy sauce and making himself understood on a restaurant table.

The complicated task of language reform was tackled almost immediately after the present government came to power. A committee for reforming the Chinese written language was set up. There were three main objectives: to simplify the written characters; to popularize *pu tong hua* ('common speech'); to draw up and put into practice a scheme for a Chinese phonetic alphabet to annotate the characters by sound symbols.

The task has not been finished, but a start has been made. Five hundred and forty-four of the most common characters have been abbreviated. Before this simplification these 544 characters averaged sixteen strokes each, now the average is eight. To popularize the 'common speech', it is being taught in all state schools and emphasized in films and radio; this in itself necessitated the teaching of thousands of teachers throughout the country who had never spoken it. Dialects are not interfered with — many children in China today grow up learning both their local dialect and the 'common speech'. However, it is believed that in the course of time the 'common speech' will be the spoken language all over China.

After much trial and error a written alphabet based on Latin symbols has been adopted. An impression has been gained abroad that the Chinese are scrapping their written language in favour of this. Such is not the case. The chief purpose of the Latinized alphabet is to make the language easier to learn by helping to annotate the characters phonetically, and by transcribing the 'common speech'. It is also being used to help in unifying pronunciation.

Scholars abroad have deplored the effect the adoption of these reforms may have on the ancient art of Chinese calligraphy. It is not intended that this art will be affected, although calligraphers in China are encouraged to use the abbreviated forms of the characters. Chinese language authorities apparently recognize that language is a living thing, that it must grow naturally, and that no one can arbitrarily determine what changes the future may bring.

Speaking of the future of the Chinese written language, Chou En-lai declared in January 1958:

> We all agree that they [Chinese characters] have made immortal contributions to history. As to whether or not they will remain permanently unchanged, whether they will change on the basis of their original forms, or whether they will be replaced by a phonetic language ... we need not draw a hasty conclusion. Any language is, however, subject to change, as is evidenced by the changes of the characters in the past. There will be changes in the future. We can also say that there will be a day when the languages — written and spoken — of the different peoples of the world will gradually become one and the same.... This is a good and not a bad anticipation.... On the question of the future of the Chinese language, there may be various views. We can bring them out for discussion and debate.

Appendix 2

FOOD RATIONING

THERE is no over-all system of food-rationing. Rations vary from area to area. This is partly because of differences in eating habits. North Chinese eat far less rice than southerners, but they eat more wheat and millet. There are areas where almost no rice is eaten. Moslem people eat more meat, especially mutton. Some sections grow more food in proportion to their population than others. For example, Szechuan province grows more food than it uses and thus exports it to other areas.

While there are no established national standards, there are 'norms' which give a general rule of thumb. An office worker, under this general average, would be given thirty pounds of grain per month; an ordinary factory worker would get forty, while those engaged in exceptionally heavy work would get fifty or more. That is, when it is available.

By the autumn of 1960, while I was still in China, these norms were considerably reduced because of the accumulative effects of the poor 1959–60 harvests. One feature of the Chinese rationing system — many Westerners may find it difficult to believe — is that people are asked to set their own 'norms' according to their eating habits. People realize, of course, that to claim more than is really needed means that someone else goes short; but it is another application of the 'trust the people' principle I have found to be astonishingly true there.

While it is impossible to reach a quantitative national picture of the rationing system, some priority principles are applied generally. Workers involved in exceptionally heavy work (steelworkers, coal-miners, etc.), children, and pregnant and nursing mothers get top priority; ordinary workers come next; highly-placed intellectuals, students, sedentary workers are next, in about that order. The lowest on the list are house-

378

wives (unless they are pregnant or nursing their babies), street hawkers, and shopkeepers. Artists, actors, and performers; students at the dance and theatre schools, and writers, get extra rations of meat and edible oil and are in many ways the most favoured group of all, but they represent, of course, a very small proportion of the population.

Cities, generally, are worse off for food than the countryside in times of national shortage, but at other times have a generally higher per capita consumption. From June 1960 on, when already it was clear that China would be facing a period of acute food shortage, the city people were being urged to plant vegetables on every available plot of ground. Outside my hotel a rough corner of yard covered with brick and rubble was tackled one afternoon by a crowd of youngsters, who in a few hours had transformed it into a neat vegetable garden. Medical students and nurses from the hospital just opposite the Hsin Chiao Hotel dug up and planted another small area. The vegetables, when they started to grow in this plot, seemed pretty sickly until one day a group of medical students doused them with anti-bug powder, and before I left it was a fairly thriving plot of Chinese cabbage.

In all cities I visited even the small strips of earth that sometimes run between the road and pavement were being dug and planted with vegetables. In some towns temporary pipes with taps at intervals were laid as an aid to these efforts. The vegetable plots were all in the open and unguarded; the vegetables could easily have been stolen at night. One man at the Ministry of Foreign Affairs told me he and his wife had planted onions in their window-boxes instead of flowers.

Such efforts, of course, could only slightly alleviate the effects of the poor harvests. In early 1961 a doctor who had recently been in China wrote to me of evidence of malnutrition in the cities — though not among the children. Peking and Canton were hard hit. Although information about daily calorie intake was hard to come by, my doctor friend estimated that in the cities, steelworkers were getting 3,000 daily, ordinary workers 2,500, students 2,000, and housewives 1,500 or less. This friend, who spent many years in China before 1949 and has been back to China several times since, noted that there was no famine. The situation was tight, rationing strict, but no starvation. If 1961 proves to be another poor-harvest year the slim rations will become even slimmer.

Appendix 3

THE MARRIAGE LAW

MORE than any other single act, the Marriage Law of May 1950 revolutionized the social structure of China. In one step immemorial feudal customs were made illegal.

Great care was taken with the wording of the law. It had to be simple, so that all could understand, and exact, so that there should be no ambiguity of intention. Under discussion even before the new regime formally took power in October 1949, a draft of the law was formulated by the legal division of the Communist Party in association with women's organizations. Before and after October, forums and discussions were held with numerous groups; the draft was sent for examination to groups at the local level, and many changes were made. It took seventeen months of discussions and revision before the draft was finally approved by the national government.

The nature of marriage in China before the Marriage Law is described by Teng Ying-chao, Vice-Chairman of the All-China Democratic Women's Federation:

A special feature of the feudal marriage system in China was that marriages were arbitrarily arranged by parents and forced on their children. Marriage was a sort of bargain. Girls were usually betrothed in their early childhood by arrangement of their parents, who would receive money and gifts as a betrothal or marriage present. Not only was this kind of marriage not free, it was also contracted on the basis of the idea of the superiority of men over women. Many were the victims of this system; many were the unhappy couples forced to share the same roof while their hearts were far apart. This was one of the forms of oppression suffered by the whole people, but women were its special victims. They were required to 'follow their husbands no matter what their lot', as the saying went. Under the patriarchal system of old China a woman was required to wear widow's weeds for the rest of her life when her husband died ... 'to die faithful to one husband and not to remarry'. A woman divorced by her husband was an object of social contempt.

An old Chinese saying, 'A wife married is like a pony bought; I'll ride her and whip her as I like', vividly describes the position of women in old China. They were not only denied political and economic rights and held in servitude, but were also stripped of the right even to manage daily domestic affairs. At home their husbands could and did beat them and curse them, and their parents-in-law were free to insult them with impunity. The sufferings endured by luckless daughters-in-law were proverbial. Such miseries resulted in unhappy family life, filled with sorrow and hatred. And this in turn had its direct adverse effects on the physical and mental health of the younger generation.

In the struggle against these evils the women of China learned through bitter personal experience that the feudal marriage system, deeply rooted in the past, and the feudal outlook of men on marriage and women, were inseparable from the whole system of feudalism in China.

The aim of the Marriage Law was to uproot totally this ancient marriage system. Traditionally there was no such thing as freedom of marriage either in law or in practice. During the Kuomintang regime there was legal provision for freedom of marriage. It was not carried out in practice except in the upper circles of society. For most Chinese it was a freedom that existed only on paper. In the same way, freedom of divorce was largely a theoretical freedom, for the provision was surrounded with so many qualifications that it was hardly ever applied. In rural areas the freedom of divorce was unthinkable. In areas where feudal attitudes were most deeply rooted, women who applied for divorce were sometimes put to death.

Polygamy in China was fairly widespread among the upper classes in the form of concubinage, and adultery was either recognized or tolerated by law. The Kuomintang made some attempts to prohibit concubinage but never succeeded.

A nation-wide educational campaign was instituted following the promulgation of the Marriage Law. In general, this Magna Charta of women's rights in China was widely supported, especially in the cities and towns where, through the newly formed women's federations, the educational groundwork had been laid. Nevertheless, what was being attempted was a gigantic effort to overthrow deep-rooted traditions and there was some opposition, particularly in the more remote rural regions.

The abolition of any form of slavery always finds some who resist their new freedom, and the women of China were no exception. Despite its initial success, progress in carrying out the new law was uneven, and in some places there was real difficulty in persuading the women that the new law was to their benefit. (There had to be a complete halt for a time in certain sections.) But the educational campaign continued and in almost all areas the population gradually learned that the change was desirable. As the Chinese put it, 'step by step' it moved forward.

In 1953 the government, reassured by its general acceptance, launched a final drive to close the remaining gaps, and a new programme of education was carried out. Today, the new position of women is accepted by a great majority of the Chinese, including many of the men who had earlier reservations. However, it is undeniable that some of the old attitudes crop up from time to time, as was shown in the divorce case described in Part 5, Chapter XIX.

Appendix 4

THE GREAT COMMUNIST DEBATE

Some Notes on the Sino-Russian Controversy

THE open dispute between the Soviet Union and China has led to a wide variety of speculations as to the nature of the argument and its likely outcome. Unfortunately, the Western press has been more eager to make cold war propaganda over this debate than to explore its real meaning and we have — even from the self-styled 'experts' — had very little in the way of objective analysis. It is generally conceded that the debate that is in progress is of the highest significance — not only for the future of the world Communist movement but for the West as well.

There are, of course, rows in all alliances. The Western alliance is full of tensions and often ill-concealed acrimony. These tensions within our own alliance occasionally break out into more or less public disputes — during the Suez crisis, for instance, the Cuban fiasco, the U.S. arguments with Adenauer over Berlin, the differences with Britain over the Congo, and so on. The Communists have generally been more successful than we have in keeping their disagreements concealed, so that when they do break into public view it is natural for us to assume that they are serious. The Communist movement was born in struggle and communists are the first to realize the strength that comes with unity and the advantages that division will bring to their enemies. The fact that the present debate is publicly admitted and has lasted so long must be taken as evidence that it involves fundamental issues and that no immediate resolution is in sight.

It is often assumed by Western writers that one of the prime causes of the present struggle is Russian 'fear' of China. The unexpected rapidity of China's industrial growth, her mastery of large-scale production techniques, the abundance of her natural resources (even in oil she is now known to be well-endowed) and finally, of course, China's enormous and diligent population — all these point to the probability of China one day becoming the foremost power in the world. I do not, myself, think however that fear of her growth is an underlying cause of Russia's current difficulty with China. Especially while the East-West struggle remains unresolved it would seem likely that the U.S.S.R. would welcome, rather than deplore, the growing industrial and military power of China.

It would appear to me that a more likely cause of friction is presented by the uneven stage of development in the two countries involved. The present enormous discrepancy that exists between the level of Russian and Chinese industrialization and per-capita output must lead to certain Chinese misgivings. How far, they must wonder, are the Russians ready to decelerate their own advance in order to be able to help the more backward socialist countries? We have here a kind of 'have' and 'have not' problem within the Communist bloc itself. In his Report to the 22nd Congress, Khrushchev introduced a programme that envisaged an increase of 500 per cent in Russia's total national product within twenty years, with a growth of real per-capita income in this same period of 350 per cent. At the end of this time it was claimed that the Soviet people will be enjoying the *highest standard of living in the world* with the most comprehensive social welfare system. (Many competent foreign economists, less bemused perhaps than some of our own by cold-war attitudes, believe these Soviet targets rational and likely to be fulfilled.)

But how would the more backward members of the Communist alliance look upon such an ambitious programme — however much it validates their belief that a socialistic economy is the way to rapid progress? They undoubtedly wonder how much is to be put aside for aid to the less advanced nations. Very little was said by Khrushchev in his report regarding aid to the less developed Communist nations, nor is it likely that the Russian people would be ready to postpone to any significant extent the fruits of half a century of tremendous toil to help the struggling Chinese and Koreans. The Chinese today are passing through the most difficult initial phases of their economic development and for the past few years were hampered by a series of natural disasters. Though the Chinese would not deny the economic aid received from Moscow, they have consistently relied on their own efforts as far as this was possible. Nevertheless they cannot help but speculate how far a prodigious expansion of living standards in the Soviet Union is compatible with socialist solidarity and fraternal mutual help.

It has become almost a cliché with Western writers that China is 'passing through a Stalinist phase' and that Russia has now gone beyond that stage. 'Stalinism' means two things. On the one hand it means the system of economic austerity, discipline, and the forced marches towards higher production goals. On the other it means the gross abuses of power, blind intellectual dogmatism, the glorification of the leader, etc.

One of the most significant features of Khrushchev's leadership of the U.S.S.R. is his formal and uncompromising repudiation of Stalin's repression, violence and dogmatism, and his public promises that the excesses and brutalities of the Stalin era are a thing of the past. Such a dramatic and major political upheaval could not be partial; it required the fullest possible publicity. Stalin's henchmen everywhere had to be uprooted and the fullest possible exposure was given to Stalin's abuse of power for personal vengeance and self-aggrandizement. Khrushchev has made it abundantly clear by his speeches and actions that liberalization of the prevailing atmosphere was long overdue.

The Chinese leaders have conspicuously refrained from joining the chorus of Stalin-denunciation. His picture is still seen in China; Premier Chou En-lai made a point of laying a wreath on Stalin's tomb in Moscow's Red Square — and this only hours before Stalin's body was removed and transferred to an ordinary grave within the Kremlin walls. This persistent refusal on the part of the Chinese leadership to support the Khrushchev line of denigrating the memory of Stalin has, I think, been widely misinterpreted in the West. It has been assumed that the Chinese see no wrong in Stalin's brutal methods because — so it is implied — they use these same methods against their own people.

Nothing, I think, could be further from the truth.

The Chinese leaders do not, and have never, endorsed the excesses and horrible abuses of Stalin's regime. Historically they have, as far back as 1935, educated their cadres to distrust the Stalin-type mass purges. Once their victory in the civil war was assured and the regime established, the Chinese Communists attempted to make social changes in ways that would cause the minimum of social friction. Though Mao Tse-tung is everywhere revered as a father figure, his rule has never been a one-man despotism such as Stalin's; nor have we seen in the Peking government the savage jealousies and purges, or jockeying for power and favour that was such a horrifying feature of Stalin's rule. And far from being blindly dogmatic in its policies, Peking has shown extraordinary flexibility and pragmatism.

The Chinese nevertheless believe that Stalin's basic economic policies were correct (not only correct but inescapable) for backward countries passing through the initial phases of industrialization — the policies of severe austerity, the curtailment of production of consumer goods, the unquestioned subordination to central authority and a concentration on industrial production targets. Sacrifices and suffering, they believe, cannot be avoided during the initial period of 'primary accumulation'. Immense work must be undertaken with production increasing faster than the improvement in the conditions of the workers. The allocation of inadequate industrial resources requires centralized industrial planning.

It is true that the U.S.S.R. has now developed beyond this stage of 'primary accumulation' and — as Khrushchev clearly recognized — many of the policies essential at an earlier stage would today only act as obstacles to further growth. But not so China. China today can no more relax her national efforts than can a nation at war. Centralization, austerity, limited consumer goods, the encouragement of a single-minded purpose to increase production at all levels, an insistence on social disciplines are positive and inescapable requirements for a nation at China's stage of development. These are the policies which brought the Soviet Union forward with such success, policies which are linked inseparably in the eyes of the Chinese with the name of Stalin. This is the strategy of economic development that the Chinese leaders cannot be expected to jettison. To the Chinese people, who were themselves never subjected to Stalin's reign of terror, and who were very little, if at all, aware of it, to denounce Stalin would be taken as a denial of the very policies that brought such success to the Soviet Union and which the Chinese people for fourteen years have attempted so ardently to emulate. The Chinese leadership has shown by its behaviour that

Stalin's 'correct line' can be followed without the terrorism and abuse of power that were part of the Stalin regime.

There have, of course, been other causes for friction, such as the dispute regarding the Soviet technicians and the reluctance of the Soviet government to give China nuclear weapons (about the latter argument we have more guess-work than knowledge). But all these differences and tensions might well have been contained 'within the family' and without public notice if a more fundamental conflict had not developed — one which involved basic questions of international revolutionary strategy which could no longer remain hidden.

Just as for the United States the problem of Russia's growing strength dominates all other international issues, so American global military and commercial power constitutes the basic problem for both the U.S.S.R. and China. The real conflict between the U.S.S.R. and China revolves around the question of *how to deal with America* and how far traditional Marxist-Leninist doctrine and strategy must today be adjusted to meet wholly new historical circumstances. Neither Marx nor Lenin could have foreseen the problem that today faces Russia and China — how to confront an enemy equipped with weapons capable of global destruction. We must not forget that China and Russia are in full agreement that the United States represents the greatest threat to their interests and the greatest threat to world peace.[1] *It is on how to deal with this threat* that the two countries find themselves in profound disagreement. Each side appears genuinely convinced that the future of world peace as well as the future of world communism is at stake in this debate. And we would be wholly mistaken to think that this debate is about an abstruse and abstract Marxist doctrine. It is essentially a debate about *action* and *strategy*, not merely an argument about doctrinal theories.

There is a prevailing view in the West that the Russians and Chinese are arguing as to whether or not a third world war is 'inevitable'. Writers in the West — taking their cue from each other — have repeatedly assumed that China believes that war between the Communist

---

[1] The Moscow Statement of 1960, signed by eighty-one Communist Parties, including the U.S.S.R. and China, states: *International developments in recent years have furnished many new proofs of the fact that U.S. imperialism is the chief bulwark of world reaction and an international gendarme, that it has become an enemy of the peoples of the whole world.* (Italics in original.)

powers and the West is inevitable. In none of my talks with Chinese officials in China, nor in any Chinese statement that I have seen, has there been any reference to the inevitability of war. Some commentators have gone so far as to say (attributing it to a completely unverified and undocumented speech by Mao Tse-tung for authority) that the Chinese would actually *welcome* an atomic war since it would leave her with a relatively large population. (The inevitability of *small* wars is not the issue here — there is no country in the world that today believes local wars a thing of the past.)

Followers of the Sino-Soviet dispute are seldom afforded the opportunity of seeing at first hand full accounts of the statements made by both sides. Thus, even Mr Edward Crankshaw, noted expert on Communist affairs, could write in the London *Observer* on April 1st, 1962, about 'the Chinese attitude which still sees in war a possible way to the triumph of global Communism'.

Crankshaw here ignored innumerable Chinese statements to the contrary. For example, commenting on the Moscow Conference, the theoretical magazine *Hongqi* (*Red Flag*), No. 20–21, 1960, stated:

At present, the primary task of the people of the world is to form the broadest united front against imperialism headed by the United States, resolutely oppose U.S. imperialism's policies of aggression and war, stand firm against colonialism, promote the growth of the national liberation movement and facilitate the progress of the revolutionary struggle of the working people in the imperialist countries against the bellicose groups and monopoly capital, *so as to achieve the aim of preventing imperialism from starting a world war and safeguarding world peace.* (Emphasis added.)

And just two days after Mr Crankshaw's declaration on April 1st, 1962, about the supposed Chinese belief in war, the following appeared in the Peking *People's Daily*, the official organ of the Chinese Communist Party:

We are in favour of holding disarmament talks to achieve general disarmament. At a time when socialism has become stronger than imperialism, when the demand of all peace-loving people of the world for disarmament is mounting steadily and when the imperialist policies of war and aggression have met with one setback after another, it is possible through struggle at disarmament talks and pressure from various sides, to force imperialism headed by the United States to accept certain disarmament agreements (on the banning of nuclear weapons, for instance). If the imperialist countries can be compelled to accept even a partial agreement on disarmament and guarantee its implementation, that will benefit the cause of world peace and we will welcome it. Moreover, through disarmament negotiations the people of the world can be enabled, from the different attitudes and stands adopted by the various sides, to further distinguish right from wrong and to see clearly the true nature of imperialism — warlike and opposed to disarmament. This will make the people of the world unite and strengthen their struggle.

In addition to their written and spoken statements I have seen no evidence in any Chinese actions that would indicate any support for the view that nuclear war is inevitable. The Chinese continue to behave (as do the Russians and Americans) as though they believed a major war could be avoided. If they wished to provoke a war they could do so at any moment in the Taiwan Straits. Far from their actions having been provocative the Chinese appear to be extraordinarily cautious. Even at the height of the Quemoy crisis in 1958 they very carefully refrained from firing on any American vessel, nor have they attacked American ships or planes that encroach on their legal territory. Quemoy — only four miles from the mainland — is still in enemy hands, though Mao's forces could presumably take it. It is Russia, not China, that has sent military equipment to Laos, and in April 1962, Mr McNamara, the U.S. Secretary of Defence, stated that there was no evidence of Chinese penetration into South Vietnam. Their actions so far would indicate that Peking wishes to *avoid* a major conflict rather than to provoke one.

The real issue between the Russians and Chinese, it seems to me, is in a sense the very opposite of the inevitability of World War III — namely it is an argument *as to what policies the Communist countries should follow to minimize the danger of such a war.*

The Soviet position, as I understand it, could be briefly described as follows. A premature show-down with the Western alliance must at all costs be avoided. The nature of war today is such that a major conflict would bring ruin to all and advantage and victory to none. What is more, the Soviet leaders believe that the spiralling armaments race must be brought under some control — partly because it may itself (through accident or design) lead to nuclear war and partly because its cost is now so enormous that it jeopardizes the social and economic aims which the Soviet government has promised their people. The Soviets would prefer to compete with the United States on the economic level where they feel they would decisively win, rather than continue a military race which no one can win.

Some accommodation with the United States, therefore, is both desirable and attainable, based on the peaceful co-existence of the two systems. Such peaceful co-existence does not however imply a freezing of the *status quo*. Some issues (the Berlin and German issues, for example) cannot be considered as settled and a real *détente* with the West will not be possible while they remain unresolved. Nevertheless, accommodation with the West remains (in the eyes of the Soviet leaders) a primary strategic objective if nuclear disaster is to be avoided.

The Soviets have put themselves on record in the last few years that a relaxation of tension with the U.S. is desirable and possible. In a meeting of the Warsaw Treaty Members they described the thaw in the cold war as real and:

> the recognition of its necessity by the decision makers of the West as genuine and reliable. For the first time, after many years of the 'cold war' normal peacetime relations are beginning to be established ... tension has been markedly reduced and prospects are opening up for a strengthening of mutual confidence ...

At the 22nd Congress of the Communist Party of the U.S.S.R. held in Moscow in March 1962, the Soviet leaders developed what this implies in theoretical terms. Even before 'capitalism is overthrown' the working classes can achieve much:

> By uniting large sections of the working people, the working class can make ruling circles cease preparations for a new world war, renounce the idea of starting local wars, and use the economy for peaceful purposes ...

And

The working class, supported by the majority of the people and firmly repelling opportunist elements ... can defeat the reactionary, anti-popular forces, win a solid majority in parliament, transform it from a tool serving the class interests of the bourgeoisie into an instrument serving the working people, launch a broad mass struggle outside parliament, smash the resistance of the reactionary forces and provide the necessary conditions for a peaceful socialist revolution.

If these statements mean what they say they are a clear repudiation of traditional Leninist theory. The new theory here expounded implies that the working classes can force a change in capitalism without overthrowing the system itself — that the popular will expressed in parliament and in extra-parliamentary demonstrations and strikes can force capitalistic societies to basically change their own nature.

This profound and far-reaching abandonment of traditional Marxist theoretical doctrine is required, presumably, because in 'the new historical situation' all other methods of overthrowing capitalism would involve the risk of nuclear disaster. The avoidance of direct military confrontation with the West, having become the primary and over-riding policy, even time-honoured theoretical doctrine must be adjusted and abandoned.

To the Chinese — equally determined to avoid a major nuclear war — the Russian position appears profoundly erroneous: a turning back of the principles by means of which Communism has achieved so much and an approach which may well lead to the very disaster which it is intended to avoid.

If I understand the Chinese view correctly, it could be summarized as follows:

The Chinese do not deny the possibility of peaceful coexistence — the leaders have stated this on innumerable occasions. But, as with the Russians, the acceptance of the principle of peaceful coexistence must not be construed to mean the freezing of the *status quo*. Just as Russia is determined to come to a settlement with the West over Berlin and Germany, so China insists that a settlement of her claim to Taiwan and the unification of Korea and Vietnam are a *sine qua non* of a *détente* with the West.

In addition, the Chinese are not convinced that under present conditions Washington has the slightest intention of relinquishing any of her military power: not only can the U.S. not afford to disarm — so heavily is her economy today underpinned by military expenditures — but that it would be contrary to the very nature of imperialism to agree voluntarily to disarmament. Any temporary decrease in American aggressiveness (as during the 'spirit of Camp David' days) the Chinese believe is a result of the impact of the brute facts of world power which is shifting against her and not to goodwill. The Chinese are never tired of pointing out that in spite of all the words calling for 'peace' the Kennedy Administration has continually increased U.S. military expenditures. American words are in contradiction to her actions and 'a mere smokescreen for war'. Under cover of the smokescreen the real policy of the U.S., according to the Chinese, is to establish an over-all world military supremacy with which ultimately to smash the power of the socialist countries.

> ... the fundamental policy of the United States still rests on two sets of facts (one set is to prepare actively for war and the other to hang out a peace signboard), both having a single objective — to destroy socialism. (*Peking Review*, January 5th, 1960.)

Thus, while supporting the principle of peaceful coexistence, the Chinese warn the socialist countries that they must not fall into the error of thinking that imperialism can ever be conciliated. They fee, that in his attempt to 'come to an understanding' with the United Statesl Khrushchev is obscuring the real nature of imperialism, and is misleading the world peace movement with false hopes. This does not imply that war is inevitable. As stated in the Chinese Communist Resolution on the Moscow Conference adopted January 18th, 1961:

> The defence of world peace, the realization of peaceful coexistence and peaceful competition among countries of different social systems and the prevention of the new world war which is now being planned by the imperialists constitute the most pressing tasks for the peoples of the world. The imperialists headed by the United States are stubbornly persisting in a 'cold war' policy

leading to the catastrophe of nuclear war, intensifying the arming of the militarist forces of West Germany and Japan and fanatically engaging in armaments expansion and war preparations. Facts have proved that the aggressive nature of imperialism has not changed. As long as imperialism exists there will be soil for wars of aggression. The danger is not yet over that imperialism will launch a new and unprecedentedly destructive world war. It is more imperative than ever that the peoples should be especially vigilant. However, owing to the fundamental change in the international balance of class forces, a new world war can be prevented by the joint efforts of the powerful forces of our era — the socialist camp, the international working class, the national-liberation movement and all peace-loving countries and peoples. Peace can be effectively safeguarded provided there is reliance on the struggle of the masses of the people and provided a broad united front is established and expanded against the policies of aggression and war of the imperialists headed by the United States. Marxist-Leninists have never held that the way to socialist revolution necessarily lies through wars between states.

To support her thesis of the inherent aggressive nature of imperialism, Peking points with telling effect to the Cuban invasion, the U-2 incident, to the sending of troops into South Vietnam and Thailand and Washington's support for unpopular dictators in a variety of places in the world — and above all to her ever enlarging arsenal of weapons.

Thus the Chinese as they look at the realities of their world position can see no answer to the problem of America either in a major war (because of its global destructiveness) nor in any immediate reduction of American power through disarmament. They look, therefore, to a furtherance of the struggle with the United States in an area where *America's military strength is of little advantage to her* — namely in the support of wars of national liberation. In these popular uprisings Washington is at a disadvantage — for nearly always it is supporting regimes which the people themselves have repudiated. Furthermore, superior military strength cannot be deployed without accelerating the movements for popular liberation elsewhere.

When Mao Tse-tung annunciated his famous 'paper tiger' theory, he was not, of course, implying that the United States was harmless, but that it was not invincible and need not be feared. For power in Mao's eyes is not power if it does not have the 'spirit of the people' behind it. But there was another nuance to this 'paper tiger' concept which we usually miss — that power itself under certain circumstances is itself powerless. I think the Chinese would cite Cuba as an excellent historical example of this. America, with all its prodigious military equipment and a navy that would dwarf all the other navies of the world combined, is confronted and challenged by six million people on a puny island not one hundred miles from America's shores — *and is unable to use her power against them.* Here indeed, the Chinese would say, America has proved herself a paper tiger. America finds herself unable to deploy her massive military strength against the Cuban people because to do so could set off a chain reaction of revolutions through Latin America.

It is this view of the Chinese — the necessity of continual and unremitting struggle on a world scale against the forces of imperialism — that is responsible for the widespread Western belief that the Chinese regard World War III as inevitable. The Chinese would reply that this struggle is precisely what is required to bring America to her senses, and make her accept the realities of her reduced global position. She can no longer act as if she was the top nation. She must, in other words, be prevented from unleashing a world war in the mistaken belief that she could win it.

As for the abandonment of traditional Marxist doctrine the Chinese, I think, would say something like this. They recognize that the world has undergone many changes since the days of Marx and Lenin and that some adjustments in doctrine are certainly required — they do not cling to doctrine as to holy writ. But they see nothing in the world today that leads them to believe that capitalism can change its basic nature by parliamentary legalism or by extra-parliamentary strikes and demonstrations. (It is, for instance, highly unlikely that any administration in the U.S. could be made to abandon its armament policy by mere popular disapproval.) The Chinese would suggest that confusion about what changes can and what changes cannot be expected under capitalism will lead to all kinds of errors — and the assumption that a 'peaceful socialist revolution' can be brought about by parliamentary means is one of them.

It can be seen from this thumb-nail sketch that the positions of the Russians and the Chinese are indeed far apart. The history of the Chinese revolution shows that the Chinese can not only show remarkable flexibility but that once they believe that they have found the 'historically correct' line of action they are not easily deterred even by apparently overwhelming odds. It was this spirit that enabled a mere handful of rebels to pit themselves against the huge American supported armies of the Kuomintang and with a total certainty of eventual victory. One cannot but be impressed by Mao Tse-tung, at a time when his struggles against Chiang Kai-shek appeared doomed to failure, sitting in his cave calmly preparing the programme that would be required after victory. This Chinese firmness and confidence on matters which they consider involve basic issues of principle will not make accommodation with the U.S.S.R. an easy matter. There is nothing more unshakeable than a Chinese who feels that he 'has history on his side'.

It is not easy at this stage to see how the divergent attitudes of the two countries will be bridged. My own view, for what it is worth, is that both sides involved in the dispute will agree that they have more to gain in remaining unified in the face of a common enemy than any advantage that a diplomatic break in their ranks could bring. I believe the essential unity of the Sino-Soviet alliance will not be broken; that new strategic concepts will be formulated that can embrace views which today seem to be far apart. But if this is indeed found to be impossible we may yet see the alliance lose its coherence — with world revolutionary leadership passing from Moscow to Peking.

MAY 1962

Appendix 5

A POSTSCRIPT ON CHINA'S ECONOMIC PROBLEMS, 1960–62

THOSE who have read the Appendix 'Food and Rationing' will have realized that by mid-1960 it was already apparent that China was moving towards a period of acute food shortage. Climatic conditions in 1959 had been serious enough; in 1960 they were worse and by the end of that year 70 per cent of China's agricultural land had been affected either by flood or drought. Hopes for improvement were centred on 1961 but this also turned out to be a year of exceptionally bad weather. This series of natural calamities was, according to the London *Times*, the worst climatic period that China had suffered for over a hundred years.

Bad harvests for three years in succession (in a country where the margin is so narrow that any reduction in food is likely to bring distress) confronted the Chinese government with a very serious crisis whose effect extended far beyond the problem of supplying food for nearly one quarter of the world's population. China was relying almost wholly (for she had no other choice) on the export of agricultural products to enable her to purchase the essential equipment for her rapidly developing industry. Not only had she to curtail her foreign trade (trade fell by 25 per cent between 1960 and 1961), but her valuable reserves of foreign exchange were spent on large scale purchases of wheat from Canada and Australia. Thus China's crop failures directly impeded her economic growth on other fronts.

The Chinese government acted as any government would confronted by these same stern realities. The increase of her over-all agricultural production was given top priority in the national effort; much heavy-industry construction was postponed; a large number of those who had come to the cities were resettled in rural areas where they could help

396

with food production; the making of tractors, fertilizer, irrigation equipment, etc., was expanded as rapidly as possible; and in the rural communes special incentives were given to the peasants to grow food for themselves and for local private trade. The Chinese government hoped that by these measures the most damaging effects of the agricultural failures could be minimized.

The question arises: Could this crisis have been avoided? How far was the food shortage, with all its ramifications, a result of natural calamities and how far of just sheer bad management? There is no question that the climate dealt China a cruel blow, and at a moment in her economic development when it hurt her most. But the Chinese today (with the benefits of hindsight) would probably agree that they had over-extended their efforts and had attempted to do too much in too short a time, and that in their wish to develop rapidly an industrial base agriculture was too long neglected.

It has become fashionable in the West to blame the communes for the agricultural failures; and to give this as the reason for their 'abandonment'. But the communes have not been abandoned, though it is true that in the light of experience considerable changes have been made in their administration to give, among other things, a larger place for private incentive and wider initiative on the village level. However, some Western economists who have watched developments in China have expressed the view that far from the communes having been the cause of the agricultural failures it was because of their administrative machinery, spread throughout China, that the consequences of the food shortage have not been more serious and that all available food was equitably distributed.

But having exonerated the communes to this extent it must be clearly stated that climatic conditions were only one of many interrelated causes that led to the 1960–62 crisis, and among these undoubtedly was the withdrawal of much technical assistance by the Soviet Union. Readers of this book will have realized that China is a nation forging ahead on many fronts and each has taken its toll of available resources. The establishment of local industries in all villages, multiplied economic activities, intensive social and educational programmes have each deflected manpower from the land. One report estimates that of 220 million full-time agricultural workers, only 80 million were available for grain production, afforestation and land reclamation. It is just conceivable that China could have managed to get by with this reduced labour force at a time of good harvests. With three successive bad harvests it proved disastrous.

It must not be thought, however, that this reduction in the number of available food-producing workers was not to some extent compensated for in other ways. China has been one of the few backward countries which has solved the problem that faces them all — the chronic under-employment of the rural population.[1]

One of the paradoxes of China's food predicament was that her success in finding full employment for the people was itself one of the causes of the food shortage. People who work need more food than those who are idle or partly idle. The average *per capita* calorie *requirement* of food is higher than it has ever been before in China's history. When dealing with a population the size of China's even a very small increase of only 2 ounces of grain in the daily ration would involve additional food consumption of more than 43,000 tons a day or 16 million tons a year.

How bad was the food shortage? The general impression conveyed by the Western press in 1961 and 1962 was that China was in the grip of a vast famine and that many Chinese were starving. This does not appear to be the truth.[2] Unquestionably there is much suffering; rations were tighter than when I was in China and even these rations were not always available. But there has, I think, been a general tendency to exaggerate the food situation.

This tendency to make the worst of any setback in China has been a marked feature of the Western press ever since Mao established his regime. With a kind of desperate regularity American newspapers, radio and TV have over the years reported 'famine', 'starvation' and

[1] See Chapter 14, 'The National Picture'. It might be also noted here that by 1960 male peasants in China worked 50 per cent more days a year than the equivalent workers in India; women worked twice as much as women in India.

[2] This is being written towards the end of May 1962, too early to have reports of this year's harvest. If China suffers yet another year of bad harvests then a real disaster may be in store for the Chinese people — though even so it is highly unlikely that it would compare with the famines we usually associate in our minds with the China of the past. As mentioned earlier in this book, some million people died in Honan province alone during the famine of 1942-43; this despite ample supplies of American relief, much of which never reached those who needed it.

'death' for millions of Chinese. As far back as 1950 (January 17th) an AP dispatch from Hong Kong spoke of '40 Million Chinese Face Threat of Famine Death'. In 1952 (June 23rd) the United Press (from Formosa) reported 'Shanghai is a city of hungry millions ... there is no rice for the vast bulk of the population ... the average Chinese is afraid to buy meat'. On March 11th, 1954, the *Christian Science Monitor* stated that 'Famine Stalks Red China' and on April 24th, 1955, the *New York Times* informed its readers that 'Red China in Grip of Spring Famine'.

Depending upon the year the 'famine' took place there have been various and often contradictory reasons given for the terrible state of affairs in China. At the beginning it was because China was forced to send food from its starving millions to feed the Russians. At the time of land reform, when each peasant was given his own small plot of land, it was said that this prevented any real modernization of ancient farming methods. When the Chinese began their co-operative farms the 'experts' pointed out that the inherent individualism of the Chinese peasant was preventing agricultural success. And so on. *The fact is that up to and including the present food shortage there has been no starvation in China.* During many of the years when the Western press was either falsifying or greatly exaggerating the food situation in China the majority of the Chinese were eating better than they ever had before.

It was, therefore, not surprising that when China faced food shortages in 1960–62 the same type of reporting took place. Thus, the *New York Times*'s Far East correspondent, Mr Tillman Durdin, wrote on September 10th, 1961, of Chinese 'mass discontent ... apathy ... mounting deaths', and of a daily intake of 600 calories. (On April 9th, 1962, *Newsweek* painted a less dire picture than Mr Durdin's and spoke of a 1,600 calorie intake.)

I have before me a copy of a letter written on October 2nd, 1961, by a Chinese-speaking British doctor, J. S. Horn, F.R.C.S., addressed to the *New York Times*, questioning Mr Durdin's report. Dr Horn had just returned home after a leisurely journey through central China. 'As a doctor,' he writes, 'I should be quick to notice signs of malnutrition and a daily intake of 600 calories would rapidly produce severe symptoms. Yet the general health of the people appears to be good ...

I found that the problems resulting from successive years of severe drought were being tackled with energy and confidence.'

(In view of the loose usage of 'starvation' and 'malnutrition' concerning the food situation in China some light was shed on the matter as far back as mid-1961 by the scholarly *China Quarterly* of London. This conservative magazine is often sharply critical of Peking. In its July 1961 issue it attempted a careful assessment of the state of nutrition in China; and the following conclusion was reached:

It is not always understood that man can be brought to a state of nutritional equilibrium at a reduced level of energy intake, well below his habitual consumption. Nutrition surveys during and after the last war revealed in Europe as well as in Asia that man can live on a low plane of nutrition for substantial periods without necessarily suffering any serious physical damage or becoming unduly susceptible to illness or disease. Food satisfies basal metabolism, maintenance requirements and energy needs for work. Shortage of food thus means in many cases a decline in work rather than incidence of malnutrition. This is the meaning of Chinese official instructions in 1960 to extend the hours of rest of the working population.

Under Chinese conditions, an average food intake of 2,200 calories per day is likely to provide the population with ample food for heavy work. At the level of 2,000 calories the population will remain in reasonably good physical condition. Below that level there is bound to be loss of body weight, retarded growth among children and reduced output among working men and women. This is what happened in 1960 ... It would be prudent not to overrate the effects which mediocre harvests have had in the last two years ...)

Acute shortage of food — even if it has not reached actual famine or starvation proportions — is among the most agonizing of human experiences and it should surprise no one that peasants who are within reach of Hong Kong, where food is much more plentiful, should attempt to go there. Hong Kong has often in the past been a magnet for many peasants in Kwangtung province during times of distress, and it is sometimes forgotten that when Hong Kong was ceded to Britain it was laid down in a supplementary treaty that all Chinese were to be able to enter freely — though this provision is not, of course, always implemented.

For a brief period in May 1962 the number of Chinese entering Hong Kong increased to such an extent that the British were impelled to put up a barrier against them and to return many who had entered illegally. True to form, this sudden influx from the mainland was greatly publicized by the United States press and our newspapers were full of accounts of refugees 'fleeing the horrors of the Communist regime' — complete with photographs of Chinese pitifully stretching out their hands through the barbed wire for food.

The conservative *Far Eastern Economic Review* of Hong Kong on May 24th, 1962, wrote in a somewhat different vein:

> Everyone who has seen the refugees has commented that they do not seem to be starving ... some reporters from the local press have interviewed a few and their stories are roughly the same; they are all people from the rural areas of Kwangtung, some of whom have worked in Canton and been sent back to the farms in the 'aid agriculture' drive ... They all give the food shortage and the general discomfort of life as their reason for coming. None of the refugees has claimed political asylum, or said that he was escaping from the Communist regime as such. That many would welcome the opportunity to go to Taiwan even were the Generalissimo's government prepared to accept them is doubtful.

In London on May 22nd, Reginald Maudling, British Colonial Secretary, gave the House of Commons (as reported the following day in the *New York Times*) much the same story: 'There was little evidence that the Chinese refugees attempting to enter Hong Kong were suffering malnutrition.'

There has been little effort in our press to present the Chinese situation in its world perspective and her food supply is rarely compared to that of other Asian nations. It is not generally realized that even during this period of severely reduced harvests China was growing more than 50 per cent more grain *per capita* than India. (India's 1960–61 target was only 75 million tons for her population of 420 million, as against China's production of 185 million tons for a population of 650 million.) Nutritionally the average Indian (in spite of

American aid) is significantly poorer than the average Chinese, as is the case of tens of millions in other backward areas.

As we have said, the rate of China's industrial growth has been, without question, seriously reduced by her agricultural failures and it has caused immense dislocation of her plans — but here again we need to set this in some kind of perspective. China's Second Five Year Plan (ending in 1962) fulfilled or surpassed all major industrial targets ahead of time. As Mr Tibor Mende pointed out in his book *China and Her Shadow*, though India started with an industrial base more advanced than that of China, China's economic growth has been about three times faster than that of India's. By 1960 India's rate of investments was barely a tenth of her national income, in China it was three times higher. 'Moreover,' Mr Mende commented, 'these high Chinese investments came entirely from the country's own current production; India has been relying on very large-scale foreign assistance in the form of loans as well as grants.'

Mention cannot be evaded of one regrettable feature of China's food problems — the political capital made of it in the West. We are apparently so anxious to convince ourselves that China's system is bound to fail that one can detect almost a note of glee in some of the newspaper reports of the difficulties facing the Chinese people. Everything apparently is grist to the cold-war mill; the human suffering that is involved when a country experiences shortages of food is all but forgotten.

In 1962 the International Trading Corporation, a private American firm in Seattle, applied for permission to sell 10½ million tons of American wheat and barley to China — worth about $585 million. We do not know whether Peking was involved in this proposal; we do know that it was turned down by Washington.

Commenting on this decision, the *Far Eastern Economic Review* on March 29th in a notable editorial entitled 'A Bad Decision', said:

From all accounts China is in very great need of foreign grain: last year she imported about $290 million worth, principally from Australia and Canada, and this year — and for several years to come — she appears to want something of the same order ...

The supreme irony may now be unveiling — that America is probably the only country that can supply the grain that China wants ...

China's position seems to be that (unlike India, which benefits from virtually free United States surplus food) she would rather starve than accept charity, but that she would also rather do business with the Americans than starve. She wants to pay for her wheat but probably cannot any more in cash: she requires credit. On humanitarian grounds there is a case for allowing this trade, and the dogged spirit of wanting ultimately to pay must evoke admiration. It is a pity that Peking has in the past refused to separate trade from politics now that the separation would suit her interests.

On the American side the position seems to be that law and public opinion forbid all exports to China; and that if China does need United States grain she should ask, as it were, on bended knee, and accept aid — with each sack or crate clearly labelled 'from Uncle Sam' so that the Chinese people cannot be misled into believing the Americans let them starve or that some other party eventually came to the rescue. This seems a very much less admirable position than China's. Both sides should free this pressing question from politics and allow commercial dealings on the world's normal commercial terms.

While the reporters and commentators wrote about China facing ruin, some economists were warning us in calmer tones not to underestimate China's capacity for rapid recovery. It was felt that once the immediate difficulties are over, China may surprise the world by speedily regaining her industrial momentum. The Chinese meanwhile are not idle, waiting for things to improve. Reports from Western observers in China described how the Chinese were busy standardizing accounting procedures, expanding and refining national statistical methods; and individual factories, no longer trying to beat records, are concentrating on improving the quality of their products and increasing their diversity and range. It is quite probable that given a year, or two years, of good harvests China will again be increasing her economic growth at her former remarkable rate.

On April 18th, 1962, the eminently respectable *Times* of London published an editorial which, in my opinion, was a rational appraisal of the China situation. (It is significant that I. F. Stone, in his weekly

Newsletter, quoted from this editorial under the heading: 'What United States Newspaper Would Dare Speak So Objectively of China?')

For all the errors, China's plight should not be exaggerated ... Sympathizers see tremendous dedication and presume immense progress; opponents hear of shortages and difficulties and presume suffering and collapse. The truth is that the sufferings of the ordinary Chinese peasant from war, disorder, and famine have been immeasurably less in the last decade than in any other decade in the century.

MAY 1962

A Later Note

Throughout 1961 and 1962 writers in the American press were forecasting the imminent 'collapse' of the Communist regime due to the widespread 'famine' conditions in China. Even a well-known author like Mr Joseph Alsop could write in the *Saturday Evening Post* (a magazine of enormous circulation) about the 'Coming Explosion in Red China' and argue, with apparently irrefutable logic, that China's economy was on a 'descending spiral' that nothing could arrest. The over-all impression conveyed by the American press was that the people of China were in the grip of starvation, were desperate, and might at any moment rise in open rebellion against the government.

By 1963 it was clear to almost everyone (as it had been to readers of the more responsible British press) that conditions in China had never been as dark as had been pictured. The 'downward spiral' of the economy was not behaving as it should. Mr Alsop's 'explosion' never occurred. The 1963 harvest was likely to be a good one. Food was again adequate and in some areas even plentiful. Industrial production — especially that concerned with agriculture — was again moving into a higher gear.

In certain American newspapers some more sober assessments made their appearance. For example, the *Christian Science Monitor*, one of America's better newspapers (but one that had regularly been reporting dire calamities in China) made a new appraisal of the situation. In a report on March 20th, 1963, written by Saville R. Davis, one of the senior editors who had just completed an extended tour of S.E. Asia, the *Monitor* struck an altogether different note of warning:

... there remains the implacable question: What of the race between Communist and non-Communist standards of living? What of the race between India and China?

It is best not mentioned in a loud voice.

The American press tends to overemphasize the rural set-backs in Communist China ... Being so anxious to prove the falsity of Communist economics they do not notice that ... the Communist system is a good deal further ahead than it was before. British and French correspondents, with access to China that is denied to the American press ... uniformly say that the Chinese challenge, even on land, is more formidable than the West yet will recognize.

The slow progress [in India and S.E. Asia] seen by this reporter then drops down into a lower level of importance. The kind of agricultural drive that the Communists themselves attempt, the all-out effort with the entire country mobilized to propel it, is India's and South Asia's next and greatest need.

For those who had followed the American press reporting of events in China, based so often on wishful thinking rather than on news, this suggestion by a writer for the *Christian Science Monitor* that some social and economic techniques applied in China are applicable to other underdeveloped countries, was a very new, and a very unusual admission.

MAY 1963

Appendix 6

THE DISPUTE WITH INDIA

Some later notes

SINCE this book was first published in 1961 relations between China and India have deteriorated sharply. Sporadic clashes between border guards became more frequent, and in October 1962 large-scale fighting broke out along most of the disputed territory. The long exchange of arguments, the border clashes, the Chinese advance, cease fire and the subsequent withdrawal of the Chinese forces at a moment when they had gained almost total victory over the Indian army left most people in the West bewildered. The areas under dispute, high in the distant Himalayas, seemed to most Westerners hardly worth fighting about; the legal claims and counter-claims were intricate and confusing; the places involved bore unfamiliar names difficult to remember.

The U.S. press, always eager to find grounds for criticism of China, was virtually unanimous in its condemnation of China for 'naked and unprovoked aggression' against India.[1] The British press and the B.B.C. did little better in providing the public with an impartial assessment of the merits of the conflict. As a result it is probable that the overwhelming majority of the people of America and Britain, unaware of the basic facts, have accepted the 'Chinese aggression' explanation without much question. It would probably come as a surprise to them that the majority of neutral governments do not support the Indian-American-British interpretation of what actually took place. Having re-read the exchange of letters and telegrams between the Indian and

[1] Once more an exception must be made in the case of the *Monthly Review* of New York. I am greatly indebted to an article that appeared in the January 1963 issue and have taken the liberty to quote freely from it. Another excellent account of the dispute and its implications was published in pamphlet form by the *Far East Reporter* (New York) and I have also made much use of this. *Whither India-China Relations?* by the Ceylonese writer Theja Gunawardhana, published in Colombo, is another very useful review of the dispute.

Chinese leaders, and having carefully studied the maps, I have come to believe that anyone who approaches the facts impartially can come only to a conclusion which is almost opposite to the one that is generally presented. It will also become clear, I think, to any one who makes such a study that this conflict — though apparently about the demarcation of a disputed boundary — has in actual fact a far greater, and for the Indian people a far more tragic, significance.

It is not my intention in this appendix to give anything but the briefest account of the dispute and some of the implications as I see them.

It would be hard to find any part of the world with a longer or more chequered history than the vast mountainous region which separates China from Burma, Nepal, Pakistan and India. These borders, undefined and often previously disputed, are a legacy of history. Almost all conflicting claims along this border can find some support in history, ethnography or in common justice. The history of this area supplies enough material for any party to support any claim. Under these circumstances it is obvious that the only way to a peaceful resolution of the various claims is through a process of compromise. And this was in fact exactly the way the borders between China on the one hand and Burma, Nepal and — later — Pakistan on the other were settled. In none of these cases were there armed clashes. In each case the *status quo* was taken as the basis of negotiations, and adjustments were then made, one way or the other, taking into account historical and geographical factors and the interests of the parties involved. All three borders were demarcated and recognized in formal international treaties. On balance in the process of give and take, it has been generally acknowledged, China gave considerably more than she took.

Between China and India matters took a very different course. No basis of negotiations could be agreed upon. Numerous armed clashes occurred, culminating in large-scale warfare. Why did this happen? Has China's attitude been more 'aggressive' towards India than it was towards Burma, Nepal and Pakistan? Or has India, unlike these other countries, been unwilling to compromise?

On this question the record is absolutely clear. China unquestionably was seeking an amicable settlement through discussion and mutual accommodation, suggesting that pending a settlement both parties should maintain the *status quo* as it existed in 1959 when the border clashes began. India has at all times insisted that all her principal claims must be conceded before the discussions could begin. There can be no doubt in the mind of anyone who studies the record that it has been India and not China that has stood in the way of a settlement through mutual compromise.

So, we must ask, was this because the *status quo* of 1959 was specially disadvantageous for India? Were there reasons why the choice of this particular moment was unacceptable to her? Before we can answer this question we must examine the border situation in 1959.

The Sino-Indian border is divided into three sectors. The western sector separates the Ladakh area of Kashmir from China's Sinkiang province and Tibet. The middle sector separates three Indian states from Tibet (the disputed areas in this middle sector were quite minor and need not be discussed in this appendix). The eastern sector separates the Indian state of Assam from Tibet.

In the eastern sector the Indians controlled the disputed area, claiming what is known as the McMahon Line — a line drawn up unilaterally by the British — to be the legal boundary. The McMahon Line was named after the British delegate at a conference held at Simla in 1914 which was attended by representatives of Britain, China and Tibet. The Chinese Government refused to sign the draft Convention and no Chinese Government since has ever accepted the McMahon line. The Chinese today still claim, as they did then, that the traditional and legal boundary included the southern slope of the Himalayas and was never based on the water-shed which was the basis used for drawing the McMahon line.

The Chinese say that some of the area between the traditional border and the McMahon Line (about 35,000 square miles, including much good farming land and valuable forests) had been taken by the British from China at a time when China was too weak to resist. This area was organized by the British and was known as the Northeast Frontier Agency (N.E.F.A.) and it retains that status today under Indian rule, together with the additional territory occupied by India in 1951. The Indians reject the Chinese claim and state that the McMahon Line merely confirmed the natural, traditional, ethnic and administrative boundary in this area'.

This Indian interpretation of the McMahon Line is, according to the Chinese, greatly weakened by the fact that the official *Survey of India* map published by the Indian Government in 1917; the map attached to the 1929 edition of the *Encyclopaedia Britannica*; the 1940 edition of the *Oxford Advanced Atlas* (Bartholomew); and the 1942 edition of the *Philip Atlas* all show the border as claimed by China and not the McMahon Line as claimed by India. In the course of a long note addressed to the Indian Government on December 26th, 1959, the Chinese Foreign Office pointed out that the McMahon Line

> was not adopted on the official map 'Tibet and Adjacent Countries' published by the *Survey of India* in 1938 ... Neither was the so-called McMahon Line followed in drawing the eastern sector of the Sino-Indian boundary on the map 'India 1945' attached to the 1951 third edition in English of the *Discovery of India*, written by Prime Minister Nehru himself ...

Even when the McMahon Line appeared on the official maps of India in 1950, 1951 and 1952 it was marked as 'undermarked'. Up to 1958 the *Times Atlas of the World* included both the traditional line and the McMahon Line with the words 'Disputed area' printed between them. The weight of these facts overwhelmingly indicates that the Indian claim that the McMahon Line merely 'reaffirmed' what was always accepted as the legal boundary cannot be supported.

The situation in the western sector in 1959 was different. In this sector the Chinese and not the Indians were in possession of the disputed area — about 13,000 square miles. The Indians claim that the legal border is considerably to the north and east of where it is at present. But here again, in 1950 the official Indian maps show this area as 'undefined'. It was only in 1954 that the *Survey of India* map for the first time showed the boundary precisely drawn. What had happened between 1950 and 1954 to justify the Indian Government (without reference to China) in claiming an area that had until then been acknowledged by them to be undefined?

The explanation is that after the Chinese entered Tibet in 1950–51 what Britain and India had considered a buffer state between India and China was removed. As Mr Nehru, in a speech to the Lok Sabha on February 21st, 1961, expressed it:

When the Chinese first entered Tibet ... frankly we did not expect any trouble on our border but, naturally, looking at things in historical perspective, we thought the whole nature of our border had changed. It was a dead border, it was now becoming alive, and we began to think in terms of the protection of that border ...

Our attention was first directed, naturally or not, to these borders, and a high level, high power committee was appointed, the Border Defence Committee, right then in 1951 or 1952, I forget. This Committee presented a comprehensive report, and many of the suggestions were accepted by Government, some were not. This was ten years ago.

It seems clear that one of the things that this Border Defence Committee did was to define what border it proposed to 'defend'. This was done unilaterally without consultation with China. From then on a border which had never been defined became in the Indian view precisely determined.

But now — still considering this western sector — we enter a phase of the dispute which even the Indians find it embarrassingly difficult to explain. Across territory in the Aksai Chin area (which India had now unilaterally defined as being hers) the Chinese had been constructing a highway. This road, which follows an ancient caravan route across the high Aksai Chin plateau, provides the Chinese with the only practical communication between Sinkiang and central Tibet. The transformation of this old caravan route into a modern highway was (in Chou En-lai's words) a 'gigantic task'. Thousands of Chinese must have been engaged in the work. The survey work for this road was started in 1954, and the road itself was not completed until 1957. But though this road was crossing land that India was claiming as hers *no protest was made until 1958* — a year after the road was completed and four years after it was begun. Why, we must ask, did the Indian Government wait so long before complaining of these Chinese 'incursions' into Indian territory? The answer is simple: *the Indian Government had no idea what was going on in this area.* This is how Mr Nehru explained it to the Lok Sabha on February 23rd, 1961:

It was not clear to us whether this proposed motorway crossed our territory. The first suspicion that this might be so came to us in

1957, from a map published in Peking. We did not even then know definitely whether this transgressed our territory. The map was a small map, but half a magazine page. We did not know, but we began to suspect it ... as we did not have proof, we did not protest then.

But even with their suspicions aroused the Indian Government made no effort apparently to confirm the presence of this road or its location for no protest was made until 1958.

How is it possible that a government does not know what is going on in part of what it claims to be its territory? The answer again is an obvious one. India had never actually exercised jurisdiction over the territory it was now claiming. Though readily accessible from the Chinese side, the Aksai Chin plateau can only be reached from India after weeks of difficult travel across barren and unpopulated mountain ranges.

With these facts in mind we can now get an over-all picture of the situation as it existed in 1959 — the situation which China wished to take as the basis for negotiations and which India rejected. In the east the Indians were in possession of the disputed area — 35,000 square miles. In the west the Chinese were in possession of the disputed area — 13,000 square miles. It was in 1959 — in August and October — that the first serious armed clashes occurred. Reacting to these encounters the Chinese Government on November 7th (a date that was to figure frequently in subsequent correspondence) proposed that both sides should withdraw at once twenty kilometres from the actual line of control to avoid further incidents and that negotiations to settle the location of the boundary should be begun. The implications of this proposal were quite clear. The Chinese were in effect offering to accept the McMahon Line in the east provided the Indians would accept a line in the west which would secure for China the important highway which they had built. This proposal was rejected by the Indian Government. No negotiations could take place they said until the Chinese accepted not only the McMahon Line but India's definition of the boundary in the west which she had unilaterally defined on her maps without discussion with China.

The rejection of this sensible compromise put forward by China was, we can now realize, the real turning point in the dispute. It is very hard to see how any rational person could regard the Chinese suggestion as arising from anything but a sober sense of realism and a desire for a peaceful settlement. India would be getting legal recognition of 35,000 square miles in the east, including much farm land and forests, in exchange for giving up her claim to 13,000 square miles over which she had never exercised any jurisdiction, which by no stretch of the imagination could be considered to have value to her and which (on the Indian side) could only be reached with the greatest difficulty.

The Chinese were offering to swallow a bitter pill by accepting the McMahon Line — the very name of which denotes its imperialist origin and a reminder of past humiliations at the hands of the Western powers. The Indians were in control of the area up to the McMahon Line and the Chinese knew they could not be dislodged without military conflict. Though subsequent events showed they had ample power to throw the Indians back, *the Chinese did not want a war with India and proved it by being willing to make very considerable concessions to avoid one.*

All the tragic events that have happened since were the inevitable results of India's rejection of the only compromise that could have led to a peaceful settlement of the border dispute. What in fact followed? Having defined the Chinese occupation of the Aksai Chin Plateau as 'aggression', the Indians began, logically enough, to apply military pressure to oust the Chinese. During the next two years the Indians pressed forward, clashing increasingly with the Chinese, and they were successful in advancing against relatively light Chinese resistance. As Mr Nehru put it in addressing the Lok Sabha on June 20th, 1962:

> India had opened some new patrol posts endangering the Chinese posts and it was largely due to movements on our side that the Chinese had also to make movements. It is well known in knowledgeable circles in the world that the position in this area had been changing to our advantage and the Chinese are concerned about it.

Throughout the summer of 1962 there were indications of Indian preparations for military action, which undoubtedly were watched carefully by the Chinese. Addressing Parliament on August 13th and 14th, Mr Nehru described the government's preparation:

> We have concentrated on increasing our strength, military strength, strength in communications, roads, etc. We have a special border roads committee which has done very well — I do not know exactly — thousands of miles in very difficult terrain. We built up our air supply position by getting aircraft — big aircraft — from various countries; we have got some helicopters too; but in the main it consisted of big transport aircraft; there were some from the United States and some from the Soviet Union ... We improved our military position, our supply position, and we have got our troops in various areas there with forward posts. If they (the Chinese) have got nine posts, we have got 22 or 23 or 24.

With India openly improving its military position along the frontier areas, the Chinese must undoubtedly have been making their preparations also. With India consistently refusing to negotiate on reasonable terms and her 'nibbling' tactics from 1959 on, the Chinese must have been convinced that they would sooner or later have to administer a severe defeat to the Indians before any negotiations were possible. It is hard to see what alternatives they had. They were certainly not ready to accept the prospect of a border in perpetual conflict.

This, then, was the general background to the large-scale fighting that broke out all along the border on October 20th, 1962. China had already repeatedly put forward proposals for negotiations which India had rejected. India's rigid attitude had by this time caused some adverse comments. The events which immediately preceded the hostilities (with our present knowledge of what was about to happen) are interesting to recall and can be summarized as follows:

July 26th   India offered to negotiate the boundary dispute on the basis of the study undertaken jointly in 1960.

August 4th   The Chinese responded and proposed that discussions begin as soon as possible.

August 22nd   An Indian note said that before discussions could take place the border in the western sector must be restored to its *status quo* (the border as defined by India.)

September 13th The Chinese said there could be no pre-conditions. They again proposed that each side withdraw 20 kilometres to avoid further incidents and suggested that the representatives of the two countries meet on October 15th in Peking and then in New Delhi alternatively.

September 19th The Indians agreed to the proposed date and place but insisted that the talks should have the specific object of 'defining measures to restore the *status quo* in the Western sector'.

October 3rd A Chinese note reiterated the proposal that both sides should enter speedily into discussion and that neither side should refuse to discuss any question that might be raised by the other side.

October 6th The Indian Government rejected the Chinese proposal and called off the talks scheduled to begin in Peking on October 15th.

October 12th Nehru announced that he had instructed the Indian army to 'throw the Chinese' out of the disputed areas. (This was considered by the New York *Herald Tribune* – October 15th – as 'tantamount to a formal declaration of war'. The *Guardian* [England] described Nehru's order as an 'ultimatum'.)

October 13th China called upon Nehru to 'pull back from the brink of the precipice'. China was 'absolutely unwilling to cross swords with India'.

October 14th Krishna Menon (still Minister of Defence) declared, 'We will fight to the last man, to the last gun.'

October 15th Nehru called upon his people for discipline and sacrifice.

October 16th The Indian Defence Ministry instructed ordnance factories to start maximum production even if it meant having three shifts on a round-the-clock schedule.

October 17th China charged India with repeatedly violating China's air space and invited India to shoot down any Chinese planes if they flew over Indian territory. (*New York Times*, October 19th.)

October 20th Large-scale hostilities began along the entire front.

And we are asked to believe — by the Indian Government and by numberless Western editorial writers, politicians and radio reporters — that this fighting came as a 'tremendous shock and surprise' to the Indians!

Who actually started the fighting?

The general assumption in the press of the United States was that the Chinese had initiated the fighting on October 20th. Some British papers indicated otherwise. For example, the *Sunday Telegraph* on October 21st reported: 'India made a secret high level approach to the West for support *shortly before launching her offensive against the Chinese on the Himalayan border*, it is now learned ... ' (My italics.)

Further light was thrown on this matter by a report in the *New York Times* of April 19th, 1963, based on a UPI dispatch from Washington:

TAYLOR INDICATES INDIANS STARTED CLASH
WITH CHINESE

General Maxwell D. Taylor, Chairman of the Joint Chiefs of Staff, indicated in secret Congressional testimony made public here today that India might have started the border fight with Communist China.

The previously accepted version of the border fighting that flared last fall was that Communist China had attacked Indian troops ...

By October 24th military operations on all fronts were decisively in China's favour. On this day Chou En-lai made one more attempt to bring the hostilities to an end and to settle the dispute peacefully. He sent Mr Nehru a three-point proposal:

1. Both parties affirm that the Sino-Indian boundary question must be settled peacefully through negotiations. Pending a peaceful settlement the Chinese Government hopes that the Indian Government will agree that both parties respect the line of actual control along the entire Sino-Indian border, and the armed forces of each side withdraw 20 kilometres from this line and disengage.

2. Provided that the Indian Government agrees to the above proposal, the Chinese Government is willing, through consultation between the two parties, to withdraw its frontier guards in the eastern sector of the border north of the line of actual control;

at the same time, both China and India undertake not to cross the line of actual control....

3. The Chinese Government considers that, in order to seek a friendly settlement of the Sino-Indian boundary question, talks should be held once again by the Prime Ministers of China and India. At a time considered to be appropriate by both parties, the Chinese Government would welcome the Indian Prime Minister to Peking; if this should be inconvenient to the Indian Government, the Chinese Premier would be ready to go to Delhi for talks.

India's response to these practical suggestions was swift. On the same day (October 24th) they were rejected. Three days later Mr Nehru wrote: 'My colleagues and I are not able to understand the niceties of the Chinese three-point proposal, which talks about "lines of actual control", etc.' (One cannot help but wonder whether Mr Nehru would have adopted this supercilious tone if he could have foreseen the resounding defeat that was in store for his armies!)

On November 15th, the Indian Ministry of Defence announced a large-scale attack in the eastern sector, and the next day the Chinese counter-attacked and resumed their advance. By now the Chinese armies were looking down towards the plain of Assam and in a position to threaten India's main oil-fields. Sela, nearly 14,000 feet high, the main Indian position south of Tawang, was stormed and outflanked. Tezpur was evacuated in panic. The heartland of India now lay virtually defenceless before the Chinese armies. Wild speculations appeared in the American press as to how far China would advance; it was almost taken for granted that China's objectives were to capture the rich Assam plain, the oil-fields — even the city of Calcutta. The precision shown by the Chinese command in the planning and execution of their advance and their mastery of the incredibly difficult problems of supply astonished military experts throughout the world. (Kingsley Martin reporting from New Delhi in the *New Statesman* called it 'one of the most brilliant operations in history'.)

With total victory over the Indian armies assured the Chinese Government on November 21st made their dramatic announcement — that they had ordered a unilateral cease fire along the entire line to start the following day; and that from December 1st the Chinese armies would withdraw in the eastern sector to a line 20 kilometres behind the McMahon Line and elsewhere to a line 20 kilometres behind the line of actual control on November 7th, 1959. On November 22nd all fighting stopped; in December the withdrawals of the Chinese armies were completed; and later Indian prisoners, and even captured weapons, were returned to India.

Thus the Chinese were at last able to impose *precisely those arrangements which she had so repeatedly offered as a basis of negotiation* — including her acceptance of the McMahon Line — and which India had so consistently and stubbornly refused.

The crucial question must now be asked: Why was the Indian Government so reluctant, while there was still time, to reach a peaceful agreement with China — like Burma, Nepal and Pakistan have done? What were the pressures which prevented such a settlement? The answer to this riddle will not, I think, be found in any further examination of the legal rights and wrongs of the border dispute itself, but rather by examining the extraordinarily difficult problems that were at this time facing the ruling groups in India.

Although India's economy is part 'socialized', part 'capitalist', the nation's ruling class (the big industrialists, the bankers, the upper ranks of the civil service, the army; in short, the 'power elite' which makes the major decisions and sets the nation's direction) is by origin and mental habit deeply committed to a capitalist future for India. But in the conditions prevailing in the world today capitalism cannot solve the pressing problems of the backward countries. Where some development does occur — such as in Mexico, for example, or some of the Latin American countries — the benefits go almost entirely to the few who are already privileged, and the gap between them and the poor grows wider. In India the circumstances are especially unfavourable for any rapid capital accumulation under the present system. But at the same time there are signs that the great masses in India will not indefinitely endure without protest their present condition of appalling poverty.

Nor can India's ruling groups ever allow themselves to forget that her northern neighbour and the country most like their own in population and stage of economic development, only fourteen years ago overthrew its own ruling class and since then has far outstripped India's advance. The nutritional level of the Chinese people, even during the recent period of acute shortage, was significantly higher than that in India; China's per capita grain production is almost 50 per cent higher than that of India; her steel production in 1960 was nearly five times that of India; her rate of growth and rate of capital investment have been three times higher than India's; the provision of education and progress in public health and hygiene have been far swifter in China than in India. The Indian ruling classes are well aware that India's rate of progress must at all costs be speeded up if the Indian people are not, sooner or later, to follow China's example and attempt to seek a better life through social and economic revolution. The large Communist gains in the Indian elections in 1957 were the first warning signals.

Nehru, it is true, remains an immensely popular leader, and while he is in control he provides some reassurance to the ruling circles that India will not move decisively to the left. But his popularity tends to conceal, except to those most sensitive to it, the growing political restiveness of the Indian masses. But when Nehru goes, as eventually he must, what then? Who will provide the unifying force? How can the ruling elite ensure that Nehru's successor will keep India moving to the right rather than to the revolutionary left?

Far from expanding rapidly, India's economy is stagnant. By 1960 it was clear that something was seriously wrong. 'Our resources,' said India's Finance Minister, 'are almost at rock bottom; there is no scope for running them further down; we have to depend wholly on foreign aid for the financing of our development plans.' By 1962 the conditions were, if anything, worse. On July 16th, *Barron's* magazine wrote, 'India's Finance Minister is chasing through the capitals of Europe in pursuit of $220,000,000 to finance the second year of the 3rd Five Year Plan; meanwhile India's liquid assets have been dropping inexorably to new all-time lows.' 'The World Bank provided another billion dollars towards India's economic development; without this sizeable sum of money, India would be unable to achieve the goals set...' (New York *Herald Tribune*, August 6th, 1962.) But in spite of their help three months later, on November 15th, 1962, the *Christian Science Monitor* was writing, 'Today, India's foreign exchange reserves practically have disappeared and there is no money to pay for maintenance imports ... India is increasing, not decreasing, its reliance on foreign capital.'

More aid would be one — quite temporary — solution; but India's dependence on foreign aid was already enormous. In eleven and a half years from 1949 to August 1962 the United States alone had granted or promised $4,754,000,000 in aid to India, and if the funds given by international monetary agencies are added the sum India received in aid reaches the staggering total of six and half billion dollars.

Thus we see some of the complex and interlocking problems that confronted the leaders of India. A seriously faltering economy, an ageing leader, a population living always on the very edge of subsistence and showing signs of looking to other means to solve their wretched poverty, and northward a China moving forward far more quickly than their own country. And above all, the most immediate need — the absolute necessity of getting yet more assistance from the only country that could provide it.

Even before the outbreak of fighting in October 1962 the United States had not concealed the fact that one purpose of aid was to keep India out of the Socialist bloc. 'The Administration is defending its request for a boost in economic assistance to India on grounds that India is a bulwark against Red Chinese encroachments in the Far East.' (*Wall Street Journal*, July 9th, 1962.) 'We know right now,' said Senator Sparkman, Acting Chairman of the Senate Foreign Relations Committee, on June 9th, 1962, 'that India is pressing very hard against Communist China on her northern boundary line ... we ought not to be discouraging India at the very time she is moving in the direction we have been wanting her to move for a long time.'

It has been said that just as the U.S. economy 'needs the cold war', so India needed the border dispute with China. These propositions are of course oversimplified, but their meaning is clear. Was it, in fact, ever possible, *within the terms of India's present economic and social system* which the ruling elite are so determined to maintain, for the Indian movement to come to a settlement with China and move once more towards friendship with her? I think it is doubtful, for a friendly settlement with China would probably have ended the foreign aid which alone was keeping the system going.[1]

[1] U.S. aid to India for 1962 totalled almost a billion dollars, lifting the Nehru.

The results of *not* coming to a peaceful settlement with China were apparent almost immediately after the large-scale fighting broke out in October. Additional foreign aid on a very massive scale was swiftly made available to India; a nation that was politically divided found a new and almost hysterical national unity in the drive to 'resist Chinese aggression'; (and a unity it should be noticed directed at precisely the country whose revolutionary experience might under other circumstances have held a dangerous attraction for the Indian masses); and the Indian Communist Party was in disarray. Under the stress of the emergency measures were passed to curb freedom of speech and which severely restricted left wing political activity (it is not generally known in the West that since May 1961 it has been illegal in India to question the rights and wrongs of the border dispute).

To sum it up the immediate result of the rejection of any peaceful settlement with China was to move India decisively to the right politically, and decisively into the Western camp internationally.

This I believe is the real significance and meaning of India's dispute with China. It was a conflict which India was able to provoke by refusing any compromise and by making demands on China which were certain to be rejected. One thing is clear: if the ruling groups in India had felt that a settlement was in their interest they could have reached one with as little fuss as Burma, Nepal and Pakistan did; and with not the slightest loss of national honour.

To the U.S. of course, the Indian move into the Western camp is a source of satisfaction. All fears that a neutral India — the largest and most influential neutral nation — would one day move into the Socialist bloc, can now be laid aside. The military 'containment' of Communist China is strengthened. The Indian economy will be increasingly militarized (already in 1963 vast increases in taxation have been announced to pay for the largest military budget ever) and India's future dependence on U.S. military and economic aid will undoubtedly make her more responsive to suggestions from Washington.

But the price of all this will be paid by the Indian people. Already

---

Government to first place in the world picture. An AP dispatch from Washington on March 21st, 1963, citing figures provided by the Agency for International Development, reported: 'In 1962, India was the biggest recipient of United States aid, with $838,000,000.'

the increased taxation for military purposes has doomed any hope of real economic improvement for a long time to come. No amount of U.S. aid can compensate for the damage that has already been done. A deteriorating economy will inevitably shift the government yet further to the right. Political democracy — India's greatest experiment — will be abandoned except perhaps in name. And eventually the military will take over.

The significance of the dispute with China does not lie in the demarcation of boundaries high in the Himalayan mountains, but rather in India's rejection of a settlement with China in favour of involvement in the cold war. The benefits that this decision will bring — and there are benefits — will be enjoyed by the few who are already among the privileged. The cost in suffering and continued poverty will have to be borne by the great masses of the Indian people.

JULY 1963

Bibliography

I. BOOKS

Barnett, A. Doak, *Communist China and Asia* (Council on Foreign Relations), Oxford University Press, London, 1960.

Beauvoir, Simone de, *The Long March*, Deutsch and Weidenfeld & Nicolson, London, 1958.

Belden, Jack, *China Shakes the World*, Harper and Bros., New York, 1949.

Bodde, Derk, *China's Cultural Tradition*, Rinehart and Co., New York, 1957. (Source Problems in World Civilization.)

Boorman, Howard L., Eckstein, Alexander, *et al.*, *Moscow-Peking Axis* (Council on Foreign Relations), Oxford University Press, London, 1957.

Boyd Orr, Lord, with Peter Townsend, *What Is Going On in China*, Macdonald, London, 1959.

Cameron, James, *Mandarin Red*, Michael Joseph, London, 1955.

Chao Kuo-chun, *Agrarian Policies of Mainland China* (1949-1956), Harvard University Press, Cambridge, Mass., 1957.

Clark, Gerald, *Impatient Giant: Red China Today*, W. H. Allen, London, 1960.

Faure, Edgar, *The Serpent and the Tortoise*, Macmillan, London, 1958.

Fei Shiao-tung and Chang Chih-i, *Earthbound China: A Study of the Social Life of a Chinese County Seat*, New York: Frederick A. Praeger, 1945.

Feng Yu-lan, *A History of Chinese Philosophy*, Princeton University Press, Princeton, 1952-3.

Fitzgerald, C. P., *Revolution in China*, The Cresset Press, London, 1952.
—— *Flood Tide in China*, The Cresset Press, London, 1958.

Gale, G. S., *No Flies in China*, George Allen & Unwin, London, 1955.

Granet, Marcel, *Chinese Civilization*, Meridian Books, New York, 1958.

423

Guillain Robert, *600 Million Chinese*, Criterion Books, New York, 1957.

Harrer, Heinrich, *Seven Years in Tibet*, Pan Books, London, 1956.

Ho Ping-ti, *Studies on the Population of China, 1368–1953*, Harvard University Press, Cambridge, Mass., 1959. (Harvard East Asian Studies 4.)

Hughes, T. J., and Luard, D. E. T., *The Economic Development of Communist China, 1949–1958*, Oxford University Press, London, 1959.

Isaacs, Harold R., *Scratches on Our Minds*, John Day Co., New York, 1958.

Levenson, Joseph R., *Liang Ch'i Ch'ao and the Mind of Modern China*, Thames and Hudson, London, 1959.

Lindsay, Michael (Lord Lindsay of Birker), *China and the Cold War*, Cambridge University Press, Cambridge, 1955.

Lippmann, Walter, *The Communist World and Ours*, Hamish Hamilton, London, 1959.

Mao Tse-tung, *Selected Works of Mao Tse-tung*, Vols. 1–4, Lawrence and Wishart, London, 1956.

Mende, Tibor, *China and Her Shadow*, Thames and Hudson, London, 1961.

Needham, Joseph (research assistant Wang Ling), *Science and Civilization in China*, Vols. I and II, Cambridge University Press, Cambridge, 1954 and 1956.

Panikkar, K. M., *In Two Chinas: Memoirs of a Diplomat*, George Allen & Unwin, London, 1955.

Payne, Robert, *Chungking Diary*, William Heinemann, London, 1945.

Peck, Graham, *Two Kinds of Time*, Houghton Mifflin Co., Boston, 1950.

Peking Opera, New World Press, Peking, 1957.

Prawdin, Michael, *The Mongol Empire*, George Allen & Unwin, London, 1953.

Riencourt, Amaury de, *The Soul of China*, Jonathan Cape, London, 1959.

Rostow, W. W., *The Prospects for Communist China*, Chapman and Hall, London, 1954.

Roy, Claude, *Into China*, MacGibbon & Kee, London, 1955.

Schuman, Julian, *Assignment China*, Whittier Books, New York, 1956.

Segonzac, A. de, *Visa for Peking*, William Heinemann, London, 1956.

Snow, Edgar, *Random Notes on Red China*, (*1936–1945*), Harvard University Press, Cambridge, Mass., 1957.

— — *The Other Side of the River, Red China Today*, Random House, New York, 1962.

Sues, Ilona Ralf, *Shark's Fins and Millet*, Little Brown and Company, Boston, 1944.

Sulzberger, C. R., *What's Wrong with U.S. Foreign Policy?* Harcourt Brace, New York, 1959.

United States Relations with China, Department of State Publication 3573, Far Eastern Series 30, Division of Publications, Office of Public Affairs, 1949.

Van Bergen, R., *The Story of China*, American Book Co., New York, 1902.

Wales, Nym, *Red Dust*, Oxford University Press, London, 1952.

Waley, Arthur, *Analects of Confucius*, George Allen & Unwin, London, 1938.

Wollaston, Nicholas, *China in the Morning*, Jonathan Cape, London, 1960.

II. PERIODICALS, PAMPHLETS AND DOCUMENTS

Eastern Horizon, Hong Kong (monthly).

Foreign Affairs, Vol. 36, No. 3 (April 1958), Council on Foreign Relations, Lancaster, Pa.

Greene, Felix, *What's Really Happening in China?* City Lights Books, San Francisco, 1959.

The Agrarian Reform Law of the People's Republic of China, Foreign Languages Press, Peking, 1959.

Brown, Harrison, and Real, James, *Community of Fear*, Center for the Study of Democratic Institutions (Fund for the Republic, Inc.), Santa Barbara, California, 1960.

What's Going On in China, American Friends Service Committee, 1959.

International Affairs, Vol. 36, No. 3. Oxford, July, 1960.

Die Weltwoche, Zürich, Switzerland, September 6th, 1958.

Mineral Trade Notes (*Rich Mineral Resources Spur Communist China's Bid for Industrial Power*), U.S. Department of the Interior, Bureau of Mines, Special Supplement No. 59, Washington, D. C., March 1960.

'Red China's Hidden Capital of Science', by J. Tuzo Wilson, *Saturday Review*, November 8th, 1959.

Chinese Trade and Economic News Letter (monthly), British Council for the Promotion of International Trade, 15 Hanover Square, London.

'China's Economic Growth', by Professor Charles Bettelheim, of the Sorbonne, Paris, *The Economic Weekly*, Bombay, India, November 22nd, 29th, December 6th, 13th, 1958.

Article on Chinese Agriculture by Chou Pei-yuan, *Bulletin of the Atomic Scientists*, October, 1958.

'Chinese Agriculture', by René Dumont, Professor of Comparative Agriculture at the Agronomic Institute, Paris, in *Le Monde*, Paris, October 12th, 1958.

Article by the Editor of *Reuters*, *New York Times*, February 27th, 1958.

New Republic, January 5th, 1959.

Letter to *New Statesman*, London, January 31st, 1959.

'The Chinese are "liquidating" their disease problems', by Dr. Brian Maegraith, *The New Scientist*, London, December 5th, 1957.

'Visit to China', by F. Avery Jones, M.D., F.R.C.P., *British Medical Journal*, November 9th, 1957.

'The New China – Some Medical Impressions', by T. F. Fox, M.A., M.D., F.R.C.P., *The Lancet*, London, November 9th, 16th, 23rd, 1957.

'A Letter from Peking', by Dr. Joshua Horn, F.R.C.S., published by Britain-China Friendship Association, London, 1959.

'Party Resolutions on Questions Concerning People's Communes', December 10th, 1958, Hsinhua News Agency, London.

Article by R. H. S. Crossman, M.P., *New Statesman*, London, January 10th, 1959.

'China May Soon Be *the* World Power', by Edward B. Jolliffe, *McLean's* magazine, November 22nd, 1958.

'The Challenge of China', by James Muir, souvenir edition of the *Royal Bank Magazine*, Royal Bank of Canada, October 1958; also in *Congressional Record*, July 15th, 1959.

BIBLIOGRAPHY

Memorandum to American Diplomatic Missions setting forth official reasons for non-recognition of China, State Department, August, 1958.

Statement on China adopted by the Fifth World Order Conference, Cleveland, Ohio, November 18th–21st, 1958; convened by the Department of International Affairs of the National Council of the Churches of Christ in the U.S.A.

'Contemporary China and the Chinese', *The Annals of the American Academy of Political and Social Science*, January, 1959.

Department of State, Public Affairs Area – Policy Advisory Staff (Special Guidance No. 28, December 23rd, 1949).

'The China Impasse', by Li Thian-hok, *Foreign Affairs*, April, 1958.

Far Eastern Economic Review, Yearbook, 1961, Hong Kong.

Index

(Topics covered by chapter headings are not included (*see* Contents). All topical entries are to be understood as coming under the general heading: Chinese People's Republic.)

JONATHAN CAPE PAPERBACKS

DATE DUE

DEC 30°			
FEB 14 '71			
IN			
FEB 21 '73			
E H			
APR 8 '78			
FE 26 01			
GAYLORD			PRINTED IN U.S.A.